England's Apprenticeship

1603–1763

CHARLES WILSON

PROFESSOR OF MODERN HISTORY IN
THE UNIVERSITY OF CAMBRIDGE

LONGMAN

LONGMAN GROUP LIMITED
London

*Associated companies, branches and representatives
throughout the world*

© Charles Wilson 1965

First published 1965
Fourth impression and first paperback edition 1971
Sixth impression 1979

ISBN 0 582 48222 4 cased
ISBN 0 582 48234 8 paper

*Printed in Hong Kong by
Wah Cheong Printing Press Ltd*

Contents

Maps

Introductory Note

Interest in economic history has grown enormously in recent years. In part, this interest is a by-product of twentieth-century preoccupation with economic issues and problems. In part, it is a facet of the revolution in the study of history. The scope of the subject has been immensely enlarged, and with the enlargement has come increasing specialization. Economic history is one of the most thriving of the specialisms. Few universities are without an economic historian. New research is being completed each year both in history and economics departments. There are enough varieties of approach to make for frequent controversy, enough excitement in the controversy to stimulate new writing.

This series, of which Professor Wilson's volume is the third, is designed to set out the main conclusions of economic historians about England's past. It rests on the substantial foundations of recent historical scholarship. At the same time, it seeks to avoid narrow specialization. Economic history is not lifted out of its social context, nor are the contentious borderlands of economics and politics neglected. The series is described as 'a social and economic history of England'.

The bracketing together of the two adjectives is deliberate. Social history has received far less scholarly attention than economic history. A child of the same revolt against the limited outlook of the political historian, it has grown less sturdily. Its future depends on the application of greater discipline and more persistent probing. Developments in recent years are encouraging, and many of them will be reflected in these volumes. So too will developments in historical geography and, where they are illuminating, in demography and sociology. There is hope that just as the economist has provided useful tools for the study of economic history, so the sociologist may be able to provide useful tools for the study of social history and the demographer valuable quantitative data. There is no need, however, for economic and social historians to work in separate workshops. Most of the problems with which they are concerned demand co-operative effort.

However refined the analysis of the problems may be or may become, however precise the statistics, something more than accuracy and discipline are needed in the study of social and economic history. Many of the most lively economic historians of this century have been singularly undisciplined, and their hunches and insights have often proved invaluable. Behind the abstractions of economists or sociologists is the experience of real people, who demand sympathetic understanding as well as searching analysis. One of the dangers of economic history is that it can be written far too easily in impersonal terms: real people seem to play little part in it. One of the dangers of social history is that it concentrates on categories rather than on flesh and blood human beings. This series is designed to avoid both dangers, at least as far as they can be avoided in the light of available evidence. Quantitative evidence is used where it is available, but it is not the only kind of evidence which is taken into the reckoning.

Within this framework each author has had complete freedom to describe the period covered by his volume along lines of his own choice. No attempt has been made to secure general uniformity of style or treatment. The volumes will necessarily overlap. Social and economic history seldom moves within generally accepted periods, and each author has had the freedom to decide where the limits of his chosen period are set. It has been for him to decide in what the 'unity' of his period consists.

It has also been his task to decide how far it is necessary in his volume to take into account the experience of other countries as well as England in order to understand English economic and social history. The term 'England' itself has been employed generally in relation to the series as a whole not because Scotland, Wales or Ireland are thought to be less important or less interesting than England, but because their historical experience at various times was separate from or diverged from that of England: where problems and endeavours were common or where issues arose when the different societies confronted each other, these problems, endeavours and issues find a place in this series. In certain periods Europe, America, Asia, Africa and Australia must find a place also. One of the last volumes in the series will be called 'Britain in the World Economy'.

The variety of approaches to the different periods will be determined, of course, not only by the values, background or special interests of the authors but by the nature of the surviving sources and the extent to which economic and social factors can be separated out from other facts in the past. For many of the periods described in this series, as in the period covered by Professor Wilson, it is extremely difficult to disentangle law or religion from economic and social structure and change. In addition, facts about 'economic and social aspects' of life must be supplemented by accounts of how successive generations thought about 'economy' and 'society'. The very terms themselves must be dated.

Where the facts are missing or the thoughts impossible to recover, it is the duty of the historian to say so. Many of the crucial problems in English social and economic history remain mysterious or only partially explored. This series must point, therefore, to what is not known as well as what is known, to what is a matter of argument as well as what is agreed upon. At the same time, it is one of the particular excitements of the economic and social historian to be able, as G. M. Trevelyan has written, 'to know more in some respects than the dweller in the past himself knew about the conditions that enveloped and controlled his life'.

ASA BRIGGS

Preface

'"Tis opportune to look back upon old times, and contemplate our Fore-fathers.' *Sir Thomas Browne*

Men study history from a variety of motives. Not the least is a simple but compelling curiosity about the past. As a great Dutch historian, Johan Huizinga, has said:

> The direct, spontaneous, naïve zeal for antiquated things of earlier days which animates the dilettante of local history and the genealogist is not only a primary form of the urge to historical knowledge but also a full-bodied one. It is the impulse towards the past. A person thus impelled may want to understand only a small bit, an insignificant interrelationship out of the past, but the impulse can be just as deep and pure, just as gravid with true wisdom as in the person who wishes to encompass the heavens and the earth in his knowledge.[1]

No century offers a richer mine for this kind of searching, antiquarian curiosity than the seventeenth. And this is not only because it is rich in human genius, in human achievement, in social and political crises, in innovations and the like; but also because, standing at the end of the Middle Ages, it was itself rich in the instinct of curiosity. Its antiquarians — Coke, Spelman, Cotton, Selden, Browne, Aubrey — gathered abundantly from the rich storehouse of their past, preserving it for their descendants and transforming their contemporaries' outlook on their own world. To them we owe much of our heritage of knowledge.

Another impulse towards the past, and one more professionally regarded in our day, is the need to understand our own world, to see how it is related to what happened in history. In this sense too, the century and a half that form the subject of this book have a strong claim on the student's attention. For it is a time of preparation, economically and socially as well as politically, for the changes and convulsions that were to revolutionize society in Britain in the late eighteenth and nineteenth century. From there, the inventions and institutions of this Industrial Revolution were to be transmitted overseas until, in our day, they have encompassed and transformed the world.

The economic and social history of our period has been written many times. The justification for writing it again is that research is continually modifying, even revolutionizing, our ideas about it. Like summer visitors to the sandy beaches by the North Sea we return to find that since we were here last the beating of the tides has altered the contours of the sand beyond recognition. New views have emerged regarding the alternating phases of depression and

---

[1] J. Huizinga, *Men and Ideas*, 1960.

ix

prosperity, stagnation and growth. Closer examination of the probable movements of population has suggested new explanations of price movements and
industrial change. Behind the overt economic conflicts of the times over taxation, historians using the sociologists' tools have discerned longer, deeper
changes in the social structure and the fortunes of social groups. Such new acces-
sions of knowledge are reflected in the boundaries of the period I have chosen
and the way the period has been subdivided for study. The divisions are not
sacrosanct. To have left it undivided would have risked obscuring all but the
longest-term changes. To have subdivided more would have risked losing the
real continuity that runs through the story. To preserve continuity I have
occasionally repeated a fact or comment. The boundary posts – 1603, 1660,
1700, 1763 – are placed at dates familiar in political history. This has been done
partly because there is still something to be said for reminding ourselves that
history is a unity when we can conveniently do so, partly because our statistical
evidence is still capable of such differing interpretations that it would be pedantic
to claim that any particular year marks a turning-point on economic grounds
alone.

Broadly, this century and a half was a time when commercial enterprise,
often closely allied with state power and aided by legislation and military or
naval force, was changing the face of the old agrarian customary economy.
Agriculture remained the source of income for by far the majority of the people,
but it was itself increasingly marked by the application of capital, enterprise,
novel methods and the quest for markets. The dynamic of the time was commercial. The economic legislation of the day was concerned increasingly with
trade, foreign trade especially, and it was crowned by the Acts of Trade of the
Restoration. Most of the economic literature of the day likewise turned on
problems of trade: and though they did not intend the word to exclude industry
(or what they still called 'manufactures') most writers would have regarded
manufacturing processes as inferior in economic importance to the business of
exchange and distribution by merchants, manufacturers as the social inferiors
of merchants. James I's best economic adviser, Cranfield, was a merchant by
training. The period ends with Pitt, the son of an East India merchant, denounc-
ing the Peace which (he said) betrayed Britain's trade, security and future to
France. In between, the national destiny was powerfully influenced by a score
of merchants and advisers on trade policy who ensured that in due time a
Britain moving towards industrialization was already equipped with the commercial skills and financial institutions that she needed for the next great phase
of expansion.

Economy and society alike were poised between medievalism and modernity.
The economy was, in important respects, still a *congeries* of local or regional
economies rather than a genuinely unified whole. Some areas, in the North
and West and the Fenland, were still virtually enclaves with their own peculiar
economic and social customs, often isolated from what we discern as the national
trends of development. Yet a growing fleet of coastal shipping, inland navigation

and a network of mapped roads of a sort, increasingly gave reality to the idea of an economic nation state. And this was strengthened by the dominant influence of London as a centre of import and export trades, manufactures, government, administration and fashion. Customary rule, whether represented by lordship or gild, was everywhere being eroded by the combined forces of centralized government and individual economic initiative. Yet the social, political and legal system as yet did not become one of freedom in the full or modern sense. Serfdom had gone. The last recorded case about villeinage was heard in 1618. The plaintiff, one Pigg, was declared free. For more than a century the royal courts of law had been enforcing manorial custom. Yet law and government were still inextricably entangled with property rights. The landed classes and the recruits from trade and the professions who joined their ranks enjoyed the greatest privileges society could confer. But they also bore heavy responsibilities. They paid the heaviest taxes, discharged unpaid offices like those of Sheriff and J.P. and generally bore the burdens — no light matter in these years — of preserving law and order. The freeholder on the land and the freeman of the town were the 'accredited elements in society'.[1]

The classes below them were inferior, less a part of society than one of its problems. 'Freedom' in legal language still meant special exemption from a general rule of compulsion; 'liberty' still implied a special privilege to do something forbidden to others. Yet the rapid rise of the 'free' elements in society had forced a change in such conceptions. When a law dictionary defined 'liberty' in 1729 it gave the old meaning, 'a privilege held by grant or prescription by which men enjoy some benefit beyond the ordinary subject', but it added that the word could also be used in a different sense: the power to do as one thought fit unless restrained by law.[2] Poets, divines and politicians had been familiar with this broader conception since the late Middle Ages. Parliamentary 'freedom' might still be identified with landed freehold, but the possession of property by M.P.s was seen as a defence of Parliament's independence against royal attempts to manage Parliament by bribery. This was the main forum where the conflicts of interest great and small were fought and settled. Such conflicts were a major dynamic of a freer society and a creative force moulding the larger conception of liberty.

Economic progress in a society still heavily trammelled by custom could be neither smooth nor uninterrupted. The first of our periods — from the accession of James I to the Restoration — was not marked by conspicuous growth: on the contrary, it was a time of painful economic readjustment in a darkening European context. The historian's task, with regard to this period, as Professor Fisher has written, 'is less that of demonstrating the expansive force of economic ambition than that of examining the impediments which contained it, less that of proclaiming its successes than that of recording the strains and

[1] See the penetrating chapter 'Freehold and Status' in David Ogg's *England in the Reign of James II and William III*, 1955.
[2] Ibid, p. 54.

stresses to which it gave rise'.[1] The impediments — lack of skill, lack of money, lack of transport — are examined here. So are the ambitious attempts at improvement and the correspondingly disastrous failures — failures to learn and apply the skills of finishing and dyeing woollens so vital to the export trade, to build and handle shipping and exploit the coastal fisheries. Meanwhile the stresses that arose from the efforts of government and individuals to adapt themselves to the changed economic conditions that were the aftermath of the great price inflation of the previous century were revealed. Those who did best in such times were those who adapted themselves most swiftly and ingeniously, spreading their risks and seizing their opportunities. The grand climax to this era of problems came with the Civil War. This was the explosion of many forces besides the economic: but recurrent economic troubles and in some sectors an almost chronic state of economic depression were among the factors which contributed powerfully to the deepening political confusion and frustration.

Yet not all was loss and regression in these years. The country's major manufacture, cloth, was painfully adjusting itself to the new techniques of worsted production and to new markets. The coastal shipping fleet was expanding as the Newcastle–London coal trade developed. The colonial trades, small and often unprofitable as yet, were to prove the source of great wealth and power later in the century. Finally, the Civil War was to sweep away the old monarchy, with its concomitants of irrationalism, paternalism and monopoly, and substitute a new and earthier conception of government. This was in time to pave the way for a new economic regime that combined industrial freedom at home with commercial regulation of overseas and colonial trade that was hardly conceivable in the conditions of earlier times.

The second of our periods, from 1660 to 1700, opened as the preceding period had done, with a burst of economic optimism. Once again it looked as if these early gains were to be lost in depression, war and confusion. Yet, in spite of the wars which broke out in 1664 and recurred periodically throughout the period, these forty years were to prove one of the most fertile and progressive periods in English history down to this time. Cradled in a protective covering of legislation enforced by naval power, the nation's trade and shipping expanded. Its geographical extent was no longer bounded by Europe though inter-regional trade in Europe remained of major importance. Its flow was no longer focused (as it had been earlier in the century) on the Dutch market nor channelled through the hands of Dutch middlemen and shipowners. England was becoming a world entrepôt on its own, and though 'England' in the context of foreign trade still meant to an overwhelming extent London, there were already signs that the Western ports were stirring. These were the most obvious and striking signs of growth. Less spectacular movement was also present, though often semi-concealed. Home production of food was steadily increasing.

[1] *Essays on the Economic and Social History of Tudor and Stuart England, in honour of R. H. Tawney*, ed. F. J. Fisher, 1961, p.3.

Britain was, through the extension of cultivated acreage and a slow, modest, but widespread improvement of agricultural skill, turning from a corn importing to a corn exporting country. This, with the continuing export of coal, helped to create a bulk demand for shipping, giving a new dimension to an economy that had previously equated the greater value of its export trade with cloth. It is possible that the later decades of the century also saw population numbers on the increase again. Certainly men continued to move into London and to a lesser extent to smaller cities and towns. Scientific curiosity gave a renewed impetus to manufactures and new technologies. Increasingly rational tariff arrangements offered protection to home industries as varied as paper-making and shipbuilding. Commercial and financial booms alternated with depressions. Not least in importance, the machinery of both public and private credit became more sophisticated and confident. Thus, the formative age of the so-called 'mercantile system', was one of impressive, perhaps unique, growth in the pre-industrial age. It does not yield itself easily to conventional explanations of economic growth that rest on price inflation, population increase, freedom from war or fertility of invention and innovation. But growth, visible and measurable, there was. It was a time when (as Mr Davis has said) 'the English merchant class was able to grow rich, to accumulate capital on middleman's profits and on the growing shipping industry which was needed to carry cheap sugar, tobacco, pepper and salt-petre on the ocean routes'. Maybe, as he has added, we should look 'with a little more favour on those historians of the past who dubbed this century with the title of "The Commercial Revolution" '.[1] Yet the commercial revolution does not stand alone as a *deus ex machina* that of itself 'explains' the other phenomena. That it was a source of wealth and capital is true, but it was also obviously the response to demand for the goods it provided. Dim and unsystematic as our knowledge is of the growth of urban population and of agricultural wealth, these must have been the major source of the growing demand for colonial imports.

Comparison with the more varied fortunes of the next period strengthens this assumption. From 1700 onwards, until the end of our period, the movements in the economy are less marked and more debatable than in the previous forty years. The impression of bustling growth goes out of the economy. For a time the people of England seem to be marking time, digesting their earlier spectacular gains. Population grew little, if at all, in the first half of the eighteenth century. Prices were pretty stable. So, in many places, were wages. The growth of London slowed down, and with it metropolitan demand, and perhaps thus accentuated those difficulties experienced by the agricultural community: agricultural production, though not growing in any spectacular fashion, may well have overtaken demand, precipitating the agricultural distress of the 1730s and 1740s. Foreign trade, on the other hand, showed more movement. Exports

[1] Ralph Davis, 'English Foreign Trade 1660–1700', *Economic History Review*, vol. VII (New Series).

grew until 1715, stagnated for another fifteen years, recovered until the mid-forties. Then followed an advance 'almost as spectacular, if not nearly as regular, as in the years after 1780'.[1] The period 1745 to 1760 was likewise a landmark in the history of the import trade, where growth had been slow since the start of the century. These movements in foreign trade probably reflect and contain similar movements in manufacturing industry — a modest growth from 1700 to 1725; then a check for another two decades before the momentum is resumed after 1745 to last until the 1760s. It is in this last fifteen years or so that general progress is once again identifiable. Paying for expensive wars in its stride, the economy creeps forward. In field and workshop technological change begins to offer answers to shortages of labour and of profits. Here in the middle years of the eighteenth century we seem to be within sight of spectacular, economic progress of a truly modern kind. What in 1603 had been 'the Manor of England' was ready by 1763 to become the workshop of the world.

The society which was the human aggregate owning, operating and benefiting from this economy was roughly stratified by contemporaries into the nobility, gentry, merchants, professions, yeomen, freeholders, customary tenants, leaseholders, shopkeepers, craftsmen, labourers and that great mass — perhaps a third or more of the total — they called 'the poor'. Yet, nobles apart, these labels did not imply legal definition of social status, though a man might be labelled knight, esquire, gentleman, yeoman or husbandman, in order to be assessed when a direct tax was being raised. Throughout the period there was a remarkable degree of social mobility, especially between the middle and top ranges of society. Many families contained representatives of the peerage, gentry, merchants, and professions, to say nothing of poor relations, at the same moment in time. The man of enterprise who made money by luck, good management or good marriage could move upwards. The number of men who did so probably never represented more than a small proportion of the total, but they were enough to influence powerfully the character of English society, and of English economic and social policy. The social categories invented by nineteenth-century historians — feudal, bourgeois, working class — do not sit happily on such a society. The simple idea of large and more or less solid social 'classes' distinguished from each other by different interests is not only unhelpful in interpreting the course of events: it can be positively misleading. Society was not revolutionized. It evolved, and its rich and complex evolution eludes — just as it constantly invites — the snap judgement. Even over purely economic affairs, each large 'class' — nobility, gentry and City merchants — is found to be divided into quarrelling factions. There are Court factions, Country factions, ins and outs, haves and have-nots. New Merchant Adventurers battle against Old Merchant Adventurers, London Companies against interlopers, the New East India Company against the Old, the Russia tobacco contractors against the

[1] P. Deane and W. A. Cole, *British Economic Growth 1688–1959*, 1962, chs. I and II for these and other measurements.

Preface

Old Russia Company, fundholders against taxpayers: and so on. More important, the turning-points in the nation's political development — especially 1642 and 1685-8 — revealed that the 'ruling classes' were sharply divided amongst themselves over non-economic questions, especially the attitude towards religion and the nature of government. No attempt to analyse the relation between economics and politics in this age will get far unless it begins by recognizing that in the Civil War and the Glorious Revolution men of similar economic interests and social class were prepared to fight each other for reasons that had little or no connexion with economics. Down to the great Reform Bill of 1832, the same two classes that were the focus of opposition to the Stuarts — the country gentry and the City merchants — continued to provide the main recruiting grounds of opposition to Ministries.

To guide us through the economic problems of the times we have nothing that can strictly be regarded as statistics. But in recent years the work of scholars like Sir George Clark, Professor T. S. Ashton, Mrs Schumpeter, Professor Harper, Mr Ralph Davis, Miss Phyllis Deane, Mr W. A. Cole and others has enabled us to convert to statistical purposes the residual labours of customs clerks, excise men, parish clerks and tax gatherers of several kinds. The picture of our economy and society that emerges is one of epic contrasts of opulence and poverty, of economic gains precariously won and easily lost, of wide fluctuations between periods and wide differences of fortune between one locality and another, of a society still frighteningly at the mercy of the weather, of the good or bad harvest that meant prosperity or ruin for many; heavily dependent on competition in overseas markets (for late in the century perhaps a third of our total manufactures went abroad),[1] and on the outcome of the wars which were in part wars for trade. Yet for all the fluctuations and backslidings, the outcome was a material increase in living standards for a sizeable proportion of a slowly growing population. This increase is, still, conveyed more vividly by observable facts — the new and grander houses that rose throughout England, by the novel additions to the clothes men and women wore and the new foods, drinks, and luxuries they consumed — than by calculations of national or *per capita* income in these early stages of growth. I have tried therefore to use social history from time to time to supplement our meagre 'statistics', as a means of looking at consumption, at the way men enjoyed the fruits of their labours.

Throughout, the English economy has been placed in a broader European and world context. For Britain was already closely linked by trade, technology, migration and the flow of ideas with a wide world beyond her own shores. In this period more perhaps than in any other she owed much to these economic energies that seem to be the peculiar distinction of refugees and 'displaced persons'. References to British colonies and settlements make no claim to be an adequate account of their development. They are only intended to explain their economic impact on Britain.

Finally, since history — not least economic history — was made by men, and

[1] Deane and Cole, op. cit., p. 42.

xv

in turn helped to make men what they were, I have tried to give examples of those men, representative and sometimes unrepresentative, whose qualities, good and less good, contributed to economic progress. They were the men who seized their economic opportunities, responded to economic challenges. Economic history is compounded of their actions.

The historian can never 'explain' history precisely or finally as a scientist can explain the working of the internal combustion engine or the thermometer. As G. M. Trevelyan once wrote: 'The causes that produce genius in individual men, and outbursts of activity in nations, are mysteries which only become more impenetrable as one theory after another is flung out to account for that which is beyond knowledge.'[1] But if we can never achieve final explanation in history we can, and must, go on trying to enlarge and deepen our understanding of it. Economic history is one means, and a fairly new one, of doing that. It demands to be studied separately, for it possesses its own inner rhythms and dynamics that help us to understand the nature of change itself. Economic history cannot therefore be understood merely in terms of other kinds of history; equally it does not itself provide any total 'explanation' of other kinds of history. Yet in separating it for study we must never forget that it forms part of the ultimate unity of history; we must always be aware of this unity even if we cannot always explain or analyse the complexity of human and social motives that compose it. 'Of all varieties of history', Sir John Clapham wrote, 'the economic is the most fundamental. Not the most important: foundations exist to carry better things.' With the material wealth created by economic activities, an increasing proportion of mankind has been enabled 'to practise high arts, organize great states, design splendid temples, or think at leisure about the meaning of the world'.[2]

The bibliography will make it clear that this general study owes a heavy debt to many scholars whose specialized labours have helped to describe, measure and explain the change and growth of the period. It owes another to colleagues and pupils too numerous to mention with whom I have discussed its problems over the years. Two special debts, however, I must acknowledge. To Asa Briggs for his penetrating editorial advice and suggestions, and especially for encouragement to face the hazards of what is now Ch. 6; and to David Joslin of Pembroke College, Cambridge, who read the manuscript, generously shared with me his own deep understanding of the period and gave me wise counsel on a number of problems. To both I am deeply grateful.

CHARLES WILSON

[1] G. M. Trevelyan, *England under the Stuarts*, 1904, p. 51.
[2] J. H. Clapham. *A Concise Economic History of Britain*, 1949 Introduction.

PART ONE

The Lean Years, 1603-1660

CHAPTER ONE

The Seventeenth-Century Setting: Social Degree and Social Mobility

WHEN John Aubrey, the antiquarian and biographer, tried to gather his scattered memories and observations together in the years after the Restoration, he saw history dividing at a point somewhere between the times of Henry VIII and Elizabeth. Until King Henry's reign was the 'olden time', when government was 'like a nest of boxes: for the copyholders (who till then were villains) held of the Lords of the Manor, who held perhaps of another superior lord or duke, who held of the King'.[1] This was a world still nostalgically remembered in many a country house in the early seventeenth century, a world of established feudal rank and order, based on the possession of land. Its antecedents seemed to stretch back beyond Tudor times to the ancient Britons. Then, great lords had reigned in their counties 'like petty Kings', with *jura regalia*, and gallows within their liberties where they could try, condemn, hang and draw. Only an annual visit to London, to sit in Parliament or do homage to the King, had taken them away from their broad acres and armies of retainers, from the feasting and jollification that seemed to Aubrey to compete for their energies only with fighting – either against each other or, more lawfully, for the King. This still-remembered world was above all one of a caste society organized for warfare. 'Upon any occasion of bustling in those dayes', wrote Aubrey, 'one of the greate lords sounded his trumpet (all lords then kept trumpeters, even to King James) and summoned those that held under them: those again sounded their trumpets, and so on downwards to the copyholders.' And (as an afterthought): 'Old Sir Walter Long,[2] grandfather to Colonel Long, kept a trumpeter: and rode with thirty servants and retainers to Marlborough and so for others of his ranke and time.'

Within living memory, this military society, deeply rooted in local

---

[1] John Aubrey, *Wiltshire Collections*, Introduction (1862).
[2] Whom Aubrey knew of Draycot in Wiltshire.

soil, stratified into peers, knights, esquires, yeomen, retainers and customary tenants, had crumbled and decayed. In the Civil Wars a commander like the Marquis of Newcastle still rode to battle at the head of a force largely his own tenants. But this was the last echo of military feudalism. The war itself destroyed many of the great castles like Basing and Latham House. Others, like Rockingham, were 'slighted' after the war was over. With them went the great armouries and the stables of great horses for the armed men. The petty manors had been disintegrating from Henry VII's time. With all these had gone the pilgrimages, the revels. The times when 'all things were civill and without scandall' had given way to a more relaxed age, the severity of parents towards children to looser discipline and morals – or so it seemed to Aubrey. The country, then 'a lovely *campania*', with few enclosures 'except new houses', and 'a world of labouring people mayntayned by the plough', had mostly been replaced by enclosures ('for the private not for the public good') and England swarmed with paupers.

In this conception of a lost Golden Age, there was an element of picturesque exaggeration, a natural feeling of nostalgia that sprang from current reflections on the troubled age by which the 'olden time' had been replaced. Yet Aubrey was not the first to see the preceding century as the hinge of change. The same consciousness of profound economic and social change permeates the earlier survey called by its author, Thomas Wilson, a versatile if disappointed antiquarian, *The State of England Anno Dom. 1600*.[1] Here again is a picture of changing customs, changing relationships between social classes, above all the rising fortunes of the Tudor yeoman and farmer class, a churning, restless society where established ideas of 'degree' had been disturbed and perhaps destroyed for ever by forces beyond human control. To Wilson, the sequence of events was clear. The low prices and sluggish demand for land of the fifteenth and early sixteenth centuries had encouraged the landowning gentry to lease land out at low rates for long periods. Then, to finance his wars, Henry VIII had debased the coinage, prices had risen steeply, to the great benefit of the active, commercial, farming class and the corresponding disadvantage of the *rentier* landlords. Hence the King had 'weakened the ability of his nobility and thereby clipped the wings of their insolvencys'.[2] To this (as Wilson suspected) half-conscious policy, the Tudors had added policies designed

[1] Edited by F. J. Fisher, *Camden Miscellany*, 1936, vol. LXVI.
[2] Wilson, p. 39.

for the mutual enrichment of great merchants and traders; charters for the monopoly of trade to this company 'to trade into such a part of the World and for such and such Commodityes, to another Company another, the 3^d a 3^d' and so on. Statutes to protect artisans and encourage local trades and fishing were added to others designed to stop the export of treasure and coin, 'by reason there is little store of silver and gold mynes in the land'. As these and other solvents eroded and destroyed the ancient local sovereignties and privileges, they had been replaced by a new national authority; that 'supreme and awfull authority which the Prince hath over all subjects great and mean, noe man, not the greatest in the whole land, haveing more authority than the meanest but as he deriveth it from the Prince by Commission . . .'[1]

Wilson and Aubrey were only two out of many who speculated on the nature of contemporary social change. The peculiar fascination of the times is, indeed, not merely the rate at which old habits and institutions were giving way to new; it is also the self-conscious awareness of change widely spread among contemporaries. That most of them found such change disturbing is hardly surprising. Their dislike of it was not merely snobbery, nostalgia or irrational conservatism, though no doubt it contained an element of all these things. They knew no living society based on any principle but that of rank; they could not conceive of one that could be based on anything else. The view of society as essentially hierarchic was almost universally held in the sixteenth century and was still powerful in the seventeenth. Shakespeare's history plays abound in its imagery, and from *Troilus and Cressida* (1602) comes the classic statement of the social function of what men called 'degree':

> The heavens themselves, the planets, and this centre
> Observe degree, priority and place,
> . . .
> O! When degree is shak'd,
> Which is the ladder to all high designs,
> The enterprise is sick. How could Communities
> Degrees in schools, and brotherhoods in cities,
> Peaceful commerce from dividable shores,
> The primogenitive and due of birth,
> Prerogative of age, crowns, sceptres, laurels
> But by degree, stand in authentic place.

Such was the orthodox Elizabethan view of society. It had developed through the Middle Ages. Statutes had attempted to devise a common

[1] Wilson, p. 41.

measure for the status of knights, esquires and gentlemen against merchants, citizens and craftsmen by a kind of points system based partly on rank, partly on wealth: so that an esquire with £200 a year was equated with a merchant worth five times as much. Dress was taken to indicate calling and station. Such outward signs continued into the seventeenth century and the conception of degree itself remained strong. The hierarchical principle is as central to *Paradise Lost* as it is to *Troilus*. Milton not only accepted the principle; he was (as Professor C. S. Lewis has written) 'enchanted' by it.[1] To him, as to Shakespeare, freedom could only be achieved within a society made stable and secure by a discipline of a divinely ordained and permanent kind. He would have echoed the Elizabethan query:

> Take but degree away, untune that string,
> And hark, what discord follows. Each thing meets
> In mere oppugnancy.
> This Chaos when degree is suffocate,
> Follows the choking.

Characteristically, such thoughts were evoked most often, and with a wealth of poetic imagery drawn from astronomy, astrology and anatomy, when the feudal stratifications were breaking down most rapidly. Not the least important witness to the social and economic transformation of late sixteenth- and early seventeenth-century England is the growing band of antiquaries — Spelman, Stow, Cotton, Coke, Selden. Mostly lawyers, they were in part the product of the social changes that went with the metamorphosis of land from being a source of power into a source of wealth. A vigorous land market meant more litigation, more legal fees and in time lawyers turned landowners once more. But the lawyers' curiosity about change seemed to some as dangerous as change itself. What disastrous precedents might be sought, and therefore found, in the obscurity of the past which they alone could penetrate? In 1604, James, 'suspecting their loyalty and attachment to his government', closed down the Society of Antiquarians. When an attempt was made ten years later to revive it, the members were still informed that 'His Majesty took a little Mislike to our Society'.[2] James might hinder the scholars. He could not stem the tide of change.

From Bacon to Defoe, there is a steady change in the attitude of writers towards technical innovations, from reluctant and suspicious acceptance towards a positive welcome. The world conceived in

[1] Preface to *Paradise Lost*, 1942, pp. 78–9.
[2] H. Butterfield, *The Englishman and his History*, 1944, p. 37.

Bacon's Essay 'Of Innovations' was a world slowly deteriorating from a Golden Age now past. Innovation is for Bacon 'a medicine' to arrest decline in conditions where a 'forward retention of custom could become as turbulent a thing as innovation'. But the mistrust of change lingers. Innovation should not be cataclysmic or indiscriminate: it should be 'quiet innovation' — 'innovation by degree'. A later pamphlet, *The Discovery of a Projector* (1641) by Thomas Brugis, a Hertfordshire physician, reveals a similar mixture of suspicion and approval. Projectors, drawn from amongst lawyers, merchants, mongers, craftsmen and especially foreigners, were half dreamers, half technocrats, 'begotten on a faire Faggot pile between the man in the Moone and Tom Lancaster's Laundresse'. Their curse was to try and apply their theories in practice prematurely and thus bring themselves and others to disaster. The projector was 'the very Corne-cutter of the age when he lived and had a notable fault in the unsteadiness of his hand, by reason whereof he [did] often thrust his knife into the tender parts of the Common wealth to the quicke and never [left] untill he had brought out the very Coare of their purses'. Thirty years later, *The History of the Royal Society* by 'Fat Tom Sprat', Bishop of Rochester, had as a main theme the duty of the Society to ensure that 'men of Knowledge' guided the innovators aright, so that 'the Production of Necessity will be amplyfy'd and compleated' and scientific vision brought to check fraud and exalt 'the flegmatick imaginations of men of Trade'. Defoe's *Essay of Projects*, twenty years later, marked another phase. Projects were 'in general of public advantage, tending to improvement of trade, and employment of the poor, and the circulation and increase of the public stock of the Kingdom'. The wheel had turned, and public opinion had steadily become favourable to technological inquiry and change. This changing opinion was shaped in the context of a steadily changing relationship of political power, property and law.[1]

In the middle ages, land law was the basis of all public law. The later middle ages and the sixteenth century particularly had witnessed the first stages of the metamorphosis by which landholders had been peacefully transmuted into a society of landlords and tenants. The villein had been gradually freed from his praedial services. Villein status was abolished so that he survived as a copyholder, more or less secure in his rights according to the nature of the copy of court roll by which his land was held. Coke thought that about one-third of English

[1] See below, p. 188.

7

land was copyhold in the early seventeenth century;[1] but this in turn was subject to the steady process of erosion as lords, by amicable negotiation or by pressure, substituted terminable leases — commercial contracts on economic terms — for the old customary arrangements. Similarly, the fief, 'The right which a vassal has in some lands, or some immoveable thing of his lord's, to take the profits thereof, paying the feudal dues', had slowly evolved into freehold. Those dues had been rigidly enforced under the early Tudors, and much land continued to be held theoretically by knight service. In practice, the enforcing authority, the Court of Wards, that 'great bridle of feudality' as Aubrey described it, had become merely a source of profit to the Crown. Its activities were not the least source of friction that drove land owners into opposition in the Civil Wars and its abolition in 1660 has been called 'probably the most important single event in the history of English landholding'.[2] This was the last stage in the emancipation of the fief. Landholders were now free not only of obligations of service to the Crown, but of monetary substitutes for service, and of the burdensome relics of feudal theory by which, at the death of a tenant, land reverted to the lord. One after another, the barriers to hereditary title were broken down and abolished. Yet the manorial structure, though weakened, did not wholly disappear. Here and there a manorial franchise compelled tenants to grind their corn at the lord's mill. A lord could seize the estate of a convicted felon or a suicide, as the Duke of Somerset seized the house of a tripeman hanged for false coining. Sanctuaries from justice, like the Savoy, the Mint and Scotland Yard, were continued reminders of the survival of medieval custom as well as a perpetual nuisance to neighbours. But generally the social and economic purposes and consequences of landholding were changing, and with them its political significance. By the sixteenth century, even more by the seventeenth, an enterprising landlord stood to gain more from the wool, corn, timber and sometimes coal and iron on his estates than from squeezing out of his tenants his ancient rights to the profits of justice and lordship. He did not, as a rule, exploit his potential riches in person, though he might and often did keep a sizeable home farm that supplied his household with necessities and sometimes served as a model to tenants. Increasingly, the work and business of farming was

---

[1] *Lex Customaria or a Treatise of Copy Hold Estates* by S. C. Barrister at Law. London, 1701, Preface.

[2] David Ogg, *England in the Reign of James II and William III*, 1955, p. 55. See Chapter III, 'Freehold and Status', for an admirable account of this process of change.

carried on by a growing class of tenant farmers who paid rent to a land-lord according to the terms of a terminable contractual lease. Their substantial farm-houses still bear witness in many parts of England to their modest prosperity.

The changing character of landed property, far from extinguishing its social and political significance, actually broadened and increased it. For though no longer the basis of public law in the feudal sense, landed property continued to be the basis of politics. The House of Lords was still an assembly of landed magnates, but now the Commons began to include a larger landed element. The possession of land by an M.P. was seen less as an outward sign of prestige – though it certainly was that – than as the best insurance against subservience to the Crown. So that when finally in 1711 the Act of 9 Ann. 05 made high landed qualification compulsory on all M.P.s, its preamble claimed that it was 'securing the *liberty* of Parliament'. Similarly with jury service: only freeholders, it was assumed, could be relied upon to be impartial and independent. Full citizenship, in fact, was open only to the property owner. Now, however, neither political privilege nor social rank was indefeasibly attached to any *specific* unit of freehold. Both had become the natural perquisite of 'property' and property was now freely bought and sold, without hindrance, other than lawyers' delays, by anyone who could afford it. Alongside the political change by which a 'liberty' or a 'free-dom' were transmuted from a feudal privilege into a general right to do as a man saw fit, subject only to the rules of law, went a closely associated process by which successful men of enterprise from the trades and professions bought their way into landed property.

The rising, socially successful merchant was no novelty in the seven-teenth century. The wealthy medieval merchant had been regarded as of more or less equal social status with the rural knight, and the two classes had frequently intermarried. London merchants (like the famous Frowick family) had combined trade with their position as manorial lords in Middlesex over a long period of time. The Earl of Suffolk was descended from the de la Poles, merchants of Hull. The merchant class of London was recruited to a considerable extent from the younger sons of country families like the Greshams of Norfolk, the Cloptons and Cokaynes of Warwickshire and Derbyshire.[1] There was, therefore, already an element of mobility between social classes and occupations. Contrariwise, even in the seventeenth century the proportion of men who improved (or lost) social status was probably only a fraction of

[1] A. Wagner, *English Genealogy*, 1960, pp. 137–48.

those who stayed roughly where they were. But it was this moving minority which gave English life its peculiar flavour, and its size, though still small in relation to the total population, was increasing significantly.

Nothing is more characteristic of the continuity and flexibility of English institutions than this steady marriage of town and country, of merchant and landed wealth. Everywhere along the seaboards of western Europe and the Mediterranean, the sixteenth and seventeenth centuries saw trade grow, and with it, important merchant communities come into being. Everywhere, some men broke through the social barriers and improved their status. But in general the obstacles to social mobility seem to have been more formidable than in England. In the Low Countries, where a loose form of feudalism had combined with land reclamation to create prosperous trading cities and ports, the successful merchants tended to remain an urban patriciate. Likewise in Venice. In France, the noble who invested in trade faced the penalties of 'derogation' — the loss of noble privileges which was justified by the doctrine that the status of nobility was incompatible with participation in trade. Only very reluctantly in seventeenth-century France was protection against such penalties granted in special cases where investment in overseas trade (the East India trade in particular) was thought to be in the national interest. But generally the division persisted. In England the landed proprietors ceased to be a closed caste. Not only in the Home Counties but also round towns and ports, and wherever desirable estates offered, successful merchants and lawyers were to be found moving in. Eminent lawyers like Bacon, Brownlow, and Coke (rumoured to have made £100,000 in one year from fees as Attorney-General), administrators like Cranfield, Ingram, George Downing and William Blathwayt, rich merchants like William Cokayne, Josiah Child and Gilbert Heathcote, goldsmith bankers like Richard Hoare and Charles Duncombe — all bought large estates, acquired knighthoods, baronetcies and even peerages, married their daughters into the gentry and aristocracy, and sometimes founded dynasties. Contrariwise, the younger sons of old gentry families commonly took to trade to make their fortunes. Cranfield, Hugh Myddleton, promoter and engineer of the New River,[1] Heathcote, Duncombe, the Morses of Woodperry[2] and many others were typical of the social process by which such younger sons came to London, made a fortune in trade or finance and later reverted once again to their traditional status as country gentlemen. The Ishams of Lamport by Pytchley were descended from John, the fourth

[1] See below pp. 48–9.   [2] See below p. 330.

of five sons of an Elizabethan gentleman. John became a City merchant, returning home in his affluence to buy back the family estate and found a long line of baronets who still live at Lamport. It was no accident that the legend of Dick Whittington dates from 1605. Variations on the theme of social mobility thereafter became the familiar stock in trade of the dramatists. The poor but virtuous apprentice aspiring to marry the rich master's daughter, whose socially ambitious mother is selling her to a raffish and poverty-stricken country squire – such themes abound in the Jacobean theatre.[1]

This constant mingling of blood, class and occupation, the traffic between town and country, was of supreme importance to the economic and social evolution of England. Like all ages of innovation, it bred twisters like Sir Arthur Ingram, sharp monopolists and usurers like Sir Baptist Hickes and Sir William Cokayne, cranks and charlatans like Nicolas Barbon, whose adventures have caught the eye and wounded the moral sense of historians. But social intermixture did more than that. It gave assurance and influence to trade, it reinforced the declining fortunes of hundreds of landed families, and it brought intelligence and social influence to bear on the economic policies of governments which might otherwise have been swayed, as rulers in Continental Europe often were, simply by considerations of royal income and dynastic interests. The steady evolution of a national economic policy owed much to the common interest in prosperity shared by the English landed and business classes. Merchant interests were constantly consulted by successive seventeenth-century governments; so that while Cavaliers and Roundheads might disagree on many things, merchant opinion was consistently sounded both before and after the Civil Wars, by governments of all types on the merits and demerits of proposed policies on taxation, protective duties, navigation laws and the like. Even in war, economic objectives were rarely lost sight of and were often dominant, as they were in the Second War against the Dutch in 1664. By contrast, French policy was more dominated by political and dynastic objectives.[2]

The effect of this continued influx of business men into estate management is more difficult to assess. Capital it certainly brought, and, in some cases no doubt, more efficient accountancy and improved methods of management. When Cokayne foreclosed on the

---

[1] Thomas Middleton's *A Chaste Maid in Cheapside* (1613) is a good example.
[2] See P. W. Bamford, 'Entrepreneurship in Seventeenth- and Eighteenth-Century France', *Explorations in Entrepreneurial History*, April 1957.

Tresham estate at Rushton in Northamptonshire it is difficult to think he did not attempt to screw out of his newly acquired assets a higher yield on his capital than the dispossessed and spendthrift owner. Ten years after he purchased the manor of Laxton in Nottinghamshire, the great merchant prince, Sir William Courteen, had a survey made which suggests a vigorous campaign of reform and consolidation of the estates. But how typical, or how long continued, such efforts were remains doubtful. The object of the newcomers was social prestige as well as an economic return on their capital. The concern and habit of their descendants was to assimilate themselves as quickly and completely as possible to the manners of their county neighbours. In any event, business acumen is not necessarily an hereditary characteristic. But whether mercantile methods had any direct impact on rural organization or not, social mobility was certainly giving the entire upper and middle classes a common stake in economic efficiency and a common interest in economic progress.

The suspicion of business wealth as a social solvent and a certain lingering nostalgia for an ordered, traditional society was to die hard. In the eighteenth century, a simple, rather muddle-headed conservative like Oliver Goldsmith voiced doubts widely shared when he attacked commerce and commercial wealth as a disturber of that social 'equilibrium' that was the eighteenth-century image of an ideal society. Even a sophisticated mid-Victorian liberal like Bagehot could write: 'The order of nobility is of great use, too, not only in what it creates but in what it prevents. It prevents the rule of wealth – the religion of gold. This is the obvious and natural idol of the Anglo-Saxon. He is always trying to make money; he reckons everything in coin; he bows down before a great heap, and gallops as he passes a little heap.'[1] This distrust of the self-made men of money, and an instinctive belief in government by traditional means and a traditional ruling class was strong in the seventeenth century. Few successful business men passed immediately into the charmed circle of government, and the few who did – like Cranfield – had to face powerful opposition from the older incumbents of office who regarded them as upstarts. Adam Smith's picture of seventeenth-century governments as puppets of a cunning clique of merchants was a long way wide of the mark. Whether 'government' meant Privy Council under the monarchy or the Council of State in Commonwealth times, it listened to merchant petitions, sometimes accepting, sometimes rejecting. It was rarely dictated to, even though

[1] W. Bagehot, *The English Constitution*, 1933, p. 80.

the early Stuarts often stooped to folly. On the rare occasions when Government gave in to the clamour of the City – as it did over the Second Dutch War – it was persuaded less by the merchants themselves than by a court clique who thought they could further their own interests by an alliance with the City.

While relatively few of the self-made men of business themselves reached the inner circles of government or rose into the peerage, their sons and grandsons did. Now that class was no longer a legal but only a social conception, there was nothing to prevent the men of talent or of wealth from crossing the class frontiers, and the process was the easier in an age that was still feeling the impact of startling price changes on a prefabricated social structure. The *rentier* section of society, living in varying degrees on fixed incomes, had had to adapt themselves to the new price relationships or die. And when, in the latter part of the sixteenth century, the *monetary* forces of inflation seemed to be losing their momentum, they were replaced by another that worked powerfully in the same direction; between 1500 and 1600 the population of England and Wales seems to have increased by as much as 40 per cent; between 1600 and the Civil Wars by perhaps another 30 per cent. Hence another widening of the gap between the growing army of the poor and the rest of society, increasing demand for the basic necessities of life, and opportunity for the entrepreneur ready to take advantage of the abundance of cheap labour.

The apprehensions about what appeared to many the social and moral confusion of the times were reflected in its literature. The adventurous confidence and gaiety of earlier Elizabethan poetry and drama makes way for the melancholy strangeness of John Donne and the metaphysical poets, for the Italianate brand of *grand guignol*, morbid and violent. The new age of economic depression and social tension was one in which the Miltonic epic of power and morality and Bunyan's allegory were more to the taste of a rising class of thinking, troubled men. No one caught the prevailing mood of doubt, of mistrust in material prosperity and the pleasures of a dissolving social order better than the Royalist poet James Shirley:

> The glories of our blood and state
> Are shadows, not substantial things;
> There is no armour against Fate;
> Death lays his icy hand on Kings;
> Sceptre and Crown must tumble down,
> And in the dust be equal made
> With the poor crooked scythe and spade.

A brighter aspect of the social situation was noted by contemporaries. 'Many great men', wrote Ben Jonson of his own times, 'were rokked in mean cradles.' Aubrey's *Lives* supplies the chapter and verse. It was not only the world of business that offered opportunity to talent and enterprise in the seventeenth century. The divines, poets, mathematicians, philosophers, scholars, lawyers and administrators whose genius or talents gave the century its special flavour were as often the sons of grocers, brewers, vintners, drapers, clothiers, poor parsons, estate stewards, butlers and blacksmiths as they were of noblemen or gentlemen.

The continual poverty of a Court hard hit by the price rise and by its own extravagance combined with the lengthening queue of self-made men and office-holding favourites to make the Jacobean age a unique period of social mobility. Where Elizabeth had been sparing in her creation of new peers, James was lavish. The numbers of the peerage doubled between 1603 and 1629, and the new men took their place alongside the Howards, Percys, Berkeleys, Cecils, Cavendishes, Russells, Pagets and the rest. Even the established aristocracy was not proof against the prying eye of the antiquarian. 'The true name', wrote Aubrey of the Cecils, 'is *Sitsilt* and is an ancient Monmouthshire family but now come to be about the size of yeomanry.' He could not resist a final dig. "Tis strange that they should be so vaine to leave off an old British name for a Romancy one, which I believe Mr Verstegan did putt into their heads, telling his Lordship, in his booke, that they were derived from the ancient Roman *Cecilii.*' Further down the social scale, the fortunate or enterprising hastened to buy themselves grants of arms, profiting by the generous, unlegal freedom which defined a gentleman as one who could 'live idly and without manuall labour . . . and bear the port, charge and countenance of gentleman'. Trade did not derogate from that status. A Cheshire gentleman could describe himself in 1640 as a gentleman by birth and a linen draper by trade. In a case in 1634 a witness said that 'many citizens of great worth and esteem descended of very ancient gentle families, being soap boilers by trade even and yet accounted gentlemen'.[1]

Conversely, the great merchants and financiers of the City did not have to go far to buy themselves a baronetcy or knighthood in a Whitehall that found them a convenient source of ready cash. Sir Baptist Hickes, the Cheapside mercer, was knighted because he was an easy creditor not only to James but to his Scotch favourites at Court. The

---

[1] A. Wagner, op. cit., p. 114.

Harington estates at Exton in Rutland were amongst many that were mortgaged to him.[1] The physical proximity of Court and City was one of the most potent factors making for social mobility and a larger measure of economic freedom in seventeenth-century England. The same class of pushful merchants who sought social honours had an equal interest in breaking down the restrictive gild covenants that stood in the way of a large supply of cheaper goods for their markets. While the 'mere' gentry, short of capital and opportunity, might lapse into frustrated disgruntlement, the London tradesmen took full advantage of their economic and social opportunities. 'We see the tradesmen of *England,* as they grow wealthy', wrote Defoe much later, 'coming every day to the Heralds' Office, to search for the Coats of Arms of their ancestors, in order to paint them upon their coaches, and engrave them upon their plate, embroider them upon their furniture, or carve them upon the pediments of their new houses; and how often do we see them trace the registers of their families up to the prime nobility, or the most antient gentry of the Kingdom.'[2] The process had been going on throughout the seventeenth century, and was to continue. As families rose and fell in the hierarchy, the social pattern of England threw up some relationships which, for all their oddity, were characteristic of a mobile society. James I numbered amongst his living relations not only five dukes and earls but a Salisbury innkeeper and a tanner. From a seventeenth-century Warwickshire yeoman were descended Dr Johnson, and, by marriage, the Crowley eighteenth-century dynasty of Quaker ironmasters. They in turn were connected by marriage with the Earl of Chesterfield. Thus the archetypes of eighteenth-century poor scholar and aristocratic patron were linked in a common family connexion.[3]

Just as there was no legal definition of a 'gentleman', so there was none of a 'yeoman'. Romantic legend said that the yeomen of England were descended from the archers of Crecy and Poitiers. Less romantically, and more accurately, they were said to be originally serving men to the great. In 1652, the Earl of Bridgewater still describes the lesser members of his household as 'yeomen'. By 1600 they were also that substantial group of rural landholders (both freeholders and copyholders) who stood between the gentry and the working husbandmen

[1] See Hope Mirrlees, *A Fly in Amber,* 1962, pp. 95–9, 288; also Robert Ashton, *The Crown and the Money Market 1603–40,* 1960, *passim.*

[2] Daniel Defoe, *The Complete English Tradesmen,* 1726, p. 377; quoted by Wagner, op. cit., p. 118.

[3] A. L. Reade, *Johnson's Early Life,* 1946, pp. 157–8.

– sometimes equated with the 'chief Farmers' as husbandmen were equated with 'petty Farmers'. How was a yeoman defined? It is not easy to say. His acreage might be as little as 25, or as much as 600; his income £50 or £500 a year. While the freeholder yeoman had shed most of his dues to superiors, copyholders still owed monetary and other dues. As pressure on the land grew, these dues – for example, heriots – became a frequent source of litigation. Might a copyholder 'top and lop' trees in the forest? How many cattle might be put on the common? What were his widow's rights? Could he lease his land? Could he mine or make salt? If, as their enormous variations in circumstances suggest, the yeomen were not an economically homogeneous class, they were certainly not a legally definable one.

> Men, Sir, gentlemen or Yeomen, I know not which,
> But the one, sure, they are.

Contemporaries, and historians, may share the confusion and certainty of the servant in Middleton's *A Faire Quarrel* (1617). Just as a gentleman was one who was taken to be a gentleman, a yeoman was one who was taken to be a yeoman. Opinion came nearest to legal definition when it was crystallized into 'fiscal' status, that is, when the tax gatherer placed a man in his category (as knight, esquire, gentleman, yeoman, husbandman) for the purpose of a direct tax assessment. A group so varied plainly shared no single destiny. If historians have tended to regard them as victims of the new commercial age, destined to dwindle and disappear, contemporaries were apt to regard them as ambitious and grasping, justly prosecuted in bad times for offences like forestalling and regrating. In fact, we do not know how many sold out (for copyhold was more easily alienated than freehold with its cumbrous and costly proof of title), how many had their copies squeezed into leases, how many obtained enfranchisement into freehold, how many negotiated a profitable lease with the lord, how many simply plodded on.

When all the foregoing had been counted – lords temporal and spiritual, baronets, knights, esquires, gentlemen, merchants great and small, yeomen, husbandmen and their families – and the professions added in – clergy, lawyers, scriveners, naval and military officers – they probably represented a good deal less than half the population. The rest comprised men unprivileged but free, common, anonymous: the small shopkeepers, tradesmen, artisans, mechanics, innkeepers, hostlers, labourers, apprentices, common soldiers and seamen, cottagers with a cabbage patch or none, labouring people and out-servants, paupers, vagrants, gipsies, thieves, beggars. Later in the century (if Gregory King was right), they comprised 3·3 out of a total population of 5·5 million. The collective title by which the least fortunate of the lower orders of society were known — 'the Poor' — did not mean that they were all destitute. It meant that they had little or nothing to save them from destitution when times were bad or as they grew old: that a proportion of them was therefore always destitute, another proportion potentially destitute. These had to rely on charity or theft to keep alive. Their order and welfare formed far the largest and most frightening social problem that faced central and local government in any period. It called forth in the end not only great schemes of private charity but a stream of positive theories of social economics.

If the 'poor' were not a totally unleavened lump of immobile poverty the servants of the great, male and female, were sometimes able to climb perceptibly in the social scale: especially those close to a lord. Mr Paynter, Master of the Horse to the Duke of Kingston, could get himself an estate worth £200 a year with '7 miles of manor for sporting and plenty of game'. Stewards were notorious climbers. Rogers, a former steward to Lord Monson, described himself later as a 'very great *landholder*'. His neighbours were less complimentary: he was the 'intruder', 'the mushroom man'. Moralists, playwrights, novelists found a favourite theme in the rise of the upstart servant whose 'Neat's leather shoes are . . . transformed in stuff or satin ones with high heels: her yarn stockings are turned into fine silk or cotton ones . . . she must have a Trollopee and long Ruffles too, as well as her misstress and her poor scanty Linsey-Woolsey Petticoat is changed into a good silk one. . . .' The locks on tea and coffee containers witnessed to the spreading popularity of such luxuries among the servant class. Stealthily at first, then overtly, fashions of dress and consumption spread amongst the lower orders of society until there, too, they became habit.

The historian may thus categorize, as contemporaries categorized, the social material of his study. Both national income studies and sociology were born in the seventeenth century. But though convenient and helpful, the social categories mentioned above must not be insisted on too much. Just as legal definitions of status below the peerage were disappearing, so economic occupations were unspecialized. Noble landowners speculated in building and mining, merchants acquired landed estates and held them as investments in conjunction with ventures into shopkeeping, colonial exploration, grain dealing and ship-owning. In Gloucestershire lived a prosperous race of men who were proud to be known as 'gentlemen clothiers'. Yeoman farmers were found in every sort of industrial enterprise. Peasant smallholders were weavers and potters. Everywhere, even in London, the division between town and country was at least blurred, and often scarcely visible. The rigid categories of Victorian sociologists do not sit easily on the mobile confusion that was the society of Stuart England.

The pages that follow will describe many of the advantages with which England had been endowed – material resources, geographical position, ports and harbours particularly. They will also describe how English merchants and manufacturers exploited these resources, seizing upon expanding markets at home and abroad, adapting their products to the forces of competition, costs and labour supply: all this within a context of rising population and an economic policy shaped in partner-ship with a government willing to trim fiscal policy to the needs of an expanding economy. The historian cannot isolate from the economic and social context any one factor that 'explains' why England should have emerged as the original nursery of industrial revolution, mass production, mass consumption. But he can point to one factor that operated more powerfully in England than elsewhere. Here a feudally hierarchic society was dissolving, not least under the growing pressure from expanding novel, commercial elements. Only once did the ten-sions generated by change break into open conflict. The economic and social causes of the Civil War were only a part of the story but they were a real part. 'Class struggle' is too crude a term to describe the feuds and foreclosures between the fortunate and less fortunate, the enter-prising and the less enterprising, the new men and the old, the favoured and the unfavoured. Men of the same origins were to be found on opposing sides, men of different origins on the same side. Yet in some sense the conflict bore out the instinctive fears of those who had pre-dicted confusion from the ending of the old order. It came as much because the Stuarts, in their poverty, extravagance, materialism and idealism had been too willing to consecrate luck, enterprise and oppor-tunism as because they tried too hard to defend the traditional order. They had thus created frictions between 'Court' and 'Country' in religion, manners, morals and material interests.

In reality, the process by which men contracted in and out of the accepted social ranks of the time did not destroy the conception of a society ordered by degree: by putting degree up for auction, it enabled it to be preserved, strengthened and given an element of vitality and rationality it lacked elsewhere. Society remained in every respect a compromise between old and new. England, as a seventeenth-century historian has said, 'while rapidly developing into a great commercial state, was still regulated by a jurisprudence the letter and spirit of which were both, to a large extent, medieval'.[1] Compromise, improvisation and empiricism bound together much that was new with much that was old. The common law provided continuity and it was not accidental that the Civil Wars were fought in part to preserve it. Likewise, the thought and language of the age were a strange amalgam of medieval and modern. Sir Thomas Browne's largest book was called *Pseudoxia Epidemica or Vulgar Errors* (1646). Yet his own mind was full of superstitions and fantasies. He gave evidence in 1664 at a trial to show that witches existed, and could observe: 'I could be content that we might procreate like trees without conjunction.' John Aubrey could speak of Elizabeth's times as 'those darke times [when] astrologer, mathematician and conjurer were accounted the same thinges ... '. Yet even for Aubrey, earnest recorder of history, scientific learning and method though he was, they were not clearly separated. Chemistry, alchemy, astronomy, astrology, history and stories of ghost and fairy all mingle in his pages, and his account of his colleagues of the Royal Society is enlivened by references to their stars, prophecies and premonitions. The best social statistician of the age, Gregory King, was comforted to find that his calculations of the population of England were supported by Old Testament evidence.[2] When the philosophers came to try and construct systems of thought explaining the universe, or statisticians to measure social and economic movements, they were compelled to use thought and language instinct with poetical and religious feeling but ignorant of scientific terms. The language that was perfect for the play, the sermon, the ballad or the dialogue of daily life, could only painfully be adapted to the new demand for exactness and the analysis of complex situations. Intellectually, as socially and politically, the seventeenth century was Janus-headed, looking back to a world of customary values and fixed quantities, forward to a world of change, expansion, mathematics, logic and rationality.

[1] Ogg, op. cit., p. 114.   [2] See below, pp. 228–9.

CHAPTER TWO

Land and People:
The Rural Foundations of Society

EUROPE in the seventeenth century remained predominantly agricultural and rural. Britain shared these characteristics. This is not to underestimate the importance of trade — especially international trade — or of the growing industries contribu tingto trade, the growth of shipping and inland waterways, or the growing community of merchants whose enterprise created these activities and by so doing formed the truly dynamic element of change in society. It is merely to put on record the fact that in general — North Holland perhaps excepted — the majority of men everywhere and in all walks of life drew their livelihood from the soil, directly or at one or two removes. There is little in the way of reliable general statistics to illuminate the rural scene in these years. Here and there local studies will tell us about agricultural change in this county and that. But to generalize from such studies is dangerous in an age of wide regional differences. Authors will point the way to technological improvement in agriculture, but we cannot know how widely their suggestions were adopted. Not until late in the century do we have an intelligent and plausible social survey — *The Natural and Political Observations* of Gregory King (1688–96).[1] The best we can do is to form impressions by working backwards from this, remembering that between 1600 and the time when King wrote, the population may have increased by a million or more, that agriculture had improved in technique and productivity, and had become more commercial, more tied to markets, more highly capitalized as the trade and manufactures of the kingdom had increased, especially after 1660.

Out of a total population of about five and a half million souls in 1688, well over a half were directly dependent on the land. Royalty, the peerage, baronets, knights, esquires and gentlemen and their

---

[1] See below, p. 239.

families living in large measure on agricultural rents numbered perhaps 150,000. Of freeholders and customary tenants and families there were nearly a million, and perhaps another three-quarters of a million tenant farmers and dependants. A million and a quarter persons were described as labourers and out-servants, while the army of poor (cottagers and paupers) had grown to a slightly larger total. If we say that something over three million persons, in palace, castle, manor, farm or cottage were dependent on agriculture for their income we can still regard it as a conservative figure. If we look not at men but at their incomes, we reach a similar result. Out of a total estimated national income of £49·2 millions, £23·5 millions may be regarded as specifically attributable to land or agriculture in the form of rents, profits or wages. Nearly half of this was accounted for by the class known broadly as 'yeomen'; as we have seen, a highly diversified group. Of them Fuller wrote in the time of Charles I that they were 'an estate of people almost peculiar to England. France and Italy are like a die which hath no points between sink and ace, nobility and peasantry – the yeoman wears russet clothes but makes golden payment, having tin in his buttons and silver in his pocket' (*The Holy State*, bk. II, ch. XVIII). The tenant farmers, holding their land on commercial lease for a period of years from their landlords, were of less social account and throughout the seventeenth century almost certainly represented a smaller slice of the national income than the yeomanry. But their numbers were growing and were to grow ever more steadily at the expense of the small owner-occupier and customary tenant.

Careful and methodical as Gregory King was, we must not burden his figures with more conclusions than they will bear: but they certainly prove that no other economic activity could compare with agriculture as a source of income and employment. Less than half a million people, all told, earned a living directly from trade or manufactures of one kind or another; though it should be added – and the point was not lost on contemporaries – that the livings they did earn were comparatively good by the standards of the day. A sizeable merchant and his family lived in at least the comfort of a country gentleman, and a shopkeeper could expect to be as well off as many a yeoman. Trade and industry seemed calculated to earn a larger return, in fact, than agriculture – a fact which became written into the economic faith of the time and drew attention to the small proportion of the nation that was engaged in these more profitable non-agricultural pursuits – some 10,000 merchants and perhaps 100,000 shopkeepers, tradesmen and artisans. It was to be some time before the artisan was a more typical figure in English society than the domestic servant.

Most of the trades and industries which accounted for the rest of the national income were themselves based on agriculture or landed property. The cloth industry used wool, the linen industry flax, beer was made from malt and malt from barley. And because the economic process is essentially circular, the basically agricultural nature of the English economy is restated and confirmed by the consuming habits of the people; by what they spent their money on as much as by the way they earned it. Nearly half the nation's income went on food and drink. One-third of this outlay, and no less than one-seventh of total income, went on beer. About a quarter to a fifth of the whole went on what Gregory King called 'apparel' – clothing of all descriptions.

Such facts underline the essentially simple structure of the seventeenth-century economy, where trade and manufactures were still rooted deeply in the countryside. The cities and towns – London especially – drew their food and raw materials from the country. Most often the urban merchant depended for his supply of goods on rural labour organized loosely within the framework of a system known to a later age as that of 'domestic' industry. Wool, flax, leather, animal fats, malting barley, might be sold off the farm for specialized manufacture; or they might be kept at home and worked up for domestic use. A landed gentleman might be rescued from impending bankruptcy by the discovery of coal or iron on his estates, or by the increased value of sites once rural but now drawn into areas increasingly urban. Everywhere, town and country, agriculture, trade and industry remained closely entwined in Stuart England.

The basic needs of the people – food, drink, clothing and (in so far as wood may be regarded as agricultural produce) fuel and housing – were produced all over Britain, though produced unevenly. Weather, soil and, increasingly, economic calculation brought about a considerable degree of specialization, of division of labour from region to region. Farmers concentrated not only on those crops that seemed best suited to the rainfall, the seasons and their particular variety of land – light, medium or heavy, sand, chalk, clay, fen, marsh, fine or rough grazing as it might be – but also on those crops and commodities that paid the best profits.

A landlord's profits might depend on industrial activities. Forges and furnaces competed with navy contractors to devour the oak forests of

the south-east and 'oaks by the million were burned to make charcoal'.[1]
Many a ruler of an entailed estate provided a marriage portion for a
daughter from a hasty cutting of his oak groves, sold off privily for
local building or carpentry. Stone quarries, clay pits and brickworks
were likewise a useful source of profit. And since overland transport
costs were heavy, these materials were often used locally, giving a tex-
ture to manor, farm house and village that was only destroyed by the
railway age.

Towards the end of the century Gregory King calculated that England
and Wales consisted of about 40 million acres. He was a little out but
not far; 38 million acres would have been nearer the mark. How
accurate his other estimates were — 9 million acres of arable, with a
further 2 million acres fallow, 12 of pasture and meadow, 6 of woods,
parks, forests and commons — it is not easy to say. If we assume that his
figures are not too far out, and remember that the preceding three-
quarters of a century had seen a sizeable addition to the cultivated land,
in the Fens and elsewhere, we might conclude that in the first half of the
seventeenth century, England and Wales probably had upwards of 8
million acres of arable land under cultivation. That is about 75 per cent
of our present-day acreage; it was farmed by about the same number of
farmers — 300,000 to 350,000 — and it had to feed a population only
one-eighth that of its present size. That the supply of food in relation to
need had improved markedly by comparison with earlier centuries is
beyond doubt, and the marginal deficit of the first half of the seventeenth century was to turn into a surplus after the Restoration. Yet, by
later standards, agricultural output was pitifully low. A fair yield for
wheat may have been 11 bushels per acre — a bushel or two above
medieval expectation but still only a quarter to a third of what a
modern farmer hopes for. Much must have been a long way below
this if estimates of the *weight* of the national harvest were anywhere near
the truth. Even King did not rank the harvest yields of cereals at more
than 70 million bushels — a mere fraction of a modern harvest that
passes the 8 million ton mark for cereals and yields besides over 20
million tons of two crops unknown to early Stuart agriculture — turnips
and other root crops for animal feed, and potatoes.

Gregory King gave estimates for the animal, as well as the human
population, even down to the 24,000 hares and leverets, and the million
rabbits and conies that he assumed to inhabit these islands. Four and a
half million cattle, 11 million sheep and 2 million pigs were probably

[1] R. G. Albion, *Forests and Sea Power*, 1926, p. 116.

not unreasonable guesses: they represent somewhere between a half and a third of present-day figures. Though, once again, as with plants, so with animals: they were pitiful creatures by any later standards.

The traveller crossing Jacobean England from Lynn or Yarmouth to Bristol or Holyhead passed from what, since Roman times, had been a predominantly corn-growing area to one that mixed more stock raising into its economy. This was in part a simple effect of geology and climate. For whether he knew it or not, he was also crossing the belts of alluvial soil, the chalk and sand of East Anglia, the midland limestones and clays, to the rocks of Cornwall, Wales and the north-west. These ran in great belts, often from north-east to south-west, through England. The differences of terrain were combined with differences in the weather. Summer temperatures were perceptibly higher in the Thames Valley and a circle of a hundred miles radius centred on it than they were further north and west. This same area likewise had only half or less than half the rainfall of Wales and Scotland. This, then, was the natural framework within which the classic system of English farming had developed, and was to endure down to our own day. The light sandy or chalky soils of East Anglia were good for growing barley and rearing sheep, the heavier clays of the Midlands were better for wheat, the wetter uplands of north and west best for cattle. For wheat and rye the northern summer was too late, but oats were grown on a subsistence basis. Again, if King's figures can be taken as a guide, twice as much barley was grown in England as wheat. The profits of English farming owed as much to beer as to bread.

The great demand for wool that had stimulated growth and change in Tudor agriculture was levelling off by the early seventeenth century and the character of the output itself was altering. Medieval England had been famous for the quality of its fine, short staple wool. Now there was a growing trend towards a heavier fleece, a longer staple and a less fine product. Early in Tudor times, critics of the enclosure policy had alleged that sheep fed on enclosed fields failed to produce that fineness of wool associated with open grazing. A writer in 1610 was still saying the same thing: 'In those daies before the trobles wee had not so much woolle growinge as wee have nowe, for that men covet to have sheepe which bear great burdens so that one sheepe beareth as much woolle as twoe or three did in those times . . .'[1]

It was the area that formerly produced the finest wool — broadly the

[1] P. J. Bowden, 'Wool Supply and the Woollen Industry', *Econ. Hist. Rev.*, vol. IX, no. 1, 1956.

V-shaped area that ran from Wiltshire north to Yorkshire and east to Norfolk – that had been most influenced by the sixteenth-century enclosure movement. Richer grazing brought coarser wool. The quality of wool from the Midlands and from Lincolnshire therefore declined in comparison with that of regions formerly less renowned like Hampshire and Sussex. This change in the character of the English wool supply went hand in hand with a change in the market for wool. Pure woollen cloth was giving way to various kinds of worsted or mixed cloths. In so far as these used wool, they used long wool. By the mid-seventeenth century the demand for long wool was equalling that for the finer shorter wools used in the older broadcloth. Instead of going westwards to the fine cloth-making area, midland wools were being sent east and north to the Norfolk and Yorkshire homes of worsteds, stuffs, kerseys and dozens. Lincoln wools that had gone in the old days to the makers of Suffolk fine broadcloths now also went to Norfolk and Yorkshire to replace local wools that were used in the coarser cloths.

Sheep were reared widely through the entire midland area. They probably accounted for a fifth of the total of farm incomes. But the sheep-farmer was feeling the edge of the sharp competition in the cloth trade, and the recurrent crises that paralysed the industry after 1620. While grain prices held pretty steady in the long term, stimulated no doubt by government policy – the first Act allowing the export of corn 'because of the great redundancy of corn, cattle, butter, cheese etc. . . .' came under the Commonwealth – wool prices were held down by a score of Acts which prohibited wool export for the benefit of the English cloth industry, and were designed specifically to hamper industrial competitors in Holland, France, Italy and elsewhere. From 1600 wool prices fell from the peak they had attained (two and a half times their price a century earlier) until by the third quarter of the seventeenth century they levelled off at less than half their 1600 price.[1] Wool was therefore less profitable and attractive to the farmer than it had been. But as the demand for food grew, there was a bigger incentive to breed for mutton, and in combination with the sale of tallow for soap and candles this could well make more profit for a farmer than wool.

Cattle of a sort were found everywhere. They might be reared for meat, as they were in the rich pastures of Northampton, Leicester or in the Vale of Aylesbury, all the homes of graziers growing rich on the

1 See E. Kerridge, 'The Movement of Rent 1540–1640', *Econ. Hist. Rev.*, VI, vol. I, 1953, Table IV.

rising demand for meat. Or they might support the dairy farms of Wiltshire, Somerset and Gloucester. In Cheshire, Somerset and Suffolk, a thriving cheese industry worked for export as well as local markets. And wherever cattle were slaughtered there was a brisk trade in hides, the raw material for a leather industry that maintained eighty tanneries in Bermondsey and Southwark alone and was said to be second only to the leading national industry of woollen cloth. Cattle may have accounted for some 30 per cent of total farm incomes in the seventeenth century. With rising standards of living at the top and in the middle ranges of society, and demand for richer and more varied diet, stock raising was a profitable enterprise.

The barley and wheat that came down-river by barge and round the coasts by ship to feed the population of London, Bristol and other cities, and the wool that supplied the widespread cloth industry, were not the only cash crops that attracted the enterprising farmer. Since the late fifteenth century, hops had been used to season and preserve an increasing proportion of the 'ale' brewed and drunk in England. Their bitter flavour was credited with digestive and even hypnotic qualities. Hopped beer became increasingly popular, in spite of some superstitious conservatism against a foreign and newfangled idea. By the seventeenth century, hop growing had become a large-scale affair and the hop fields of Suffolk, Essex and Hereford were as famous as those of Kent and Sussex. Another crop that supplied the needs of industry was flax. Though England, with her excellent wool supply, relied less on rough linen than many countries, a good deal was made domestically from the crops grown throughout the Midlands and in other areas where there was a good rich dry soil. Many other localities had special crops. Camden, the Elizabethan topographer, noticed that Saffron Walden in Essex lay 'among the fields looking merrily with most lovely saffron'. The yellow dye was used by the textile makers. 'Carrets' and turnips in East Anglia witnessed to the influence of Dutch immigrants who brought with them the skill and knowledge of the market gardening at which the Low Countries excelled. Fruit came from the orchards of Kent and Worcestershire. Cherries and apples were of many varieties — five hundred it was said, including the kinds that made the cider of Devon and the West Country. All round London market gardening, which it was said 'began to creep in England' from Holland about 1600, flourished on the demands of Londoners, who were kept supplied with 'cabbages, colleflours, turnips, carrots, parsnips and peas'.

It would nevertheless be easy to exaggerate the extent to which English farming of the earlier seventeenth century had become specialized. Specialization there was, and it was increasing. Medieval Norfolk had had over a hundred markets and fairs. As farming became more specialized and commercial, these were reduced to thirty-five by the mid-seventeenth century. But specialization was everywhere held in check by the needs of those thousands of small men, owners and tenants of tiny holdings who looked to their land to supply their own basic needs. They maintained a high degree of diversity in the rural economy everywhere. So, for that matter, did the home farms of the great landlords, who likewise supplied much of their own household needs, especially in the times of rising prices. 'Market opportunity', that is to say, did not entirely rule the pattern of the English countryside. It was modified by the surviving elements of a subsistence agriculture and a peasant society. But this rural economy was not static. The age was already putting forth the first of those improving agricultural writers who were to tell the farmer his business for a long time to come. Some, like Gervase Markham, the author of *A Way to Get Wealth* (1625), were hacks and charlatans. Others, like Sir Hugh Plat (*A New and Admirable Arte of Setting of Corne*, 1600) and Edward Maxey (*New Instructions of Plowing and Setting of Corne*, 1601), were serious, thoughtful inventors who turned their minds to the problem of reducing the waste of seed corn which the broadcast method of sowing entailed. John Norden (*The Surveyors' Dialogue*, 1608) was a man of wide practical experience, topographer and map maker as well as a lawyer. As Crown Surveyor of woods and forests, he carried out some important reforms of the royal estates in 1614 and 1615 – one of the few who succeeded. Walter Blith (*The English Improver*, 1649, and *The English Improver Improved*, 1652) has been called 'the greatest of the mid-seventeenth century writers'[1] who set the pattern of good husbandry in almost all its essentials until the days of Jethro Tull. Blith advocated the use of water meadows, the drainage of wet soils, enclosure to intensify production, the ploughing up of old grass, and the use of grass 'leys' in worn-out arable and of manures everywhere, and systematic afforestation. For the old-fashioned traditional open field farmer he had little sympathy. 'He will toyle all his dayes himselfe and Family for nothing, in and upon his common arable fielde land; up early and downe late, drudge and moyle and ware out himself and family; rather than he will cast how he may improve his hands of imposturing and enclosing of it.'

[1] R. Trow Smith, *English Husbandry*, 1951, p. 108.

27

Richard Weston (*Discourse on the Husbandrie used in Brabant and Flanders,* 1645) was another influential Commonwealth writer. Less original than Blith, he was an important channel of agricultural news from the Low Countries and personifies that Dutch influence which was as vital to the countryside as it was to be in counting-house and workshop. In that most densely populated corner of Europe, resource and enterprise were the only alternative to starvation and poverty. Food and raw materials had to be imported on a large scale and these were paid for by the export of other goods and commodities. Agriculture itself had therefore for long concentrated on cash crops or cattle breeding, and was strongly influenced in its methods by intensive horticulture which pointed to the virtues of deep digging, heavy fertilizing, culture and continuous weeding. From the Middle Ages, Flanders had known a system of convertible husbandry that alternated a three-course system of corn and fallow with a six-year pasture for producing meat and manure. By the seventeenth century sown clover was replacing grass, and turnips and carrots were being grown for fodder. Fed to livestock in the stall they were the source of added supplies of manure which was carefully collected and added to town sewage carried out by barge into the country. This was the system that surprised and impressed Weston and that other indefatigable agricultural publicist and reformer of the Commonwealth, Samuel Hartlib.[1]

How representative, how practical were these writers? Plainly they were ahead of the traditional, conservative, superstitious rural world which it was their object to reform. Blith, who wrote of 'the scandall and prejudice among many of you against new projections', must have been voicing the feelings of other reformers too. The path of the rural revolutionary has never been easy. Even in the nineteenth century, an agricultural writer could lament the ignorant prejudice that kept the mass of farmers from following the principles laid down and proven by reformers of the century before.[2] While it would be absurd to ignore the gap between precept and practice, evidence abounds that a critical, improving spirit of curiosity and experiment was abroad, even in the first half of the century. As often in times of change, the distinction between charlatan and innovator grows thin. Charlatans or not, all these writers performed a useful function in purveying knowledge of experiment at home and abroad from the innovators to the average

[1] See G. E. Fussell, 'Low Countries' Influence on English Farming', *E.H.R.*, October 1959.

[2] *Library of Useful Knowledge. British Husbandry,* 1834, vol. I, ch. I.

rural traditionalist. That their writings were not merely academic exercises may be seen from their own close contact with innovations. Blith's plough was used everywhere for over a century. In some places it lasted until the end of the nineteenth century.

In the eastern counties turnip husbandry as recommended by Weston was already practised in the mid-seventeenth century under the influence of immigrants from the Netherlands. The poet Drayton marked it out as a special feature of Norfolk that it grew every variety of vegetable — 'colewort, coliflower, cabidge, great beans, onions, scallions, leeks, garlick' — but above all

> The savory persnip next, and carret pleasing food;
> The turnip tasting well to clownes in winter weather.

By 1660 turnips had been incorporated as an essential part of the farming economy. They were sown in mid-August, after harvest on what would otherwise have been fallow, hand-hoed, raised from Autumn to March and fed to milking cows or fattening bullocks. Suffolk, said Defoe later, 'was the first to feed and fatten turnips'. Recent research shows he was right.[1] Norfolk farmers came next. The rest of the country was much slower to follow.

Further west the great sheepfarmers of Wiltshire were experimenting with the water meadow. The main purposes of the sheep here were, first, to provide dung, and second, wool. As Latymer put it: 'if they have no sheep to help fat the ground they shall have but bare corn and thin'. The Wiltshire sheep were bred, therefore, to walk from the fold on the tillage to the pasture and back to do their good work. A thousand sheep — and there were many flocks of upwards of 400 — would fold an acre of arable overnight. So each man's land got dunged in turn. The yield of corn depended on the number of sheep; that in turn depended on the winter feed available. The purpose of the water meadow was to cover the early grass with a blanket of water that protected it from the frost, giving a stalky but luxuriant feed by mid-March — long before the normal growth. This 'early bite' for ewes and lambs, it was said, much increased the quantity and quality of a crop of barley. John Aubrey, the antiquarian, thought he could remember water meadows in Wiltshire by 1635. His recollections have been pushed back thirty years by modern inquiry. By the second quarter of the century the water meadow was widely spread. It increased the supply of hay, improved the yield of corn and made earlier lambing and larger flocks possible. Its

---

[1] E. Kerridge, 'Turnip Husbandry in High Suffolk', *Econ. Hist. Rev.*, VIII, no. 3, 1956.

benefits were not limited to Wiltshire and the neighbouring counties. Middle and eastern England knew them too.[1]

Further west still, in Devon, an early seventeenth-century writer could praise the improving urge that was reclaiming the waste grounds, and making use of ashes from old dried turf to spread as a fertilizer — the so-called 'denshiring' that was to be spread far beyond the boundary of the county that invented it. Here in the first half of the century flourished an efficient mixed husbandry which produced wool for the local cloth industry, fed the local population with beef, pork, beer, cider, biscuits, beans, and peas and had a surplus for export. 'I have been in all the Counties of England', Cromwell is reported to have said, 'and I think the husbandry of Devon the best.' The remark may have been apocryphal but it serves to emphasize that rural improvement was not limited to East Anglia or the Midlands.[2]

All the same, it was in the east that the most spectacular instance of large-scale improvement was to be found. The drainage of the Fenland cannot be compassed within the normal confines of agricultural improvement: it was that, but it was more also and many influences combined to bring it to fruition. Mooted in Elizabeth's day, it was James I's poverty that stimulated the survey of Crown Lands in 1607. This in turn suggested that it would be profitable to assert the royal rights in marsh and fen. The desire of local landlords to raise the rental value of their lands combined in the next year or two with the speculative ambitions of some London capitalists — including that ubiquitous Jacobean financier, Sir William Cokayne — to bring forth practical attempts at drainage. It was a formidable task. This was the time when Isaac Casaubon, on a visit to Ely, described a watery land where cottagers spent their lives travelling by boat, fishing and fowling amidst bittern and dotterel, walking on stilts as they drove the cattle on to the dry pastures. These were the people described by Camden as 'rude, uncivill and envious to all others whom they call Upland-Men', a people subject to ague of mind as well as body. Their opposition helped to frustrate the drainage plans of the second decade and repeatedly to hinder or undo later schemes.

It was 1620 before James I decided to take a hand in the operations himself. The story of the partnership between him and, after his death, Charles I, and the remarkable Dutch engineer and entrepreneur,

[1] E. Kerridge, 'The Sheepfold in Wiltshire and the Floating of the Water Meadows', *Econ. Hist. Rev.*, VI, no. 3, 1954.
[2] W. G. Hoskins, *Devon* (New Survey of England), 1954, p. 94.

Cornelius Vermuyden, is not strictly agrarian history, and is more appropriately told elsewhere (see below, p. 104). Its consequences are. They
can be briefly summarized thus. As a result of an agreement of 1634
between the Earl of Bedford and thirteen co-Adventurers, mainly local
landowners, Vermuyden undertook to drain a large area of the Fens. A
period of confusion and recrimination followed until 1638 when the
King, even more in need of realizable assets than his father, declared
himself the 'undertaker'. He thereby stood to gain 57,000 acres out of
the total acreage reclaimed. This was described by Vermuyden as 'a
continent of about 400,000 acres which being made winter ground
would be an unexpected benefit to the Commonwealth of £600,000
per annum and upwards . . .'.[1]

There is plenty of evidence from later writers, including Hartlib,
Pepys, Dugdale and Fuller, to confirm that Vermuyden achieved something like his target — Hartlib put the 'recovered' area at 380,000 acres.
True, the Fens were not all as bad as those 6,000 acres of Crowland
Manor leased out as 'fishing fields', or even those half-drowned parts of
the Isle of Axholme that never dried out at all, even in summer. Large
areas were already valuable summer pastures and the original drainage
schemes aimed only to bring up the worst areas to the standard of the
best. Later it was found inevitable — so it was said — to make 'winter
grounds for the plough' in order to justify the heavy capital outlay. In
this way, rich pastures became rich arable, and something like half of
the modern area of the Fens was brought into being — 'roughly three
quarters of a million acres of land unsurpassed in productivity anywhere
in these isles . . . thus it is no exaggeration to say that the draining and
reclamation of the Fens represents a permanent and important influence
on the social and economic history of England'.[2]

The new land was sown mainly with oats and coleseed, emphasizing
the trend towards fodder for livestock as the potentialities of the market
for meat and wool were realized. Coleseed, 'whereof they make oyl by
breaking it between two great black marble stones of nearly a Tun
weight, one standing perpendicularly on the other . . . in mills, called
oyl-mills', was another crop that came into methodical use through the
Dutch example. Its oil could be used for lamps and for the preparation
of wool, its straw made into fuel cakes, and the seed itself used for
feeding sheep. The oil mills (like the one at Santoft in north Lincolnshire) was to become a feature of the Fenland scene; 'some go with

[1] H. C. Darby, *The Draining of the Fens*, 1940, vol. II, pp. 23-38.
[2] L. E. Harris, *Vermuyden and the Fens*, 1953, p. 16.

sails and serve also to dreyn the Fens and are called *Engines*, being of good use and discharge great quantities of water[1].' Mill construction was to be an important technological link later on between rural and urban industry. No longer a backwater, the Fens were becoming a centre of agrarian enterprise. To fodder crops were added hemp for making ropes and canvas, flax for the rough linens commonly used by the peasantry, onions that grew excellently in the local soils, mustard and woad. The flocks of geese increased as rapidly as the sheep and cattle, crowding the roads to London in season, and providing additional profits from the sale of their feathers and quills for pens. The lakes and meres that survived the drainage were made to yield their mead of profit too, and the well-to-do Londoner could order fresh pike and eel that came up from the Fens in tanks of fresh water borne in specially designed carts.

To the north and east of the Fenland, meanwhile, other improvements were going forward. Along the Lincolnshire coast, large stretches of marsh were being reclaimed, thus compensating for those erosions of which the local inhabitants were constantly reminded (as a woman testified at an inquiry in 1636) by the church steeple which stood up out of the sea off Skegness. The Skegness marshes, like those of Kent, supported a great sheep population. It was mainly the property of rich farmers from the near-by wolds who gladly rented this additional support for their sheep and barley economy.

The historian of Lincolnshire farming has suggested that these developments, on marsh and fen, hills and lowlands, have a more than local importance. Lincolnshire, she has suggested, was a model and a microcosm.[2] What was happening here was to be repeated, sooner or later, elsewhere – on the marshes of Essex, the fens of Cambridge, the Cotswolds and in the entire midland plain. In Devon Mr Hoskins sees signs of the same tendency towards larger pastures and more stock. Likewise in the Midlands; no violent change in methods but a little more emphasis on grassland – it was already the home of the largest graziers in England. And these were in turn the reflection of changing social habits and living standards as rural methods of production adapted themselves with a modicum of skill and substantial profit to the demands of the urban market. The English – or at any rate some Englishmen – were breaking through the starch barrier into the world of protein: an elementary and universal sign of progress in living standards.

---

[1] Darby, op. cit., p. 93.
[2] J. Thirsk, *English Peasant Farming*, 1957, p. 2.

'Improvement', defined as new crops, new methods, manuring, marling and drainage, had taken place largely in those eastern and western counties that stood outside the confines of the old open-field area. Especially in those areas with easy access to growing urban markets, of which London was far and away the largest. Throughout the Midlands, the face of the land was still wrinkled and corrugated into a million small strips, the old communal farming system persisted, cramping agricultural initiative and inhibiting experiments with crops and methods. Even here, nevertheless, in the heart of the open-field country, the winds of change were blowing. For one thing, a growing acreage of arable was being created by 'assarting' — that process of winning new land from old waste and heath. This newly won land was farmed on the new principle of separate, hedged fields. The land was given the newer treatments — drainage, manure and, where suitable, as on the lighter soils of Leicestershire, sown with root crops. On many a holding these new methods were run in double harness with the old. Quite apart from the writers who preached improvement and equated the unenclosed open fields with agricultural barbarism, scores of ordinary farmers saw the lesson quite as clearly. The full benefits of drainage and root crops were not possible without enclosure. Hence a good measure of private exchange of strips was in progress between tenants and freeholders in the open fields to achieve a more rational layout of their properties. Increasingly, though often empirically, it was more widely recognized that the farmer's problem was to break the vicious circle of stagnant or declining productivity. Held in the straitjacket of the old communal cultivation, the farmer could do little. The land could yield no more until it could be drained and manured. More manure was not to be had without more livestock. Livestock could not be fed until the supply of fodder was increased — especially to keep stock through the winter months. But until there was more stock, there could be no muck. The land must be freed from communal restrictions that held back the numbers of livestock and technical improvements. The purpose of enclosure was to do precisely this, enabling the farmer to combine grain growing with stock raising, to substitute for fallow new fodder crops like turnip and clover. These, in turn, enriched the soil by adding nitrogen, instead of exhausting it as cereal crops inevitably did. The larger numbers of animals provided manure. This raised the yield of the soil. Already the advocates of enclosure and the new methods were claiming remarkable results. Yields may have been nearly doubled, especially on newly converted land. Some of the other claims – to outputs of 50 or 60 bushels to the acre – were improbable, or at any rate certainly unrepresentative.

Why, then, was technical progress so slow? The answer lies partly in the conservatism and suspicions, not always irrational, of the peasantry; partly in the attitude of a government which still feared that enclosure might bring that depopulation which it regarded as incompatible with its bounden duty to maintain the military security as well as the general prosperity and just government of its subjects. Popular suspicions broke out from time to time in riots like those of 1607, when Northampton-shire, Warwickshire and Leicestershire were shaken by violence. Three thousand men assembled at Hillmorton, calling themselves 'levellers' or 'diggers'. They were there to protest against the engrossing of farms. The Adventurers of the Fens had throughout to face the hostility of the local peasantry. In south Yorkshire, the new dykes were thrown down. In the Bedford Level, the 'fen-slodgers' took reprisals on the Dutch drainers who were destroying their franchise to fish, fowl, cut reeds and turf. The intruders were thrown into the water and held under with poles. The hostile attitude of the peasantry was supported by writers like Moore (*The Crying Sin of England*, 1653) and the extreme republican radicals who denounced the injustice and depopulation that accompanied enclosure. Successive governments, from James to Crom-well, sustained the traditional hostility, or at any rate reserve, towards enclosure. Down to the Civil War, the Stuarts took spasmodic action through the Privy Council against enclosers, fining and imprisoning offenders. These actions testified, no doubt, to the sense of social justice that is often seen as the informing spirit of early Stuart government. It would have been more convincing if the Crown's own excursions, especially in the Fens, had been restrained by an equal care for their social effects on the peasantry. For there, where the Crown claimed a third of the reclaimed land, little attention was paid to individual peasant rights. The Crown's attitude, it has been said, 'resembled that of a prospector striking gold in an uninhabited desert'.[1]

There was no official recognition, much less encouragement, of enclosure until after the Restoration. But since what was official was by no means always what was practicable, some enclosure did go on, by voluntary agreement, by stealth, by violence or simply by that flagrant inconsistency which was perhaps the leading characteristic of Stuart attempts at social and economic planning. Mr Beresford has shown, for example, that in Leicestershire, where only seven parishes had been

[1] Joan Thirsk, op. cit., p. 109.

enclosed in the second half of the sixteenth century, and only twenty-four were to be enclosed in the second half of the seventeenth, fifty-seven were enclosed between 1600 and 1650.[1]

It is doubtful whether the enclosure movement generally had anything like the momentum of Tudor times, when the urge to enclose and convert to pasture had changed the face of much of the Midlands. Now there was more enclosure by agreement. But against the background of recurrent economic depressions, even this modified improving movement could produce agrarian radicalism on a considerable scale, as the appearance of Diggers and Levellers shows. The times were working against the small landowner with no reserves of capital, against customary tenants whose rights were most often vague and ill-defined. The age of landlord and tenant farming was already dawning. In the long run it would offer great material benefits. In the short run it often created individual hardships and added to the growing social tensions of the time.

[1] Quoted by Trow Smith, op. cit., p. 113.

CHAPTER THREE

The Trade of England:
The Seventeenth-Century Crisis

ENGLAND'S trade — in wool, leather, grain, hops, minerals — grew directly out of her land and farms. Historians often divide it into two kinds: domestic and foreign. The distinction is useful: but in reality there were many organic links between the two branches of trade. Although the home market often remained highly localized, cramped by poor roads and high transport costs, it was to be slowly knit together more closely as the century progressed by improved river navigation and a growing fleet of coastal shipping. Newcastle and Welsh coal, Cornish tin, Devonshire cloth, East Anglian corn, Cheshire salt — to mention only a few of the bulkier cargoes — were marketed not only locally but nationally. The chief focus of their domestic market was London. London demand was the most powerful single influence determining agrarian and industrial investment: a magnet that drew goods, money and men south, rousing the jealousy of the outports who felt themselves dwarfed by the size and thwarted by the political power of the metropolis. In London the domestic market merged into the foreign. A high proportion of exports were sent to London before going abroad. London was the centre of the great trading companies and the finishing industries. In London sat the Privy Council and Parliament, which increasingly regulated the foreign trade of England as a whole. The wool trade, corn trade, the movement of bullion and coin, imports and exports, and the shipping industry, were a few of the economic activities that were already the subject of official intervention, prohibition or encouragement. Trade might often be largely local, but already it was conceived as the nation's business, to be regulated and administered on a national scale.

The economic nationalism of the new century was more than mere rhetoric. The Jacobean Englishman knew far more about the geography, natural resources and economic potentialities of his country

than his ancestors, thanks to the surveys of topographers like William
Camden (1551–1623), map-makers like John Norden (1548–1629), even
to the romantic verse of the monumental *Poly-Olbion* wherein the poet

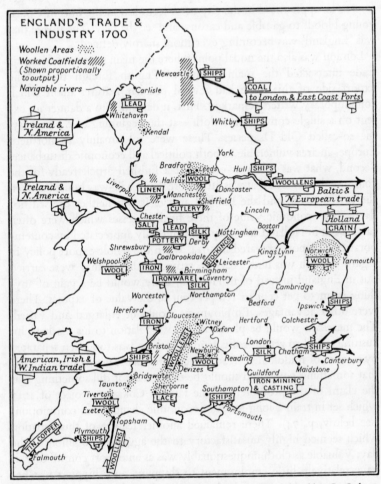

ENGLAND'S TRADE &
INDUSTRY 1700

Woollen Areas
Worked Coalfields
(Shown proportionally
to output)
Navigable rivers

Based on Sellmann, *Students' Atlas of Modern History*, Edward Arnold & Co. Ltd.

Michael Drayton enshrined the geography, flora, fauna and a generous
sample of the folk-lore of England. Probably nothing contributed more
to the sense of conscious national identity than the increasing numbers
of the upper and middle classes who visited London. Of a London

'season' it is as yet too early to speak. But hundreds of the nobility and gentry were brought together by the growing part played by Parliament in the nation's affairs. Court duties, offices and sinecures attracted others. Merchants came from the provinces to talk business, younger sons to be apprenticed in the city or to learn law at the Inns of Court, young bloods to gamble and carouse and see the play. The image that was 'England' was becoming ever more sharply defined.

London was also the nodal point where the main stream of domestic trade intersected the main stream of English foreign trade. The export side of this trade had several peculiar features upon which contemporary writers remarked. First, it depended to a dangerous extent on a single commodity: cloth – at the beginning of the century, the so-called Old Draperies. These were sold mainly to northern Europe, an area vulnerable to both political and economic disturbance. Second, what was sold was often not a finished article ready for the consumer but a cloth that was little more than a half-way house between the raw material and the finished article. It was neither dressed nor dyed. The economic value of these final processes which were often carried out in Holland was very high and fully appreciated by contemporaries. A report prepared in 1614, when the whole export policy in regard to cloth was under review, estimated that, if they were carried out in England instead of in Holland, there would be a gain of anything from 50 per cent to 100 per cent in the value of exports. There were other advantages. Employment would be enlarged and varied. The merchant would be placed in a closer relation to his markets, his customers and to retail profits from which he was too often separated by a series of middlemen. About such *desiderata* it was commonly felt that something could and should be done. That it did something was the claim of the promoters of the famous Cokayne project of 1613 which set in train a long series of economic changes and commotions (see below, p. 74). There remained another feature of this situation which seemed highly unsatisfactory to the aggressive opinion of the day. Valuable as cloth unquestionably was as an export commodity, it gave relatively little employment to shipping, and shipping was becoming a popular test of the 'national' value of trades and industries within the economy. Throughout the repeated crises in the cloth trade, pamphleteers emphasized the risks to public order from the virtually monopolistic position the cloth industry occupied in our foreign trade, adding that 'we may peradventure employ our selves with better Safety, Plenty & Profit in using more Tillage & Fishing, than to trust so wholly to the making of Cloth . . .'.[1] A glance at the Dutch seemed to prove the advantages they enjoyed by their vigorous exploitation of e.g. the fisheries, which had stimulated the growth of their economy, especially its shipping industry. This contrast between the bulk trades which the Dutch had managed to monopolize, and the specialized but relatively meagre tonnage of England's trades, became a stock comment as time went on. It was pithily summarized by George Downing, a shrewd observer of the Dutch scene. Pleading that the Government should pay more heed to the fisheries, he wrote from Holland:

> . . . the [Dutch] *herring* trade is the cause of the *salt* trade, and the *herring &* *salt* trade are the causes of this countrey's [Holland] having, in a manner, wholy the trade of the Baltique Sea, for that they have those bulky goods to load theire Shippes with thither; whereas the Shippes which goes from England thither are faine to goe in a manner empty thither, which makes the fraight backward from thence to England to be double of what it would be.[2]

Yet how was this to be done? The expansion of fisheries and of foreign trade of the right kind was to prove an arduous struggle, one step forward invariably neutralized by another step back. Recent inquiries seem to confirm the opinion of contemporaries that the real foundations of progress — the techniques of deep-sea navigation and seamanship — were laid by the pioneers of the coastal trades, especially by the colliers that rolled down from Newcastle, past Flamborough Head, Spurn and Cromer to the Thames. Conventionally, this is a part of the 'domestic' trade of England. It was also an exacting school of seamanship that produced the sailors without whom overseas expansion would have been impossible: even, in later days, the greatest of all, James Cook, apprenticed at Whitby in 1746.

The statistics of shipping tonnage are not easy to interpret. Different historians calculate them differently. Mr Harper thinks that total tonnage grew between 1615 and 1660 from 102,000 to 162,000 tons. Mr Davis suggests a larger increase. Between 1629 and 1660 he thinks the total rose from 115,000 to 200,000 tons.[3] Calculations are bedevilled by the absence of any systematic registration, by the purchases and

---

[1] Thomas Mun, *England's Treasure by fforraign Trade*, reprinted 1933, p. 73.

[2] Lister, *Life of Clarendon*, vol. III. Downing to Clarendon, The Hague, 8 July 1661, N.S.

[3] L. A. Harper, *The English Navigation Laws*, 1939, pp. 339, 343; R. Davis, *The Rise of the English Shipping Industry in the Seventeenth and Eighteenth Centuries*, 1962, ch. 1 and Appendix A. The figure of 200,000 in 1660 seems high. It depends on the capture of prizes in the First Dutch War. Contemporaries thought that most of these were lost in war against Spain after 1655, when building was likewise stagnant.

captures of Dutch ships, and by subsequent losses in the war against Spain. It does not seem so difficult to agree that the biggest increase in the years before the Civil War was in the coastal trades, especially in the coal trade between the north-east coal ports and London. The collier tonnage, according to one calculation, rose from 28,000 to 71,000 tons between 1615 and 1660. Foreign-going ships probably increased more slowly, certainly down to the 1650s with the exception of the rapidly growing Newfoundland cod fishing fleet. The increase in foreign trade, judged by the shipping figures, was certainly less than that which England enjoyed between the time of the Armada and the accession of Charles I; much less than she was to enjoy between the Restoration and the Glorious Revolution.

Writers on trade and shipping regularly praised the coal trade, exalting its claims to be 'if not the only, yet the especial Nursery and School of seamen': 'the chiefest in employment of seamen'. The sailors were trained in a hard school; if war came they were near at hand for naval impressment. More than that, coal was a bulk cargo that employed big ships. Along with the corn Londoners needed for food and drink, the coal they needed for their houses and industries constituted England's earliest and largest need for those bulk cargoes which had brought the growing Dutch merchant fleet into being. Coal had already established the claim it was to reinforce down to the twentieth century to be a main promoter of shipping and shipbuilding. It offered certainly the brightest prospect in an age that was to see the disastrous collapse of export trade. For the chronic depression that engulfed the English economy for more than a quarter of a century had its roots in that collapse and in the disintegration of the old European economy under the pressures of war and currency manipulations. To offset this, new types of manufacture, the so-called New Draperies in particular, were being devised for new customers in new markets in the Mediterranean and elsewhere. Governments, administrators and merchants were fumbling their way towards a new and aggressive conception of a mercantile economy, protectionist, self-sufficient, exclusive. A bellicose colonial push was to expand the perimeter of England's commerce eastwards to India and the Archipelago, westwards to the Caribbean and North America. But as yet much of this was the stuff that dreams were made of. The gulf between aspirings and reality remained obstinate and wide. The reality was empty bellies in the old cloth-making areas, the slow decline of the Merchant Adventurers as the traditional exporting interest, riot, frustration and war, both civil and foreign.

Steadily the opinion gathered conviction, became indeed an obsession, that England's economic problems reflected her unsatisfactory relationship with the leading economic power of the day; the Dutch Republic. In the interval between the declining threat of a Spanish and the later rise of a French, hegemony, Englishmen allowed themselves the luxury of a temporary but virulent campaign against the Dutch. It had its roots in the knowledge that the English economy was, in many respects, still a junior partner in a system of European and extra-European trade which, though centred once upon Antwerp, now revolved around Amsterdam. Freed from Spanish suzerainty, the new republic had made astonishing strides in the first decades of the new century. These years witnessed the foundation of the Bank of Amsterdam, a new Bourse, the Dutch East India Company, the rise of a great new woollen textiles industry at Leiden, important technological advances in refining and finishing industries which sprang up in the wake of a prodigious flow of commodities through the Dutch entrepôt. Baltic corn, timber, iron, guns, were shipped through the Danish Sound southwards for customers throughout Europe. They were paid for by a countervailing stream of goods brought or collected in Europe, and ·increasingly in Asia and America. When these were not available or saleable, Spanish American silver won in the trade with Spain flowed north and east to fill the gap between inward and outward trade. A Dutch fleet sailed each year from February to September from the Shetlands to the Thames, close in to the coast, fishing up herrings. Salted and barrelled, these provided food at home and valuable exports abroad. English-made cloths were finished, dressed and dyed in Amsterdam, German linens bleached at Haarlem, Norfolk barley distilled or brewed, Caribbean sugar boiled and refined, Baltic timber converted into ships, barrels, planks. And a sizeable proportion of these trades, so far as they were driven with England, came and went in Dutch ships, especially in the relatively newly designed 'flyboats', built for cheap freightage. In all the arts of commerce, and many of industry, the Dutch were indisputably ahead. They had cornered the most profitable economic activities. They dominated world markets, standing at all points between the English and their suppliers and customers. Their demand for wool drove up prices to the English clothier. They removed a half-finished cloth and extracted the largest profit margin from dyeing it. They stood in the way of the direct shipment of naval stores and colonial wares from their place of origin to England. England, it seemed, stood only on the periphery of an international system of trade dominated by superior skill and cunning. All this helped to provoke the growth of that school of thought and action later dubbed 'mercantilist'. It was dedicated, first and foremost, to rectifying what it saw as the defects and humiliations of the state of affairs just described. In short, to establish the economic independence of England; and if, in a static scheme of trade, independence meant, perforce, domination, the logic was acceptable. Exaggerated, hysterical, bloody-minded as it frequently became, there was enough logic in the diagnosis to give the economic nationalism of the age an irresistible appeal.[1]

I. THE HOME TRADE

The chronology of western European economic development in the early modern period points to the dominant influence of communications – above all of water transport. The great permanent entrepôts that now replaced the annual or periodical fairs of the Middle Ages – Venice, Marseilles, Antwerp and Amsterdam – were all seaports with access by river or canal to a wide hinterland. The Dutch Republic was the latest and most spectacular example of a country, small in size, population and natural resources, rising to wealth and pre-eminence almost entirely by the skilful exploitation of sea, river and canal transport. Seventeenth- and eighteenth-century evolution extended the process. From Danzig and Hamburg round the western seaboard of Europe to Marseilles and Genoa, a score of ports grew fat on ocean trades. So far, the prosperity of London and Bristol abundantly, Hull, King's Lynn, Yarmouth, Harwich, Exeter and Liverpool in varying degree, spoke to the same effect.

The rate of England's economic growth is to be explained only by a combination of economic and non-economic factors. That she was relatively free from internal disorders, that the military ambitions of her dynasties were relatively restrained, that English society was characterized by an unusual degree of social mobility between class and class: all these have their importance. That her resources – of land, minerals, fuel, wool – were abundant by comparison with those of her Dutch

---

[1] For more or less contemporary accounts of the Dutch economy see *The True Interest and Political Maxims of the Republic of Holland* (English translation 1702). Published originally in 1662, this is often described as 'The Maxims of Jan de Witt'. Sir W. Temple's *Observations on the United Provinces* (ed. G. N. Clark) is the fullest and best known of a number of English descriptions. Relationships with the Dutch are a major theme of Thomas Mun's *England's Treasure by fforraign Trade* (published 1664 but mostly written in the 1620s).

rival is likewise important. But none of these advantages could have operated had she been divided by political and customs barriers or dependent, as France and Germany largely were, upon inland transport. Of English roads it is not necessary to add much to the already ample witness to their condition: they were everywhere deplorable and getting steadily worse. In many places they were little more than grassy tracks tracing a wayward and fitful passage through open fields, and liable to disappear under flood water which retreated to leave only a sea of mud behind it. In this coaches, waggons, trains of pack horses and travellers wallowed helplessly. For a long time to come, the risk of drowning was real, as Celia Fiennes and John Wesley both found. So was the lesser risk of getting lost; even at the end of the century signposts were still a novelty. As population and the volume of inland trade grew the chronic neglect made things worse than ever. Especially near London, where a never-ceasing army of cattle, sheep, turkeys and geese converged in its march on the capital, the roads became mere quagmires. Beyond lurked the threat — a very real one, as the elaborate precautions for convoy testified — from thieves and highwaymen.

Such obstacles threw into vivid relief the blessings of the 700-odd miles of navigable river which were vouchsafed to Englishmen, affording a cheap and reliable means of moving goods, especially heavy cargoes like corn, coal, fish, iron and salt. The Thames, Severn, Trent, Yorkshire Ouse and Great Ouse connected the inland producer with the ports that served as outlets and inlets. Sheffield steel used the Don, Yorkshire cloth the Aire and Calder, Cheshire salt and cheese the Weaver and Dee, Lancashire textiles the Mersey. The rivers were, as an early writer phrased it, 'the cherishing veines of the body of every countrey, Kingdome and Nation', but of none more than of England. The improvements and extensions that were to mark the later years of the century were already foreshadowed in a number of proposals. The men of Exeter even continued their attempts (begun in the Queen's day) to cut a navigable canal for lighters from the sea up to their city: but failed, against the determination of the men of Topsham to keep their monopoly intact at the mouth of the Exe. The Great Ouse was the centre of a network of rivers linking an area from Lincoln in the north, Bedford in the west and Bury St Edmunds in the south, to the Wash. When this 'goodly fair river' was surveyed in 1618 it was 'generally foul and overgrown with weeds'. Thus began the onslaught on the succession of mills, weirs, shallows, and fords, as well as the riparian rights of all descriptions which lasted well into the eighteenth century.

Armed with Letters Patent and where necessary Acts of Parliament, local gentry, tradesmen and even London merchants carried forward the assault. Works, often involving costly locks and sluices, called for heavy capital outlay. The return came in the form of tolls levied on the valuable cargoes that flowed along the rivers. The inward traffic from Lynn included coals, salt, iron, grindstones, hemp, stone, bricks and wine: Wisbech still had a famous wine cellar until a few years ago. In the opposite direction went grain of all descriptions, mainly for transshipment to London. As an investment, one of these projects might yield up to £400 a year to the promoter. It was a worth-while prize, but it was not always easily won. Local opposition, like that of the miller of Hemingford who 'fell into a crossness', might lead to a score of lengthy lawsuits. Some investors lost rather than gained, like a local squire, Arnold Spencer: 'His being concerned in the navigation did much waste his estate.' Cumulatively, nevertheless, the Ouse improvement progressed and profited. It reflects 'almost all the main elements of the general movement for river improvement in the seventeenth century'.[1] The best surviving evidence of the economic expansion that followed is the group of inland ports – Bedford, St Neots, St Ives, Wisbech – with their solid seventeenth- and eighteenth-century merchant houses.

Many seaports, London, Bristol, Hull, Lynn, Exeter, Newcastle, Glasgow included, stood at the mouth of navigable rivers which brought from the hinterland the outward-bound cargoes – corn, cloth, iron, dairy produce – that provided one-half of their trade. Beyond lay the sea, 'a river' as it has been called 'round England'. In all, there were twenty-one 'head ports' with inlets capable of taking coasting ships, and there was more navigable coastline to every square mile of territory than anywhere in Europe. When roads were universally bad and even river traffic liable to obstruction, the sea was free and uninterrupted for the larger part of the year. Even allowing for the taxes levied on the coasting trade to provide piers, harbours and lighthouses, coasting still remained the cheapest form of transport, twenty times as cheap, it has been said, as wheeled transport. For carrying corn and coal it was indispensable, but its utility even to the cloth industry emerged clearly in 1639 when the Government prohibited the carriage by sea of fuller's earth in order to stop the leak of this vital material to the rival Dutch clothiers. The York clothiers immediately protested that this would

[1] T. S. Willan, 'The Navigation of the Great Ouse between St Ives and Bedford in the Seventeenth Century', *Publications of the Bedford Historical Record Society*, XXIV, 1946.

force them to obtain fuller's earth by land transport and thereby bear a ruinous increase in costs. The prohibition was withdrawn.

As the volume of trade grew, merchants, shipowners and shipbuilders began to exploit the evident economies of size offered by the coaster. The average coal cargo in 1600 was 60–70 tons: by the end of the century it was to be four or five times as large. The small open boat made way for the corn sloop and the square-rigged collier, which could be seen from the east coast sailing south, deep in the water 'topsails out, full bunted and bows rustling'. Ships improved in efficiency, too. Early in the century it took twenty men to handle 100 tons; by 1660, ten men could manage a 250-ton collier. But the numbers of the colliers went on growing, too. The fleet of 400 smallish ships of 1600 had grown into one of 1400 large ships by 1700.[1]

The uninterrupted growth of river and coastal traffic was vital to the entire economic life of the country. Without the supplies of food and materials brought in by sea, the phenomenal growth of London would have been impossible. Conversely, London's growth created ever-increasing demands. These, in turn, stimulated agricultural and industrial production and fed the flow of traffic. The population of the *congeries* of parishes within and without the City of London proper, of Westminster and the nearer suburbs had been growing fast in Tudor times. The 50,000 inhabitants of Henry VIII's time had grown to a quarter of a million by the early seventeenth century. Of these, some 76,000 lived within the walls of the City itself, still a picturesque but unhygienic jumble of merchant houses, half-timbered, gabled, red-roofed, many arranged in the form of courts, with ancient churches whose towers looked down to the Thames. There the wharves, filled with shipping, stretched along a frontage a little over a mile long. This formed the Southern boundary of the City area. The northern boundary was the medieval city wall, still in good order in 1600, which circled and enclosed it in the shape of a bow, joining the river frontage at its west and east ends. The great ditch beyond was blocked in many places with the refuse which Londoners traditionally dumped beyond the wall. So was the Fleet river, which came in from the north and crossed Fleet Street, though the Lea, entering from the east, was a valuable source of water and of transport. This rich and smelly profusion was linked to the alleys, innyards, hospitals and churches of Southwark and the parishes of Lambeth and Stepney along the south bank by only one bridge — London

---

[1] T. S. Willan, *River Navigation in England 1600–1750*, Oxford, 1936; also *The English Coasting Trade 1600–1750*, Manchester, 1938.

Bridge, carrying its grotesque burdens of houses and shops. Hence the need for hundreds of boatmen to ferry passengers across the Thames. As the congestion within the walls grew, people were spilling over into the extra-mural parishes, especially into the 'Liberties' between the old wall and the Bars (or gatehouses) beyond. There were 'Bars' at the Temple, Holborn, Smithfield, Shoreditch and Whitechapel. These 'Liberties' already contained far more people than the City — 113,000 in 1605 — and building was going on rapidly. Another 36,000 lived in the outparishes beyond the Liberties, many of them Irish, Scotch, French and Dutch immigrant artisans. All this eastward conglomeration and its overflow south of the river accounted for well over 80 per cent of the people inhabiting the parishes known as London. Their occupations were mainly in trade, handicrafts and money, or in the shipping that crowded the new frontage, down even to the 3,000 Thames watermen who worked the 2,000 small wherries on the river.

But in 1600 London was still two cities, not one. The sprawling, expanding commercial metropolis was linked to the real capital of England, Westminster, only by a row of palaces, not long built, which fringed the Thames. Here, as the names of the palaces denoted, lived great nobles: York House, Essex House, Somerset House, the last surviving witness today of this fashionable epoch of the Strand. Already the days of these great houses were numbered and it was not to be long before they were to fall victim to the common fate of districts deserted by fashion and decline into squalid overcrowded tenements, sitting target for the ambitions of the speculative builder.

As the population of London grew, its pressure added ever greater incentives for politics and fashion to move westwards. Our detailed knowledge of population growth we owe to the attacks of plague which, in 1603 and again in 1625 and 1636, gave an horrific foretaste of 1665. This evident threat to health and order lay behind the constant but totally unsuccessful attempts of Government to check the growth of London and, immediately, to the regular publication of the so-called Bills of Mortality within the London area. The area within which deaths and the causes of deaths were recorded was gradually extended. By 1660 it covered 130 parishes — all those inside the old city and thirty-three outside, including Westminster and the 'Liberties'. Deaths were attested by two searchers ('ancient women'), notified to the parish clerk and collected and published weekly by the Company of Parish Clerks. But whatever gaps were made by plague were soon filled by immigration, and to the normal influx was added, it was believed, a stream of refugees who came 'to shelter themselves from the outrages of the Civil Wars during that time'.[1]

In 1600, perhaps one-twentieth of the total population of England lived in London. A century later the proportion was nearer a tenth. Fear of plague, fire, overcrowding and shortage of water kept King and Council, Star Chamber and, spasmodically, the City Government, busy against unauthorized building: but with scant success. As the tension between Charles and the City grew — over Ship Money, the seizure of the City's Irish estates and other frictions — the suspicion took hold that here, as elsewhere, the royal solicitude was financial rather than social. The Commissioners charged with executing the planning regulations found themselves targets for the indignation of the City Fathers. They were charged with selling privileges to Scottish favourites while obstructing the proper enterprise of the City. The allegations were enshrined in Article 30 of the Grand Remonstrance which protested against 'the sale of pretended nuisances, as building in & about London'.

While the armour of regulation showed more and more such chinks, trade continued to spread outwards and westwards from the City. The Strand, Fleet Street, Covent Garden and neighbouring areas lost their social attractions. The new Banqueting Hall at Whitehall, synchronizing as it unfortunately did with the worst economic depression in history, seemed to symbolize more than the new Italianate trend of fashion at Court. Palace and architect (Inigo Jones) became the symbol of extravagance and tyranny. And when Inigo Jones in 1626 became the Secretary of the Commissioners for Building, the suspicions of the opposition were confirmed beyond doubt. The nobility moved west, attracted to the Court, repelled by the growing congestion of the middle areas, also perhaps by smell and fumes of the growing commercial area. The movement (Evelyn later remarked) 'must be westward, because the Windes blowing near ¾ of the year from the west, the dwellings of the West End are so much more free from the fumes, steams & stinks of the whole Easterly Pyle; which when Sea coal is burnt is a great matter'. Congestion, trade, coal fires and the Civil War itself completed an estrangement between Court and City which was to be perpetuated in a peaceable, veiled but extended feud between City and West End.[2]

---

[1] Norman Brett-James, *The Growth of Stuart London*, 1935, p. 501, quoting William Petty.

[2] See Chapter 15 for the eighteenth-century distinction between the City and West End banks.

The economic expansion of London promised a golden harvest for many sorts and conditions of men. But for none were the prospects brighter than for those fortunate ground landlords in the areas being rapidly 'colonized' between the City and Westminster. Before the Restoration development was only fractional and spasmodic by comparison with what was to follow, but it was the acumen of great landowners like the Earls of Bedford, Holland, Salisbury and Clare which pointed the way for later developers. Most of the new building represented a partnership between landed and mercantile capital. The ground landlord allowed the developer to take a building lease of thirty-one to forty-one years. The lessee-developer provided the capital, the lessor provided the land and took the reversion of the property when the lease expired. By 1650 the Earl of Clare was drawing an income of £2,800 a year from the ground rents of his property in Drury Lane, Princes Street and elsewhere. The Earls of Cleveland and Northampton drew perhaps £1,000 a year each. There were occasional exceptions to this popular method. Occasionally a landlord was able to provide the capital for direct freehold development. The Earl of Salisbury built the 'New Exchange' on the south side of the Strand in 1608 for £11,000, 'a sort of multiple store for fancy goods, serving the upper class clientele passing from the City to the Court'.[1] In 1630 the Earl of Bedford obtained a dispensation to develop land in Covent Garden lying behind his house in the Strand. Bedford was not of the Court set. He was at least half a Puritan, with a strong interest in 'improvement'. The result was the famous Piazza at Covent Garden, long since destroyed but preserved in spirit in the present design of the fruit market. A few years later William Newton, a speculative builder, was at work in Great Queen Street and Lincoln's Inn Fields. The result has been called 'the first regular street in London' and was to set the pattern for the next two centuries.[2]

Such was the main contribution of capital, and enterprise of a sort, by the nobility. One other great 'project' connected with the expansion of London appealed to the imagination and pockets of the Court: Sir Hugh Myddelton's New River Company. Its purpose was to bring fresh water from Amwell, near Ware in Hertfordshire, to Islington, thence to be piped to the houses of London. This remarkable feat of engineering occupied the years from 1609 to 1613 and was financed in

[1] L. Stone 'The Nobility in Business', *Explorations in Entrepreneurial History*, December 1957.

[2] J. Summerson, *Georgian London*, 1945, p. 18.

part by the King, who scented a good investment. The notorious Sir Giles Mompesson and Sir Robert Killigrew were amongst those let in on favourable terms. In the financial straits of the thirties, Charles disposed of the royal shares and probably the Court shareholders followed suit. Other aristocratic investors took part in mining, drainage, shipping and colonial joint stock enterprises. But their part should not be exaggerated. Coming up beside the nobility and the more affluent gentry was a growing nucleus of London merchants whose wealth overshadowed that of all but the greatest noble landowners. Trading occupations in London were numberless, rising from those chapmen and pedlars suspect of J.P.s and housewives, the city hawkers of cat's meat, rhubarb or slippers, through the ranks of the broggers, bodgers, factors, jobbers and crimps to the great men who governed the twelve great livery companies, handled vast deals in corn, coal, salt, spices, cloths and lent money to the King.

Through the hands of this community passed a high proportion of the nation's trade. Out of a yield at the customs houses that increased tenfold in the course of the century some three-quarters was accounted for at London. It was not only that London was, in Professor Fisher's phrase, a centre of 'conspicuous consumption' connected with the Court, the nobility and high fashion, and represented by the activities of the goldsmiths and other purveyors of luxuries.[1] It was also a centre of *mass* consumption. The demand for corn for food and drink rose from half a million to a million and a half quarters. The expansion of the coal trade has already been mentioned. Local demand and trade led inevitably to trade with third parties. Slowly the business of corn importing was to give way to corn exporting. The great specialized markets — Billingsgate for fish, Southwark and Leadenhall for leather, Blackwell Hall for cloth — expanded. London attracted not only what it needed for itself but increasingly materials and manufactures for redistribution. Clothiers from the West Country and from the north brought their cloths, some to be dressed and finished, the rest to be exported. Warehouses, retail shops, workshops, breweries and glasshouses multiplied.

In this mercantile society, economically expansive, bursting the bounds of the ancient city, the power of capital was becoming dominant. Producer and distributor were now different people. The great livery companies were absorbing subordinate crafts, as the Skinners' Company had already absorbed the tawers, the Blacksmiths' the

1 F. J. Fisher, 'The Development of London as a Centre of Conspicuous Consumption in the Sixteenth and Seventeenth Centuries', *Tr. R.H.S.*, 1948.

spurriers, the Girdlers' the pinners. Within the companies, the mercantile elements were dominating the handicraft elements. The great leather industry of London, which kept eighty tanneries busy in Bermondsey and Southwark and set 3,000 shoemakers to work, was dominated by the Leathersellers. In 1619 they were under fire from the handicraft workers. A petition to the Privy Council illustrates a common complaint of the time: that the leathersellers were no longer men who 'made drest and sold wares of tanner's leather' (as they had once been) 'but men of other trades'. And while they 'pretend themselves to be of the same trade with the Glovers, Pointmakers, and White Tawyers, if once they part their griping hands betwixt the Grower or Merchant and any of the said Trades they never parte with the Commodities they buy till they sell them at their own pitched rates without either regard or care whether the workman be able to make his money thereof or no'.[1] Similarly in the textile companies, the old functions of industrial regulation were falling into disuse as the mercantile elements displaced the handicrafts. The official duties of the Merchant Taylors were perfunctory by the 1620s. The 'yeomanry' was disbanded in 1661. The Drapers' Company had abolished their wardens of yeomanry in 1657. The cloth workers likewise were dominated by the merchant element. In all these tendencies, the logic of an expanding economy was to be seen working itself out. The old regulation of industry was slowly being abandoned as the handicraftsmen lost power to the merchant. The new emphasis was on trade. Echoes of the old mistrust of middlemen was still to be heard. Were there not too many merchants? Were their activities not injurious to the Commonwealth? Even a liberally inclined economist like William Petty could doubt whether they were not 'merely a kind of Gamesters that play with one another for the labours of the poor; yielding of themselves no fruit at all, otherwise than as veines & arteries, to distribute back & forth the blood and nutritive juyces of the Body Politic, namely the Product of Husbandry & Manufactures'. Another writer could doubt whether England could ever support 'such a prodigious Increase of Retailers and Shopkeepers as are in and about London, being near 100,000 in number when in Amsterdam they are not 5,000'.[2] Such prejudices against the merchant were a commonplace, to be consecrated by Adam Smith a century and a half later. They could not prevent the inexorable growth of the

[1] G. Unwin, *Industrial Organization in the Sixteenth and Seventeenth Centuries*, 1904, pp. 128–9.

[2] N. S. B. Gras, *Evolution of the London Corn Market*, 1915, p. 204.

power of mercantile capital required to minister to an expanding urban economy. While the great livery companies turned into symbols of social prestige and charitable organizations, domestic trade became increasingly the province of individual merchants. Many of these were relative new-comers. Of fifty-three Lord Mayors of London between 1591 and 1640, more than half were born countrymen. Cranfield came from a family of minor country gentry. So did Cokayne. So did Hugh Myddleton and his brother Thomas, a Lord Mayor of London. These and many others reflected the common practice by which the younger sons of the gentry, and even, occasionally, of the peerage, for whom no estate or profession could be found, were apprenticed to trade: 'the boy baptised Septimus or Decimus', as Sir Lewis Namier has said, 'was almost certain to be found in the counting house'.[1] Artisans and unemployed poor were certainly not the only ones who emigrated to London from the country. Maybe this influx from the gentry brought to the English merchant class a little more breadth of vision and experience, a little more social assurance than was enjoyed by M. Jourdain. Maybe it explained also that nostalgia which repeatedly sent the successful tradesmen back to the peace and pleasures of rural life. Thus Sir Dudley North and Sir Hugh Myddleton fled from the smoke and dust of the smithies round Basinghall Street to their country seats at Wroxton and Edmonton.

The outports felt themselves in these early years of the century oppressively overshadowed by London, thwarted by its monopolistic grip on many branches of trade, resentful of the political manipulations by which those close to the seat of power seemed to secure and streng-then their hold. By comparison with London, these outport communi-ties of merchants were tiny. Bristol, far the largest, was a place of some 12,000 people in 1600. It included about 150 merchants — strictly defined as those admitted to the freedom of the city: but there were besides several hundreds of woollen and linen drapers, soap boilers, grocers, clothiers, victuallers and brewers who also traded. The Bristol merchants, like the London, came from diverse social origins. The younger sons of gentry and the episcopacy rubbed shoulders with the descendants of merchants. Edward Colston, the greatest merchant of Stuart Bristol, was the last of a long line of merchants.[2] The same was

1 *England in the Age of the American Revolution*, 1930, p. 9. See also W. E. Minchinton, 'The Merchants of England in the 18th Century', *Explorations in Entrepreneurial History*, December 1957.

2 P. M. McGrath, 'Merchants & Merchandize in 17th-Century Bristol', *The Bristol Record Society*, 1955. For details of merchant families see H. R. Fox Bourne, *English Mer-chants*, 1886.

true of the other ports, all still tiny by any standards – Glasgow, where the Lyon family descended from Lord Glamis, held sway over trade; Liverpool (which Chester men could still claim was 'but a creek' of their own port) where the ancient family of Moores disputed valuable territorial rights with upstarts like the Johnsons.

The early Stuarts had to steer a precarious course between the claims of the outports to their reasonable share of the nation's trade and the tempting financial convenience of yielding to the London 'establishment', affluent, ambitious and monopolistic. As yet, the outports were caught in the trough of economic change. On the east coast, they were the victims of a troubled European economy, and sustained mainly by the rise of the coastal trade in coal and corn. On the west side, the reviving breezes of the transatlantic colonial economy had scarcely begun to blow.

2. ENGLAND'S TREASURE BY FOREIGN TRADE: AN OLD ORDER PASSES

The first years of the new dynasty were marked by an apparent burst of prosperity that contrasted with the last sombre years of Elizabeth, especially with 1603, when plague and depression had made a joint and disastrous visitation upon England. The new-found peace, the Anglo-Spanish Treaty of 1604 and the Truce of 1609 in the Netherlands, seemed to provide a background against which economic normality might return. The export of cloth from London rose from about 100,000 pieces in 1600 to 127,000 pieces in 1614, their highest recorded level. The Merchant Adventurers, chief agents of the nation's export trade, had never been so prosperous. Yet this brilliant overture belied the gloom of the economic drama that was to follow. Eight years later, cloth exports from London had fallen to little more than half the figure of 1614. After a brief recovery, another joint visitation of plague and poverty recurred in 1625. War with Spain and France paralysed trade in 1629 and the abysmal harvests of the following two years accentuated and prolonged the depression. Another slump descended in 1636. By the late thirties, depression was generally regarded as chronic. In the two years that preceded the Civil War 'the decay of trade', as a contemporary wrote, 'is in everybody's mouth from the sheep shearer to the merchant, and even a weak statist, without Galileo's prospective glass may see both our wealth and safety therewith declining'. As the Civil War began, the Venetian Ambassador wrote home from London that 'the trade of this city & Kingdom is stopping altogether'.[1] Nor did the troubles end with the Civil War. 1649 saw a return of acute depression, and the lamentations of contemporaries were borne out by the fall in the yield of the Customs. The generally successful war against the Dutch from 1652 to 1654 raised morale, but Cromwell's Spanish war brought another depression that touched bottom in 1659. Its effects were still felt after the Restoration.

The historian plotting economic trends learns to take the lamentations of the business man with a grain of salt. But all the evidence supports the view that the fluctuations of the time did reflect a real and prolonged crisis arising from a radical adjustment of England's foreign trade. This depended in a dangerously high degree – perhaps some 90 per cent in the early seventeenth century – on the export of undressed woollen cloth to northern Europe. At the heart of the problem of these years lay a catastrophic fall in this trade: between 1606 and 1640 alone, a drop from a total of 120,000 pieces exported by London alone to about 45,000 pieces.[2] Plainly, a whole international economy was collapsing. The pressures behind the collapse were vividly illustrated by the spectacular crisis of the early 1620s. This can now be seen to be not only a watershed in English economic life, but a starting point for new ideas, new politics, and – ultimately – new growth.

The recurrent crises of trade were popularly explained at the time in terms of the intervention of Providence – plagues and bad harvests; or the even more disastrous intervention of man – the failure of ill-conceived schemes like the Cokayne project, restrictive practices by merchants or the machinations of Dutch rivals. That plague could, by paralysing the business life of London, bring exports to a virtual standstill was proved in 1625. The Merchant Adventurers were scattered by the plague, as the rich usually were. The Levant Company could not convene a directors' meeting. And so on. Here was a plain demonstration of one danger of a London export monopoly. Yet plague did not explain other crises. Nor did bad harvests, though there was some basis for the popular belief that a good harvest brought general benefit and vice versa. When grain was plentiful and prices fell, buyers – and already a large proportion of the population had to buy their food – had more money left over to buy other commodities. High grain prices left no such margin. A bad harvest also necessitated the import of

[1] On this period see B. E. Supple, *Commercial Crisis and Change in England 1600–1642*, 1959, esp. chapters 1–6.
[2] Supple, op. cit., Table 10b, p. 266.

Baltic grain and this was paid for in specie. Hence (they believed) one source of that 'scarcity of money' often associated with low prices for cloth and general unemployment. Since weather in western Europe was apt to be fairly uniform, the same phenomena often occurred in the export markets simultaneously.

Much of the blame for the disastrous export slump of 1616 was placed at the door of the notorious Alderman Cokayne and his partners, and their attempted reorganization of the cloth export trade. The promoters proclaimed that their object was to destroy the existing Merchant Adventurers' virtual monopoly of the export of unfinished cloth and replace it by a new company. This would export a dyed and finished article of much higher value, creating higher export values and a larger volume of employment. Whether this was its real aim or whether it was merely an unscrupulous plot to replace an old group of monopolists by a new is still uncertain.[1] The scheme had all the plausible qualities of a seventeenth-century take-over bid. Technically it was premature; diplomatically it was disastrous. The dyeing and finishing of cloth was a highly skilled business and England could not then or for some time to come provide a competitive supply of skilled labour to fulfil the professed aims of the projectors. The Dutch, the target of the plot, immediately took reprisals against all English cloth exports and markets collapsed completely. The Government then tried to put the clock back. The old Company got back its privileges. But even this did not end the troubles. Trade remained bad, and now the inbred monopolistic habits of the Merchant Adventurers came under fire – 'above three-fourths parts of all broad cloth transported, is driven [it was said] by less than forty persons'. By 1624 the Commons demanded, and got, freedom for outsiders to join the cloth export trade. Parliament had already emerged as the champion of the unprivileged merchant. The Merchant Adventurers, significantly, did not regain their monopoly till 1634, when there was no Parliament.

Domestic conflicts and disasters certainly played their part in bringing about the great depression of the early 1620s. It is doubtful whether they were more than contributory factors. More fundamental were events in Europe. In the short term, the years from 1617 to 1623 witnessed a series of currency manipulations which dislocated some of the main markets for English cloth in Germany, Poland and the Baltic. Briefly, the effect of this tampering with the coinage – the so-called

[1] See Supple, op. cit., p. 51. See below Ch. IV for the industrial implications of the project.

Kipper-und-Wipper-Zeit — by local princes in order to snatch a quick profit, was to raise the price of imported goods to local consumers. English exporters therefore found trade difficult or impossible. Conversely, since prices of local manufactures fell in the countries concerned, traders were encouraged to buy goods for sale in England. The contemporary anxiety about the growing deficit on the English balance of trade seems to have sprung from the assessment of a real problem of foreign trade. It was worsened by the stimulus given to export *bullion* overseas where it was worth more, and to bring home the proceeds of overseas sales in *goods*. Here was the immediate problem of the 1620s.

The exchange problem, like plague and murrain, was a short-term, soluble problem. By 1623 it had been dealt with, though the dislocations of European markets by war were to continue for another thirty years. The larger, and, as it seemed, permanent problem was created by foreign, above all Dutch, competition. Throughout the early decades of the seventeenth century, the Dutch continued their expansion beyond the European periphery. Within it they were exploiting the shrinking markets of a war-ravaged Germany with all their customary skill. Their most concentrated cloth industry, at Leiden, had taken on a new lease of life with the arrival of a stream of refugees from the southern Netherlands. Beginning in the 1560s they had brought to Leiden new enterprise and new skills, replacing the Dutch 'Old Drapery' by the 'New Drapery' — bays, says, camlets, fustians, etc. Another stream of Flemings and Walloons had fled to England. Here in East Anglia especially the 'New Drapery' took root, though less rapidly than in Holland. The Leiden industry was to reach its peak in the 1660s. Until then, the 'New Draperies' of East Anglia had to fight an uphill battle. With northern markets closed or unpromising, the Mediterranean offered the best hope of compensation, and it was here that merchants of both countries deployed their major effort. Lighter, brighter and cheaper than 'pure' woollens, the new cloths sold well in semi-tropical climates.[1] Hence the Anglo-Dutch rivalry for the Spanish and Levant trades, where the English evidently made some progress. In the markets for finer, more costly cloth they did less well, though the so-called 'Spanish' cloths of Wiltshire made reasonable headway. The English advantages lay in lower labour costs, and in a supply of home-grown long-staple wool specially suited to the manufacture of the 'New Draperies' and similar cloths, often fairly cheap ones.[2]

[1] See Chapter IV for the technical differences between the old cloths and the new.
[2] F. J. Fisher 'London's Export Trade in the Early Seventeenth Century', *Econ. Hist.*

The progress of the 'New Draperies', welcome though it was, did not as yet offset the loss of the old markets in Germany, Eastern Europe and the Baltic, where the older 'regulated' companies — Merchant Adventurers and Eastland Company — held sway. Another regulated company was trading with rather more success to Russia, but its transactions, especially in cloth, were relatively small. A glimmer of optimism came from the Levant Company, which was driving profitably a multilateral trade in the Mediterranean. 'Turkey merchant' was a synonym for wealth, and some of London's richest men drew part of their incomes from the Levant. The Elizabethan penetration of the Mediterranean had continued. Trade had expanded, and expanded in a way that for once satisfied the criteria of the times. Much of it consisted of raw material imports — silk especially for a growing English manufacture, cotton too. The premium charged by a Turkey merchant to an aspiring apprentice was as large as any charged for entry to a trade. It was a suitable pointer to the potential wealth it offered.[1] But otherwise the condition of the joint-stock companies was generally far from prosperous. The largest and oldest was the East India Company, founded in 1600 as an offshoot from the Levant Company. Down to 1616 it had done well, but then it had fallen into what was to prove a protracted and costly struggle with its Dutch rival. A series of conferences to settle these differences had broken down, and an ambitious proposal to merge both companies had aborted. Now its affairs were in confusion. It was, and was to remain, a controversial aspect of the Indies trade that it was an import trade rather than an export trade. Obviously there was little sale in India for England's staple export: woollen cloth. The valuable spices and, later, fine textiles that the company imported had therefore to be bought with bullion. And bullion export contradicted all the deeply held popular convictions of the day. The company defended itself by arguing that the re-export of its purchases brought back far more bullion than it exported to India. But the opposition were not convinced. The debate was to continue into the eighteenth century.

The rush of newly promoted companies to settle the Americas and West Indies did not at once bring profits or employment. These were, in every sense, 'adventures' and as yet their importance was largely

[1] R. Davis, 'England and the Mediterranean' in *Essays on the Economic and Social History of Tudor and Stuart England*, 1961.

Rev., second series, III, no. 2, 1950; C. Wilson, 'Cloth Production and International Competition in the Seventeenth Century', *Econ. Hist. Rev.*, second series, XIII, no. 2, 1960.

potential. Most were divided by discussions over policy, often as much a source of loss as of gain to their promoters. So it was to continue until late in the Interregnum. Here and there some individuals might reap a personal profit from these new ventures beyond Europe. A few made large fortunes. But for some time they were not to bring much comfort to an economy in the throes of reorganization. For another forty years cloth was still to dominate the export trade, though with a greater variety of types.[1] A high proportion of imports, especially in the important Anglo-Dutch trade, still came in Dutch ships.

Yet it was out of this unpromising situation that there emerged in the early 1620s a new vision of a national economic policy, a new understanding of the criteria by which its success or failure might be judged, and a new grasp of the appropriate division of trades into those which called for company organization and those better left to the enterprise of individual merchants.

3. IDEAS, POLICY AND LAW

English economic policy in the seventeenth century was to reflect an increasingly effective blending of two elements: the interests of private individuals and groups, and the interest of the State. It therefore represented a middle way between the lack of central policy to be found in the Dutch Republic where hostility to dynasticism threatened to destroy the federal power, and the economic authoritarianism of a state like France, where private interest might reluctantly be consulted but played little part in policy-making. Between English 'mercantilism' and Colbertism and its derivatives, there was all the difference between a tailor-made suit and a ready-made. The geographical proximity of Court and City might be a marriage of convenience that led to many quarrels, but at least it ensured that 'trade' had a voice in public affairs. The economic difficulties of the turbulent years down to 1660 themselves created a developing machinery of discussion, consultation and decision between Government and trade.

The early Stuarts inherited and insisted on the tradition that the regulation of economic affairs fell under the King's prerogative. The burden of decision fell on the Privy Council and down to 1622 it discharged its office without formal assistance by committees.[2] In

---

[1] See M. P. Ashley, op. cit., Appendix B, 'The Character of English Exports and Imports in the Mid-Seventeenth Century'.

[2] Charles M. Andrews, *British Committees, Commissions and Councils of Trade and Plantations 1622–1675*, Baltimore, 1908, p. 10.

that year special Commissions of Trade were appointed, to inquire, *inter alia*, into the depression in the cloth industry. Temporary commissions gave way in 1630 to one that was to be virtually permanent and ruled down to 1640. During the early part of the Interregnum, Parliament assumed the duty of economic control. For the first time merchants were brought into full membership of the appropriate committees. In 1650 the first Board of Trade was created, though the Council of State swiftly resumed full control (as the Privy Council had earlier done) in face of the growing weakness of Parliament. The Protector continued the custom of consulting expert merchant opinion. It was the representations of financiers like Martin Noell and Thomas Povey which led to the creation of the 'Trade Committee' of 1655 headed by Cromwell's son Richard and comprising seventy members. In the range of mercantile interests of its somewhat unwieldy membership, and in the breadth and variety of its inquiries, the Committee of 1655 went beyond its predecessors. But it did not renounce their character: the interest of the State remained paramount. The Protectorate was no more at the bidding of merchants than the monarchy it had replaced. But it preserved and extended the habit of economic government by consultation that had been evolving since 1622. What Adam Smith was to call 'the mercantile system', and later writers 'mercantilism', emerged from the streams of petitions from private parties directed to these various Committees of State, from the continuous discussions that arose from the frictions between competing private interests and from attempts to reconcile the demands of the mercantile elements in the State with needs deemed to be those of the Commonwealth as a whole. 'The Government', Mr Hinton has written, 'had a will of its own.' Its decisions were based on 'ancient and conventional ideas about the common weal, which the subjects abundantly shared and which easily transcended the interests of particular groups'.[1] Without some recognition of this genuinely public function of government it is impossible to explain seventeenth-century social and economic policy.

Puzzled by the complexity and gravity of the depression of 1622, the Government called mercantile experts to its aid. Among them were Gerard Malynes, Edward Misselden and Thomas Mun. Malynes, a Fleming by origin, was a currency expert and mint contractor. He had only just emerged from the Fleet prison into which he had been cast for debts incurred in an unsuccessful contract for making farthing coins.

[1] R. W. K. Hinton, *The Eastland Trade and the Common Weal in the Seventeenth Century*, 1959, p. 164.

Misselden was closely connected with the Merchant Adventurers and was later to play an important part in their negotiations in Holland. Mun was the stepson of an East India merchant, already experienced as a merchant in Italy and himself an East India Company director since 1615. He and Misselden were close neighbours at Hackney. In the early stages of their historic controversy, all three started from the assumption, a legacy from the debates of the previous century, that the key to the mysteries of foreign trade lay in the 'exchanges', in the mechanism of payments by which it was believed bullion and specie moved across national frontiers – in this particular instance, the malign attraction by which disastrously large quantities were drawn abroad from England. Like most other commentators, they both agreed with Malynes that 'the want of money ... is the first cause of the decay of trade'. From this followed the dwindling of the currency and 'the want of a convenient stock of money to maintain the prices, and to beat or maintain our home commerce'.[1]

Some twenty years earlier Malynes had formulated the view that England's problem was the result of her currency being undervalued. There was thus a permanent stimulus to the export of specie, and to the movement of the terms of trade against England. To this explanation, conceived entirely in terms of monetary and price factors, he still clung obstinately in 1622. Malynes's remedy was straightforward: to stop specie export by controlling the rate of exchange. To this 'old soiled project of his, of 22 years' growth', as he impolitely described Malynes's programme, Misselden replied with a different analysis. To him the main problem was the manipulation of the European currencies which had caused English *coin* to be undervalued and drawn off into the foreign mints. It was 'not the rate of exchange but the value of monies, here low, elsewhere high, which cause their exportation ...'. The remedy was therefore to raise the valuation of silver coins. In the early stages of the discussion, Mun seems to have shared some of the views of both his fellow controversialists. Like Malynes, he criticized the 'abuse of exchange' as a cause of the trouble. Like Misselden, he blamed currency manipulations for the loss of bullion. But by 1623, possibly by 1622, he had emerged with an entirely different and more coherent theory, the most influential before the rise of the *laissez-faire* school a century and a half later. Monetary factors were not the cause of changes in the demand and supply for currencies and the loss of treasure. They

---

1 See Supple, op. cit., chap. 9, for the fullest and most recent discussion of the controversy.

only reflected the state of the flow of trade. 'For it is a certain rule', he wrote in a memorandum of April 1623, 'that in those countries beyond the seas which send us more of their wares in value than we carry unto them of commodities, there our monies are undervalued in exchange, and in other countries where the contrary of this is performed, there our money is overvalued.'[1]

Forty years later, this emerged as the central theme of the work by which Mun is best known and which was to be the matrix of popular economic thinking for another century and a half – *England's Treasure by fforraign Trade* (published in 1664).

> The ordinary means therefore to increase our wealth and treasure is by *Forraign Trade* wherein wee must ever observe this rule; to sell more to strangers yearly than wee consume of theirs in value. For suppose that when this Kingdom is plentifully served with the Cloth, Lead, Tinn, Iron, Fish and other native commodities, we doe yearly export the overplus to forraign countries to the value of twenty two hundred thousand pounds; by which means we are enabled beyond the Seas to buy and bring in forraign wares for our use and Consumptions, to the value of twenty hundred thousand pounds; By this order duly Kept in our trading, we may rest assured that the Kingdom shall be enriched yearly two hundred thousand pounds, which must be brought to us in so much Treasure; because that part of our stock which is not returned to us in wares must necessarily be brought home in treasure.[2]

Concern with the trade balance was nothing new. It was implicit in the whole argument of the Tudor *Dialogue* of *the Commonweal* written three-quarters of a century earlier. A few years before the commissioners began their inquiries in 1622, Lionel Cranfield and John Wolstenholme, a London Merchant Adventurer with wide business interests, had also conducted an exhaustive inquiry into the balance of trade problem. But Mun's formulation was the most succinct and striking so far, though it contained logical flaws which were not corrected till later in the century. Like other mercantilists Mun's aim was not primarily to construct a universal set of economic principles, but to explain a pressing economic problem; not to amass bullion but to explain its loss. And, as Keynes pointed out in the 1930s, while economists might later have come to regard the favourable balance of trade as 'a puerile obsession', those more immediately concerned with policy in the centuries that followed have continued to regard it as a prime object of practical statecraft.[3] The central concept of the trade balance was, then,

[1] Quoted in Supple, op cit., p. 214.

[2] T. Mun, op. cit., reprinted by the Economic History Society, 1933, p. 5.

[3] J. M. Keynes, *The General Theory of Employment, Interest and Money*, 1936, ch. 23, p. 333. See also C. Wilson, 'Treasure and Trade Balances', *Econ. Hist. Rev.* II, no. 2, 1949.

the product of crisis. But from it flowed a series of proposals crystallizing into ordinances, proclamations and statutes that formed the dynamic of a new economic policy. Such regulations frequently served private ends; collectively their object was to raise the economy to a new level of productivity and profitability. In the interests of trade and industry, the export of raw materials — wool and its ancillaries, fuller's earth, pipe clay, wool fells — was strictly prohibited, so as to keep prices down for the native manufacturer. The inflow of skilled artisans was encouraged, bounties were granted to producers. The import of raw materials and goods, especially from the colonies, was to be stimulated, and the purchase abroad of luxuries and competing manufactures was to be restricted by tariffs. These principles became interlaced with complementary ideas in later decades aimed primarily at eliminating the Dutch middleman from the dominant position he occupied in the economy and at constructing by deliberate planning an entrepôt system not unlike that which had grown up spontaneously at Amsterdam. Collectively they amounted, as a recent writer has said, to the economics of diversification.[1] The germ of this is clearly present in Mun's proposals. The danger of allowing the national economy to rest on a single industry — cloth — was obvious, and his Commission itself recommended that the colonial trades, the fishing industry and the mercantile marine should be protected and developed.[2] Such ideas were developed by other writers who, like Mun, were merchants or men closely associated with the merchant community. Lewis Roberts, whose *Treasure of Traffike* was widely read during the Interregnum, was a London merchant whose son held high office in the Treasury under Cromwell. Henry Robinson, whose *England's Safety in Trade's Increase* (1641) was the ablest exposition of economic diversification, was the son of a London mercer and himself auditor of the excise under Cromwell. Benjamin Worsley, the author of *The Advocate*, the classic justification of the need for a navigation policy to exclude the Dutch middlemen, was Secretary of the Council of Trade, and a go-between between the trading companies and the Government. All this conscious economic re-orientation from the 1620s onwards reached its climax in the first Navigation Act of 1651.

The Act, recommended to Parliament on 5 August 1651, was the immediate product of two events, closely linked — or so it seemed to contemporaries. One was the failure of English attempts to reach a

[1] Supple, op. cit., p. 221.
[2] Astrid Friis, *Alderman Cockayne's Project and the Cloth Trade*, 1927, pp. 421 et seq.

comprehensive alliance with the Dutch. These had broken down — in the English view — because the Dutch had insisted on concentrating their efforts to *expand* their share of Anglo-Dutch trade, whereas the English wanted to combine a diplomatic treaty with plans to *restrict* the Dutch economically. This breach had come hard on the heels of another of those recurrent depressions of trade that had set in in 1649 and which had created the usual demands for protection against Dutch economic encroachment. It was significant that Oliver St John, one of the principal negotiators in the abortive diplomatic talks in Holland, was closely connected with the drafting of the Act that followed close on their failure.[1] The formula of the 1651 Act was simple: merchandise imported into England was to come from the country which produced it or first exported it — not via the Dutch entrepôt. It must be carried in English ships, or ships belonging to the country where the goods originated or were first shipped — another blow at the Dutch, whose technical superiority as shipbuilders and skill as ship managers had concentrated a large volume of European freight in their hands. Pursuing its autarkic logic, the Act then prohibited the import of any Asian, African or American goods in foreign ships. A clause forbidding the import of fish in any ships other than English was aimed primarily at the Dutch herring fishers, whose lucrative enterprises off the coast of Scotland and England had been an annual humiliation to English patriots since the early years of the century.

Few statutes have aroused such controversy amongst later writers. Some have regarded it as the product of powerful economic lobbies — the great importing companies especially, like the Levant and Eastland Companies — to whose demand for protection against Dutch competition the Government was finally compelled to yield. Others, following Adam Smith, have seen it as essentially a measure of national naval defence, of which the merchants were but the fortunate and more or less incidental beneficiaries.[2] It can be accepted that the governments of the Interregnum yielded nothing to their predecessors or successors in their belief that it was the business of Government to govern. Moreover the Act came at a time when the companies, both joint stock and regulated, were weakened by the current revulsion of sentiment against company privilege, especially in the provinces, where they were

[1] See L. A. Harper, op, cit., p. 47. For the genesis of the Act see C. Wilson, *Profit and Power*, 1957, ch. IV.

[2] For a full discussion see my *Profit and Power*, ch. IV. More recently R. W. K. Hinton has contested the view that the Act was the concession to mercantile pressure in his *The Eastland Trade and the Common Weal in the Seventeenth Century*, 1959, pp. 90–4.

associated with metropolitan monopoly and intrigue. The Government was certainly no mere puppet dancing to tunes called by company monopolists. While the Act did not meet in full the demands of any particular interest it did recognize in general the need of English merchants and shipowners for protection against Dutch rivalry. Its general mode of operation automatically placed the Dutch exporters of foreign and colonial produce at a severe disadvantage in the English market. In short, the debate as to its objects — whether it sought the advantage of private trade or the military security of the State — is in reality irrelevant. It sought, and sought to reconcile so far as it could, both objects. And its method — a general regulatory statute that applied regardless of particular companies — marked a vital stage in the evolution of national economic planning. So far, successive governments had most often tried to control overseas trade through the grant of privileges to private companies, just as they had delegated the control of domestic industry to the gilds. These methods were to continue for those distant areas and types of trade that demanded specific assurance against risk. For the areas of established trade in Europe a new policy was adumbrated. Henceforth the merchant was here to work out his destiny, free of formal organization, within a general protective framework of national legislation. It would not be long before the franchises of the regulated Companies — the Merchant Adventurers, the Levant Company and the Eastland Company — would wither away as those of the feudal magnates and gilds had withered. With the Navigation Act we have arrived at a fully fashioned conception of economic policy in an essentially national form. Its dynamic was no longer the achievement of social justice through Christian ethics working against private greed or exploitation. It was the welfare of Leviathan.

It is impossible to calculate how effective this first experiment in statutory control was. The remaining years of the Interregnum were economically abnormal and the evidence of its workings is meagre. But the latest historian to investigate it has suggested that its lawyer-like formula was too neat to be enforceable. At the Restoration it was to be revised with a keener eye to administrative practicality. Its essential objects were to remain the same.[1] The belief that the Act by itself brought about the First Dutch War which followed in 1652 can be dismissed. The immediate cause was a matter of maritime etiquette and national pride: a dispute at sea which arose out of the English allegation that a Dutch fleet under Tromp, then cruising off Dover, refused to

[1] Harper, op. cit., ch. v

lower its flag in the conventional gesture of respect. Yet undoubtedly the Act was part of the mounting volume of grievances, mostly economic, between the two states: the Cokayne project, the disputes over the North Sea fisheries, the Amboyna massacre and other quarrels in the East, brushes off Africa and in the West Indies and North America. It was itself the product of the same wave of economic nationalism as the disputes themselves. Mercantilist logic was the logic of violence in an age of violence. In a situation where economic policies were producing few if any signs of progress towards the desired goals, Englishmen appealed willingly, even eagerly, to the arbitrament of war. All the more because, strategically, Providence seemed to have smiled on the English (much as she seemed to have smiled on Germany two and a half centuries later). The Dutch might have achieved economic and technical advantage, but at a high cost. They were in almost every respect vulnerable to attack. Their shipping was in large measure unarmed, their sea lanes exposed. Much of the food and raw materials needed by their peoples was imported. Even the Dutch recognized their peril, and as the war of 1652 began the Dutch Grand Pensionary himself reflected that 'the English are about to attack a mountain of gold; we are about to attack a mountain of iron'.

His fears were well grounded. The First Dutch War brought disastrous losses to Dutch trade and shipping, and heavy privations to the Dutch people. To a large section of English mercantile opinion it was a highly satisfactory episode. Its supporters did not find it easy to forgive Cromwell for winding it up for political and religious reasons. Contrariwise, the war against Spain in 1656 was largely ideological in origin. Politically misconceived, it brought severe and immediate losses of shipping and trade; yet by a not uncommon paradox, the genuine expansion of the English economy is often dated from this initially unprofitable experiment in imperialism. When the war against the Dutch was resumed, with misplaced confidence, a decade later, its course was to demonstrate how the theatre of trade had expanded, commensurately with the range of naval operations, into the western and southern Atlantic and the eastern seas.

All this investment – of capital, enterprise and, no less important, of intellectual energy and the lust for adventure – was slow to yield dividends. The returns did not as yet compensate for the collapse of the old economy. England remained an underemployed nation. But her economic pains were growing pains. Beneath the recurring crises and palpable failures, there lay a rough coherence of policy, ideas and action that reflected the unique advantages of a centralized — as some believed an over-centralized — economic administration. For all the risks it entailed, the geographical proximity of the political and economic centres, the power of the monopolistic capital of an expanding and dominant metropolis, had drawn together the threads of policy. To this, neither the loose federation of the Dutch Republic, with its obstinate traditions of local autonomy, nor the French State, its energies still dispersed over widely separated regions, could as yet offer effective rejoinder. It is probably significant that French 'mercantilism' was to remain relatively incoherent and unformulated, even in Colbert's day. Industrial, as distinct from commercial, regulation may owe its protracted dominance in France to the absence of anything comparable to that combination of expanding commercial capital and government influence represented by the Westminster–City axis in London. The economic innovators, speculators and gamblers of the earlier seventeenth century often tried to storm citadels far beyond their powers to breach. But even their failures were prophetic: by the end of the century many of their objectives had been reached.

CHAPTER FOUR

Manufactures, Markets and Technology

MEN did not use the words 'industrial' or 'industrialism' in the seventeenth century. Occasionally they spoke of an 'industry' but more often of 'trade' or 'manufacture' to describe the processes by which raw materials were made into more elaborated articles of sale; the emphasis was still on the intimate relationship between those who made (by hand) and sold. If we use the word 'industry' to describe such processes we must rid our imagination of the accretions of two centuries that have associated it with urban life, with a clear division of capital and labour, with heavy accumulation of fixed capital in the shape of factories, plant, machinery and so forth. Here and there the beginnings of the later economy may be discerned. Some towns were already centres of certain specialized industries, as London was of leather manufacture, brewing and shipbuilding, or Norwich and Exeter of cloth working. Most cloth workers were already supplied with materials and even tools by others and were economically so placed that they were unlikely to rise in the economic and social scale except by migration or change of occupation. A few industries like brewing, salt making, iron working and paper mills began in the seventeenth century to use metal vats, pans, forges and pumps, and presses. A ship and its components represented a substantial aggregate of capital, often shared between a number of owners. Both buyer and builder needed a substantial capital. Yet these were not characteristic of the economy as a whole.

What we may call the social structure of industry varied from industry to industry, region to region. Generally, in textiles, the finer the article, the more likely it was that the industry making it would be dominated by big capitalists capable of making the bigger outlay on finer materials, expensive dyes and tools. Where the article was coarser, nearer the rough cloths peasants made for themselves, the less need there was for capital. In such industries – like those of the Devonshire or Yorkshire kerseys and the cheaper kinds of New Drapery in East Anglia—plenty of small masters would be found. A memorandum on the woollen industry prepared for the Privy Council in 1615 made this distinction between 'rich' and 'meaner' clothiers very clearly.[1] But everywhere the nation's leading industry was a household industry, full of rural cottage workers working for a capitalist who 'put out' materials to them and collected their product. It is difficult to know whether to regard earnings in such work as a helpful bonus to families that were basically agricultural, or as a prime source of income. Wages, though crawling upwards, were still low, and in the half century that ended with the Civil Wars the workers were living through hard times. In many places, the J.P.s continued to assess wages — mainly on a piece-work basis: 'for a weaving of a broad listed white of this making IXs.' and so on. Until the 1680s most wages seem to have been paid at assessed rates. The system died harder than historians used to think.[2]

The burden of this manufacturing system on the workers lay less in the low wages it paid (though they were low enough) than in the precarious nature of the employment it offered. The fact that their merchant employers had in general few fixed capital assets on which they had to earn a return meant that they moved into production when times were good and out of it when they were bad. In depressions, stocks of materials were liquidated and not renewed. There was thus chronic unemployment, and for most workers busy times alternated with spells of idleness and poverty. The chronic depressions of the first half of the century threw thousands of workers on to the mercy of the charitable.

Almost everywhere, and especially in the remoter parts of the countryside, there survived the remains of an ancient and unspecialized economy in which many people lived a more or less self-sufficient life, growing a substantial proportion of the food they ate or drank, making their own clothes and footwear, cutting their own fuel, boiling their own soap, and so on, as they still do in the more primitive parts of Asia, Africa and even Europe today. This phase was passing but not yet past. More or less specialized industries were growing up to perform services formerly provided by the consumers themselves, and providing for the simple, basic human needs — food and drink, clothing and footwear, housing and fuel. Much of the manufacturing involved was of the simple kind performed by rustic craftsmen — tinkers, tailors, weavers,

---

[1] *State Papers Domestic*, James I, vol. LXXX, 13, 1615.
[2] J. Clapham, *A Concise Economic History of Britain*, 1949, p. 215.

carpenters, joiners and the like. But from this world of Bottom and his rude mechanics, craftsmen of immense skill and ingenuity were already emerging. In 1600 Thomas Dallam, a Lancashire blacksmith turned organ builder, could construct a mechanical organ which the Queen sent as a present to the Sultan. Its clockwork action worked singing birds, bells, trumpeters, suns, moons, planets, crowing cocks and striking clocks, besides the organ which played pieces in counterpoint on the hour. If Dallam had lived a century and a half later he might well have turned his talents to textile machinery.[1] Occasionally craftsmen could rise to a high pitch of excellence to produce exquisite pieces in gold, silver and jewels, rich silks, damasks, tapestries and other trappings of aristocratic living. More often, late Tudor or Jacobean manufactures were crude and simple. They usually abandoned simplicity only at the risk of the vulgar ostentation characteristic of the great family tombs and ornate chimney-pieces of the great houses.

The rise of specialized industries had its origins either in the desire of the richer or more discriminating customers for articles – clothing especially – of a higher quality than their local makers could supply: or, in the case of mineral industries, in the universal demand for commodities which were only found in particular regions. Iron and salt were the classic instance but, as timber grew scarcer, coal – sea coal as it was known since it travelled by sea from Newcastle to London and from Glamorgan to Bristol – was added to the list. The list was to grow longer through the century as the standard of living rose and with it the demand for glass, pewter, soap and the colonial goods imported to London, Bristol, Liverpool, Glasgow – sugar, tobacco, cotton and dyes. The extractive industries grew therefore around the mines or workings – coal in the north-east, north-west, South Wales, Scotland; tin in Cornwall, lead in Derbyshire, iron on the Sussex Weald but increasingly in Shropshire and the west Midlands. Other manufactures that refined or processed imported raw materials, like sugar boiling or tobacco cutting or cotton manufacture grew up near the ports where their materials were loaded. Tanning and soap making, which used hides and tallow, developed in or near towns – London especially – where there was a large consumption of meat and consequently a large supply of by-products.

It is less easy to account for the growing tendency to concentration in the largest industry of all: cloth. Yet the trend is plain. Wool was still spun nearly everywhere in England. Englishmen were proud that

[1] Stanley Mayes, *An Organ for the Sultan*, 1956 *passim*.

they wore woollen cloth, just as they were proud of wearing leather shoes rather than wooden clogs. Perhaps it was a mark of Scottish poverty that Scotland spun flax, as much of Europe did. The wool was spun now on the wheel, and the distaff was disappearing. Even in districts where there was no longer much special manufacture of cloth, the village weaver survived till late in the eighteenth century and even later. But this only emphasized the real concentration that was taking place in the cloth counties. The clothier and his network of workers were beginning to disappear from the south and the Home Counties, from Kent and Berkshire and from the ancient cloth areas of Suffolk; from the old cloth towns of earlier times like Coventry, York, Lincoln and Beverley. The future was to lie with three main areas; Norfolk and Essex in eastern England, the West Riding of Yorkshire in the north, and a long area from Gloucestershire to Devon in the west. The reasons why this concentration took place are many and complex and will be examined later.[1]

Seventeenth-century pamphleteers were fond of boasting of England's natural riches. Not without reason. What Thomas Mun called 'Naturall Wealth'[2] lay in her 'excellent Fleecewools, Iron, Lead, Tynn, Saffron, Corn, Victuals, Hides, Wax and other natural Endowments'. At every point English 'manufactures' were intimately connected with the land. A series of judicial decisions in the sixteenth century concentrated the rights to work or lease mineral deposits in the hands of the lord of the manor. Thousands of yeomen and farmers were concerned with the price of the wool and barley which they sold to the clothiers and the brewers. Thousands of smallholders and their wives and children depended on wages earned as spinners, weavers, fullers and shearers to eke out a living. Elsewhere the mines and iron works similarly offered part-time work to small farmers. Crops like flax, hemp, saffron, woad were grown specifically for manufacturing. The basis of the entire economy was agriculture and the land.

The woollen cloth industry, which by any token – employment, turnover, profit, exports – was England's largest industry after agriculture, entered the Stuart period with a flourish. The boom lasted approximately for a decade, if the export figures are any guide. Woollen cloth had by this time come to represent at least three-quarters of England's total exports by value. Having ousted the Hanseatic merchants who had previously played a leading part in the trade, the Merchant Adventurers had come to control the export from London

[1] See below, pp. 75–8.   [2] T. Mun, op. cit., reprint, p. 71.

69

to northern Europe which accounted for about half the total trade. At the very end of the sixteenth century the grand export total for London was reckoned to be about 105,000 cloths, of which 75,000 went to Germany and the United Provinces, 12,000 to the Baltic, 6,500 to the Levant, about the same to France and 2,000 each to Italy, Russia and Barbary. These exports were made up largely of the so-called 'Old Draperies', much of them the heavy undyed broadcloth that was made throughout Wiltshire, Gloucestershire, Somerset, Worcestershire and Oxfordshire. In East Anglia, the 'Old Draperies' of Suffolk, Norfolk and Essex might be either undyed or dyed. They were spun and woven from the fine, short-staple wool that was England's pride in the Middle Ages. There was less of it now than formerly but throughout the seventeenth century it was still to be the basis of the 'woollen' manufacture proper. The short-staple wool was not combed, as the increasing volume of the less fine, long-staple wool was, but carded, i.e. the fibres were worked between two boards covered with spikes until they were interlocked to form the basis of a cloth at once fine, heavy and costly. The trade in these broadcloths continued at a high level until 1614. In that year London sent over 127,000 cloths abroad. Now and again a shudder had run through the cloth areas as though men felt some premonition of trouble ahead. In 1613, a grim year of plague and depression, Wiltshire magistrates drew up rules attempting to regulate the flow of capital and labour into the local industry as though they were nervous it might exceed a safe level and encourage young people to marry on prospects that might turn out only a mirage. Output slumped in 1610 when the Merchant Adventurers feared the competition from rival manufacturers abroad where stocks of unsold cloth were said to be ominously high. These seemed, nevertheless, to be only passing fancies to the great body of traders and clothiers, and in July 1614, when the blow fell, trade had never been better.

In that month James I decided to forbid the export of undyed cloth — 'in the white' as they put it — in favour of a group of 'projectors' led by Alderman Cokayne. Cokayne was an Eastland merchant who had for some time been urging upon the Government a plan to dye and dress all cloth exported.[1] In December the Merchant Adventurers' Charter was rescinded and Cokayne and his friends were left in control of the trade to Germany and the Low Countries. It was the first move in a

---

[1] The fullest account is by Astrid Friis, *Alderman Cockayne's Project and the Cloth Trade*, 1927. The most recent critical account is by B. E. Supple, *Commercial Crisis and Change in England 1600-1642*, 1959. For the purely commercial aspects see supra, Ch. III.

long process of painful adjustment which was to keep the English cloth industry in a state of chronic instability for the next half century and more. Two major changes were involved. Cokayne himself claimed that the object was to substitute a fully manufactured article for a semi-manufactured article and thereby achieve a higher value for English exports. Unfortunately, this attempt at economic planning chanced to coincide with a number of natural happenings over which neither he nor anyone else had any control. Succeeding decades saw European markets decimated by war and upset by the manipulation and debasement of currencies on an unprecedented scale. Meanwhile the nature of the wool supply was changing to the detriment of the 'Old Draperies' and to the benefit of those 'New Draperies' which necessarily competed with the old broadcloths both at home and abroad to an extent that is still unknown. Add to this sharp and efficient competition of foreign manufacturers, especially from the Dutch, and the omens for Cokayne's project were not bright.

Cokayne's plan was not, on the face of it, without a certain *rationale*. A high proportion of the Merchant Adventurers' exports were of un-dyed and undressed cloth. England was therefore losing turnover, profit and employment because of her technological weakness. This compelled her to leave the finishing processes to others, especially to the Dutch who were never slow to corner the most valuable lines of business. A Dutch schedule of the costs of making a piece of cloth in the sixteenth century gives some idea of the probable division of profits between the branches of manufacture carried on in England and those which were still controlled by foreigners.

	Percentage
Raw materials	10
Combing	6
Spinning	2
Weaving	7
Fulling	5
Dyeing	47
Miscellaneous	10
Profit	13
	100

The first four items were indubitably 'English'. The English clothier bought his wool and distributed it, as he had done for centuries, to be worked up into cloth, amongst a scattered variety of cottage workers. The unfinished, undyed cloth that resulted was not more than a half-way house between raw wool and a completed article. Indeed, it was only a quarter-way house. The very high 'value added' by dyeing explains why Cokayne's scheme appealed strongly to a number of different interests. Merchants from organizations other than the Merchant Adventurers, jealous of their monopoly, saw here an opportunity to break it in a popular cause. A strong section of the Cokayne group hailed from the Eastland Company, old rivals of the Adventurers. Members of the Levant Company were not far behind. Powerful support came also from the London cloth workers and dyers, for London was the reception centre for much of the country-made cloth before it was exported. Some was already dyed for exporters outside the Adventurers' areas of monopoly. Why not extend and expand the process and increase employment? It was a plausible argument. Finally, James and some of his less prudent advisers were attracted by the idea of national economic gain and by the promise of larger royal revenues that went with it; £20,000 more from the customs on dye-stuffs, another £20,000 on the higher value exported from exports. The prospects were irresistible. The old company was swiftly replaced by a new, the so-called 'Kings Merchant Adventurers'. Naturally they included Cokayne.

Retribution came equally swiftly. The new organization made sure of securing the powers possessed by the old, i.e. to export undyed and undressed cloth until (as a sage observer said) 'they can provide sufficient store of workmen and materials, which will be God knows when'.[1] Was it really possible to develop the dyeing and finishing industries quickly enough to execute the plan and fulfil the promises? Or was the whole scheme merely a manœuvre by the anti-Adventurers to capture their monopoly without any real intention or hope of changing the system? Probably the latter.[2] The slippery Cokayne was up to almost any trick.

By 1616, the new men had run into every kind of trouble. The Dutch had retaliated against them by prohibiting the import of their finished cloth. Their staple in the Dutch Republic was in danger, and the flames were only fanned by James's proclamation – one of scores of such prohibitions – against the export of English wool, so valuable to the Dutch cloth industry. Stocks of cloth piled up, unemployment was rife in the western counties. Exports fell catastrophically; but still James

---

[1] Quoted by Supple, op. cit., p. 35.   [2] Ibid., p. 39.

went on with his project, against the judgement of all his best advisers – possibly because Cokayne had more than once proved good for a loan when the royal credit was strained. Not till late in 1617, after three disastrous years during which exports had fallen by about one-third, was James finally persuaded to drop his plausible friends. In October the Privy Council, never friendly to Cokayne, put the gears into reverse with a plain announcement that it was 'now his Majesty's pleasure and resolution not to disturb the trade of whites with any further essay, but to leave the same to the train and course of trade now in practice and according to the use before the late alteration'. Always short of capital and of the necessary skills, the project of Cokayne and his friends was dead.

Thus ended the attempt, or what was claimed to be the attempt, to achieve a spectacular rise in the value of England's exports by capturing those finishing processes which in turn gave strategic control of a large part of the contemporary world textile markets. In the 1630s three-quarters of the trade to Germany and Holland, once again restored to the Merchant Adventurers, was still in undyed cloth, and it is doubtful whether any substantial increase in the ouptut of dyed woollens as a whole was achieved until late in the seventeenth century. In this, as in so many matters of technology, English industry was a long way behind the Dutch, and the advances that were made, shadowy though our knowledge of them is, seem to have come from Dutch sources. One Dutch resident whose name is linked with a process of dyeing with a solution of cochineal and tin was a figure characteristic of this Janus-headed age in the history of science. Cornelius Drebbel, a Dutch immigrant, was half alchemist, half scientist, contriver of stage effects for the royal masques, alleged inventor of a submarine boat that travelled under the surface of the Thames and of a patent brand of fireship for naval use. The scarlet 'Bow dye' for cloth was the result of experiments by Drebbel and his son-in-law Kepler, himself of Leiden and presumably, therefore, well versed in the technical knowledge of the great cloth industry of that city. Later in the century, there is talk of other Dutchmen, Germans and Portuguese being enticed to England to spread their skills in cloth dyeing. But progress was evidently slow and little certainly had been achieved by the Restoration, except that in Wiltshire the so-called 'medley' cloths were dyed in the wool and became popular and profitable. The technology of dyeing was still a good problem for the infant Royal Society to cut its teeth on in 1662.

Two years after the old Merchant Adventurers, by a sizeable bribe to James, had managed to restore the *status quo* and Cokayne was fading into history, the whole cloth industry fell into a new and paralysing depression. Once again exports fell to a record low level, little more than half that of the best years of the early century. Many Merchant Adventurers went out of business as stocks piled up. In the West Country and Suffolk, home of the 'Old Draperies', unemployment and poverty spread; to make matters worse a bad harvest in 1621 sent food prices rocketing. The Privy Council watched the situation anxiously as local J.P.s reported that many poor people were 'ready to mutiny for want of work'. This was the major economic dislocation of the first half of the seventeenth century and it proved a fruitful source of debate and reform, throwing up a revolutionary economic analysis by Thomas Mun and the proposals of the special Committee for Trade of which he was a leading member. The reasons for this catastrophic situation were complex. It was not merely the aftermath of the Cokayne scheme and its failure, as used to be thought, though it may well be that Dutch competition was sharpened as a result of that fiasco. Nor was it merely the result of restrictive practices by organizations like the Merchant Adventurers, though these again may have contributed. One effect of the crisis was the freeing, from 1621, of cloths other than undyed woollens from their monopoly. New manufactures were thus released to expand outside the old framework of company regulation. Most important among the immediate causes of this short but violent depression that went on till 1624 was the manipulation and debasement of currencies that was in progress on the Continent, especially in Germany and Poland, and the outbreak of the Thirty Years War, both interlinked phenomena. These were responsible for major interruptions to international trade which made it difficult for English merchants to export cloth profitably and brought about that unfavourable balance of trade which Mun placed at the centre of his analysis of contemporary economic ills. It was to haunt economic thought for two and a half centuries.

That was not the end of the story. 1625 was another year of depression and plague which scattered the London merchants and dislocated manufactures. 1629 saw another major fall in which even the 'New Draperies' of East Anglia found themselves sharing the now almost chronic troubles of the 'Old', no doubt because of the wars against Spain and France which blocked their major outlet to the Mediterranean. This was followed by a renewed quarrel between the Merchant Adventurers with the Government of the Dutch Republic over their privileges in that country. Stocks of English cloth were confiscated and tempers ran high. The worst sufferers, as always, were the clothiers and their employees in the West Country. So matters continued throughout the thirties, with distress general but particularly severe amongst the white-cloth makers in the western counties. A commission set up in 1638 to investigate the causes of declining trade published a gloomy picture. At home, trade was stagnant. Abroad, competition was sharp and powerful. From then until the Civil War broke, the air was filled with laments of 'scarcity of money'.

The decline of the 'Old Draperies' was indicative of more than immediate intrigues, clashes of interests and currency difficulties. In retrospect it is clear that they were the victims of one of those major revolutions in trade and fashion which have periodically turned the textile industries upside down, and still do so. The older 'woollens' proper (whose modern descendants are such things as blankets and baize cloth) were being replaced in public favour by newer, lighter, brighter and frequently cheaper fabrics. These were, most often, the 'stuffs' of East Anglia, cloths of the worsted type manufactured from the coarser, long staple wools that had overwhelmed the production of the old, finer, short-staple wools. These, the so-called 'New Draperies', all stemmed — as did competing stuffs manufactured by the chief rival industries at Leiden — from those country clothiers and artisans who had fled before Alva's troops from the cloth-making villages of Flanders round Ypres, especially from Hondschoote and Poperinghe. In the late sixties and seventies of the sixteenth century, the refugees had settled principally at Leiden, and in England, not unnaturally, in those areas where the manufacture of worsted-type cloths not wholly dissimilar to their own was of long standing. Neither Worstead nor Kersey (which had given their names to earlier textiles) was very far from Colchester and Halstead, which had welcomed 200 'Dutchmen' by 1570 'making bays, says, perpetuanos, shaloon, grosgraines and serge . . . trades not commonly known', as the Colchester bailiffs told the Privy Council. The strangers were 'very honest, godly, civil and well-ordered people, not given to any outrage or excess'. The aspiring immigrant was scrutinized carefully for any signs of dangerous fanaticism before he was accorded the clearance certificate with its standard label: 'Jan Gelison, dyer, of Flanders. No fanatic. His conversation is honest.' In the seventeenth century the Colchester cloth industry was still under the rule of two governors, with twenty-two assistants, elected by the whole body of makers each 28 December, with powers to make statutes to prevent frauds and abuses. Their contribution was a matter for local rejoicing in

King James's time, when the bailiffs marvelled 'how beneficial the strangers of the Dutch Congregation there have been and are unto our said Towne, as well in replenishing and beautifying it, as for their trades, which they daily use there, setting on work many of our poor people . . .'. By 1622 it was said there were 1,500 'Dutchmen' in and around Colchester. They included sixty-eight makers of bays and says, 104 weavers, forty-six fullers and a variety of other traders and skilled craftsmen, and amongst the 'congregation' were some of the richest men in the town – the Fromenteels, Hornes, Buskins and Volls, whose efforts had given Colchester a thriving export trade. Their main pro-ducts – bays and says – differed from 'pure' woollens in that the pattern of the weave (whether both warp and weft were of combed wool or whether the weft was of cotton or silk) was still visible in the finished fabric. The varieties of make were bewildering even to contemporaries. 'Says' were a hard-wearing worsted used for men's dress, monk's shirts in Italy and Spain, and in a green version for Quakers' aprons. 'Bays' – the Colchester speciality – were said to be a 'kind of coarse open woollen stuff – exported in considerable quantities to Spain, Por-tugal and Italy . . . for the monks and nuns, and as linings for military uniforms. The looking-glass makers also use them behind their glasses to preserve the tin and quicksilver.'

The Colchester makes spread northwards, through Halstead and up along the Essex–Suffolk borders. Bays and says and perpetuanas – not unlike bays – were made in Suffolk. Lavenham specialized in 'Callim-ancoes', a light worsted in striped colours much in favour with the Eastland merchants. They sold well in Russia where the Tartar and Siberian tribes were said to use them for sashes. So northwards to Nor-wich, where again, as at Colchester, the 'New Draperies' were sprung from refugees from the Low Countries in Elizabeth's time. The original settlers were licensed by the Privy Council 'to exercise the faculty of making bays, says . . . and other outlandish commodities as hath not been used to be made within this our Realm of England . . .'. They were divided into two communities; the Walloons had the Bishop's Chapel and St Mary the Less, the Dutch the Church of the Blackfriars, as their headquarters. From the one came the cloths known collectively as the *Cangeantrie*, from the other the *Baytrie*, or goods of the 'bay' type. The particular strength of the Norwich industry came to be in the light, bright 'stuffs', often made of a mixture of wool and silk. Such were the so-called *bombazines*, an early imitation of Indian fabrics which came to be the popular wear of the not-too-affluent squire's lady or the tradesman's wife. Between them, the Flemings and Walloons and their New Draperies helped to turn Norwich and the surrounding countryside into a flourishing scene. Writers contrasted its well-distributed prosperity with the poverty they saw in Suffolk, where for some reason the new industries never did so well.[1] 'I should judge this City to be another Utopia', wrote Sir John Harrington of Norwich. 'The people live so orderly, the streets kept so cleanly, the tradesmen, young and old, so industrious, the better sort so provident and withal so charitable, that it is rare to meet a beggar there, as it is common to see them in Westminster.' It was no mere rhetorical flourish. The prosperity and the charity are demonstrated from many sources.[2] Drawing its yarn from Yorkshire and Suffolk and organized under the leadership of capitalist clothiers who watched the fashions, dictated patterns, supplied capital, material and wages and played the markets, the Norfolk industries were buoyant and expansive.

So, in the west, were the rising industries of Devon. Here, since the late Middle Ages, was an industry, mainly in the north of the shire and round Exeter, that turned out 100,000 yards of roughish cloth a year. The principal make was then kerseys, as it was in many parts of Yorkshire and the northern counties. The kersey was a cheap type of woollen, but with one feature of the worsted: the pattern of the weave was visible to the eye. But kerseys were no match for the New Draperies which began to reach Devon in the early seventeenth century. Soon Exeter was making a series of new lines — serges and perpetuanas — which were later in the century to oust the kersey from its preeminence. Before the Restoration, Tiverton seems to have held fast to the kersey; after, it turned over to serges. Serges were something like bays and says but heavier, and the type known as 'perpetuana' advertised their durability. The strength of the serge lay in its combining a woollen weft with a worsted warp. Hence it required two kinds of wool. Devon was conveniently placed to get both. The fine, short wool came from overseas, increasingly from Spain; the coarse, long wool from Ireland. Serges were to make a rapid conquest of those north European markets lost to the Merchant Adventurers. The loss of London and the mid-western counties was the gain of Exeter and Devonshire.

There was, then, a broad contrast between the fortunes of the Old and the New Draperies. The New Drapery areas in East Anglia and Devonshire did not suffer as badly as the Old Draperies of the 'middle'

[1] See Drayton's *Poly-Olbion*, p. 646; *Collected Poems*, ed. J. Buxton, 1953, vol. II.
[2] See p. 234, below.

west in the 1620s. In the 1630s there were occasional signs of overproduction of New Draperies but they were not prolonged. By 1640 their output had risen to a point where, as exports, the New Draperies could compete with the Old. There was, nevertheless, one outstanding success amongst the 'woollens' proper. The so-called 'Spanish' cloths which began to be made in Wiltshire and Somerset early in the seventeenth century, and the 'stammels' or 'scarlets' of the Stroudwater district in Gloucestershire, rapidly acquired a European reputation. In 1640, England was exporting nearly 14,000 of these cloths as against just over 3,000 in 1628, and since these cloths, made of imported fine Spanish wool, were fully finished in their home areas and did not create employment for the London finishers, they roused protests from London in the 1630s. Although they were, like the 'Old Draperies', a pure woollen cloth, the Spanish cloths were a new departure. They came in many colours, they were exceedingly finely made and they catered for an expensive market. Like the New Draperies, they incorporated a good deal of immigrant Dutch skill, especially for dyeing.

Collapse of the Old Draperies, the rise of the New, the appearance of mixed serges and fine, coloured Spanish cloths in the west – the whole structure of the cloth industry was undergoing a radical transformation. In part, this was the response to the changing character of raw materials and of markets, to wars and currency problems abroad. But it was also the result of sharp competition for the shrinking markets of northern and central Europe and the fitful and capricious trade in the Mediterranean. There, one old competitor was in steady decline after about 1620: Venice, whose industries had been a powerful rival in the late sixteenth century. The dead hand of the gilds and high costs had somehow whittled down her competitive spirit and Venice had never entered the arena for the 'New Draperies'. In vain, as the decline of the mid-seventeenth century overtook them, her merchants lamented that they could not compete with the 'more pleasing & less costly' textiles supplied by their western European rivals to the Levant. More formidable than the Venetians were the Dutch. Between the still dispersed, mainly rural industries of England, and the concentrated industries of Leiden and its immediate vicinity, a fierce contest was in progress from the 1620s to the end of the century, which we can follow almost blow by blow. Each side had advantages and disadvantages, and the structure of the English industry in the later seventeenth century is explained to a considerable degree by the success with which advantages were exploited and difficulties overcome. As regards wool, England was strongly placed to injure her Dutch rival by forbidding the export of all wool. This she did. Whatever success smugglers may have had in selling wool to France (not yet a powerful competitor) they evidently had little success with Holland. All the evidence suggests that the prohibitions were effective, and though the Dutch got wool from elsewhere, they had to pay more dearly for it as a result of the cutting off of English supplies. This affected their cheaper makes – they too had a 'Nieuwe Draperie' that corresponded very closely to the English, and sprang from the same Flemish roots – because the profit margins were smaller than on the finer and more costly makes. They seem to have done rather better in their search for fine wool. Here, their skill as buyers in world markets stood them in good stead and they were able to outpace their English rivals for favours in Spain, the principal source for really fine sheep's wool: in Turkey, too, whence came fine mohair and angora wool. As a result of these raw material problems, the pattern of output at Leiden was in complete contrast to that in England. While the Dutch were able to develop their fine expensive cloths – very comparable to the Wiltshire 'Spanish' – their cheaper 'New Draperies' quickly began to feel the draught of competition from East Anglia and Devon. By the 1650s, lower wages, lower taxes and cheaper, more abundant supplies of the coarser wools had enabled the English industry to make its mark on the rival Dutch industries. In the struggle for the more expensive markets, the honours were more evenly divided: maybe the Dutch kept a little ahead, though their technical lead was certainly shortening as England slowly learnt the techniques of finishing and dyeing and acquired new sources of colonial dyestuffs. There was even an elaborate English plan in 1651 to pre-empt the entire crop of Spanish fine wool and thus put a stranglehold on the Dutch woollens trade. It seems to have remained armchair strategy.

While the rural textile industries were jostling for position and adjusting themselves to new tastes and changing markets, a revolution of a different order was overtaking other industries. Mining and processing of mineral ores made up an important part of this vital, though still localized type of industry. The others were mainly what a later age would have called 'consumption' industries – malting and brewing, salt making, sugar boiling, soap making, glass making and the like. There was an important link between these two groups: both were using coal on an increasing scale. The figures of coal output and the nature of the growing trade in coal are an important measure of the larger industrial change that was in progress.

The increase in coal production in the various coal-fields of Britain between mid-Tudor and late Stuart times was as spectacular as any of the economic happenings in the period. The 'statistics' are conjectures rather than scientific data, but they probably give a reasonably accurate picture of the trends:[1]

ESTIMATED ANNUAL PRODUCTION OF COAL (in tons)

Coalfield	1551–60	1681–90
Durham and Northumberland	65,000	1,225,000
Scotland	40,000	475,000
Wales	20,000	200,000
N. and W. Midlands and North	65,000	850,000
Cumberland	6,000	100,000
West	10,000	100,000
Forest of Dean	3,000	25,000
Devon and Ireland	1,000	7,000
Total	210,000	2,982,000

The approximate increase was therefore some fourteen-fold, of which a considerable proportion took place between 1600 and 1660. The most striking growth occurred in the north-east coalfield and the related east coast trade to London, stirring even poets to comment:

> England's a perfect world! has Indies too!
> Correct your maps: Newcastle is Peru.

as an enthusiastic troubadour sang in some verses in 1651 entitled 'Upon the Coal Pits about Newcastle upon Tine'. The names of individual mines (like 'Stella' and 'Blaydon') were household words to the citizens of London. Yet the expansion was common to all the coal-producing districts and markets, though the *rate* of increase may have slackened during and immediately after the Civil War.

Any attempt to explain this extraordinary growth of coal mining must begin with an inquiry into the demand for coal and the means by which so bulky a product was transported from mine to market. There were two uses for coal: domestic and industrial. Both had their roots in a single problem; that acute shortage of timber which had been growing steadily ever since the accession of Elizabeth and reached in the seventeenth century the dimensions of a national crisis. This was not restricted

[1] J. U. Nef, *The Rise of the British Coal Industry*, 1932, vol. I, p. 19.

to England. It was felt in other countries and voices were raised in alarm from most western European states. But the crisis may have been sharper in England than elsewhere, since England was less well wooded than the Continent. Her population and her industries were increasing substantially, maybe faster than elsewhere; certainly people were flowing into towns and cities at a faster rate, above all into London, which was growing at a pace which, as we have seen, alarmed governments and citizens.

The timber shortage did two things. It persuaded householders to turn over from warming their houses and cooking their food with wood, and use coal instead; and it sent manufacturers of many kinds — brewers, brick makers, soap boilers, sugar boilers, metal workers, bakers — in search of processes which would allow them to substitute coal for wood in their manufactures. The first revolution is often associated with King James, who is credited with setting a fashion for coal burning and thereby giving added impetus to the movement of fashionable society to the West End. There may be some substance in the story. James certainly knew 'Auld Reekie' where the timber shortage had already turned Scotland over to coal. By the Restoration, London was taking somewhere between two-fifths and a half of the total shipments from the north-east producers. The coal fire and the chimney stack had already become peculiarly British institutions. But this change in social and manufacturing habits had a serious disadvantage: it created the one real chink in England's economic armour. During the Dutch wars of the seventeenth century, the coal supply to London was a constant anxiety to English governments and an ever-present target to the Dutch fleet, whose raids were swift, sharp and lethal. In 1653, in the middle of the First Dutch War, the price of coal rose from £2 to £5 a chaldron. The cooks had not 'wherewith to dress their meat', the brewers were idle and the cries of the poor 'very lamentable for want of fuel'. When Newcastle was blockaded in the Civil War, it was observed how many of those 'fine-nosed Dames' who had been in the habit of objecting to the smell of sea-coal 'now cry, would to God we had Sea-coal, O the want of fire undoes us, O the sweet Seacoal we used to have, how we want them now, no fire to your Seacoal . . . etc.'. Against such hazards those responsible for the security of the State had to set the employment and training for naval seamen created by the growing fleet of colliers that plied between Newcastle and the Thames. Here was that 'Nursery of Mariners', from which the Commonwealth and later navies were chiefly manned.

The London demand for domestic coal created the largest single market; but it was not the only one. The entire Thames valley drew on London for coal. It went along the Thames as far as Eton, Henley, Reading and Oxford, and was then hauled overland to towns and villages at least ten to twelve miles from the river. Other areas got their supplies through ports like Hull, Lynn and Yarmouth, and then by river or overland. The south-west got its coal by sea from Glamorgan, the north-west from Whitehaven, east Scotland from Fife. Inland, large quantities travelled in sailing barges along the rivers of the west and the Midlands, by Severn, Avon and Trent. The coal routes were already getting busier before the Civil War, as the exchange of coals going outward against corn coming inwards from the east coast ports and up the rivers gave merchants opportunities for profitable business. England was fortunate in her network of navigable rivers in the pre-canal age, for the cost of overland carriage doubled the price of the cargo every two miles. A paper read in 1675 before the Royal Society calculated that it cost as much to carry coal overland for 15 miles as it did to carry it 300 miles by water. Probably the calculation was equally true half a century earlier. Overland traffic of coal was therefore mainly local. Round each coal pit, the inhabitants came to fetch their own supplies. In midland England, Lancashire and Yorkshire, hundreds of thousands of people lived within half a day's ride of a pit. Villages and sizeable towns were supplied by pack-horse, as Coventry was supplied from the Warwickshire pits or Leicester from Nottinghamshire and Derbyshire. A proportion of the increased output of coal must, then, be attributed to a change of people's habits with regard to household fuel.

But that was far from being the whole story. In many areas, including London, there was a rising demand for coal, or coke, in industries where it could be substituted for wood or charcoal. As early as 1610, Sir William Slingsby, the lessee of coal mines at Seaton Delaval and a notable entrepreneur of the north-east, divided manufacturing processes into two categories. The first included brewing, dyemaking, alum and salt manufacture. These were processes in which coal could already be substituted for wood without difficulty. The second, including malting, baking, brick, tile and pottery manufactures, as well as copper, brass, corn, lead and glass making, comprised those processes where successful substitution was still in the future. Yet with the cutting of timber for house building, shipbuilding and charcoal going on apace, the pressure to find methods of substitution was very strong. In London alone the annual consumption of wood by the brewing industry in the middle of Elizabeth's reign was probably some 20,000 wagon loads. To bake 2,000 bricks took one load. A ton of salt consumed in its manufacture four loads of wood. So did a ton of lime. One glass works was said to consume 2,000 wagon loads in James I's time. The metal industries as a whole were thought to cost England the best part of a quarter of a million trees a year. Little wonder that the substitution of coal for timber became a task of high priority from Elizabeth's time onwards.

In some industries, the use of coal was already well established. By the seventeenth century, the ancient (and presumably frustrating) habit of trying to reduce brine to salt by the heat of the sun had been long abandoned. In the north-east coal – 'pan coal' as it was called – had replaced wood for firing the pans in which the brine was poured. Shields and Sunderland were using 90,000 tons of coal a year in their salt works before the Civil War. (At the 'wiches' in Cheshire and Worcestershire, on the other hand, the salt makers were further from the pits and so stuck to wood firing longer.) Alum, saltpetre, copperas and gunpowder makers likewise turned over to coal.

Even larger users of coal were the 'consumption' industries, mostly in London and in the larger cities like Bristol and Norwich. Goodish soap for town dwellers was made from olive oil and tallow 'boiled for many hours together'. Chandlers and contractors who boiled pickles for the navy were conspicuous consumers of coal before the Restoration. So were dyers and brewers, though with some opposition from doubting Thomases who thought the smell or dirt of a sea-coal fire might be transmitted to cloth or ale in the process. Already wool was scoured, dyeing vats heated and yarn dried by coal fire. Beer, ale and cider were brewed, spirits and vinegar distilled, over coal fires.[1] In London especially, brewing victuallers (who brewed solely for retail customers) were giving way to the great 'Common Brewers' — manufacturers brewing for other publicans who did not brew for themselves. Some of them were already very big men indeed. Even an average brewer could speak of himself casually as owning £10,000 of capital and turning over £2,000 of business a year.[2] Here were the ancestors of the great brewers of today. They were most prominent in London with its mass market. North of the river they clustered round the Tower: on the south side, most of the twenty-six common brewers

---

[1] Nef, op. cit., vol. I, pp. 214–15.

[2] *The Manuscripts of the House of Lords, Vol. XI, 1514–1714,* ed. M. F. Bond, 1962, pp. 240–3. The Case of John Ayliffe.

had their plants in Southwark. They were German or Dutch by origin, reflecting the European origin of 'hopped' ale, and it seems unlikely that they could have expanded as they did in the seventeenth century without the aid of Newcastle coal. Malting barley flowed in to serve London's needs by coaster and barge from the barley-growing areas of Herefordshire and Norfolk. Thus the growth of London led to a concentration of brewing in the metropolis that was not challenged till the railway age.

In other industries the objections to coal were more than prejudice. In malting and baking it was said that the gas of raw coal left a disagreeable taste in the product. Hence Derbyshire beers, made with a special coke free of gas, acquired a special reputation. The use of coal fuel in brick-kilns was said to damage the brick-clamp 'by makeing it run together in a lumpe'. In glass making, too, technical problems were raised by the gases freed into the crucibles when the potash and sand were fused. It was a condition of the grant of a royal monopoly to the notorious monopolist Sir Robert Mansell in 1615 that he had a partner who had overcome the difficulty, apparently by using anthracite. Between then and 1624 it was claimed that ways had been found of making white, crystal, bottle green and all other types of glass with common Newcastle 'sea-coal'. Smelting of metals presented the most intractable problems of all, and it was still possible for a writer in 1750 to say that 'iron-ore is not converted into malleable iron with any fire but wood or charcoal'.[1] This was not quite true. Throughout the seventeenth century, experiments in ore smelting were going on, including those of the famous Dud Dudley, who was only one of a dozen 'projectors' who played with the idea. Dudley was unlucky. Floods ruined his works, Parliament abolished his patents and the charcoal iron masters drove him from Worcestershire into Staffordshire, where he was more fortunate. The problem was not to be solved in the seventeenth century though the experiments of that age were to bear fruit early in the next century.[2] The economic effects of the increased use of coal may be summarized as follows. First, it was an enabling condition of the growth of London, and of other great ports and cities near the sea or waterways. Without coal the citizens could neither have kept warm, nor fed themselves, nor have been supplied with the necessities and luxuries that made city life tolerable, let alone preferable. A reciprocating action thus began between the emergent coal industry, especially in the north-east and the

[1] Quoted Nef, op. cit., vol. I, p. 251.
[2] See below, p. 301.

Midlands, and the growing aggregation of people in towns and certain of the industries that catered for them, where the substitution of coal for the dwindling supplies of wood created no insuperable technical problems. More coal meant a bigger London, more breweries, more soap and sugar boilers, more salt pans. And a bigger London and more industries meant a bigger demand for coal. Ultimately it was to mean deeper mines, though as yet most coal came from fairly shallow pits. With deeper pits, longer hauls, bigger tonnages came a demand for more carts, more horses, more ships, anchors, tackle, sails, cordage, victuals and so on. The consuming industries called for more and larger vats, pans, furnaces and pipes. The size of the producing unit was freed from ancient limitations. Breweries, salt works, soap workers, sugar houses all grew, mostly on urban sites where demand existed but where wood fuel would have been difficult to acquire in sufficient quantity.

The success with which coal was substituted for wood as fuel, and the growing output of the coal industry, must not be regarded as a *deus ex machina* which can be invoked to explain every development of British industry outside textiles. It was probably the factor in the economy of the early seventeenth century most favourable to expansion. The failure to substitute coal for wood in metal smelting was, conversely, a serious check to expansion in the mining and metallurgical industries. But there were other complications. The Cornish tin mines were kept down to a production of about 500 tons a year and perhaps less by simple lack of demand. The main users were the London pewterers, who were beginning to encounter the competition of the potters of Staffordshire and the glass makers of east London and the north in the market for utensils and plate. The Worshipful Company of Pewterers were even complaining in 1636 of competition from what they called 'Crooked Lane wares' — goods made there of imported German tinplate. Bronze goods (in which tin was used) were giving way before brass, which was a mixture of copper and zinc. Brass replaced bronze in church bells, cannon and cannon balls and all sorts of ordnance, and in a growing range of small wares such as the 'cards' used for carding wool. These new demands sent up the production of copper and stimulated the search of monopoly companies like the Society of the Mines Royal and the Company of Mineral and Battery Works for the metal. Lead was needed for roofing houses, especially in London, and for bullets and shot, and sheathing the hulls of men-of-war. The Derbyshire lead industry therefore flourished throughout the century. In Charles I's time the total annual output of lead was put at 12,000 tons; by 1800 it was only to be 30 per cent higher.

Evidently technological difficulties and innovations are not the whole explanation of industrial trends. Markets were also important.

A combination of technological and market difficulties seems to have kept the iron industry fairly static between 1600 and 1660. The total number of blast furnaces probably remained fairly steady at around eighty, but the proportion on the Kent and Sussex Weald was falling slowly, while the number in the Forest of Dean and Herefordshire was rising. The Weald had been a great producer of cannon – the local ore was good for a hard iron. The move away from the Weald may have owed something to a change in demand for goods like nails and wire that could be made better from the west midland and western ores that yielded a softer metal. Certainly it was influenced by the exhaustion of timber supplies near the mines and furnaces. The new iron masters were often landlords who wanted to realize the value of standing timber as fuel. In the Forest of Dean they improved the smelting of the ore and refining of the pig iron into wrought iron so as to achieve a more continuous and economic process which gave more iron for less fuel; roughly 3 tons a day instead of 1. For all that, the total output probably did not increase more than from about 18,000 to 20,000 tons between 1600 and 1650, in spite of the growing demand of hundreds of small manufacturers in the Midlands and north. These men, mostly smiths or metal craftsmen, were great users of coal. Birmingham – 'Bremicham' – in 1637 was 'full of inhabitants and resounding with hammers and anvils for most of them are smiths'. So it was also in the Black Country. No technical obstacle prevented their using coal to heat the forges where the ploughshares, axes, horses' bits, nails, scissors, scythes and a hundred other implements were made. To meet such demands, more iron was being imported from countries like Sweden and Spain, where ores were richer and costs lower. This import of foreign metals may well have been one aspect of that balance of payments problem which publicists were making much of in these years. Be that as it may, the metal workers accounted for a growing proportion of coal consumption, especially of midland coal. Industrial use did not yet anything like equal domestic use, but it already gave England a ponderable advantage over foreign competitors in certain industries.

It is easy for a later generation to forget how parochial this all was. Different regions and different industries enjoyed or suffered different fortunes. Sometimes the loss of one area or industry was the gain of another. Just as, in the textile industry, the Old Draperies of the west were in general losing to East Anglia, Devonshire and the New Draperies, so Cornish tin was losing to lead from Derbyshire or the Mendips, and the Weald was losing to the Forest of Dean. So, on the whole, the outports, especially on the east coast, were losing to London, often represented in the seventeenth century as a greedy maw that gobbled up men, wealth and power alike. Can any general trends at all be observed? Tentatively, yes, though any judgement remains largely impressionistic. From the twenties to the Restoration, recurrent crises, stagnation, decline even, seem to predominate, obscuring those industries and areas where profits, employment and sentiment were more buoyant. The rise of new industries was no certain remedy for the decay of old and there was an unavoidable hiatus between the collapse of old and the rise of new manufactures. Labour made redundant by change did not move easily. As agricultural improvement made it increasingly difficult for part-time workers in manufactures to return to their smallholdings, the victims of changing fashion, disrupted markets and technological change tended to drift downwards into that anonymous mass of human misery and dereliction known everywhere to contemporaries as 'the poor'.

Did any social or economic group do well out of the reshufflings and shifts that make up this confused patchwork of an economy? Did, for example, the landowners of this period as a class derive great profits from coal or other mines on their land? It is doubtful. Mining has always been a speculative game. Prospecting was expensive and unreliable. Mines were flooded or became exhausted. Markets collapsed. Fuel supplies ran out. Harbours had to be financed. It is hardly surprising that even colliery owners often sank back to be mere miners, as did Thomas Robinson, one of the proprietors of the great colliery at Bedworth. By 1640 he was working for a friend at Nuneaton Colliery, 'under whom he gets that small meanes of livelyhood that he hath'.[1] A few noble landowners, like the Earls of Cumberland, Arundel and Rutland, seem to have done well out of coal mines and metal workings. John Robartes (later Earl of Radnor) owed his barony largely to the profits of mining Cornish tin. But these were not typical. Commoner were those cases where landowning gentry found themselves faced with mortgages, debts and foreclosures as a result of ill-managed agreements with city merchants and financiers sharper than themselves. And not all these succeeded in making mining pay.

Those who did best were men like Sir John Lowther of Whitehaven, who managed to acquire most of the coal-bearing land in his district, get

---

[1] Quoted Nef, op. cit., vol. II, p. 422, and ch. iii, *passim*.

control of the wharves and shipping, and monopolize the trade to
Ireland. The Delavals of Northumberland and the Pagets of Staffordshire prospered by well-managed partnerships with outside capitalists
through which their coal deposits were exploited. Here, as everywhere,
it was that elusive quality called enterprise – the ability to seize and exploit economic opportunity – that often decided a man's· fortunes.
'The financial history of the [coal] industry', writes Professor Nef, 'is
largely the story of the control which the great town merchants obtained over the mining and transport of coal.'[1] So it was at Whitehaven,
so at Newcastle and many other places. Mr Stone has summarized suc-
cinctly the results of aristocratic excursions into such ventures: 'On the
whole, industry was not the road to great wealth.'[2] In short, the countryside was repeating the experience of the towns, where salesmen and
middlemen came to dominate the crafts collectively and individually.
This was the age of the middleman, the merchant, the entrepreneur.
Urban growth multiplied his opportunities. Economic fluctuations
affected him less than they affected more conservative and narrowly
based members of society, for a large part of his skill lay in spreading
his interests and risks.

[1] Nef, op. cit., vol. II, p. 448.
[2] *Explorations In Entrepreneurial History*, December, 1957, X, no. 2, p. 59.

CHAPTER FIVE

Public Finance:
The Cost of Kingship

'THE only disease and consumption which I can ever apprehend as likeliest to endanger me', wrote James I to his Council in 1607, 'is this canker of want, which being removed, I could think myself as happy in all other respects as any other King or Monarch that ever was since the birth of Christ.'[1] The canker was to plague him and his heirs throughout the century and to provide a focus for many other grievances besides the purely economic. It was profoundly important for the future that the early Stuarts inherited arrangements for royal revenue and public finance that were antique, inadequate and ambiguous. Serious as it was that natural causes made them short of money, it was more serious still that the Stuarts aggravated their want by extravagance, and disastrous that they attempted to remedy it by means which alienated not one but many different sections and interests. The Civil War was fought for ends other than economic, its allegiances cut clean across social and economic groupings – nobility, gentry, merchant, yeoman, etc. But that economic irritants were important in the phases when opinion was forming and hardening there can be no doubt.

The roots of the trouble were deep, its origins far older than the Stuarts. Elizabeth herself had needed all Burleigh's skill and all her own woman's sagacity to make the permanent revenue of the Crown stretch far enough to meet the ordinary expenses of government. The cost of government was always increasing as royalty became more royal, even though the Queen ingeniously induced her richer subjects to share as much of the cost as possible. New and larger palaces were built, navies and munitions became more expensive, lay bureaucrats replaced their clerical predecessors who had been paid in benefices, all prices rose. Although Elizabeth cut back on her father's extravagances she barely succeeded in holding her 'ordinary' expenditure at about somewhere

1 Strype, *Annals of the Reformation*, 1824, vol. IV, p. 560.

between £225,000 and £300,000 a year towards the end of her reign.[1] The income which provided for this was not primarily taxation regularly adjusted (as it is in most modern states) to current needs in the light of changes of prices or other circumstances. The royal income remained in essence a feudal income obtained from land and incidents. Over half the ordinary revenue came from 'Rents and Revenues', the properties of the Duchy of Lancaster, and the yield of the Court of Wards which screwed feudal fines out of the landowners. The phrase still used to describe the administration of the ordinary revenue was, appropriately, 'the manor of England'. It emphasized the point that the monarch was still, in a financial sense, a feudal magnate writ large. The preoccupations of royal ministers were, as Professor Tawney has said, 'less those of a financial statesman than of a prudent steward or bursar'.[2] To these feudal rents had to be added the customs. They too had risen with Elizabeth's prosperity but far less than they should have done in proportion to the growth of trade. They were farmed out to contractors for terms of years, and yielded in the Queen's latter years between £100,000 and £130,000 net to the Crown. The largest remaining item came from taxes on the Church and fines on recusants.

On top of this 'ordinary' revenue intended to meet normal expenditure came 'extraordinary' revenue justified only by emergencies, the main item of which was the 'subsidy'. This was nominally a tax on land or on goods or chattels voted by Parliament; but the basis of valuation had, in the manner of early tax systems, become fixed and formal. The county, as the administrative unit, was expected to yield so much, and each 'subsidy' man paid his share. In the year of the Armada, Elizabeth had £88,000 from this source. Yet Elizabethan England was very lightly taxed. Rich men paid far less than some thought they should, poorer men paid nothing, and for this they had to thank the Queen's saving spirit. Raleigh could protest in the 1601 parliament against the absurd under-assessment of rich estates. 'The Englishman', said Bacon, 'is most master of his own valuation and the least bitten in purse of any nation in Europe.' Elizabeth herself had not escaped the effects of her liberality towards her subjects entirely. In the last five years of her reign she had had to sell £372,000 worth of Crown Lands and piled up a debt of £300,000.[3]

---

[1] W. R. Scott, *Joint Stock Companies*, vol. III, pp. 507–9 and 517; also R. H. Tawney, *Business and Politics Under James I*, p. 139, n. 1.

[2] Op. cit., p. 136.

[3] *Parliamentary Debates in 1610*, ed. S. R. Gardiner, p. ix.

With the accession of James, who saw his new Kingdom as a new Peru, the brakes were off. His insolvency was 'immediate, continuous and gross'.[1] James began with a recurrent annual deficit on his 'ordinary' account of about £30,000. To this had to be added exceptional expenditure connected with his coronation and with Ireland. By 1606 his debt had already risen to nearly £¾ million and by 1608 it stood at nearly £1 million. Where Elizabeth's ordinary expenditure had normally run at less than £300,000 a year, James was soon spending £½ million or more annually. Some of this increase he could, with justice, blame on price levels which may have risen as much as 50 per cent between Elizabeth's accession and his own. But this was not the whole story. The rising cost of monarchy did not consist, during the first fifteen or so years of the new dynasty, of unavoidable necessities for the good of the kingdom. The cost of defence, diplomacy and security did rise, but by nothing like the amount that was sucked away by pensions, luxuries, entertainments and the like. Amongst the immediate beneficiaries of this lavish spending were royal favourites. From the accession to 1610, Scots received in annual payments between £10,000 and £11,000 a year and over £¼ million in cash. The annual outgoings on 'English' fortunates were double those on the 'foreigners'.

The situation which Robert Cecil, Earl of Salisbury, faced when he took office as Lord Treasurer in 1608 was a debt of nearly £1 million, and this in spite of a rise in the ordinary revenue in the preceding quinquennium that derived largely from buoyant trade and customs revenue. In two years Salisbury had managed to reduce the debt to £300,000 but the annual deficit on current expenditure continued. It was the need to tackle this that brought forward the so-called 'Great Contract' — a proposed arrangement between King and Parliament — and Salisbury's proposals for new levels of 'impositions' (extra customs dues) in 1610. A new 'Book of Rates', which had considerably raised the imposts on many articles of merchandise, had been issued in 1608 after consultation with the trading companies. The new rates affected not only imported goods but beer and wine sold by alehouses, and coal from the north-east coast. The 'Great Contract' was an attempt to negotiate a permanent increase in the King's ordinary revenue from taxes on trade in return for abolishing certain antiquated and vexatious forms of feudal revenue. One such was the system of wardship enforced through the notorious Court of Wards. Although in practice landed states now normally passed at the owner's death to his heirs, the notion

[1] Tawney, op. cit., p. 517.

lingered that they might in certain circumstances still revert, in feudal fashion, to the lord. Even an heir coming of age still might be required to pay a 'relief' to the lord. A manor would surrender rents and profits to a lord who had the wardship of a minor's body or the disposal of marriage when there was an heiress. The Tudors had enforced such rights to the full, evading somehow the consequences of the widespread unpopularity of the system. The new financial crisis of the seventeenth century gave the opponents of the system a renewed opportunity. It was a vital point in the 'Great Contract' that wardship be abolished in return for the substantial compensation of £100,000 a year from other sources. Purveyance, the compulsory supply of provisions at arbitrary rates to the King and his retinue while on itinerary, was likewise an anachronistic grievance now that the monarchy was no longer itinerant but had 'a fixed seat and constant access to fair markets'. All such feudal relics were to be abolished in return for an annual settled income of £200,000 a year. Yet large concessions such as these left a gap in the royal revenue which had to be filled from some other source. The obvious one was trade. But here the merchant interest was rallying support against proposals which were beginning to look suspiciously like those forms of vicious internal taxation of the excise type which had been all too successfully imposed in continental Europe. Here was a risk of unending burdens upon the food, drink and necessities of the people. What made it worse was that such taxes were in some cases granted by the King for the specific benefit of particular favourites. The result was a wave of opposition that had not spent itself by Walpole's day.

The proposals for the 'Great Contract' could not survive the conflicts of interest they aroused. They foundered, as the monarchy itself was to founder, on the rocks of mistrust. With them went the best opportunity to reform and rationalize the anachronisms of royal finance. Whereas 'feudal' features had disappeared from the management of the great noble estates, giving way to more or less rational and economic methods, they continued to characterize this, the largest and most important of 'manors' – the 'Manor of England – and to act as a chronic irritant in the body politic.

The end of the wrangles of 1610 was prophetic of a pattern that was to be more and more familiar. The King offered to withdraw some of the impositions, and the Commons agreed to pass a bill for a fifteenth and tenth and a subsidy. But this temporary and uneasy compromise did not disguise the real nature of the impasse.[1] This was the vicious circle

[1] Dowell, *History of Taxation*, 1888, vol. I, p. 189.

of Stuart finance. The extravagance and poverty of the Crown made frequent parliaments a necessity. They were asked for subsidies to fill the gap between ordinary income and expenditure, in violation of the tradition that such demands were justified only by genuine emergencies such as war or rebellion. Parliament, freer now of that 'management' which the Queen had raised to an art and which James despised as beneath the dignity of a king, insisted that redress of its grievances should precede any supply. Rather than yield, the King thereupon set out to increase his extra-parliamentary revenue, invoking in the process rights against individuals which were, even if legal, highly impolitic. Hence further grievances which embittered yet more the relations of Crown and Parliament.

After Salisbury died, the situation became steadily worse for half a decade. Under the influence of the new Scottish favourite, Robert Carr, originally a page who ran alongside the royal coach, then raised first to be Viscount Rochester and later Earl of Somerset, the royal debt rose in a year to £680,000. Expenditure was now outrunning revenue at the rate of £200,000 a year. Such deficits could not continue indefinitely, even at the Court of King James. By the time Bacon, as Lord Keeper, made his report on the finances in 1617, there had evidently been some retrenchment. In the following year James discovered a rescuer better than he deserved. Lionel Cranfield, formerly a great merchant, had become Surveyor-General of Customs in 1613. In 1621 James made him Lord High Treasurer. Brave and dutiful, Cranfield was essentially a financial administrator, not a politician. His task was to restore solvency. His method was a rational administration that increased income and cut expenditure. Pensions, gifts and sinecures for favourites were tackled first. Then military outlay in Ireland and the United Provinces was pruned. Unprofitable lands and royal estates were sold off.

The general trend of royal revenues was clear by Cranfield's time. In James's reign so far, the royal revenue from land had fallen by a quarter as estates had been sold to realize cash; on the other hand customs duties collected at the ports had more than doubled in the same period.[1] This was the general consideration which determined Cranfield to look sternly at the current methods of realizing customs revenue. His tough policy here, as elsewhere, no doubt contributed to his ultimate fall.[2] So did his efficient reformation of the Court of Wards — disastrously efficient, as it was to prove.

[1] R. H. Tawney, op. cit., p. 93 and n. 4.
[2] See below for the system of customs farming.

93

There is little doubt that Cranfield, now Earl of Middlesex, was within an ace of achieving his immediate aim when he was brought down in 1623 by a combination of old enemies and ungrateful masters. In a time of unprecedented depression, and in face of fierce and entrenched opposition, he had come within sight of, if he had not actually achieved, a balanced budget.[1] His plans were wrecked, in February 1623, by the revelation of the costs of the futile Spanish perambulations of Charles and Buckingham. Cranfield was never consulted on this or any other aspect of foreign diplomacy. His task was merely to pay the bill. The incident shows how impossible his task was. Add to this that he had often been brusque and even truculent with royal favourites and M.P.s alike and it is not difficult to explain the malevolence with which he was pursued through his impeachment by those whom he deprived of the plums of office and those who regarded him as the banker of despotism. James, never at a loss for a sage philosophic comment to cover an ungrateful desertion, remarked that: 'All Treasurers, if they do good service to their masters, must be generally hated.' His administration of the Court of Wards was certainly a major cause of hostility. His impeachment included four separate charges relating to this Court. 'All the rich families of noblemen and gentlemen', Clarendon wrote, 'were exceedingly incensed and even indevoted to the Crown, looking upon what the law had intended for their protection and preservation to be now applied to their destruction: and therefore resolved to take the first opportunity to ravish that jewel out of the royal diadem.'[2] Cranfield had served James well. He 'had merited well of the King and had done him that service that few had ever done', said Sir John Eliot. Like Bacon before him, like Strafford, Laud and many later royal servants, Cranfield was the victim of that embryonic, brutal Stuart version of the doctrine of ministerial responsibility. When unpopularity became too great, the servant was sacrificed to his enemies. But why were the enemies so numerous and so ferocious? Natural jealousy of upstart ministers was inevitable. At St Albans, where even the servants kept their own coaches and racehorses, Bacon might expect to suffer for a rise to power that had thwarted and offended many on the way. Likewise, Cranfield's wealth and power could hardly fail to injure the pride of the established ruling clique. To them he remained an upstart from trade. Neither minister was politically minded enough to realize

[1] R. H. Tawney, op. cit., p. 221.
[2] Quoted H. E. Bell, *An Introduction to the History & Records of the Court of Wards and Liveries*, 1953, pp. 148-9.

the strength of the social and political forces arrayed against him. Yet that was not all. The failure of the 'Great Contract' of 1610, the unwillingness of the landed or commercial interest to accept rational reform of the tax system, and the growing mistrust between King and Parliament all condemned Cranfield to spend his time applying essentially superficial remedies to deep-seated ills. Nor can the problem be understood simply in economic terms. Decline in royal prestige had gone along with a fall in public and social morale. Culturally the fresh humanism of the Elizabethan renaissance had grown stale, its fruit ripe to rotting. The darkening mood of contemporary literature reflected in the grotesque horrors of Webster's tragedies, the morbid imagery of Middleton's *Women Beware Women* (1621), the moral earnestness of Massinger, the troubled, involuted fantasies of Donne, was not merely the caprice of individual imaginations. The dramatists and poets were not insulated from their social context. All were in some measure affected by the mounting problems, doubts, and tensions of the times.

How far was the Court itself responsible by its example for the slide down into confusion and pessimism? Or how far was it the mounting burden of the times, with unemployment, riot and bankruptcy rooted in crises that were essentially international? There is no simple answer. Not all the problems of the early Stuarts were of their own making, but in the last analysis they drowned themselves: they were not merely submerged. To this extent James must be held responsible for the changing mood of the times and in a measure for the reaction into Puritan dictatorship that was to follow.[1]

The immediate effect of the frustration of Cranfield's limited proposals was to accelerate the run into the era of 'shifts and bargains' that followed James's death — monopolies, feudal exactions, Ship Money and the like: in fact, as Clarendon wrote, those 'new projects (which) every day were set on foot for money, which served only to offend and incense the people, and brought little supply to the King's occasions'.[2]

The new Court of Charles I was certainly the most cultivated since the Reformation. Its civilized elegance was in every way an advance on the buffoonery, pedantry and indecency of the Jacobean Court. But it was not less expensive. 'Administrative' costs were enormous. An army of lucky candidates swarmed round Whitehall and the other royal residences, administering — theoretically at any rate — the business of the Household. The salaries of this host of feodaries, filazers, aulnagers of the linen, comptrollers of the tents and pavilions, clerks of the pipe,

[1] R. H. Tawney, op. cit., p. 139.   [2] *The History of the Rebellion*, vol. I, p. 32.

carvers and chirographers were necessarily insecure: hence the scramble for the larger perquisites of office – a few shares in the New River Company, a cut of the Fen drainage profits, a place on the new Fishery Company or the Cokayne Adventurers board. Nor were the embellishments of van Dyck, Rubens, Inigo Jones and the rest to be had for nothing. The costs of court life rose sharply. So did the costs of Charles's military and naval adventures, though they remained as monotonously unsuccessful as his father's. In a period when the Court needed to reform, not to recuperate, it was for once unfortunate that only a mile or two from the seat of government in Whitehall lay the City. Within its courts and alleys were the counting houses of merchants passing rich; rich enough to contemplate a temporary lodgement of some of their surplus wealth with the Crown in return for some degree of security and an understanding that a baronetcy or a peerage was not an unthinkable favour.

When relations between Charles and his Parliament finally broke down in 1629 and the period of personal government began, three different modes of finance are discernible. All represented in some measure a continuance of practices begun under James, but they were now pursued with a new exigency required by the more urgent needs of a government whose moral tone was higher but whose extravagance was no less than that of its predecessor. The first was the exploitation of the customs revenue, still rising in importance. The second was the combination, deliberate and fortuitous by turns, of social policy and fiscalism. The third was the use of the prerogative powers of the Crown for monetary purposes. Closely connected with these was the use of the prerogative courts as an instrument of enforcement. The result was that royal policy, in spite of its high, and by no means wholly insincere, pretensions, became associated on the one hand with privileged groups, on the other with exactions regarded as burdensome and illegal, and with a system of enforcement that was arbitrary and tyrannical. The result was to alienate considerable sections of opinion not only amongst the commercial classes but amongst gentry and nobility too. The effects cannot be measured in sociological or even geographical terms. The loyalties of some individuals and families were stronger than the loyalties of others. Some pockets were better lined than others. Customs farming, monopoly and patent grants created some obliged beneficiaries. For the great merchant in the financial swim – a Cokayne, a Garway or a Cranfield – or a magnate in high favour at Court, the pickings of the system might be rich. But the effect was the creation of a thousand cracks in the social edifice.

The Customs were now a main source of revenue. But they were not easy to collect. The trade upon which customs duties were levied fluctuated with seasons and, less predictably, politics. Between December and March, storms and gales put an end to seaborne trade in the coastal waters round Britain. At such times, sailors (it was said) 'would rather run the Hazard of an East Indian voyage than be obliged to sail all the waters between London and Newcastle'.[1] At other times, naval wars might interrupt the flow of trade, as did the first Anglo-Dutch War and the Spanish War in the 1650s. Even in peacetime, the timing of sailings and the arrival of cargoes was linked to the traditional dates of fairs and auctions. The Hamburg cloth market, vital to Yorkshire exporters, was in April. If their fleet missed it, half a year's employment was lost. In such a world, prey to weather, war and poor communications, trade moved not smoothly or continuously but in jerks. So, necessarily, did revenue based on trade. How to iron out these fluctuations and give the King a steady, certain income?

The answer that was given from 1604 onwards and throughout the larger part of the seventeenth century was to place the collection of the customs revenue in the hands of syndicates of business men, the 'farmers', who paid an annual rent to the Crown in return for the privilege of appropriating the customs duties to themselves. When this system was established in 1604 it was justified by the claim that it enabled the King 'to know exactly how much he has'.[2] More doubtfully, it was claimed that the net revenue produced was larger when it was farmed out than if it was collected directly. Theoretically the farmers paid over their receipts, minus of course their 'expenses', once a month to the Exchequer. In practice – since income fluctuated widely – the Crown simply drew upon the farmers by means of 'tallies'. It was as if they accepted cheques drawn on them and then reduced by that amount their own obligation to the Exchequer. Gradually the farmers became, as it were, government bankers, advancing loans on the security of the customs, granting short-term overdrafts and even meeting advances on duties payable in the future. Only men of substance could undertake such risks. Even under James, sums ranging from £10,000 to £45,000 were involved, on a total annual customs rent that had risen to £160,000 by the end of the reign. Under Charles, the farmers' responsibilities became even larger. James had often managed to negotiate his

---

[1] Quoted by T. S. Willan, *The English Coasting Trade 1600–1750*, 1938, p. 25.

[2] For a full discussion see Robert Ashton, 'Revenue Farming under the Early Stuarts', *Econ. Hist. Rev.*, second series, VIII, no. 3, 1956.

longer-term loans from the Corporation of London, from 'alien merchants', and from private individuals like the farmers, Sir William Cokayne, Sir Peter van Lore, Sir Baptist Hickes and others in search of commercial privileges, monopolies and favours. By 1630 the credit of the King had so declined that such operations were increasingly difficult. Charles was in dispute with the Corporation of London about earlier loans, all the old lenders were dead or, like Philip Burlamachi, 'the greatest sponge of all',[1] bankrupt. In this new situation, the farmers of the customs emerged increasingly as long-term lenders to the Crown, the financial 'Establishment' which seemed to reap all the profits of a privileged position as well as the obloquy which increasingly accompanied these along with other monopoly profits. What they lent to the King was, in reality, 'his own revenue' (as one contemporary critic put it). But this was supplemented by borrowings from other private individuals with spare capital looking for employment at interest. This was also channelled through the farmers, who acted as a kind of collective banking syndicate, able to lend on a scale that no one individual could any longer face.

In the late thirties, two rival groups of financiers competed for the farm. One consisted of such well-established City men as Sir Paul Pindar and Sir John Jacob, the other had Lord Goring, the original of the guinea-pig director, as its head. The latter won. It is plain that the older farmers were becoming nervous of the increasing demands made on them to anticipate the revenue further and further ahead. As the political climate worsened, the whole farming system was falling into disrepute. The farmers themselves were held guilty of connivance at the King's invasions of parliamentary rights and were amongst the first to suffer. In 1641 their lease was sequestered and a Bill prepared for the confiscation of their estates. Eventually they were allowed to compound for their delinquency by payment of a huge fine of £150,000.

During the thirty-five years or so while the labyrinthine politics of the customs farm were being played out, other and more public forces were deployed in efforts to sustain the royal income. Widely as the methods varied, they all derived in one way or another from the prerogative powers of the Crown, that residuum of the ancient duty of the king to act in the national interest, especially where speed or force was needed in an emergency. Such extraordinary powers included the conduct of relations with foreign states, and these could be held to include economic relationships. As early as Bate's case in 1606, the implications

[1] Ashton, op. cit.

of this aspect of prerogative power were made plain. Bate, a Turkey merchant, refused to pay an additional impost placed on imported currants. Bate lost. 'The matter in question', the judges in Exchequer argued 'was a matter of state, to be ruled according to policy by the King's extraordinary power. All duties on merchandise are the effects of foreign commerce; but all affairs of commerce and all treaties with foreign nations belong to the King's absolute power. He, therefore, who has power over the cause, must have it also over the effect. The seaports are the King's gates, which he may open and shut to whom he pleases'.[1]

More than three decades later, John Hampden challenged the same interpretation of prerogative power in the more spectacular Ship Money case. The Petition of Right was designed to suppress taxes on property other than aids or subsidies consented to by Parliament. The issue of the so-called 'Ship writs' offered (as its opponents suspected) a convenient escape clause from the royal undertaking. Ship Money had been often levied in the past in time of war to collect a navy. As lately as 1626 the ports had been mulcted for the war against Spain. William Noy, a hard-headed lawyer who had shifted his allegiance from the Opposition to the King and been rewarded with the office of Attorney General in 1631, was the author of a new scheme which proposed to turn Ship Money into a tax on the plan of ship-geld in Anglo-Saxon times. The issue of the first writs – still only against the maritime towns – was accompanied by broad hints that the whole realm ought to bear the burden of defence, and though London protested, it submitted without fight. £105,000 was raised. Encouraged but unsatisfied, Charles now proceeded to the second stage: in August 1635 the second issue of writs extended to inland towns as well as ports. It raised £209,000, and bitter opposition in Oxfordshire and Devonshire. Asked for an opinion in 1636, the judges found that the King might levy Ship Money when 'the whole Kingdom' was in danger. Who determined whether such an emergency existed? 'We are also of opinion that in such case your Majesty is the sole judge, both of the danger and when and how the same is to be prevented and avoided.'[2] The third issue followed a few months later. Then the fourth. When Hampden, a Buckinghamshire squire, contested the case in the Court of Exchequer late in 1637, he lost to a decision that was essentially based on the judicial opinion of 1636. A fifth issue followed in 1638, a sixth in 1639.

---

[1] *The Great Case of Impositions*, Lane's *Reports*, p. 22; Howell, *State Trials*, vol. II, pp. 371–534; Dowell, op. cit., vol. I, p. 186.
[2] Dowell, op. cit., vol. I, pp. 218–19.

It was now clear that there was, in practice as well as in theory, a short answer to the question – 'when is a tax not a tax?' It was: 'when it is an act of policy, deemed to be in the national interest'. And to the question, 'who determines when such an act is necessary?' the answer was shorter still. 'The King.' Where mutual confidence was already weak, such a demand for a blank cheque could only destroy it utterly. It was, as Selden said in his *Table Talk*, 'like putting in a little auger that afterwards you may put in a greater. He that pulls down the first brick does the main work; afterwards it is easy to pull down the wall'. Hence the attack on Ship Money by the Long Parliament[1] as 'contrary to and against the laws and statutes of the realm, the right of property, the liberty of the subjects, former resolutions in Parliament and the Petition of Right'. Kill it they could and did. They did not succeed in obliterating the example it provided to the Government of a tax conveniently and efficiently collected and administered. A future parliamentary tax, the land tax, was to owe much to the principles of assessment first employed in connexion with Ship Money.[2]

The King's prerogative in relation to defence was not the only aspect of his personal power that involved him in dangerous, if lucrative, ambiguity. He was also, by tradition, the source of authority on matters of economic and social regulation. Here, as with defence, many decisions were taken throughout the early Stuart period which were capable of conflicting interpretation. A royal concession – a charter, a monopoly, a patent – was graciously granted. The fortunate individual or corporation made payment. Was the motive to achieve social betterment, economic stimulus, social justice? Or was it merely to raise the wind? The answer can never be a simple one. The motives were usually mixed. Politically, the objection to these often half-baked essays in social and economic planning was that they created more problems than they solved. Invariably inconsistent, often frivolous, the numbers of those who lost by them seemed usually to be larger than those who gained. All the disputes centred on the grant of economic privileges of one kind or another to favoured individuals or institutions. Most were essentially bound up with monopoly rights. Paternalism and fiscalism combined to make the first half of the seventeenth century a record time for the royal incorporation of new companies. While some had a genuine economic or social purpose, there were many cases where the

[1] *The Act against Ship Money*, 16 Car. I, c. 14.
[2] See below, p. 130.

only justification seemed to be the ability of the petitioners to pay for the economic privileges they sought.

Under pressure, Elizabeth had made a skilful retreat from the monopoly controversy, protesting that she had no idea how her people had been vexed by the 'harpies and horse-leeches' then discovered to her. The new broom of 1603 had continued to sweep clean, but not for long. Soon James was caught up in a dozen schemes where fund-raising was inextricably mixed up with schemes to inaugurate new trades and industries or to reform old ones. Impressive claims were naturally put forward on behalf of such projects. The Cokayne scheme claimed to be a tactical move in the nation's economic war against the Dutch cloth makers. The Bartlett scheme was similarly said to be directed against the Dutch pin importers, in the interests of employment and the balance of trade. In order to obtain a charter the promoters of the local pin industry bargained with a courtier who was to receive in return for his help a commission on every 12,000 pins sold for the next forty years. By 1616 the wrangle had crystallized into a plan where the contact man at Court, Sir Thomas Bartlett (who was carver-in-ordinary to the Queen), was to form a company with a monopoly of pin making, protected against competition from imported Dutch pins. The dispute was still unsolved in 1635. Even after the Restoration Charles II had to be reminded that it was by becoming involved in such patent disputes that his father had lost his head.[1] Such disputes frequently involved the Crown and Privy Council in the complex quarrels of the gilds and City companies. There is no need to question the claim that the royal motives often included a genuine desire to support the struggling outsider against powerful vested interests, to promote employment, improve the balance of trade and protect the working poor. But the consequences could, even so, be embarrassing and thankless, as in 1639, when Charles found himself solemnly attempting to define for eternity the boundaries that separated the calling of felt maker from that of beaver maker, and forbidding the 'mixed hat' as injurious to public morals.[2]

The rate at which patents were being granted was more than doubled in the early years of the century. In the last half of the sixteenth century, rather less than a hundred had been granted, many to refugees from Alva. In a little over two decades James granted 108. Some were of

[1] G. Unwin, *Industrial Organization in the 16th and 17th Centuries*, ed. T. S. Ashton, 1957, pp. 166 et seq.
[2] Ibid., pp. 142–6.

dubious originality and limited economic value (like 'Back-frames for the Bed-Ridden' and a monopoly for importing lobsters) but the majority could claim to have a *prima facie* connexion with economic processes of genuine importance – smelting ores, dyeing textiles, making explosives, swords, boats, ploughs, mills, locks, soap, glass, oil, pumping engines, etc. The origins and effects of such grants have been much disputed. They existed in many countries. Probably the idea derived from the earlier habit of granting privileges to individuals or companies ready to carry out geographical explorations. Their vigour in England may have been due to the fact that England could offer a larger area and better enforcement than most other countries. Cumulatively, the list of patentees gives the impression of a genuine desire on the part of Government to infuse life into a relatively sluggish economy: hence the favours to enterprising foreigners – Venetian and Dutch in particular.

But, as the grants proliferated, the suspicion grew that the policy concealed taxation in a new form. In 1614 Parliament protested against the grant of a patent for the manufacture of glass. The patent to license alehouses in 1617 caused a furore, that of 1618 for manufacturing gold and silver thread a greater one, for existing makers were fined and imprisoned. Hence the proceedings against Sir Giles Mompesson, the thread monopolist (said to be the prototype of Sir Giles Overreach, the cruel extortioner in Massinger's play *A New Way to Pay Old Debts* (1633)).

These discontents with monopoly and patent policy culminated in the Act of 1624 which restricted the grant of monopolies to patents for fourteen years and no more. They were to be reserved, in theory, for genuine innovations. However, the Act specifically excepted from the ban on monopolies all charters granted to towns or to 'corporations, companies or fellowships, of any art, trade, occupation or mystery or to any companies or societies of merchants . . . for the maintenance, enlargement or ordering of any trade or merchandise . . .'[1] Incorporation, in fact, was henceforth the obvious way of getting round the Act. Where previously monopolies had been granted most often to individuals, they were now granted to corporations. By a strange irony, William Noy, who had led the attack on Mompesson as a monopolist, now emerged as the ingenious contriver of a corporate soap monopoly. The project was to transfer by charter certain privileges of soap manufacture to a new 'London Society of Soap Boilers'. The beneficiaries,

[1] J. R. Tanner, *Constitutional Documents of the Reign of James I*, ed. 1952, p. 271.

it was alleged later, were government favourites — 'Knights, Esquires and Gentlemen never bred up to the Trade'. The victims were the established makers whose 'Pannes were broken and destroyed, their houses of a great yearly value made unuseful: their families dispersed and necessitated and their estates almost ruined'. Making all allowance for the heated rhetoric of a Long Parliament debate, it seems that this was, like the Cokayne episode, usurpation masquerading as an innovation. In the last analysis, the soap monopoly was taxation — a kind of embryonic excise — in another form. For besides the £10,000 cash payment for their charter, the new corporation was to pay £8 a ton on all soap manufactured, a charge which was naturally passed on to the consumer. Hence the violence of Culpeper's attack in the Long Parliament on these 'frogs of Egypt . . . who sup in our cup, dip in our dish, sit by our fire. . . . They have a vizard to hide the brand made by that good law in the last parliament of King James; they shelter themselves under the name of corporation; they make bye-laws which serve their turns to squeeze us and fill their purses.' Here was adumbrated not a little of the later hatred of excise, as well as the suspicion of privileged corporations that was to produce the Bubble Act of the eighteenth century.

These were urban, even London, discontents. But the attempt to combine social welfare with fiscal convenience had its effects on the countryside in equal measure. No aspect of early Stuart policy (if a collection of shifts can be dignified with such a title) illustrates the desperate ambiguities of the royal situation better than the manipulation of Crown Lands. Throughout James's reign, estates acquired at earlier dates were being granted away or sold off to syndicates of city business men. Yet at the same time, the royal poverty, and especially perhaps the English Crown's lack of mineral assets of the kind continental monarchs could so often pawn or sell, led it to search for wastes and unimproved commons that could be turned to financial account. Hence the great survey of Crown Lands of 1607. In the numerous schemes of drainage and improvement that followed — at Hatfield Chase in Yorkshire and Lincolnshire, the Fen drainage schemes, Canvey Island and elsewhere — the King's private and public interests were inextricably intertwined, not only with each other, but with those of a swarm of courtiers, hangers-on and contractors, who came either to invest or to scrounge. Here, as elsewhere, the royal actions were a typical mixture of the idealistic and the squalid, the politic and the immediate. Both James and Charles were genuinely impressed by the possibility of

improving the land agriculturally, providing better for the existing population and perhaps increasing both the yield of food and the number of
inhabitants. More immediately they were attracted by the rise in their
rent roll that was obtainable by drainage in, for example, the west Fen.
Here, on Crown Land, a revenue of £18 a year became £600 a year.

In such ventures, the King had the support of large local landowners
and Crown tenants who foresaw similar rates of increase for themselves. The trouble lay with the existence of commoner's rights adja-
cent to Crown Lands or large estates. Vermuyden, the King's Dutch
drainage engineer and 'undertaker', might drain the royal chase at Hatfield, but near-by commoners of the Isle of Axholme rose, rioted and
destroyed all his works as an invasion of their rights. Yet the Crown's
profit on the Hatfield enterprise had been temptingly large: £16,000
cash and a new rent of £1,200 or more a year.

A monarchy committed to a high view of its social responsibilities
towards the poor was thus tempted to betray its own professed ideals.
It was the royal advisers who invented an ingenious method of extinguishing common rights to make way for improvement. The Commissioners of Sewers would lay an impossible tax on land (usually common) judged to be 'hurtfully surrounded' by water. If the tax remained
unpaid, the community would be adjudged in arrears with its rates and
the commons could be sold to an 'undertaker' to drain. His reward was
a proportion of the land drained. In the earlier stages of the drainage
craze – as late as the early 1630s – the largest beneficiaries seem to have
been the large local landowners – men like the Earl of Lindsey, Sir
Anthony Thomas, Sir John Monson and others. As the King's finances
declined, he began to exact a larger share of the profit and demand more
say in the management. After seven years of wrangling, Charles took a
full third of the acreage drained in 1637–38. The King had, in effect,
had to assume the role of entrepreneur himself in order to make sure
that he secured a large enough bite out of the improved acreage disputed between King, local landowners, drainage contractors and peasantry. The monarchy thus became a party to local feuds, sharing the
hatred that was vented on the local improvers. (In the Civil War, much
of the drained land was seized back by the peasantry, some of it permanently.) Worse still, the need for capital outran local resources, making
it necessary to import 'foreigners', Dutch and Cockney. To the feuds
between gentry and peasant was added the feud between the local
gentry and the court favourites and city financiers who joined in the
scheme. As usual, 'Sir William Cokain, of London, Skinner' put in an

early appearance in 1608.[1] Hildebrand Prusen, 'citizen and salter of London', Cornelius Drebbel, a Dutch pensioner of James,[2] were typical candidates for 'undertakings'. But most characteristic was Sir Robert Killigrew, whom Charles employed to negotiate his share of the drainage of the east and west Fens.[3] Killigrew came of a Cornish family who had long contrived to stave off the consequences of extravagance and high living by their good services to the Crown in the House, at Court and elsewhere. Robert, though rash and violent of temper, seems to have had enough business acumen to strike a goodish bargain for his master and himself. By 1640, the allocation of the lion's share of the land to Killigrew's court clique had needled the local gentry into opposition. Lord Lincoln, Sir Henry, and Lady Dimoke, were said to be headed for London 'pregnant with designs' to persuade the Short Parliament to revoke the intruders' privileges.

Such troubles were not confined to eastern England. In the west, too, what was called 'arbitrary' enclosure, often the clearing of forests also, led to violent riots which put in doubt the claim of the twenties and thirties to be years of civil peace. Again, the beneficiary was often less the King than some court favourite, like Christopher Villiers, Buckingham's brother, who got Melksham Forest and Chippenham. Especially in the dairy country, where the disintegration of the manorial system had left many social tensions behind, the ineptitude of Stuart policy roused opposition not merely from the peasantry but from all ranks of men – and women – including the gentry. 'It was these popular revolts', an historian of Wiltshire has written recently, 'that ushered in the Great Rebellion, and the extreme discontent expressed in them must shatter all the illusions that have been conjured up of the beneficence and benevolence of Stuart absolutism'.[4]

While the lucky few were reaping the rewards of the royal favour at Court, the aristocracy and gentry at large were sharing the burdens of an imprudent and absurd revival of feudal dues in a desperate campaign to stop up the leaks in the Crown's financial boat. The obsolete jurisdiction of the Forest Courts was deployed against land owners who were accused of infringing the royal rights. Compulsory knighthood was revived, 'and no less unjust projects of all kinds, many ridiculous,

---

[1] H. C. Darby, *Draining of the Fens*, 1940, vol. II, p. 32 n.

[2] See above, p. 73.

[3] Margaret Albright, 'The Entrepreneurs of Fen Draining', in *Explorations in Entrepreneurial History*, VIII, no. 2. 1955.

[4] E. Kerridge, 'The Revolts in Wiltshire against Charles I', *Archaeological and History Magazine*, Wiltshire, July 1958.

many scandalous, all very grievous [as Clarendon later wrote] were set on foot'. The city had been exasperated by the manipulation of patents, monopolies, charters, impositions. The rural gentry and even the peasantry had been alienated by the cynical or ignorant tactics that awarded stretches of countryside to the fortune-hunters who infested the Court, in defiance of all those high professions of regard for his subjects' welfare uttered at regular intervals by the King.

Steadily, in every stratum of society, significant sections of opinion and interest were being lost to the King, all for the sake of extracting absurdly small yields of tax. Cranfield emerged from retirement in 1637 to advise Charles to retrench and abandon 'projects and extraordinary courses'. The shifts to which he was descending combined 'the minimum advantage to the Crown with the maximum exasperation of the public'.[1] Only by placing his finances on a rational basis would the King convince his subjects that he was acting *pro salute rei publicae* and secure 'their hearts and their love, wherein consists the real glory and safety and content of the Kingdom'. But the rot had set in. What Tawney has called 'that fatal loss of moral authority by the ruler',[2] begun in James's time, was difficult to repair. Not only the King, but the Church of which he was Supreme Head, was now inextricably involved in a turmoil that was taking on the aspect of a social conflict. Laud, in his attempt to restore the economic situation of the Church, was engaged in a parallel struggle to recover impropriations and tithes or restore them to their old levels of real value. Here, again, was a policy as politically tactless as it was economically barren. Laud, it has been justly said, was 'trying to revive the Middle Ages not only in ceremonial but in economics'.[3] Like the King's own devices, this, too, alienated not only 'Persons of honour and great quality', but the City of London (with whom a great tithe battle ensued), the gentry everywhere and even the yeomanry, who hated tithe as much as the squirearchy did. Worst of all, these arbitrary exactions were followed up by arbitrary enforcement. As the idealism of Charles's social planning crumbled and degenerated into expediency, it became more necessary to apply ruthless sanctions to enforce it. The instrument was at hand: the prerogative courts were there to impose unpredictable penalties for offences themselves created by the exercise of the same prerogative, 'holding (as Thucydides said of the Athenians)

[1] R. H. Tawney, op. cit., p. 294.
[2] Ibid, p. 291.
[3] C. Hill, *Economic Problems of the Church from Archbishop Whitgift to the Long Parliament*, 1956, p. 341.

for honourable that which pleased, and for just that which profited'. Thus Clarendon summarized the moral collapse of an entire system of government.

How far back did the trouble really go? To Clarendon, the outbreak of the Great Rebellion was not a premeditated thing. 'I am not so sharp-sighted as those who have discerned this rebellion contriving from (if not before) the death of Queen Elizabeth, and fomented by several Princes and great Ministers of State in Christendom, to the time that it broke out. Neither do I look far back as believing the design to be so long since formed. . . .' There was in it, he thought, so much that was accidental — 'not capable of being contrived'. No four men of the opposition were 'of familiarity and trust with each other'. All these judgements refer to the mechanism by which the powder train was fused. But even Clarendon saw that the train had been some time a-laying. Alongside all the personal emotions, rivalries and follies one factor stood out: 'the excess of the Court in the greatest want, and the parsimony and retention of the country in the greatest plenty . . . like so many atoms contributing jointly to this mass of confusion now before us'. The possibility that there was in progress, independently of the fiscal policies of the Crown, a slow, deep change in the social structure of England which brought social conflict into the open is discussed elsewhere.[1] That religious convictions and conflicts played a major part in precipitating the war, only the materialist pedant would deny. Such wider and more general causes do not subtract from the importance of the economic factors discussed above. The poverty of the King was in part the product of inflation: much more, of his own extravagance and his obstinate refusal to retrench or reform. It was Stuart ineptitude in seeking a way out of the impasse thus created that led directly to methods of public finance no better than a racket. At Whitehall the royal household had become an administrative rabbit warren. Public business was turned into a Dutch auction that accentuated social tensions and set up the favoured against the unfavoured, family against family, faction against faction, Court against country.

---

[1] Chapter Six below.

CHAPTER SIX

Economic and Social Aspects of the Great Rebellion

I. THE NATURE OF THE PROBLEM

EARLY in 1642 the discontents of England erupted into open violence. By the autumn of that year organized military operations had begun. In the Civil War that followed, some 100,000 Englishmen were killed — getting on for 10 per cent of the adult male population. In Ireland many thousands died by massacre or starvation. Many others were maimed, injured or taken prisoner. Great cities like Bristol were besieged and sacked. Cathedrals and churches were desecrated and pillaged. The Catholic population of Bolton was massacred. Homes, rich and poor, were looted, farms and ricks burned, great flocks of Cotswold sheep slaughtered. The standard-bearers of local feuds seized their opportunities: the drama of famous pitched battles like Marston Moor has obscured the tale of scores of small local wars between magnates and their neighbours. Family fortunes, rentals, hoards of gold and silver plate were all sacrificed in the royal cause. Crown Lands to the value of £3½ million, Church lands worth nearly £2½ million, were sold. More than 700 Royalists had their lands, valued at over £1 million, confiscated and sold.

Why and how did this 'Great Rebellion' come about? What part did economic factors play in causing it? Earlier chapters have drawn attention to some of the disputes that arose over specific fiscal acts and policies of the Stuarts. It is doubtful whether these would of themselves have caused men to fight each other. The fear of arbitrary rule was real and important, but here it is impossible to dissociate constitutional causes from religion. It is probably true that 'if we are asking what went on in the daylight of men's conscious emotions, the answer is . . . that their differences over religion raised the temperature to battle point'.[1]

[1] H. N. Brailsford, *The Levellers and the English Revolution*, ed. C. Hill, 1961, p. 7.

Yet behind the political, fiscal, religious and local interests that all helped to split England into Cavaliers and Roundheads, writers of many kinds and periods have thought they discerned also broad economic and social differences between the contending parties, as well as shifts of wealth and power which, variously interpreted, have been advanced to explain the Civil War. Clarendon was surprised to find that Henry Marten, 'a gentleman possessed of a very great fortune', should be anti-monarchical. Elsewhere he noted that the King's troop of guards possessed 'estate and revenue' equal to the entire wealth of the rest of the Lords and Commons. Such comments, combined with his observation that the cloth towns of the north were puritan and 'factious', have led some later historians to find in Clarendon's thought a theory that the war was 'a class war' or something like it.[1] A more comprehensive theory of the fundamentally economic nature of the Civil War came from James Harrington in his *Commonwealth of Oceana* (1656). This was one of a numerous crop of Utopian schemes produced by writers in these years, and probably Harrington's own chief interest was in his proposals to equalize wealth, especially landed wealth, as soon as possible by setting a top limit on the acreage one man might hold, and by abolishing primogeniture. But these proposals in turn were justified by the theory that they would remove the causes of civil strife, which historically could be traced to a politically disastrous shift of wealth and power from the Crown and nobility. 'Domestick Empire', wrote Harrington, 'is founded upon Dominion. Dominion is . . . in Lands, or in money or goods'. Under the Tudors, the argument went, 'the nobility being abated, the balance fell into the power of the people'. Harrington might have found it difficult to follow some of the more recent arguments between historians about the relationship of the nobility and the gentry. To him they were the same. '*Nobility*', he wrote, 'in which style . . . I shall understand the *Gentry* also, as the French do by the word *Noblesse*.'[2] If Harrington had a consistent theory it must therefore be that power fell to a non-noble middle class. This view that the Civil War arose because the Tudors put power into the hands of the middle-class commoners is more interesting as an exhibit in the history of social thought than as a scientific explanation of the Civil War. Nevertheless, it has had a marked influence on later writers, blending in the nineteenth and twentieth centuries with Marxist thought to produce the still current hypothesis that the war was the peak of a class struggle in which 'bourgeois' England triumphed over 'feudal' England.

[1] See Brailsford, op. cit., p. 6.   [2] *The Commonwealth of Oceana*, 1656, pp. 4, 44, 143.

England's Apprenticeship 1603–1763

One point needs to be established before the responsibility and motive for the resort to arms is discussed. Most contemporaries regarded the war, in its initial stages at all events, as a war that principally concerned the nobility, gentry and the upper urban classes generally. Hobbes (whose inclinations were royalist and authoritarian) and Hazelrigg, the parliamentary politician, could at any rate agree on this: that the mass of the 'people' were indifferent to the great issues at stake. 'They care not what government they live under, so as they may plough and go to market.' Their observation was borne out by the husbandman who was warned off Marston Moor because the battle was about to begin. 'What!', he inquired, 'has them two fallen out then?'[1] Later on, the war was to reveal the existence of social tensions not only in the City, where the 'people' were to be an important element in the military strength of Parliament, but also in the northern towns of Yorkshire and Lancashire, where Puritanism emerged as the natural habit of the small masters and workers in cloth manufacture. But this came later. It followed upon the division of the gentry and upper classes into Cavalier and Roundhead. It was not in itself a sufficient dynamic or vocal force to start the trouble, which began as fratricide, not class warfare. In Yorkshire, for example, where the 'Clubmen' have sometimes been credited with seizing the initiative from the timid leadership of the gentry, the Fairfaxes had already been at arms for half a year before the Clubmen appeared. True, neither here nor anywhere else did the gentry accept the inevitability of armed conflict with anything but reluctance. When the Battle of Edgehill was fought (October 1642) the majority of the nobility and gentry were still uncommitted. Only the depredations against private property of those who had decided one way or the other, slowly drove the neutrals into one camp or the other. Fairfax described what was probably a fairly typical situation in his *Short Memorials*. In Yorkshire the Royal Commission of Array became so oppressive that it upset 'many honest people; whom, by way of reproach, they called Roundhead: they being (for religion, estates and interest) a very considerable part of the country . . .'. The offended parties entreated the Fairfaxes to join them. In the end, after being 'much importuned,' they resolved to join the opposition.

Even here, then, the division of the gentry followed the usual course – hesitantly and at first with obvious reluctance; for the countervailing arguments of loyalty and risk were persuasive and poignant. Not everybody chose sides and some who did later changed their minds. Some

[1] Quoted by A. Woolrych, *Battles of the English Civil War*, 1961, p. 36.

110

chose in ways that showed how little the fiscal exactions of the Stuarts counted when it came to the final decision. Almost all the Northamptonshire gentry who had been mulcted for fines under the revival of the forest laws still fought for the King.[1] Nevertheless, if we accept that in its *origins* the war was rooted in the convictions and antipathies of the nobility and gentry and upper classes, how are we to relate these to the course of their fortunes in the years that preceded the war? The possibility that, behind the sharp clashes over taxation and privilege, deeper and slower changes in the balance of social wealth and power were taking place has been briskly debated in recent years. Were the 'gentry' in the ascendant or were they in decline? On one interpretation, the aristocracy, conservative and extravagant, were burdened with large estates which were, by mere size and geographical dispersion, beyond their capacity to reorganize. Reduced to living 'like a rich beggar, in perpetual want', the conservative aristocrat saw his affluence and influence melting away as the rise in prices reduced the reality of his means. Contrariwise, the enterprise and organizing ability that was lacking in the nobility is held to have been present amongst the gentry. Accordingly, the rise of this last class becomes the organizing concept of English social history between the Dissolution of the Monasteries and the outbreak of the Civil War.[2] By applying business methods to the administration of their estates, the gentry (it is argued) kept their heads above water. It was they who set the pace and staked their claim to social pre-eminence and political power. In this work they were less hampered by the somnolence of the *rentier* outlook of the aristocracy, by the cumbrous administrative machinery of the great household or the counter-attractions of social and political life. The task of substituting business leases for customary rents, enlarging the demesne, enclosing, draining, clearing woodland, marketing produce could all go ahead under the personal supervision of the squire himself. Hence the advance of those classes which represented a more businesslike, less traditional, agriculture.

Such assumptions have been vigorously challenged.[3] That the Crown was losing its landed assets is not disputed. The thesis that 'the centre of

[1] P. Pettitt, 'Charles I and the Revival of Forest Law in Northamptonshire', *North, Past and Present*, 1961, III, no. 2.

[2] R. H. Tawney, 'The Rise of the Gentry', *Econ. Hist. Rev.*, XI, 1941 no. 1, See also H. J. Habbakkuk, 'English Landownership 1680–1740', *Econ. Hist Rev.*, X, no. 1, 1939–40.

[3] H. R. Trevor Roper, 'The Decline of the Gentry', *Supplement* to *Econ. Hist. Rev.*, April 1953. See also J. P. Cooper, 'The Counting of Manors'. *Econ. Hist. Rev.*, second series, VIII, no. 3, 1956.

social gravity' was shifting is revised, and against texts drawn from Harrington has been placed one that Sir John Oglander wrote in 1632 'with his own blood'. 'It is impossible for a mere country gentleman ever to grow rich or raise his house. . . . By only following the plough, he may back his word and be upright, but will never increase his fortune.'

The distinction between aristocracy and gentry, this counter-argument runs, is arbitrary. Both classes were extravagant, both were burdened with debt. While a peer had a definite legal status, a gentleman did not. He was only 'one who can live idly and without manual labour, and will bear the port, charge and countenance of gentleman' — or at least should 'be taken for a gentleman'. Movement from one group into the other was not necessarily economically significant: it might equally result from accident of inheritance or marriage. Many a gentle family expired for want of a male heir. High death rates among children thus often spelt the end of individual families and contributed to the brisk market in landed property that marked the seventeenth century. There were many examples of gentry breaking themselves by hospitality, hunting and living beyond their means, while great lords like the Earls of Worcester, Newcastle and Bedford were growing rich. The statistics that have been adduced to prove 'the rise of the gentry' (the critics continue) are invalid. The figures which show the aristocracy losing half its manors while the gentry gained one-fifth are rejected, for they assume that the newly created peers of Tudor times were aristocrats, not gentry. Adjusted to meet this criticism, calculations suggest that the gentry gained (and the nobility lost) but little ground.[1] The critics go on to challenge the validity of the 'manor' as a measurable unit of wealth. To count the number of manors a lord owned is like 'counting sheep: it introduces us to a dream world in which, as in all our dreams, reality may not be entirely absent but appearances are often deceptive'.[2]

---

[1] In his preface to Miss Finch's study *Five Northants Families* Professor Habakkuk has suggested that agricultural conditions favoured the families concerned, who all enjoyed a substantial increase of income. He also adds, however, that they were probably not typical of landed families generally. Their large properties lay in rich pasture country and they drew a large part of their incomes from direct farming rather than rents. Even so, it is worth noting that the Treshams broke, the Fitzwilliams only survived ruin by a lucky marriage with trade, the Brudenells were up to their ears in debt: only the Spencers and the Ishams, exceptionally shrewd and frugal, seem to have escaped being permanently in the red. (M. E. Finch, *Five Northants Families 1540–1640*, Northants Record Society 1956, p. xiv and *passim*.

[2] Cooper, op. cit.

Which of the gentry, then, did rise? In general, not those who had to rely on land, even when reorganized on more economic principles, but those who were lucky or ingenious enough to find an office at Court, insinuate themselves into lucrative projects like fen drainage or company promotion, or — most often — unite their families by marriage

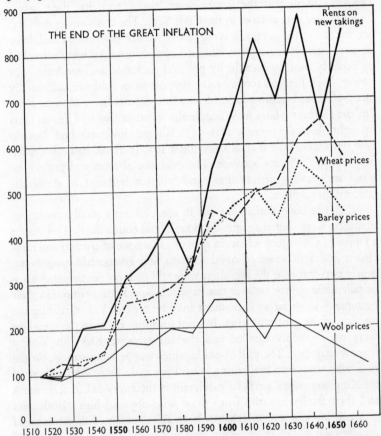

THE END OF THE GREAT INFLATION

Rents on new takings

Wheat prices

Barley prices

Wool prices

Note: the data are taken from Eric Kerridge's article 'The Movement of Rent 1540-1640', *Econ. Hist. Rev.* VI, I, 1953, Table IV, page 28. The rents are those of the Herbert estates in Wiltshire. The price sources are general and are explained in Mr Kerridge's note to his Table. Observe conflicting trends after 1620.

with mercantile wealth. Those who had neither the luck nor capacity for this kind of diplomacy found their plight getting worse in these years. There were no longer tit-bits of church lands to be had, no openings for privateering against Spain. The peasantry were putting up tougher resistance to increases in rent than formerly. On top of this came the new exactions of the Stuarts. Hence the retreat of an embittered and impoverished class of gentry into Puritanism and opposition. A moderate statement of this view stops short before drawing political conclusions, and is content with a verdict of non-proven on Professor Tawney's thesis that the gentry were 'rising' and that their newly found power was at stake in the Civil War. The crisis of the nobility, like the rise of the gentry, it is suggested, has not been established. In so far as the gentry were provoked into opposition, they were provoked by poverty, not by wealth, by political exclusion and weakness, not power. Such theories receive some support from evidence, admittedly incomplete and fragmentary, of rent movements from 1600 to 1660. On the Herbert estates in Wiltshire the inflation that had driven rents up eightfold in the century 1510–1610 faltered and levelled off. In 1660 new rents were little if at all above their 1610 level and had often fallen below it in the years between. The evidence of rents and prices — of wool and grain — proves that rural inflation had lost its sixteenth-century momentum.[1]

When the Long Parliament met in 1640, all but a small minority of members were united against the King's 'evil counsellors'. This was in a House of Commons where, in spite of an increase of lawyers and merchants and a decrease of royal servants and aristocratic hangers-on, nearly two-thirds of the members were still country gentlemen.[2] Risen or fallen, the gentry were at this stage temporarily unanimous in their opinions — in so far as Parliament may be regarded as mirroring the opinion of the gentry at large. But not for long. By 1642 the members were pretty evenly divided and the anti-royalists had only a very narrow majority. The pull of old loyalties was proving strong. Of the men who went into Parliament, it has been said, 'those who supported the King were not superficially different in their way of life, their status and their family histories from those who opposed him'. Both sides returned lawyers and merchants. Both sides contained descendants of middle-class Tudor profiteers in land and speculation. Rather more of the parliamentary Puritans came from eastern and southern England. Royalists were evenly drawn from all areas. *Both* sides in fact included a large *bourgeois* component. Not only the Fairfaxes but Cromwell, Ireton, Whalley, Fleetwood and many other Roundhead leaders were landowning squires. Were they different in outlook from the older

[1] E. Kerridge, 'The Movement of Rent 1540–1640', *Econ. Hist. Rev.*, VI, no. 1, 1953.
[2] D. Brunton and D. H. Pennington, *Members of the Long Parliament*, 1954, pp. 176–85.

Cavalier squires? Were they men who regarded their estates 'merely as assets in the money market, who had here no rest for the spirit or home for the heart, who so long as they were sojourners upon earth, lived "in Mesheck which they say signifies Prolonging; in Kedar which signifieth blackness"?' Were they less attached to the land, ready to migrate rather than live under the military despotism of an Anglican king?[1] Were these the 'mere gentry', deprived, embittered, driven into Calvinism? We cannot be sure. All we know is that on the eve of the Civil War this section of the ruling classes was split from top to bottom. In each party are to be found families and individuals who by our over-simplified exercises in sociological arithmetic ought to have been on the other side of the fence. To quote only two cases out of scores: at Wilton House, the heart of the English Renascence, the Earl of Pembroke, formerly an intimate at Court, became disaffected on the eve of the war. Henceforth the favours of his great family, the Herberts, were skilfully distributed between King and Parliament. In Suffolk, one of the leading families in organizing the resistance to the King was the Barnardiston clan. Closely intermarried with rich city merchants, the Barnardistons were nevertheless not a 'new' family. They had dominated their part of Suffolk since the days of Richard II. Many other families were divided between the contestants, as the Cokes and Hobarts of Norfolk were. Many changed sides.

Such cases, and they are numerous, will make us chary of supplying any single social or economic answer to the question: Why did the Civil War break out? And if the landowning class was divided along lines infinitely difficult to explain, the loyalties of the merchant class and the office holders are hardly more easy to analyse. Like the gentry, the merchants were deeply divided in their allegiances. Seventeenth-century writers exclaimed against the 'proud, unthankful, schismatical, rebellious, bloody City of London ...' and later historians often echoed their words. But things were not so simple as that. During the fifteen or so years that preceded the Long Parliament, the Crown's poverty, combined with its determination to guide the social and economic policy of the nation, had split the City of London into 'haves' and 'have-nots', royalists and anti-royalists. Great customs farmers like the Crispes, Hickes, Garways and Salters had a large stake in royal survival and victory. So had a great interloping merchant like Sir William Courteen who had paid the King heavily for the privilege of infringing the East India Company's monopoly. Yet so confused and contradictory had

[1] G. M. Trevelyan, *England under the Stuarts*, 1904, p. 226.

royal 'policies' become under pressure of poverty and weakness that even those who might have been expected to show gratitude to the Crown for the most material of reasons found their supposed privileges and monopolies invaded and worthless. Charles behaved no better as a party to a contract than as a master to his servants.

> There were few concessionaires whose interest in the survival of the old regime could stand the sort of shock which Charles was prepared to administer indiscriminately to institutions and persons as diverse as the Corporations of small masters, the East India Company, the Merchant Adventurers and, in the realm of finance, to a great financier like Philip Burlamachi, whose bankruptcy due to his over involvement in royal finances provided a spectacular example for all to ponder.[1]

The rifts in the London merchant community were reflected in the City government. From 1625 to 1638 the City showed itself ready to lend money to the King in need on reasonable security. As late as 1641 the City government was more sympathetic to King than to Parliament.[2] The majority of the aldermen were closely connected with the King either as magistrates or officeholders or customs farmers. Not until early in 1642 did this state of affairs alter. But from 1640 onwards the anti-royalists in Parliament were egging on their Puritan sympathizers in the City, and in January 1642 under Pym's leadership the new men — supported by an extraordinary medley of peers, merchants, shopkeepers, craftsmen and apprentices — were confirmed in office as the City government. Out went the old gang. The new government was an unstable alliance, doomed to a relatively short life, and its unifying principle is not easy to discern. Most probably it was simply dislike and jealousy of those who, like the customs farmers, monopolists and directors of the big chartered companies, seemed to constitute the inner 'establishment' of City affairs. The new rulers of London were more often manufacturer-merchants, interlopers, brewers, shipbuilders, or clothiers. New companies in the transatlantic business like the Providence or Massachusetts Bay Company were their particular rendezvous — the latter ingeniously announcing its business to be 'the propagation of the Gospel of Jesus Christ and the particular good of the several Adventurers'.[3] Yet the economic and social differences between old and new men were not absolute. Parliamentary Puritans were also to be found on the

[1] Robert Ashton, 'Charles I and the City' in *Essays in the Social and Economic History of Tudor and Stuart England presented to R. H. Tawney*, ed. F. J. Fisher, 1961, p. 162.
[2] Valerie Pearl, *London and the Outbreak of the Puritan Revolution. City Government and National Politics 1625-1643*, 1961, pp. 276-7.
[3] Ibid., p. 169.

boards of the rich, established companies like the East India and Levant Companies. And one of the most powerful of the new radicals was an alderman, Thomas Soames, of a very rich and old City family and brother-in-law of Sir Nathaniel Barnardiston, head of the ancient Barnardiston clan of Suffolk.

The merchant community, like the nobility and gentry, was split, and the nature of the split is only a little clearer than in rural society. Likewise the nature of the opposition party's popular support. Some of it derived genuinely from religious or political differences and from the economic distress in the export trade, for the London suburbs were the great centre of the textile finishing trades. Beyond this, the astonishing growth of London had created, besides the risks of fire and disease, intractable problems of law and order. The expanding city had outgrown its antique and confused mode of governance. Crime flourished. When depressions came, as they did thick and fast in these years, employment in the textile, leather, glass and metal trades provided ready fuel for discontent, riot and upheaval. Unemployment, poverty, hunger and crime went hand in hand.

To return to the question of the underlying economic causes of the rebellion. Plainly, no neat formula of the rise or decline of a single class will explain the outbreak of the war. What we have to explain is why the ruling classes of town and countryside were split between King and Parliament. Into any explanation many non-economic factors enter — religious, conscientious, constitutional, regional, local, family, personal. As students of the economic problems of the time, we cannot with certainty say much more than this: that the middle decades of the seventeenth century were a time of dislocation and major readjustment in the English economy. The great price rise and the increase of population that had marked the preceding century were levelling off. Markets for most farm produce were unsteady and that for wool never recovered its old buoyancy after the first decade of the new century. The European war had finally thrown export markets for cloth into confusion. Old Draperies were giving place to new, northern European markets yielding to southern European markets. These and other economic changes were only half accomplished and their future promise was less evident than the immediate hardships they inflicted.

For at least a century society had felt the effects of a long slow rise in population and, more spasmodically, of a price inflation. Our knowledge of the dimensions of the population increase is slender. One recent estimate suggests that it had increased by some 40 per cent between 1500 and 1600, by which time it stood at a figure of over 4 million. The highest recent estimate for 1603 is 5 million.[1] One recent investigator suggests that in 1600 the population stood at 4·2 million. During the seventeenth century there was a further increase which brought the total to about 5½ million.[2] Between 1480 and 1660, then, the population of England and Wales may have doubled itself. The reasons remain almost entirely a matter of conjecture. The long period of internal peace, order and good government may have brought an increased number of marriages and thereby births. Alternatively, or additionally, plague may have carried off fewer victims. The consequences of the increase are easier to observe. Rural parishes found themselves everywhere with a labour surplus that was not easily absorbed into a relatively rigid and inelastic agrarian society. The gild organization of local town handicrafts put barriers in the way of growth in the old corporate towns. Even London, expanding rapidly as it was, could digest only part of a growing army of surplus poor who were neither skilled nor even mobile. And many of the traditional cloth areas were suffering from the decay of the Old Draperies. Hence proposals such as those of Richard Eburne, a Somerset clergyman, in his *A Plaine pathway to Plantations* (1624). The only remedy for the 'multitude and plentie of people' was mass emigration to the colonies, at a rate of at least 16,000 a year, two from each parish.

A large proportion of those who looked to the cloth industry for employment were all the more vulnerable because the organization of that industry made its fortunes inherently unstable. The central figure in cloth production, who determined the volume of its output and the employment it could offer, was the clothier. He had few fixed or specific capital assets at stake, little if anything in the way of buildings or plant. In a boom new men entered business easily, investing almost entirely in stocks of raw materials that were handed out to cottage labour to be converted into manufactured cloth. At the first signs of a slump, they could cut down their investment as easily as they had built it up. It was much less easy for the army of redundant labour to adjust itself to the change.

The effects of these fluctuations on an increasingly market economy were not limited to the purchasers. They penetrated to the heart of rural

[1] A. M. Carr-Saunders, *Population*, 1925, p. 7. This is the figure accepted by A. L. Rowse in *The England of Elizabeth*, 1951, p. 218.

[2] W. K. Jordan, *Philanthropy in England 1480-1660*, 1959, pp. 26-9, 63, 70. See G. S. L. Tucker, 'English Pre-Industrial Population Trends', *Econ. Hist. Rev.*, XVI, no. 2, 1963, for a full bibliography.

society. We know more about the prices that the consumer paid than about the prices the producer received. Between the two stood (as now) a chain of middlemen. Famine prices to consumers did not mean prosperity for producers. Writing after three successive wet summers, Sir William Pelham, of Brocklesby in north Lincolnshire, described vividly the common plight of landlord, tenants and labourers:

> ... many insufficient tenants have given up their farms and sheepwalks so as I am forced to take them into my own hands and borrow money upon use to stock them ... Our country was never in that want that now it is and more of money than of corn, for there are many Thousands in these parts who have sold all they have even to their bed straw and cannot get work to earn any money. Dog's flesh is a dainty dish, and found upon search in many houses, also such horse flesh as hath lain long in a deke [ditch] for hounds. And the other day one stole a sheep who for mere hunger tore a leg out and did eat it raw. All that is most certain true and yet the great time of scarcity is not yet come.[1]

'To the Seventeenth-Century Englishman', Dr Supple has written, 'few things were more important than the state of the English harvest – for many, it might, quite literally, have been a matter of life or death.'[2] The twenties and thirties especially saw some uncommonly bad harvests that must have hit all regions, occupations and classes of men. But behind the immediate impact of weather and harvests, other slower and deeper forces were also at work. In the previous century, currency debasement and the influx of Spanish American silver had probably played a major role in creating the long inflation of prices. By the early years of the seventeenth century this monetary force had lessened or disappeared. The other major influence – the increase of population – was still at work, though probably also slackening in momentum. The forces that had combined to create an inflationary economy had not quite lost all their vigour by the 1620s and 1630s, but the main thrust was gone. Wool prices had dipped down sharply in the 1610s, and from the mid-1620s began a long slow decline. Barley prices followed suit; then, in the mid-forties, wheat prices followed. The entire countryside must have felt the squeeze of poverty created by the change from inflation to uncertainty, from uncertainty to deflation and confusion.

Commercial farming might still offer opportunities to the enterprising, organizing man with capital. Its victim often seemed to be the small man, who knew only his customary ways and had no cushion

---

[1] Quoted by J. Thirsk, p. 192.   [2] Supple, op. cit., p. 19.

against adversity. A great part of the population never stood more than a few paces away from poverty, starvation even. The afflictions which fell thick and fast in the early seventeenth century pushed many over the narrow divide. 'Improvement', unavoidable if society as a whole was to achieve any ultimate raising of living standards, seemed to work, in the first instance, against them. Enclosures – arbitrary enclosures especially – drainage, and forest clearance brought increments to those affluent enough to provide the capital. But as to the effects of improvement it might be said of England what was said of Italy, where princes and great lords created fertile lands out of swamp, marsh and parched acres: 'The poor own the mountains: the plains belong to the rich.' The effect of applying capital to land was often to drive out the small cultivator.

Poverty and the fear of poverty had become a normal part of the daily social problem of early seventeenth-century society. But when plague, harvest failure and economic crises were added to the endemic fact of poverty, the widespread fear of the consequences turned to panic. The tenderness of successive seventeenth-century governments towards cloth manufacture was explained in large measure by the nagging fear of the social disorder which might follow if this widespread form of employment of the poor were to fail.

The deepening social crisis of poverty and unemployment and the widening gap between rich and poor throw into high relief the measures, private and public, of these years to alleviate distress. The central legislative instrument had been provided by the Elizabethan statute for the relief of the poor. Recognizing the fact of unemployment, this had provided for the care of the unemployable, setting up parish overseers and enabling them to obtain funds, set children to work, relieve the lame, impotent, old and blind. Like most legislation of the time it was not new; it gathered together earlier experience and practice into a carefully drafted code. With it went other Acts for the encouragement of charitable trusts, hospitals and workhouses, and from time to time Stuart governments amended and reinforced the Acts. But the attitude of the Stuarts to the problems of social justice, though sincere, was as fitful as to their other responsibilities. Their intentions towards the victims of enclosure, expropriation, unemployment and improvement were contradicted by the franchises they sold to favoured individuals to execute plans that created the very evils they were trying to remedy. In any event, legislation did no more than create a framework for action in case of emergency, a set of enabling conditions on which the local community could act if the need arose. The principal burden of the care of the poor continued to fall on private donors, and self-interest and a sense of social responsibility combined to make the first four decades of the century an era of social philanthropy on a scale not previously achieved.[1]

During the period 1600 to 1640, more money seems to have been given for charitable purposes than had been given during the previous century and a quarter. Between 1610 and 1630, between £$\frac{3}{4}$ million and £1 million was subscribed in charitable trusts, principally from the merchant community. Hundreds of inscriptions in churches, both in cities and country parishes, still bear witness to the Protestant conscience of a class that has often been reproached for a stony-faced disregard of the poor and their troubles. Sentiment entered strongly into this philanthropy. Many an affluent London merchant remembered in his will the needs of the poor in the distant country parish in Somerset, Yorkshire or Lancashire from which he sprang. But the bulk of the merchants' benefactions went to the urban poor. Since the Reformation, Protestant divines had hammered home the doctrine that there was no inherent virtue in poverty. It was a social evil and a danger to men's souls, to be fought and extirpated. It was in the towns that the poor lived in the most uncomfortable and unhygienic proximity to the rich. Urban poverty was more concentrated and spectacular than rural poverty. This is one reason why the merchants were far the largest benefactors of the poor: that, and the perception that the labour of the poor could be made productive. For it is doing no injustice to the donors to recognize that their charity, besides being a confluence of Christian conscience and social need, also contained an element of economic opportunism. As the law made formal provision for the poor in the shape of trusts easier, a change came over the nature of almsgiving. The medieval view that charity was directed to the moral betterment of the donor was eclipsed. The emergent view identified it increasingly with the social betterment of the recipient. While purely religious and eleemosynary purposes continued, there was a steady rise in the number of gifts for social rehabilitation and improvement: apprenticeship and training schemes, marriage grants, workhouses and the stocks of material for their inmates, loans for the enterprising – all these objects were of far greater significance by the mid-seventeenth century than in 1600. Concern with the

---

1 See W. K. Jordan, op. cit., especially ch. VII and Appendices. For criticisms of Professor Jordan's statistical methods, however, see D. C. Coleman's review in *Econ. Hist Rev.*, for August 1960 (XIII, no. 1) and C. Wilson in *E.H.R.*, 1960.

economic value of the labour of the poor was henceforth to be bonded increasingly into the 'mercantilist' thought of the time.[1]

In all this work of social amelioration, so far as it is reflected in formal charities, the merchant classes, especially those of London, Bristol and Norwich, took the lead. They were followed by the larger gentry, the nobility following a good way behind. The statistics may cloak some injustices to the landed classes. The possession of land, manorial rights and an assured traditional role in the social hierarchy conferred opportunities for informal, unrecorded benevolence by lord and lady not open to the merchant. Such charity is not susceptible to measurement but it should not be forgotten. For all that, it is likely that it was, by and large, the merchants who had the largest opportunities for creating sizeable fortunes and who were left with the largest margins of disposable wealth. This philanthropy was not merely an automatic reflex of rising prices (as it has sometimes been represented). It was to continue in times of stable and even falling prices.[2] The merchant of enterprise was able to take advantage of the inherent mobility of his capital to deal, in some measure, with whatever economic situation might arise; and the best explanation of the success of this class as a whole lies in the way in which they spread their risks. In this they had nothing to learn from the modern investment trust. A merchant like William Cokayne had his finger in twenty pies, and left six daughters married into the peerage. As a money lender to the gentry in distress he helped (and broke) many a country squire, as he broke Sir Lewis Tresham in 1616, moving into a great house at Rushton in Northamptonshire.[3] Cokayne had a hand in fen drainage schemes, in projects for a British fishery company. He was a member of the Eastland Company, and used his influence with James I, another of his debtors, to float the great cloth project of 1614. No doubt he owed his contracts for minting currency to the same royal favour. William Courteen, also knighted, a Fleming by origin, began as a member of his family firm trading between England and the Continent. By turns money lender, bullion smuggler, West Indian colonizer, East Indian interloper and creditor to the Crown for nearly £40,000, he ends as a country squire, reorganizing his estates at Laxton in Nottinghamshire and elsewhere in the Midlands. The same pattern of diversified investment can be found in the affairs of Lionel Cranfield and was true of many of the larger and most affluent merchants. The

[1] See Jordan, op. cit., Table III, p. 370, Wilson, *Tr. R.H.S.*
[2] See below, pp. 234–5.
[3] See M. E. Finch, op. cit., ch. IV.

risks they took were large. Here and there one would topple. But by and large their highly diversified business was proof against adversity. If one enterprise went down, another was almost sure to succeed. The most affluent members of the London community, where a man with less than £50,000 was not reckoned rich, did not stay in the metropolis to form an urban patriciate, as their Dutch rivals had in Amsterdam. They had (as we have seen) become country landowners, squires, even peers. But their situation was very different from that of the older squire or the 'mere' gentleman with an income that was measured in hundreds rather than thousands of pounds. It has not been established beyond doubt that this influx of merchants into the landholding classes brought about any certain or permanent improvement in methods of estate management. Here and there the new broom may have swept clean: but how long the training of the counting house lingered is less sure. The merchant who bought an estate did so more in the hope that neighbours would forget his origins, rather than be reminded of them. *A fortiori*, his descendants, who were probably anxious to conceal any *stigmata* of trade, would want to be seen to behave with all the careless ostentation proper to their newly acquired status. In any event, the idea that business acumen is heritable is one of the less plausible of the many fallacies with which this particular historical problem is riddled. The first half of the seventeenth century enjoyed no handy or widespread *nostrums* for its rural troubles. The economic problems of the 1640s and 1650s may have been less acute for the larger than the smaller landowner. The great lord's assets, opportunities and credit were all that much larger than the smaller squire's. The larger the estate, the greater the possibility of realizing the values of standing timber or mineral deposits, of profiting from improved ground rents in the growing cities, above all in London. The London property of great landowners like Bedford or Northampton had been a notable source of relatively easy increments. Again, just as the peerage were the natural recipients of court favours, so they were the greatest beneficiaries from the un-romantic view of marriages which the seventeenth century inherited from the Middle Ages. Most matches, now as earlier, were matches of interest.[1] To be absent from the estate, to be seen at Court and in fashionable places was not necessarily the deplorable frivolity that it seems to a more bourgeois age. It might well be part of the never-ending social diplomacy by which wealth was maintained, ensured and transferred, and risks distributed; to find the right heiress or to stand well

[1] See C. S. Lewis, *The Allegory of Love*, 1936, pp. 13–15.

with those in high places might be a better investment than an enclosure expensively executed. In critical times, the nobility shared two principles of advantage with the merchants: their risks were spread, their reserves were large. In such advantages smaller men might sometimes share, but it is difficult, all in all, to think that these were naturally prosperous times for the 'mere' gentry. Bearing many of the social liabilities of their class, they were often excluded from financial opportunities more readily available to their superiors. Perhaps their relatively poor showing as contributors to charity may possibly reflect the narrowness of the margin between their incomes and expenditure.[1]

The same adverse and deflationary forces which were making life difficult for many of the gentry were also felt severely by that sizeable but amorphous 'class' which stood next below them on the social ladder: the yeomanry. In later Elizabethan times the yeomanry and the farmers had done well out of inflation. Thomas Wilson, writing on the relative wealth of different social classes in 1600,[2] thought they were by then less prosperous. Certainly both the property-owning yeoman and his recognized inferior, the husbandman, with or without freehold or secure copyhold, must have felt the chill of the growing depression. Yet as a class these working farmers enjoyed some modest advantages. They were under no social or traditional compulsion to keep up any particular standard of living, as the gentry were. In good times, they had expanded their modest comforts – a little more furniture, some pewter, a cupboard of linen for bed and table. Regional differences were already important. The small men of East Anglia and Kent, with access to urban markets, were markedly better off than those of the west and south: though the very problems of poor soil were said to have stimulated the yeoman farmers of Devon and Somerset to 'marvelose metamorphoses of husbandry'. In all, their situation was more flexible,

[1] See Jordan, op. cit., ch. VII: but any such inference must be necessarily tentative. The difficulty of generalizing about the fortunes of the gentry is illustrated by the most recent detailed study: *The Wealth of the Gentry 1540–1660* by Alan Simpson (1961). Dr Simpson is very judicious. The state of our knowledge in this matter is (he thinks) one of 'mitigated ignorance'. Nor were the beneficiaries or victims themselves always better informed. Often without books or balances, they knew whether they had any cash or not. They knew the extent but not always the value of their possessions. Some of Dr Simpson's inquiries suggest that some rents, at any rate, kept up with prices. Yet it is questionable whether Norfolk, with its shortish leases, goodish roads, access to London and Dutch markets, profitable sheep and proximity to Dutch technological example, was likely to be typical of agrarian conditions further west. Dr Simpson's cautious conclusion is that while a few (gentry) may have risen and a few fallen, 'the rest may just have endured' (op. cit., p. 216).

[2] T. Wilson, *The State of England anno-dom 1600*, ed. F. J. Fisher, 1936.

if more exposed, than that of their social betters among the smaller gentry. Everything depended on their share of that country cunning which has never been rare in the countryside. In bad times they could pull in their belts and hang on doggedly until times improved, as their descendants were to hang on through the crises of late Victorian England and the 1920s, when squires and gentlemen farmers were to disappear by the hundred. Their needs and their expectations were small. If there was enough to feed the family, keep a few head of stock alive and provide seed for the next harvest, a man could pull through.

Not all of them were merely inert or conservative. Yeomen like Robert Loder in Berkshire or Henry Best in Yorkshire were intelligent agrarian experimenters and entrepreneurs who left accounts of their activities. Loder's experiments with rotations and grasses seem to have given him a wheat yield of modern dimensions. Best and his like had a shrewd eye for the right markets and the right animals. Where industrial opportunities offered, the yeomanry were a nursery of enterprise. Yeomen leased mines in Northumberland, set up forges in Shropshire, turned clothiers in Yorkshire or Devon, styled themselves 'potters' in Staffordshire.

In retrospect, one can see all the indications that England was preparing for another economic step forward. But to contemporaries, these were generally times of stagnation and poverty. Hence the anxiety with which men continually debated in those years the state of manufactures, the coinage, the balance of trade. Hence the formulation of more and more schemes calculated to promote manufactures, employment, exports. Hence the dangerous conjunction (and confusion) of projects to bridge the gap between the revenue and expenditure of an improvident Crown with plans to control and expand the national economy. Hence the invitation to ingenious and plausible schemers like the Cokaynes, Courteens and Ingrams,[1] to take advantage of the poverty of King and people to feather their own nests while paying apparent tribute to current *nostrums* for promoting economic growth. Yet if the grant of economic privileges to such as these produced no assured political support for the King, neither did the grant of offices at Court. By the 1630s the royal household and the sinecures with which it was encrusted were costing 40 per cent of the King's total revenue. Yet those who were given or who bought offices were by no means unanimous in their active support for their master. The scramble for

[1] See A. F. Upton, *Sir Arthur Ingram*, Oxford 1961.

office, the chances, the usurpations and dismissals created more grievances, intrigues and feuds than solid loyalties.[1] Officeholders, like gentry and merchants, were divided. A few, mainly those physically nearest the King, regarded themselves as his private and loyal servants; others, more remote, were beginning to regard themselves less as royal servants and more as public administrators. In the end it was the divisions within the 'administration', its inherent confusion, inefficiency and incapacity to reform itself, that explain why it was overthrown so easily. The old, balanced Elizabethan order had broken down and 'the scandal and discontent caused by a putrefying political system helped to provoke the Civil War.'[2]

These years then were in general lean years. Decay in the dying parts of the economy was not as yet fully compensated by the spring growth in the newer parts. The minority of men who were able to turn this situation to their personal advantage seemed to the more numerous remainder to do so at the general expense. The provinces resented the way current political influences established and consecrated luck, greed and cunning as the metropolitan virtues: or so it seemed. Economic conditions themselves created a context in which tempers grew short, loyalties were strained, social tensions multiplied, and even men of similar class, family, interests and attitudes found themselves at odds.

2. THE GREAT REBELLION AND ITS ECONOMIC CONTEXT

If the Civil War was not a war of a 'feudal' against a 'bourgeois' class, was it – like the American Civil War – a war of region against region, of an 'advanced economy' in the east and south of England against a retarded one in the west and north? Was there a clear division between the 'Parliamentary areas of industry' and the 'Royalist areas of agriculture'? Were 'the ports all for Parliament'?[3] Is it true that 'the mercantilist East went to war with the feudal West'?[4] And was the outcome of the war determined by the superior economic resources available to Parliament?[5]

There is a measure of truth in most of these propositions, but they are neither the whole truth, nor the whole explanation of the cause or outcome of the war. London and its wealth were, in the end, to prove

[1] G. E. Aylmer, *The King's Service 1625–1642*, 1961, pp. 342–4, 420.
[2] See Sir J. E. Neale, *Essays in Elizabethan History* (1958), p. 84.
[3] For a recent statement of this view see C. Hill, *The Century of Revolution*, 1961, pp. 120–3; also H. N. Brailsford, *The Levellers*, p. 7.
[4] Brailsford, op. cit., p. 7.
[5] A. H. Burne and P. Young, *The Great Civil War*, 1959, pp. 224–9.

a strong and decisive support for Parliament. But at the beginning the merchants were divided. Battles are not won by money bags, even by ships or cargoes. The early years of war, for all the weight of metropolitan wealth, went badly for Parliament. What of the trained bands of London, often credited with great military achievements?[1] The latest military commentator is inclined to think their prowess has been exaggerated.[2] At Bristol, parliamentary sympathies were uppermost at first, for Bristol, like many of the outports, felt itself badly treated by Charles. But the merchant community itself was not particularly Puritan in any sectarian sense. Most merchants before the Restoration were Anglican.[3] and Bristol served the royal cause well until late in 1645, paying for equipment and supplying manufactures. So did Falmouth and Chester. Exeter, with its small but useful port of Topsham, was a Royalist centre. Newcastle was a valuable funnel for Royalist supplies from Europe. At King's Lynn, in the centre of the Parliament country, the inhabitants rose and held out for a month against Parliament under a local Cavalier leader in an action which might have been decisive if they had been given support by the Royalist general, the Earl of Newcastle.

The rural manufacturing areas of Yorkshire and Lancashire and the towns on whose capital and orders they worked were certainly strongly influenced by Puritanism. This indicated, no doubt, the force of the same socio-religious link that had long created a Calvinist society of small masters and workers in the textile manufactures of Norfolk. Times had been bad for the north country cheap woollens since the 1620s. To the natural difficulties of the times were added, in the period of personal government (1629 to 1640), quarrels with the royal aulnager, heavy mortality from plague, and a protracted dispute over the oligarchical corporation which the King had set up at Leeds. The royal name had, here as elsewhere, become associated with monopoly, oligarchy, oppressive taxation and interference with everyday business. Capitalists, small masters and workers alike resented it.

Not all manufacturers or manufacturing areas were for Parliament, nevertheless. The King had his entrepreneurs in the persons of such Cavaliers as the Ashburnhams, who were iron masters in Sussex, and Sir John Byron, who had wide industrial interests. Sir John Winter, another Cavalier, owned vast iron and timber estates in the Forest of

---

[1] Hill, op. cit., p. 168. Burne and Young, op. cit., p. 33.

[2] Burne and Young, op. cit., p. 120.

[3] P. McGrath, *Merchants and Merchandize in Seventeenth Century Bristol*, 1955, p. xxix.

Dean. At the siege of Gloucester the royal army was supplied from furnaces and forges set up in the same forest under the Marquis of Worcester, the largest local (Catholic) landowner. When Parliament took
Newcastle in November 1645 they did not rest content with merely
making the coal-owning Royalist mayor and his wife wait upon the
victors at table 'with napkins on their shoulders' (as the Covenanters
had done four years earlier); they confiscated all the property of the
prominent Royalists who owned the majority of the collieries.[1]

Curiously, one of the most radical of the great crop of radical,
Leveller, pamphlets to appear in 1648–49 came from this backward
northern area. The officers and troopers of the Northumberland Horse,
descendants of those who had twice defied the Tudors, now petitioned
Fairfax to release them from the bondage of the customary tenures
which they still endured.[2] It would be rash, in this age when most small
capitalists and workers in manufactures were still closely tied to the
land in one way or another, to try to distinguish too sharply between
'industrial' and 'agrarian' areas, or even between town and country.
The two were still intermingled in fact as well as spirit. The identity of
the 'Levellers', who began to emerge after 1646, remains obscure.
Many of them were Londoners. Their leaders spoke of them sometimes
as 'the middle sort of people'; occasionally as 'the hobnails, clouted
shoes, the private soldiers, the leather and woollen aprons and the
laborious and industrious people of England'. How were they related to
the Diggers? Or to those angry but opportunist peasants who from 1640
onwards were restoring enclosed fields to open, breaking down the
Earl of Suffolk's fences in Essex, crying that 'if they took not advantage
of the time they should never have the opportunity again'?[3] Behind
such riots there was often a fairly articulate hatred of what they believed
to be servile, customary tenures. When the countryfolk of Hertfordshire
presented a petition to the army in 1647, they claimed that the copyholders had been 'very cordial and faithful to the Parliament' in expectation of having their tenure turned into freehold.[4] The importance of
such incidents can be exaggerated. The radicals of the Interregnum, like
the radicals of the early industrial age, were angrily sincere, but they
were naïve, ill-organized, without real leadership and without any
clear, unifying principles.

[1] J. U. Nef, *Rise of the British Coal Industry*, 1932, vol. II, p. 69.
[2] Brailsford, op. cit., pp. 447–8.
[3] Ibid., pp. 10–13, 417–27.
[4] Ibid., p. 439.

If the Civil War was not a class war, neither was it a war of one region or occupation against another. Everywhere, as an older historian wrote, there were two parties 'of which the weaker only waited opportunity to join hands with an invading force'.[1] Parliament had an advantage in economic *potential*, especially in the support of London. But two years of muddle, indecision and missed opportunities by Charles elapsed before Parliament was able to turn this potential into actual military superiority. The King lost the war because of the want of a unified military command in the early stages, and because this enabled the opposition leaders to seize the initiative. Charles's defects lost the war as surely as they had lost the peace.[2]

The problems of converting economic potential into reality were demonstrated vividly by the history of taxation in the war. When the Civil War broke out, Parliament had no money. The London Customs were seized but the turmoil had reduced them to a mere trickle. Lords and Commons were as slow to agree to money bills as they had been twenty years earlier. The sequestration of Royalist estates was to produce some contribution, but the main innovation of 1643 was Pym's 'excise', denounced by M.P.s as 'an unjust, scandalous and destructive project'[3] but destined to become, along with the land tax and the Customs, the principal source of government revenue down to Napoleonic times. The new tax was in all probability imitated from a Dutch model: the word itself was a corruption of the Dutch *accijns*. It was an inland duty, payable on the sale of the article, levied on a range of commodities that seemed to grow larger each year: ale, beer, cider, spirits, meat, victuals, salt, alum, hops, starch, hats, caps, saffron as well as a wide variety of imported goods. It bore a strong resemblance to those monopolies the Stuarts had imposed on articles of trade, and its collection followed the pattern of local areas adopted for Ship Money. Its imposition was the signal for an outburst of violent popular opposition and riot. Excisemen were abused and assaulted. Broadsides, doggerel verse and parodies circulated freely. One, calling down heavenly wrath on the inventors and collectors of the system, ended:

> Let all Exciseman hereby warning take
> To shun their Practice for their Conscience sake

Another blasphemously parodied the general confession and litany: 'O

[1] G. M. Trevelyan, op. cit., p. 229. For Norfolk see R. W. Ketton-Cremer, *Forty Norfolk Essays* (1961).
[2] See 'Economics and Politics in the Seventeenth Century' by Charles Wilson in *The Historical Journal*, V, no. 1, 1962.
[3] J. H. Hexter, *The Reign of King Pym*, 1941, p. 25.

God the Father have mercy upon Us, miserable Excize-men.' Excise roused violent hostility because the burden fell on the people's necessities — food, drink and clothes; because it was a dangerously convenient tax to collect, and because it was foreign in inspiration. These suspicions were well founded. In Holland, the tax had become all-pervasive. The sharp eye of George Downing noted that in that country 'a man cannot eate a dish of meate in an ordinary but that one way or another he shall pay nineteen excizes out of it. This is not more strange than true'.[1] And Hazlerigg, the old Republican, lamented: ' . . . we shall next vote canvass breeches and wooden shoes for the free people of England.' The excise reopened another old sore: it brought back the tax farmers in force. By 1654, over thirty-one counties and towns were 'farmed', and Cromwell's righthand financier, Martin Noell, was handling on his own the excise of salt, glass, wire, copperas and alum. The excise system has been described as 'a jerry built structure' that opened the way to chicanery, favouritism and the petty tyranny of assessors and collectors.[2] That it endured was due to the persistent demands of war finance, the ease with which it operated and perhaps the newly vested interests of the farmers. During the Protectorate the net yield varied between £162,000 and £238,000 a year.

The second great indirect tax continued to be the Customs. Although the rates remained stable, the *yield* increased enormously during the Interregnum – net, from £140,000 in 1643 to £502,000 in 1659. The improvement was due partly to the growth of trade, partly to more efficient administration. Even so, Cromwell was not satisfied and seems to have been ready to yield in 1657 to the eager offers of a number of 'citizens of London of good account' to farm the Customs as they had been farmed under the Stuarts. No doubt the attraction was, as before, the convenience of a smooth flow of money into the Exchequer. Customs and excise, it was said, were to be farmed for £800,000 a year which would be advanced in weekly instalments. Behind the scheme, once again, was Martin Noell. In fact, the plan never materialized and the Customs continued to be administered by commissioners until the Restoration.

The principal source of public revenue was the only general direct tax of the time. The land tax, as the 'monthly assessments' were to become known, derived administratively from the Ship Money 'assessments' of 1636. The sum needed was decided upon, and then divided

[1] *Clarke Papers*, vol. III. pp. 175–8.
[2] Hexter, op. cit., p. 26.

up proportionately between towns and counties on an assessment similar to the Ship Money assessment. County committees were responsible for collecting it. This was not, like excise, a revolutionary tax, and it was administered by methods inherited from Charles I. As a cross between a property tax and a local rate, it produced the largest part of the public revenue — nearly half of the bumper revenue of £1·8 million in 1656, for example.[1]

The course of financial policy during the Interregnum made it clear that republican governments were apt to impose heavier, not lighter, tax burdens on their subjects and extract them with a ruthless efficiency of which their royal predecessors were innocent. Most of the money raised went on war (whatever Cromwell's detractors might allege about his personal extravagance). The last year of the Dutch War (1653–54) cost £2¾ million. It was not only gentry and merchants in Parliament who disliked the taxes imposed by Pym and Cromwell: it was the country at large: ' . . . the people complain', the Venetian ambassador wrote home, ' . . . the government lets them squeal.'

In this way the three main sources of public revenue — customs, excise and a land tax—had been built into the permanent structure of English public finance. This experience may have helped to take some of the passion of principle out of the taxation issue. The second Protectorate Parliament opined meekly that excise was in reality 'the most equal and indifferent levy that could be laid on the people'. Excise remained, nevertheless, a dangerously touchy subject with Englishmen, as Walpole was to find. But it was no Ship Money. Taxation was becoming a chronic grievance, rather than an acute one. The Englishman was beginning his long apprenticeship to the art of learning to live with his taxes.

Like their predecessors the republican governments fell back on the farming system where the excise was concerned. The customs were placed in the hands of public commissioners — not apparently with wholly satisfactory results. Thurloe, Cromwell's Secretary of State, thought that farming was more efficient, and the 'backsliding' of 1657 when it was proposed to put out customs as well as excise to tender is no doubt evidence of this. But whether collected directly or indirectly, the yield still left the governments of the Interregnum with a large gap between expenditure and revenue; quite how large is still as uncertain as most other aspects of seventeenth-century public finance. The Long Parliament, with an annual revenue of, say, £2 million a year had only

[1] Ashley, op. cit., p. 96.

managed to remain solvent by squeezing its opponents by fines and by selling off royal and church property. In Oliver's time, the public debt grew, especially with the Spanish War. Richard was left some £2 million in debt and searching for credit to cover his father's funeral expenses. How, then, had the gap been bridged thus far?

Pym, with a mysterious network of connexions in the city and elsewhere, evidently managed to borrow through the City Chamber, which lent money on the security of the land tax and acted as a link between the Government and the rich London companies. But the difficulty they met with in recovering their capital made them shy of Oliver's approaches. London gave little corporate help to Cromwell, apart from a more or less forced loan wrung out of the East India Company in 1654. He (like Charles I) was perforce thrown back on a series of hand-to-mouth arrangements made privately with a small group of financiers. Of these Martin Noell and Sir Thomas Vyner were the leaders. Noell, the prince of the excise farmers, was also a navy and army contractor, with large interests in the salt mines of Cheshire. With Vyner he figured as a government agent remitting money abroad to English diplomats and troops, selling captured prizes, dealing in bullion, and, above all, lending money on the security of taxes. Both of them survived, though much battered by their experiences at the hands of their political masters, into the Restoration age. Their less well founded contemporaries, like the colonial merchant Samuel Vassall, or Samuel Avery, Governor of the Merchant Adventurers, did not. Bankruptcy, even jail, was their lot. Lending to governments was hardly less hazardous than it had been in the Middle Ages when the Bardi and Peruzzi fell victims to the caprice of princes. The theory that Cromwell's failure to understand or manage his finances paved the way for the return of the monarchy contains an element of truth.[1] Like his predecessors, he was driven by want of money to summon Parliament. Like his successors, he had to recognize the power of the landed interest by reducing the taxes on land and increasing those on trade. Most important, his poverty preserved the adumbration of a public debt inherited from the monarchy, and stereotyped and made permanent a collection of taxes that began as the hasty expedients of a civil war.

How did the Civil War end? It is sometimes argued that the Restoration represented a sinister compromise and reunion between the two halves of the divided upper class — a compromise designed to repress

[1] See H. J. Habakkuk, 'Public Finance and the Sale of Confiscated Property during the Interregnum' (*Econ. Hist. Rev.*, August 1962) for the most recent survey.

the dangerous upsurge of social radicalism represented by the Leveller movement and extreme republicanism. Thus (it is said) there emerged a two-class society, with a *laissez faire* economy and a new system of government where the propertied classes were free to pull all the strings.[1] This is, of course, one way of looking at the formation of that majority party which finally agreed to recall Charles II. It is possible to quote the fears of Cromwell (and many others) of 'the levelling principle',[2] to denounce them as self-interested property-owners guided only by their terror of a peasantry determined to inherit its own. The sporadic challenges to social authority, the breakdowns of law, must have caused many to reflect anxiously on the precarious nature of the social order, on the 'chaos, when degree is suffocate'. But it is also possible to quote other 'landlords' (like Major-General Whalley) who themselves denounced enclosures and servile tenures as bitterly as any Leveller. The anti-enclosure riots *before* the Civil War were nowhere more violent than on the royal estates in Cornwall, where practice had not apparently followed precept. That the enemies of 1642 were reconciled at the Restoration is true, but the motives behind the reconciliation were more immediate and more remote than the suppression of radicalism amongst the lower orders. The Restoration was the act of men of all kinds sick of the slaughter, violence, repression, fanaticism and (let us not forget) the extortionate public finance that had marked the previous twenty years. Few men of any class had wanted the war. They now saw a chance to end it. They had not been at war as delegates either of classes or districts. They fought, in the last resort, for ideas and ideals. Now they had had enough. Idealism was to desert politics for a hundred years.

3. THE ECONOMIC AFTERMATH OF THE CIVIL WAR

Impressive claims have been made for the economic effects of the Civil War: that it destroyed a whole class of landholders, that it freed the capitalists from Crown control, that it was a turning point in the evolution of capitalism, that it saw the beginnings of *laissez-faire*.[3] As usual, there is an element of truth in these claims: but it is an element easily exaggerated and distorted. Dramatic politically, the Civil War was not, in any economic or social sense, 'revolutionary'. The physical destruction of the war was quickly made good. Confiscated lands of

---

1 See C. Hill, op. cit., p. 308.
2 Brailsford, op. cit., p. 417.
3 For a summary see C. Hill, op. cit., pp. 145–6.

Crown, Church and Cavaliers had been bought and sold on a vast scale during the Interregnum. Some passed permanently into the ownership of gentry, merchants, yeomen. But even this process was not new: land was already being bought and sold on a growing market long before the Civil War. The war in fact saw the start of systematic retrenchment by Royalist families to *preserve* their estates: after they had paid their fines, they conveyed the estates to trustees to pay off their debts, reserving a fraction of their total income for their own use. This helps to explain 'why the perils and misfortunes of the Civil War had less permanent effect on the fortunes of landowning families than one might expect'.[1] Some Royalist gentry passed into oblivion after their lands were sold. But a larger number, including most of the nobility, managed to reassemble all or part of their estates even before Charles II returned to the throne. And these great estates were to be held together more tightly as the law relating to family settlements developed. True, the estates which were recovered by the Cavalier families were often encumbered with debts as a result of the expenses of their recovery. The reverberations of the events of the 1640s were still being felt in the 1740s as families were at long last compelled to sell out to meet the debts of nearly a century earlier.[2] But this was not a common experience. The landowning class had never been strangers to debt, and as the facilities for raising credit in various ways improved, the landowner was under less compulsion to resort to the final drastic remedy of selling his assets. More often he was able to bridge the gap by borrowing, and the pressure of repayment and interest may well have been a powerful incentive to raising the productivity of his lands through improved estate management.[3] Vis-à-vis the Crown, the landowners were strengthened by the abolition of the Court of Wards (confirmed by statute in 1660). Lands held by noble tenure were freed of their old feudal obligations of service and of the monetary payments which had been substituted for such services. In these ways a major source of friction between King and landowners was removed. Lower down the scale the remnants of the manorial system continued. Copyhold tenure went on. This has been represented as another aspect of the victory of the landed class over reformers. It is very doubtful. The lord's will was (as a legal expert wrote in 1701) 'abridged, clogged and restrained' by the custom of the manor.[4] The fact was not lost on the propertied

---

[1] H. J. Habakkuk, *Britain and the Netherlands*, 1959, p. 163.
[2] Ibid., pp. 158–9.   [3] See below, p. 259.
[4] *Lex Customaria* by S. C. Barrister at Law, London 1701, Preface.

classes. Henceforth it would be lords and bailiffs who would try to convert copyhold to leasehold.[1]

Other economic changes sometimes attributed to the Civil War were often the continuance, in an intensified form, of phenomena already apparent long before the Civil War. The great Restoration Navigation Code itself (1660–63) represented a second, and more successful, attempt to codify the laws relating to shipping which Parliament had first tackled in 1651. Yet this in turn was foreshadowed in scores of earlier acts relating to shipping[2] and especially in the attempt of 1622 to reserve the Baltic shipping trades to Englishmen.[3] Indeed, the Restoration Government spent several busy years after the King's return re-enacting a whole catalogue of 'mercantilist' statutes relating to trade and industry. These included not only those which had been torn out of the Statute Book as disaffected and invalid but also revisions and extensions of early Stuart legislation such as the prohibitions against the export of wool, fuller's earth and other clothmaking materials. An administration strengthened by the accession of a new class of royal 'public' servants and more sensitive to the demands represented by the restored Parliament was now moulding a revised set of formulae for economic policy. They had behind them the experience of the Interregnum as well as the period of personal government, and they legislated with an eye to the trade of the nation as a whole and not merely of London. The London companies, both chartered and joint stock, had been in rough waters between 1643 and 1660. Yet there was no clear-cut contrast between the attitudes of Kings and Protector to company organization. Charles had licensed rivals to the East India Company. Cromwell, in spite of the current prejudices against the old company, decided to retain it. The fortunes of a company after the Restoration depended broadly on its utility and its lobbying power. That the prejudices of the Interregnum did no permanent damage to the joint-stock image is shown by the Act of 1662 which protected stock holders in such companies by limiting their legal liability to the nominal value of their holding. The principle that monopoly might be justified in distant and difficult trades was thus confirmed: but the general enforcement of trade and maritime policy was transferred, under the Navigation Acts, from the companies to the State. After a brief period of ostentatious participation in commercial and colonial policy-making, the merchants gave way once more to the

1 See below, p. 251.
2 Harper, op. cit., chs. III and IV.
3 Supple, op. cit., pp. 88, 243.

nobles and professional administrators.[1] In traditional fashion, Government reaffirmed its right to govern.

While commercial policy was assuming more coherent patterns, manufactures seemed to be moving into a phase of freer growth and independence. How far was this the result of the Civil War and the dismantling of the Prerogative Courts and the whole central government machinery by which economic and social policy had been (at any rate theoretically) enforced under the early Stuarts? The answer must be: only partially and indirectly. Unlike the old urban crafts, the up and coming industries – textiles, metal working and mining – were not located in the narrow streets of the corporate town. They were dispersed widely over villages and countryside. 'Water power', Sir John Clapham wrote, 'had been a solvent of gild-power from the days of the first rural fulling mill.'[2] The increased industrial use of fuel and power continued its disintegration. Neither Manchester nor Birmingham nor any of the towns and villages where capital and markets for production were growing had gilds. Even in London the gilds were losing control over the workers of the sprawling suburbs. Likewise apprenticeship was in decline. Cromwell allowed demobilized soldiers into protected trades without apprenticeship. After the Great Fire the shortage of craftsmen dealt the system another blow. By the 1670s there were 'illegal' men in all occupations. All the economic forces of the day were pulling against these old forms of industrial regulation.

But this did not mean full or doctrinaire application of *laissez-faire*: nor did it necessarily mean the entirely heartless, anti-social regime described by some later historians. Wage-earners had not done well in the first half of the century. After 1650 they did a little better. The old system of wage assessment continued well into the eighteenth century. But on the whole the rise of wages seems to have come before the Justices gave it official recognition. The picture of a ruthlessly materialistic ruling class exploiting wage-earners and the poor is not borne out by the facts. That great severity and even brutality followed in the wake of e.g. the Settlement Laws of 1662 is undoubted. The power to eject immigrant paupers from a parish led to grievous hardship. But the preamble to the Act explains how these powers derived from the very measures taken by some parishes to deal with their own poor. Those parishes which most conscientiously did their duty 'were inundated by distressed paupers' from parishes which did not. The law, in fact, merely

[1] A. P. Thornton, *West India Policy under the Restoration*, 1956, ch. 1.
[2] J. Clapham, *A Concise Economic History of Britain*, 1949, p. 253.

reflected the horrific proportions of the nation's major social problem between 1660 and 1834: the poor. There was no sudden change of ethos.

To the great 'debate of the poor' the men of the Interregnum made a significant contribution: not only the Levellers and Utopians but a whole group of more practical writers like Hartlib, Chamberlain, Goffe and Plockhoy. Especially in the dark year of 1649, they had brought the linked problems of poverty and unemployment to the fore of the debate. They never ceased from that time on to occupy the attention of mercantilist writers and social reformers.[1]

Finally there is the problem of the contribution of Dissent to economic progress. In the general revulsion against Puritanism, the restored Parliament passed a series of Acts between 1661 and 1665, the so-called Clarendon Code, which divided the nation into Church and Dissent, depriving Dissenters of civic rights, civic responsibilities and education, and generally creating a second-class citizenry of chapel-goers. Those who survived the material loss and persecution were nevertheless to play an important economic role in the nation's future. Quakers, Independents and Presbyterians were to be among the leading figures of the business world. Some historians have seen this social phenomenon as a manifestation of the Puritan ethos. Others have attributed it simply and solely to the deprivations of the Clarendon Code: deprive a man of one way of life and he will contrive himself another. The problem is necessarily a speculative one, but the argument is forceful. Certainly Puritanism changed its social character after 1660. Before then it may have been, for a century, a religion for all, but it had evidently a special appeal to the small masters and artisans in manufacturing areas. After 1660, its connexion with successful trade and finance is more evident. By an apparently consistent law, Dissent became subject to increasing material success, increasing respectability; until, a century later, Methodism was to take over the role once played by 'old Dissent' as the religion of the working poor.

The permanent economic consequences of the Civil War and Interregnum owed little to any conscious or direct onslaught by one phalanx of economic interests on another. Such direct action as there was (against the great companies, for example) left little lasting impression. The effects were less direct and more subtle than that. They resulted from the abolition or reform of political and religious institutions

---

[1] See C. Wilson, 'The Other Face of Mercantilism', *Tr. R.H.S.*, fifth series, IX 1959, for a full account. See also Chapter Eleven below.

undertaken principally for political and religious reasons. The end of the absolute monarchy, of the Prerogative Courts, and the new expanded role of Parliament created a matrix of government and law within which economic change and expansion could proceed with less anachronistic interference than under the old regime. Most if not all the economic trends observable in the century after 1660 were a continuation of earlier ones. The social structure continued to evolve empirically. It was not revolutionized. But the individuals who composed it were left as suspicious of idealism as of fanaticism. Of this inquiring, cynical but above all opportunist generation, the rightful image was Charles II himself, President of a Royal Society slanted towards profitable invention; Prince Rupert, retired from war to be head of the Hudson's Bay Company; and James, Duke of York, chairman of an ambitious national Fishery Company whose real business was to exploit its monopoly of state lotteries.

PART TWO

The Turning Tide: 1660 to 1700

CHAPTER SEVEN

Agricultural Surpluses and the Spurs to Improvement

MANY of the changes and improvements to be seen on English farms after the Restoration represented the natural extensions of earlier changes. The logic of enclosure was too strong to be resisted, and the attempts of Government and of social reformers, mostly abortive, to stop men enclosing by laws and by administrative action came to an end with the Restoration. The Privy Council, which had been the engine of Stuart social policy, now ceased to perform that function. The main executants of its policies, the prerogative Courts, had disappeared. Attempts at social planning had been an aspect of that idealism so characteristic of early Stuart government and so dangerous in execution, by turns desultory and severe. The more down-to-earth and cynical rulers of the century after the Restoration abandoned them as practically fruitless, economically backward, and politically inconvenient. Enclosure could now go forward, either by private Act of Parliament, or — more commonly — by the enrolment of the enclosure agreement in the Court of Chancery.

The changed attitude towards enclosure and its merits did not bring an immediate flood of applicants. Even by the end of the century, more of the cultivated land of England was open than enclosed. In some parts of the Midlands — in Leicestershire, for instance — there was less enclosure after the Restoration than before. But the erosion of the old open-field area went on steadily and where the new 'severall' fields were created, bounded by dyke, bank, wall or hedge as local fashion, materials or climate suggested, the face of England began to assume something of its modern appearance. Throughout the Midlands, the ditch and quick set hedge appeared. The favourite hedge was white-thorn, followed by blackthorn or crab, holly and elder. Furze was the last resort when nothing else would grow.

Within the fields formed by these enclosures, arable and pasture were now divided. Manure from the pastures, or from the cattle yarded up through the winter, could be spread on the enclosed arable to maintain and improve its fertility. Dung carted in winter was harrowed into the soil between the ploughing up after harvest and sowing-time. Grassland was treated with humus from the bottom of the old haystack. If the land was too wet to be drained by the flow of surface waters along the natural contours, or by the rise and fall of ridge and furrow, the work could be speeded by the use of the 'Lincolnshire Wheel', a water wheel in reverse. Subsoil drainage was still in the future. Land that needed water was irrigated either by water scooped from pond or stream by hand or by the use of the so-called 'Persian wheel' recommended by Blith and other improving writers.

Drained or flooded as nature and experience dictated, the land was then manured. And to the natural manuring and the 'denshiring' mentioned earlier, an ever-widening number of other methods were now added. Chalk, burnt lime, marl, sea sand, seaweed, soap, ashes, soot, rags, salt, and every kind of human and animal dung and refuse were spread on the land. Barges that took malt from the great kilns at Ware in Hertfordshire along the River Lea to the London breweries, came back loaded with metropolitan dung that helped to establish for Hertfordshire farming a very high reputation for productivity.

Land thus prepared was ploughed by implements of improving design and then sown. A large variety of wheats, a rather smaller variety of barley and either black or white oats, peas and beans — these covered the larger parts of arable England. Here and there the man of enterprise could diversify with one of the many industrial crops available — flax, madder, wood, liquorice, saffron, hops, teasels,[1] aniseed. But, in general, farmers held to the staple cereals from which they had their food, drink and animal feed, fallowing the land one year in three or four. Where the soil was poorest, each alternate year was fallow — the 'two-course' rotation handed down from the early Middle Ages.

The midland peasant of the Middle Ages had often been compelled to farm virtually stockless on his open-field strips, leaving sheep and cattle raising to the specialists of marsh and wold. These old natural pastures were still filled by the sheepmasters and graziers. Those who supplied the Smithfield market could buy Lincolnshire or Leicestershire wethers, fatten them on the rich grass of the Essex marshes and sell out at the top of the Christmas market. From Romney Marsh came the biggest mutton in England. At the turn of the century more than

[1] A plant with a large prickly head used for raising the nap on cloth.

half a million sheep were said to be browsing on the sweet grass of the Downs within six miles of Dorchester. From Leicester to Peterborough lay that famous land where 'most of the gentlemen are graziers and in some places the graziers are so rich they grow gentlemen'.

Important as all this evidence was of the continuing trend towards stock raising and meat production, the crux of agrarian improvement was the *combination* of animal and arable husbandry. Here the work of the pioneers of the first half of the century — Weston, Hartlib, Loder, and others — and the experience of those who wisely followed their advice, was bearing fruit; but it was a slow process. Clover, artificial grasses like sainfoin, lucerne, trefoil and vetch, were being added to the traditional hay crop to help to overwinter a few more animals. Most important of all, the seventeenth-century husbandman could already command three kinds of turnip — round, long or yellow — which he could feed to his stock in the yard and keep them in good flesh where previously they would have had to be killed off. Just as the idea of embodying these fodder crops into the rotation had come from the Low Countries, so a sizeable proportion of clover was still imported from there. Turnip seeds were more easily provided from local sources.

For the suggestible, a new generation of improving writers still provided a steady stream of exhortation. Of these Andrew Yarranton (*The Great Improvement of Lands by Clover*, 1663), J. Worlidge (*Systema Agriculturae*, 1669) and John Houghton (*Collection of Letters for the Improvement of Husbandry and Trade*, 1681–83 and 1691–1703) are the most important. Yarranton was a jack-of-all trades characteristic of the times: amongst his many enterprises he included that of seed merchant's agent, and in that capacity claimed to have been responsible for doubling the value of lands in a number of western shires. Worlidge and Houghton, on the other hand, exemplified the new spirit of scientific observation and measurement that was beginning to permeate thought in agricultural as well as other forms of inquiry. Worlidge was the first to produce a comprehensive and reasonably methodical treatise on agriculture which had considerable influence until well into the eighteenth century. Many of his recommendations were directed towards reducing costs and increasing the efficiency of farming methods. He pointed out, for instance, that it was better to use too little marl than too much, which might damage rather than improve crops. He invented a drill to replace the traditional methods of broadcast sowing. Like a modern combine drill, it both drilled the seed and dressed it with manure. It was regarded as a failure, but a recent authority has commented that 'it is hard to resist the belief that amendment and further trial might have given Worlidge the honour which fell to Tull sixty year later'.[1]

Worlidge, a Hampshire farmer, was one of the correspondents who contributed to the agricultural newsletters circulated by John Houghton. These did a good deal to break down old prejudices and remove barriers to the flow of ideas between one region and another. This was an important function in an age when knowledge itself was often restricted – as in the case of turnips – to particular areas of specialized farming. Houghton himself was a man of parts. He had studied at Corpus Christi College, Cambridge, and became a Fellow of the Royal Society while continuing in business in London as an apothecary. (The Royal Society apologized to Charles II for electing a tradesman, but were assured that so far from being dissatisfied at the election, he would be glad to see more of the same stamp.) Houghton's weekly paper, which was pretty well continuous from 1691 to 1702, contained on one side a short article on agriculture, natural history or manufactures; on the other, a price list of grain prices from different parts of the country which is still of great value as a source of statistical information about the rural economy of the time. The essay told of other forms of rural progress – that enclosures were spreading, that the science of forestry was increasingly popular with landowners, that the people ate barley bread in times of scarcity when wheat was too dear, and so on.

Haunted by the traditional, though in fact diminishing, threats of starvation and depopulation, the influential classes in society threw their weight behind the campaign for increased food production. This was conceived to be not only a defence against national poverty and weakness but a positive contribution to the nation's wealth in the shape of an export surplus of grain and a bigger demand for shipping. Hence the keen interest of the Royal Society, its royal patron, and its agricultural committee some thirty-two strong, which proceeded to debate at length such problems as the best size of wheel for the farm cart, and the best designs of scythes, trenching spades, hedging hooks and harrows. It set its approving seal on the cultivation of hemp, which would help to reduce the nation's bill for Baltic imports and improve the balance of trade, and might even form a basis for an export trade. It weighed the pros and cons of steeping grain seed in brandy to prevent disease. More important, in the long run, its committee recommended

---

[1] Trow-Smith, p. 107.

in 1662 that the potato should be cultivated more extensively as an insurance against famine. By way of example, the members of the Society were urged to plant the tuber themselves, to encourage their friends to do likewise and to advertise its virtues in the 'Diurnals'. The potato was already common enough as a garden vegetable. Worlidge had urged its merits 'as a food for pigs or other cattle' and Wigan already had a potato market in 1680; Lancashire, outside the open-field area and near to Ireland (which had already taken to the potato), was to be the stronghold of potato growing. Market gardens outside London grew it for the market, and there is some evidence of it in the drained fens and in Yorkshire. It was slower to penetrate the east and south of England.

Houghton himself put a high, possibly flattering, value on the con-tributions of the Royal Society to agricultural progress:

> ... since His Majesty's most happy Restoration [he wrote in 1682] the whole land hath been fermented and stirred up by the profitable hints it hath received from the Royal Society by which means parks have been disparked, commons inclosed, woods turned into arable, and pasture land, improved by clover, st. foine, turnips, coleseed, parsley, and many other good husbandries, so that the food of cattel is increast as fast, if not faster, than the consumption, and by these means, although some particular lands may fall, I strongly persuade myself that altogether the rent of the kingdom is far greater than ever it was.[1]

Important as these more scientific and rational approaches to the farmer's problems were, their importance remained, *pace* Houghton, qualitative rather than quantitative. Mr Fussell has calculated[2] that the clover seed imported from the Low Countries (the principal source) at the end of the seventeenth century was only sufficient to sow a mere 4,000 acres, or 1 in every 2,250 acres of the land under crop cultivation. This suggests some 16,000 acres of land cultivated on a four-course rotation, or 1 acre in every 580. The area under turnips is even more difficult to estimate. Such figures, precarious as they must be, emphasize how small was the influence of the new ideas and methods statistically. It was not just that farmers, peasant farmers especially, were conservative, illiterate and suspicious of newfangledness. It was that the traditional communal husbandry that still dominated large areas especially of midland England presented practical barriers to alternate husbandry.

1 *Collection, 1681–3*, edn. 1727, p. 83.
2 G. E. Fussell, 'Low Countries' Influences on English Farming', *E.H.R.* LXXIV, 1959, p. 11.

The whole system of scattered strips and common rights could only be reformed by a costly and cumbersome process of negotiation and legal agreement.

The factors which encouraged the gradual changeover to new crops and new systems of rotation were many and varied; but it is possible to recognize some which operated in the 'advanced' regions north and west of London, in the West Country, especially round Exeter and Bristol, and in East Anglia and Kent. In the first place, these were all areas where the open-field system as it was known to the Midlands had never existed or had been modified or rearranged at an earlier period. Parts of Norfolk had never known the rigid three-field system of the Midlands. This had allowed a comparatively flexible agricultural economy to develop and experiment on lighter soils, often no doubt newly enclosed from waste or heath, that received the new turnip husbandry more gratefully than did the midland clays. Secondly, these areas all had access to the cities whose growth was a feature of seventeenth-century economic and social evolution. Norfolk had access not only to Norwich, the third city of the kingdom, with its satellite villages where cloth making flourished, but, almost as easily, to London itself. While Norfolk corn went thither coastwise from the thriving port of Lynn, and from a series of small ports dotted along the Norfolk coast — Blakeney, Cley and Wiveton — struggling armies of cattle, turkeys and geese made their way to Smithfield and the other London markets by road. Thirdly, legislative changes opened up the possibility of export markets. A brisk trade, mainly to Holland, developed through the same cluster of Norfolk and Suffolk ports that served London. These were the days that saw the building of Henry Bell's Custom House at Lynn and the merchant houses at Cley and Yarmouth. A rising trade, often in malting barley that found favour with Dutch brewers, is reflected in the Customs figures. From a value of a mere £4,000 or £5,000 in the sixties, the export of corn had risen to the sizable figure of well over a quarter of a £million by the end of the century and was to treble over the next half-century. Marginal figures these may be, but they were a useful cushion for the Norfolk farmer and his landlord. Again, the export trade may well have helped the farmers round ports like Lynn, Bristol and Exeter to get those supplies of Dutch clover and turnip seed which we know they used. Norwich stuffs and Devon serges were sold against imports of seed which were distributed over the countryside by travelling salesmen. Thus trade and agriculture speeded each other's progress and prosperity.

Throughout the last forty years of the seventeenth century, two broad changes were going forward in the English countryside. In East Anglia, under the aegis of landlords like the Townshends at Raynham, the Cokes at Holkham and the Walpoles at Houghton, grassland was being converted to arable, the sheep yielding to the plough, wool to corn. Similar changes were to occur, though rather more slowly, at the southern end of the chalk belt, in Wiltshire, where the emphasis moved to wheat rather than barley. Contrariwise, on heavy land, the clay soils were being laid down to grass for cattle rearing — on the Weald in Kent and Surrey, and throughout the Midlands from Chilterns to Trent, but especially in Leicestershire. Here the grazier had become the dominant figure. Agricultural specialization was under way. Both movements were a response to market prices for grain, wool and meat, and these prices were in turn influenced not only by 'natural' factors of demand like population trends but also by artificial stimuli — the corn laws, the bounty on corn export and the prohibitions on wool exports.

Grain prices might fluctuate wildly from harvest to harvest. On a long view they were pretty stable. Maximum Elizabethan prices, it has been said, had become normal Stuart prices. The 1680s, a time for good harvests, saw wheat at 34s. to 35s. a quarter, which was precisely where it had stood nearly a century earlier when the 'nine men's morris was filled up with mud'. It was this general stability of price levels, reflecting presumably adequate food supplies for the nation, which encouraged the landed interest to demand, and Government to grant, permission for the export of corn. The Scylla and Charybdis that faced statesmen were starvation and high prices if harvests were bad, and ruin for farmers and landlords if a glut sent down prices to bankruptcy levels. Until the 1670s, policy was empirical and intermittent. Merchants could export wheat if the price was below 32s. a quarter. In 1670 the emphasis switched, and export was in general allowed, with an understanding that the policy would be suspended if harvests failed. Three years later came the famous 'experimental' bounty of 5s. a quarter on wheat, and smaller bounties on barley and rye, when prices fell below certain reasonable levels. The policy was renewed again in 1689 and was applied pretty steadily thereafter. The 'mercantilist' attractions of the bounty — the stimulus to export, a contribution to a favourable balance of trade and a larger mercantile marine — have been mentioned. It should be added that like many other acts of high policy, this one had a private aspect. The first grant in 1673 was by way of a bargain between Government and the landed interest. The Government imposed a property tax on land; the landowner got his bounty, 'to the end that all owners of land whereupon this tax principally lyeth may be the better enabled to pay, by rendering corn more valuable'. Bounties on exports were coupled with duties on imports, so that England was pretty well a closed market so far as corn was concerned. Yet the bounty system did not inaugurate a Golden Age for the arable farmer. Prices from 1675 to 1700 were only poor to moderate, rising higher only in the 'barren years' of the nineties. Probably the bounty did no more than keep levels reasonably stable. The extension of new methods of arable farming in these years was therefore not a pursuit of easy profits but a means of adjusting arrangements so that a larger output at stable prices was obtained for the same or slightly larger costs.

If the bounty policy looks like another of those conspiracies between Government and the landed interest which has led some historians to suppose that government policy was wholly dictated by private interests, a glance at wool production suggests a different view. While the corn market might be the farmers' preserve, the wool market was reserved for the clothier. Here seventeenth-century policy consistently aimed at a bountiful supply of wool at low prices that helped the manufacturer to keep spinners and weavers busy, accepting it as axiomatic that it was uneconomic to export a primary material when it was possible to export it in a manufactured, and therefore more profitable, form. Scores of Acts prohibiting the export of wool testified to this belief, and it is fallacious to suppose they were of no effect. Smuggling there certainly was, especially to France, but the laments of the Dutch clothiers and the trend of Dutch industry leave no room for doubt that large sections of the old Dutch woollen export trade were killed stone dead.

The relationship between government policy and agricultural progress is not easy to state. Few Acts of Parliament have created more controversy amongst later observers than the corn laws and the bounty arrangements. What can be said about them nowadays? First, that down to 1660, corn law policy had been designed to protect the consumer in an age of shortages that were often acutely present and always potential. From 1660, policy could be designed in the interest of producers, as food production rose until it usually matched and sometimes exceeded the demand of the population. Later critics in the eighteenth century declared that in the end the system overstimulated the growing of grain, at the expense of meat and dairy products. Even this is not easy to prove.[1] In the seventeenth century the rise was slower, the surplus less reliable. The motive behind policy seems to have been a double one: to subsidize larger corn output by a flexible policy that developed the export trade when harvests were good, but diverted supplies homewards when they were bad; and to compensate the agricultural interest, which was taxed and penalized in the matter of wool production. When one asks why the landed interest were apparently powerless to abolish the prohibitions on wool export, the answer is presumably that successive governments put a high value on the economic and social services of the cloth manufacturers: economic in their contributions to export trade, social in the vital part they played in providing employment and wages for hundreds of thousands of workers. A competitive cloth industry was an indispensable condition of public order as well as of private profit.

The barriers against wool export, and the permission given to Irish producers to send wool and yarn to the English market, combined with strong competition in cloth markets to keep wool prices down. From the Restoration onwards for eighty or more years, the trend was downwards. Conversely, meat prices kept well up, reflecting a growing taste for mutton and especially beef that was not limited to the upper classes. The Civil War had seen a shortage of meat and tallow; prices reached a new peak on the eve of the Restoration and remained high till the end of the century. Taken in conjunction with low or moderate grain prices, the possibility of the new fodder crops, and the comparatively low labour costs of grazing and fattening stock, these high meat prices pointed an obvious moral. Farmers turned to fattening cattle, breeding turkeys, geese, pigs. Sheep were less popular, but where they were kept, the emphasis was on mutton rather than wool.

We may guess that by extensive as well as intensive methods — by assart and reclamation as well as by enclosure and the new husbandry — aggregate production and aggregate wealth from farming were on the increase. Not everywhere and not uniformly, but where farmers could respond to the stimulus of markets and prices through improving transport and a supply of credit. Yet on quantities we have little in the way of exact information, and almost as little regarding qualities. The horse was everywhere tending to replace the ox team at the plough, but little is known about his breed. The 'shire' there certainly was, a smaller version of the great warhorse of the Middle Ages. Suffolk had

[1] For a full discussion see D. G. Barnes, *A History of the English Corn Laws 1660–1846*, 1930, ch. III *passim*.

its 'punch' and probably other local breeds were evolving. Cattle were likewise recognizable by region. There were hardy 'runts' of Galway and Angus that were driven south by the thousands to be fattened in Norfolk for the London market each year. East Anglia bred a black beast descended from them. Wales had its upland black stock, Lincolnshire already its famous shorthorn that was said with some probability to be Dutch by origin. But the bullock, like the sheep and the pig, still awaited the attentions of the eighteenth-century breeder. The new scientific spirit that was surely but very slowly changing the farmer's methods in his arable fields, was slower still to impinge on animal husbandry. For the moment, England had more, but hardly better, animals on the farm.

Who initiated and executed the programme of improvement? Who bore the cost and who enjoyed the profit? What was the legal and social structure of land ownership, tenure and management within which the farming practices so far described were taking place? The great manorial demesnes of the high Middle Ages had decomposed into the component parts of which they were in reality a federated whole, partly because they were unsatisfactory as farming units, difficult to manage, and a standing invitation to fraud and inefficiency. Manorial organization was in origin as much military as economic. As the military functions of the system atrophied, its shortcomings as an economic organization became clearer. Only in periods that were exceptionally favourable, and under management exceptionally assiduous, was it easy to hold the large demesne estate together. Less favourable conditions pointed unequivocally to the convenience of decentralized farming. The lord had in many places become a *rentier* before the end of the Middle Ages. The landlord group – for they cannot properly be described as a 'class' – shuffled and reshuffled over the preceding two centuries by recruitment and defection, promotion, demotion, bankruptcy and inheritance, held the prime power of initiative: prime, not entire. The largest yeomen – including the more substantial and more secure copyholders as well as freeholders – were also important. So were the tenant farmers, who though socially of less consequence might well be men of enterprise and action. Somewhere between lord and tenant, squire and farmer, lay the centre of rural gravity. It varied from parish to parish, district to district, and it was to change with time.

Three kinds of landowner above the yeomen class have been descried about the mid-seventeenth century – large, medium and small; or, more specifically, the great aristocratic landowners, the large squires and the smaller squires. At the top of the first group came the older aristocracy – the Earls of Essex, the Stanleys and the Talbots, or the smaller peers of the midland shires, men whose income was unlikely to fall below £3,000 a year and might rise to five times as much, as in the case of the Duke of Bedford. At the bottom of the third group came the disgruntled, penurious Tory squire living on a few hundreds a year, jealous of those above and below him, peerage and yeomanry. The peerage he regarded as the corrupt oligarchy that represented the power of London, Dutch finance, profligacy disguised as toleration: the yeomanry he saw as a menace to his partridges, a threat to be dealt with by game laws preventing the yeomanry from shooting even on their own land and (in due course) by property qualifications that would keep them out of Parliament. This was Macaulay's country squire – hard up, ignorant, parochial, his dialect as yet uncorrupted by a public school system designed to iron out the provincialisms of its pupils. His estate and crops were, wrote Macaulay, his chief preoccupation. 'He examined samples of grain, handled pigs, and on market days, made bargains over a tankard with drovers and hop merchants.' Hard drinking, hospitable, he enjoyed his animosities, hating everything that was strange, including all foreigners, dissenters, Jews and Londoners. Poverty and the consciousness of his exclusion from politics and fashionable life commonly kept him a Tory, even a Jacobite. Yet, unlettered and boorish as he might in many ways be, he was, as Macaulay said, in some most important points a gentleman, a member of a proud if rustic aristocracy, jealous of his family pride, a magistrate, and when need arose, a soldier. He combined, in short, features that a later age was to deem characteristic of either plebs or patriciate, but not of both. Yet Macaulay was right: this mixture of ignorance and shrewdness, brutishness and authority, was the mark of a rustic *élite*. In its upper reaches, it shaded into the second of our three classes – the upper squirearchy – the Ishams and Treshams, Drydens and Osbornes of the Midlands, the Cokes and Walpoles of the eastern shires – who stood midway between the great aristocrats and the yeomanry.

It is not easy to assess the part played by the great aristocratic landowners in rural improvement. That the numbers of really large estates were increasing in the second half of the seventeenth century seems not to be in doubt, and the trend may have been hastened by changes in the law which made it easier to entail estates. Instead of being broken up by death and by debt, the large estates held together and became even larger. By making it more difficult to sell land and realize cash the new arrangements often left the larger landowner short of that working capital that was needed to run his estate most profitably. Even the biggest landowners were often short of cash. There was for them, as for smaller men, a potential stimulus towards greater efficiency. In some cases they took farms in hand themselves, profiting by more efficient methods directly rather than by the slow putting up of their tenants' rents. But probably more chose to live mainly from their rent rolls. In 1641 the Earl of Bedford's income was £8,500, but he was still heavily in debt – the penalty of neglect that stretched back to Elizabeth's days. By the Restoration a vigorous campaign of improvement on all his properties, urban and rural, had increased his income by 50 per cent and turned him from a debtor to creditor. Poverty, as the historian of the Bedford family remarks, was the spur.[1]

The great landowners seem generally to have been pretty easygoing landlords, preferring a steady tenant at a low or moderate rent to a less sound man at a higher figure. That they could afford to do this, and postpone the systematic exploitation of their assets till later, was probably because they could help themselves from other sources and resources. High social connexions brought them the possibility of offices, pensions, sinecures. Their broad properties might include acres ripe for urban development, with all the consequent increment in site values, as the Bedford properties in London were to be the sites of docks, shops and great houses. Or they might conceal mineral wealth, as the Lowther property at Whitehaven contained coal, or the Foley and Leveson Gower estates in the Midlands contained iron. Income from coal and iron mines made up an increasing proportion of the fortune of Lord Dudley on his Black Country estates. By the end of the century it accounted for nearly half a rent roll that totalled over £5,000 a year.[2] Most commonly, the heir might be prudently married to a rich heiress to restore or improve the family fortunes, as the Marquis of Tavistock was married off in 1695 to the granddaughter of Sir Josiah Child, the Grand Cham of the East India Company and one of the greatest merchant financiers of the late seventeenth-century London.

In general one must look a little further down the social scale to find the main source of 'improvement'. Not, perhaps, to the lowest strata of the squirearchy. Enterprise does not seem to have flourished conspicuously amongst this class though here and there is evidence in the Midlands of a nucleus of tenacious yeomen who were swimming

[1] Gladys Scott-Thomson, *Life in a Noble Household 1641-1700*, 1937, pp. 21, 113, 366.
[2] W. H. B. Court, *The Rise of Midland Industry*, 1953, p. 154.

successfully against the tide that engulfed so many of their kind. Some were even turning themselves into a kind of fustian gentry.[1] Small landowners and tenant farmers felt the draught of lower grain prices from time to time. Some, no doubt, fell by the wayside, but others took advantage of growing urban demand and even enjoyed modest prosperity. Those who did best were the ones who concentrated on dairy products, poultry and livestock, bought their feeding stuffs more cheaply if they did not grow enough themselves and marketed their surpluses in the near-by towns. Such working farmers, unburdened by social pretension or the need to keep up appearances, probably did better than some of their social superiors amongst the lower squirearchy.

The numbers of the latter seem to have diminished in these years, as the wars demanded an increasing share of their incomes in the shape of the land tax, as rents fell away and as poor rates rose in the 1690s. Those on the loose fringe of the gentry were liable to get detached unless they were lucky enough to have other sources of support. Hence their detestation of the war, the ministry and the City. In all this they shared their misfortunes and often their principles and prejudices with the upper gentry; yet the number of larger squires seems to have remained pretty stable. It was amongst them that most evidence is to be found of enterprise and innovation in estate management. The upper Norfolk gentry, whose estates were at this period the foremost nursery of rural improvement, illustrated the problems, opportunities and social rivalries that form the background to rural change. In a world from which many of the older names — the Pastons, the Palgraves, the Heydons — were disappearing, the new gentry were jostling for position. First in size were the Cokes, the descendants of old Edward who had bought the manor of Holkham in 1610, adding it to the portion of his wife (herself a Paston). Some ten miles to the south lay the estate of the Townshends at Raynham, grouped round the house built (if legend is correct) by Inigo Jones early in the seventeenth century. A few miles westwards, at Houghton, were the Walpole estates. While the Townshends had been rewarded for loyalty and ascended into the peerage at the Restoration, the Walpoles, though of an ancient lineage, remained plain gentry. If Horace Walpole is to be believed, Sir Robert's father had £2,000 a year, of which he spent only £64 on the pleasures of the winter season that he passed in London as a Member of Parliament. 'He little thought', wrote Horace, 'that what maintained him for

[1] W. G. Hoskins, *The Midland Peasant*, 1957, ch. VII.

153

a whole session would scarce serve one of his younger grandsons to buy japans and fans for the princesses at Florence.'

These were the years when the foundations of later fortunes and careers were laid. By the turn of the century, when Robert Walpole inherited the estates, the home farms at Houghton and Dersingham were models of crop rotation, mixed animal and arable husbandry, manuring, marling, hoeing. Walpole kept up a vigorous correspondence with his steward when he was absent from Norfolk in which all the details of management were explained and reported. The farming practice on the home farms was compulsorily applied on the Walpole tenants' farms too. 'Had he lost in his struggle with Townshend in 1730', writes Walpole's biographer, 'doubtless he would have been known to posterity as turnip Walpole!' [1]

The Norfolk gentry enjoyed special gifts of Providence – soil, weather, knowledge – which were not vouchsafed to all members of their class in other parts of England. Their problems, however, were shared almost everywhere by an aristocracy and gentry that had ever new temptations to live beyond their means. Everywhere the later seventeenth century provides abundant evidence of rising standards of upper-class living. Great mansions like Chatsworth in Derbyshire, Petworth in Sussex and Dyrham Park in Gloucestershire were being built in the eighties and nineties, massive witness to the wealth of the nobility, timely refreshed by the profits of place or office and solidified by well-ordered marriage alliances. Such palaces continued the traditions of Inigo Jones, and were to multiply and grow more magnificent as Vanbrugh's visions took splendid if sometimes uninhabitable shape in the following decades. But they were less characteristic in these years than the scores of smaller, more comfortable houses that sprang up all over England. There is hardly a stretch of country without its pleasant Wrenish manor house that dates from this period. Christopher Wren stood as acknowledged master of architectural taste and practice: most of all, as the designer of what Horace Walpole called 'the snug, middling house for middling people'. They ranged from mansions of modest size like the Moot at Downton in Wiltshire, built about 1690, to Belton House in Lincolnshire. At Belton Sir John Brownlow, descended (like the Cokes) from a successful Jacobean lawyer, built the largest and most handsome of the country houses attributed to Wren. All these mansions achieved a new elegance. Glazed windows and plentiful coal supplies freed architects and occupiers from the hazards of

[1] J. H. Plumb, 'Sir R. Walpole and Norfolk Husbandry,' *Econ. Hist. Rev.* V. no. 1, 1952.

winter faced by their predecessors. Where even Tudor mansions were often found placed in hollows out of wind and weather, the newer houses were on rising ground or in open spaces ready to survey a noble prospect of park and valley. Much of the social history of England in these years is the history of the life that went on within such houses — the purchase of tapestries and damasks, of Dutch and French furniture and marquetry work, of marbles and mirrors, of paintings, clocks and vases, of sumptuous meals of unbelievable length served by a growing army of servants, black as well as local, of topiary gardens, ponds, statues, grottoes and parks.

A not unimportant chapter of our economic history ought to be concerned with how this new phase of increasing luxury was financed. It is improbable that it could always be paid for out of income in times that were often precarious for farmers and landlords, more especially in the so-called barren years. There can have been few more prudent or thrifty squires in England than Colonel Walpole. Yet even he found the inevitable costs of family, estate and citizenship pressing him hard in the 1680s and 1690s: annuities for indigent relatives, an extravagant wife, the costs of fighting an election in 1698. New farms that were added to his estates were bought with borrowed money. When even sober living necessitated loans, one can guess the consequence of extravagance.[1] Providentially for the propertied classes, this age when new and seductive luxuries beckoned on every hand was also the time when the means of obtaining credit were multiplying. Bills of exchange and promissory notes increasingly transferable made it possible to remit money from place to place. A new banking system was growing in London from the mid-century and in a few provincial towns like Bristol and Nottingham. Bankers were recruited from a number of trades and professions. One was the profession of the scriveners.[2]

From Tudor times until well into the eighteenth century, the scrivener's work — preparing bonds, drawing up mortgages, advancing money to clients — was suspect as a form of usury; a scandal of the times, even to Defoe. The scrivener's function was not precisely that of the later banker. He was more like a mixture of land agent, investment broker and money lender, and the conditions in the nineties made him much more in demand. 'If these high land taxes long continue, in a country so little given to thrift as ours', wrote Charles Davenant in 1695, 'the landed men must inevitably be driven into the hands of

[1] *Studies in Social History. A Tribute to Trevelyan*, ed. J. H. Plumb, 1955, ch. VI.
[2] J. K. Horsefield, *British Monetary Experiments 1650–1710*, 1960, p. xiii.

Scriveners, citizens and usurers, except some few of the most wary families.'[1] That many were so driven, the papers of one of the largest scriveners, Sir Robert Clayton, 'arch-scrivener of the age' who rose to be Lord Mayor of London in 1679, provide eloquent witness. Sir Compton Reade desires to mortgage Denford Manor 'rather than to be longer in ye Alderman's debt'. Sir Thomas Peyton offers his property as security for a loan in 1669. Sir John Mayney gives details of land 'to be mortgaged for £3,000 for four or five years'. (It is already mortgaged for £4,000 of which £1,000 is paid off.) The same client wants to mortgage other property in Kent for £3,000 at 7 per cent. 1,500 acres of Sir John Cotton's estates at Farningham are to be sold to pay his debts. Lord Strangford borrows £2,000 on mortgage. And so on. Clayton's own lavish home at Bletchingly was acquired from Lord Peterboro who sold it to pay his debts.[2]

Diaries, letters and lawsuits of the time all tell the same tale of estates 'encumbered' with debt. There can be little doubt that Davenant was correct: many a country gentleman spent first and cast about for means to pay later. The commonest conception of collateral security for a loan was land: it was never more to the fore than in the nineties, when a number of schemes for 'land banks' were put forward. Of one, founded by the ingenious Dr Nicolas Barbon, it has been said that it would today be described as a building society. The essence of the scheme was that the 'bank' should borrow at 2 per cent and lend not only to Government but to landowners who would be enabled to borrow at $3\frac{1}{2}$ per cent — a comparatively low rate — up to three-quarters of the value of their land.[3] If the land bank proposal had succeeded, it would have canalized and centralized what was in fact going on all over England in scores of offices of scriveners, lawyers, attorneys and money lenders.

Much of the borrowing described above was needed to pay for that extravagance and ostentation which contemporaries saw, rightly, as a growing characteristic of the age. Its economic and moral implications were to be a popular topic with philosophers from Mandeville to Dr Johnson.[4] In other cases, the debts which burdened the land arose from unavoidable necessity. Of the so-called 'delinquents' lands that had been sold during the Interregnum, some fell into the hands of London speculators but in many cases the former Royalist owners

[1] Quoted by D. C. Coleman, 'London Scriveners and the Estate Market in the later Seventeenth Century', *Econ. Hist. Rev.*, IV, no. 2, 1951.
[2] Coleman, op. cit.
[3] Horsefield, op. cit., ch. 16.
[4] See below, pp. 351–7.

managed to buy their lands back by the time of the Restoration. The Marquis of Winchester got back all but two of his fifteen estates in Hampshire and Berkshire. Lord Arundel, the Duke of Newcastle and many others were equally successful in putting the clock back: but often only at the cost of burdening the recovered property with debt.[1]

Quite apart from these costs of political loyalty and defeat land-owners faced the continuing expense of improvement itself. To enclose the open fields, to hedge, ditch, wall, embank, drain, resite buildings and roads, clear forests, reclaim waste, fen and marsh, was a costly business which few could meet from their own resources. Sometimes, where the initiative came from the leasehold farmers and local freeholders, they might contribute to the expense of an agreed scheme. Even where the initiative came from the squire, he might be able to insist on contri-butions from tenants in times when tenants were plentiful and rents buoyant. But more often the cost fell on the landlord. He could only meet it by borrowing. And it was no worse for a squire to raise credit on the security of an improved estate scheme of this kind than it is for a modern business corporation to raise funds from the public for a sound enterprise, or for a householder to raise a mortgage on his pro-perty. In both cases, the lender receives his dividend or interest. The promoters reap the reward of their enterprise in better profits.

However the 'encumbrance' of debt may have come about, the need to pay interest on it, and ultimately to extinguish it or be extinguished by it, must have spurred on many a landlord, agent and bailiff to negotiate new leases and higher rents with the tenants. The tenant farmer and the rents he paid are two of the central features of English farming and we have no adequate study of either. Nor do we know much about a figure of crucial importance: the estate steward. On his good sense, enterprise and honesty many a landed family's future de-pended. The problem of estimating the average level of rents is com-plicated by the survival of customary tenures, but in general good enclosed arable land seems to have let at from 10s. to £1 an acre; in some areas of market gardening or commercial crops the return was much higher. Plenty of farmers in the twentieth century have paid less.

What of the commercial methods which it is often said were introduced by merchants and tradesmen seeking social status through land? Everywhere, but especially round London, successful City men

[1] Joan Thirsk, 'The Sales of Royalist Land During the Interregnum', *Econ. Hist. Rev.*, V, no. 2, 1952.

could be identified as buyers of land. Often they succeeded hereditary owners who had failed to improve their rents to keep pace with their debts. Such a one was Sir John Banks (1629-99) a self-made man, Governor of the East India Company who died worth £200,000. He had married his daughter and co-heir to Heneage Finch, later Earl of Aylesford. In the last forty years of the century Banks raised his rent roll from £800 a year to £5,000. Some surviving correspondence shows him bombarding his agent with queries about potential value of properties for sale — what rent this tenant pays, whether he has a lease, for how long, and whether the land will hold the rent. Will such and such a farm let well? Is it likely to be well tenanted? How does it lie? What are the rates for drainage? Does it lie near the markets? And so on.[1] Sir William Courteen, another prosperous London merchant of Flemish origin, with a rich Dutch wife, and varied business interests[2] bought the manor of Laxton in Nottinghamshire: obviously with the intention of making his estates pay. Customary tenures were replaced by leases whenever possible, rents raised to a more economic level. In the end his income from his midland estates totalled £6,500 a year. Such examples could be multiplied many times over. They illustrate an influence that was certainly important. Yet its permanent effects on agricultural management can be exaggerated. Many of the newcomers were getting on in years when they took to the countryside. They went there with the object of 'gentleizing' their sons and grandsons. They often had to endure a frustrating period of probation before they were fully admitted to the world of the county families. Many of the midland squirearchy were second- or third-generation descendants of merchant families. Some of them in turn fell victim to newer and sharper city men, as Sir Lewis Tresham fell to Alderman Cokayne, leaving his great house to become the seat of Cokayne's ennobled descendants. Such aspirants to social status would not always want to remind their neighbours of their commercial origins by attending too officiously to the business of their estates. If estate management was becoming more efficient, this was more likely to be the result of purely economic factors than of any hereditary commercial flair among the 'new' landowners. The scramble for land in the seventeenth century was not only the effect of a snobbish desire for social prestige among successful tradesmen. It was also caused by the absence of other channels of investment open to men looking for safety for their capital

[1] Coleman, op. cit., quoting the Clayton MSS in the Kent County Archives.
[2] See above, p. 122.

and a return on their money.[1] Competition drove up land prices to a point where even the newcomers, rich though they might be, had to consider how to obtain a reasonable return on a very large outlay of capital. This problem caused economists like Petty to doubt the merits of land as a form of investment. Some form of improved agriculture was necessary if rents were to be raised to economic levels. Improvement was therefore not merely a gentlemanly hobby amongst landowners. It was a gentlemanly necessity, especially to those who bought land at the new prices. Whether the new men were as a class more efficient managers of their estates than the old, like the Percys or the Bedfords, it is impossible to say. Henry Percy, ninth Earl of Northumberland, was evidently a match for any tycoon. But there were probably few great estate owners, old or new, who could direct their heirs (as he did) 'to understand your estate better than any one of your officers'.[2] Generally, the most precious gift Providence could bestow on a country gentleman was a good steward. Casting his mind back over the history of his family estates Roger North recalled gratefully 'the venerable old steward, careful by nature and faithful to his lord, employing all his thoughts and time to manage for the supply of his house and upholding his rents'.[3] Many a lord and gentleman must have felt the same.

[1] See H. J. Habbakuk, 'The Land Market in the Eighteenth Century', in *Britain and the Netherlands*, ed. J. S. Bromley and E. H. Kossmann, 1960.

[2] *The Household Papers of Henry Percy, Ninth Earl of Northumberland 1564-1632*, ed. G. R. Batho, 1962.

[3] See the essay by Edward Hughes, 'The Eighteenth-century Estate Agent' in *Essays in Honour of J. E. Todd*, 1949.

CHAPTER EIGHT

England the World's Entrepôt

AFTER a half century during which depression and maladjustment had been a chronic feature of English economic life, the Restoration was the occasion for economic as well as political renewal. The loyal bells, bonfires and rejoicings had their parallel in a revived economic optimism. The obverse of the earthy realism that was to pervade politics for a century was a renewed conviction that private initiative in trade could be combined with the use of government regulation and naval power to achieve a great advance in national prosperity. Charles himself entered into this new task with zest. It was to prove characteristically short-lived, but the wider hopes of the men of business were not in the end disappointed. The economy steadily assumed a new pattern, acquiring a momentum which, in spite of temporary setbacks, was not to slacken until the century was nearing its end. This remarkable era of change and growth can be briefly summarized. England's foreign trade grew rapidly in volume, geographical range and variety. Longer voyages and bulkier cargoes — not only coal, timber and grain but also colonial goods like sugar, tobacco and cotton — demanded more tonnage, bigger and better designed ships. The old staple of the export trade — cloth — changed its character and bulked less large in total trade. Above all, the transatlantic traders came to account for an increasing proportion of imports and re-exports. Such changes were gradually reflected in the figures of the trade balance. The inquiries of earlier investigators like Cranfield had revealed a balance only dubious and precarious.[1] After the Restoration the position was still far from satisfactory. In the autumn of 1669 the House of Lords appointed a committee 'to consider of the causes and grounds of the fall of rents and decay of trade within these Kingdoms'. The result was a preview of the balance of trade similar to that which was to become a regular return from 1696 onwards.[2] Adjusted for

[1] See above, p. 60.
[2] See below, pp. 229 and 354. For a discussion of the value of the figures see Harper,

errors, the figures show that in the 1660s total exports stood at about £4·1 million, total imports at about £4·4 million. On the same principles, the corresponding figures in 1700 were respectively £6·4 million and £5·8 million. That is to say, a deficit of − £·3 million on foreign trade had been converted into a surplus of + £·6 million. It can also be assumed that England was earning more by way of 'invisible' exports — shipping services, insurance commissions, etc.[1]

Exports had thus increased by more than half, imports by just over one-third in these forty years. But this differential rate of growth, with its resultant effect on the trade balance, was not the whole story. In the 60s, re-exports accounted for less than a quarter of the export totals. By 1700, they represented about 30 per cent and much of this trade was provided by the import of cargoes of raw materials, foods and textiles from the colonies and tropical areas — America, the West Indies, India and the East. These areas were supplying about a third of our total imports by 1700. Finally, although London continued to dominate England's trade overseas, the share of the 'outports' had begun a steady increase. In part it came from the growth of new industries in the hinterland of ports like Exeter, Bristol, Liverpool and Hull, and in part from the favourable geographical position of the west coast ports in relation to the expanding Atlantic economy. Profound change was overtaking the whole economy. England was becoming a world entrepôt, serving not only Europe but the extra-European world, and was herself served by a growing fleet of merchant shipping, a growing equipment of docks, shipyards, wharves and warehouses, a growing community of merchants and tradesmen. Those older historians who used to call this the period 'the Commercial Revolution' were not after all, far wrong.[2]

The economic regulations of the Interregnum were torn out of the Statute Book along with the rest of its legislation. The early years of the Restoration therefore saw a vigorous reconstruction of this apparatus of economic control and stimulation. Its principles were not new. Just as in earlier years, monarchical or republican, the aims remained those of economic and strategic self-sufficiency, expansion, and the exclusion

[1] The costs of foreign wars, embassies, etc., are imponderables left out of account for the moment.

[2] For details see Mr Davis's article referred to above and his *Rise of the English Shipping Industry*, ch. 2 and *passim*.

op. cit. *The English Navigation Laws*, p. 420 et seq, also R. Davis, 'English Foreign Trade 1660–1700', *Econ. Hist. Rev.*, VII, no. 2, 1954.

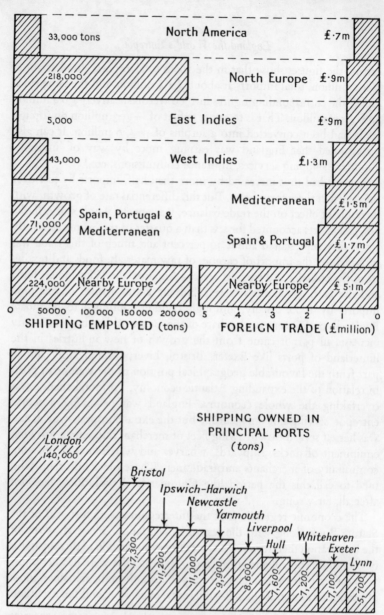

SHIPPING AND TRADE IN 1700

This chart is based on tables from Ralph Davis's *The Rise of the English Shipping Industry* (1962). They illustrate how different were *tonnage* and *value*, e.g. the East Indies tonnage is very low in relation to the high value of its cargoes. The North European trades, contrariwise, employed a large tonnage carrying cargoes of comparatively low value. 'Nearby Europe' employed only slightly more tonnage than North Europe but the *value* of its cargoes was more than five times that of the latter.

of the Dutch from their dominant position in the economy. But the revived system was constructed by men with a greater skill and cunning that derived from longer and keener observation of the problems to be tackled, and with a shrewder awareness of the loopholes in the older legislation. Now, more than ever before, the legislator looked to the New World and Asia and Africa to seek freedom from the thraldom — as they saw it — to Dutch economic superiority in Europe.

Cloth no longer enjoyed quite its old and dangerous domination over exports: but it still remained far the largest manufacture, representing somewhere between three-quarters and a half of total exports by value. In September 1660, therefore, the King lent a ready ear to a petition from the clothiers. 'For some years past', they asserted, 'the Dutch have designed to beat down and discourage the manufacture in this realm, and to gaine the same to themselves, which they have in great measure effected . . . in order to that designe thay have imposed immoderate imposts upon English cloth imported into their countries.' Demanding that such tariffs be revoked before any treaty was made with Holland they went on to ask for the old penalties against the export of wool, yarn, fuller's earth, etc., to be renewed, and the import of rival luxury textiles to be forbidden. Renewed they were; and the old regulations reserving the supply of local raw materials to this major English industry were to be primed watchfully by successive administrations down to the Napoleonic wars.

The inadequacy of the Navigation Act of 1651 had become evident long before the Restoration. Even if the Act itself had not been repudiated it would have been necessary to amend it. The Masters of Trinity House, representing the shipowners, declined to agree that the 'Act or pretended Act' (as they called it) was of benefit to English shipping 'unless it had been more Exactly performed'. Its chief weakness was that it had done nothing to make sure that the ownership and nationality of ships could be identified. If a master chose to swear that his ship was English-owned, it was impossible to disprove him. In any case many ships were Dutch built. In the European trades, it had proved impossible to enforce the Act and even in the colonial trades it seemed to be more honoured in the breach than in the observance. The new Act of 1660 derived from the same principles and ambitions as its predecessors, but more effort was now directed to making its provisions workable, even if this meant limiting its objectives. To make enforcement more practicable, all foreign-built ships in English ownership were to be registered. (Two years later, the Act of Frauds added that any foreign-built ship not registered by 1 October 1662 was to be deemed alien.)[1] Again, the master and three-quarters of the crew of English-owned ships were to be English. Again, the main concern of the new Act was to control imports. But whereas the old Act had tried to enforce a blanket prohibition on imports in Dutch ships, the new one limited itself to ensuring that *specific* commodities should be imported in English ships or ships belonging to the country where the goods originated. From the Baltic, timber and naval stores, from the Mediterranean, fruits, oils, wines, spirits and salt, were so named. In all, about half Europe's trade to England was reserved — as it was said, 'enumerated' — in this way. Equally stringent rules were then applied to the colonial trades. Sugar, tobacco, cotton wool and dyes for the cloth industry from English colonies might only be exported to England in English or colonial ships.[2]

By 1662, then, two of the pillars of the Navigation or Old Colonial System, as it came to be known, had been set up. In the next year came the third, the so-called Staple Act (or Act for the Encouragement of Trade), which bound the colonists to buy nearly all the European goods they needed in England, and carry them in English-owned and English-manned ships. Further Acts of 1673 and 1696 were necessary to complete the arrangements for enforcing the Act, but in principle the legislation of the first three years after the Restoration laid the foundations of the system by which English overseas trade was to be regulated for more than a century and a half. Many ideas, old and new, were combined in its workings. The rules affecting shipping found their roots in a myriad of laws, mostly confused and confusing, that dated from the Middle Ages. Its spirit derived from the Committee of the 1620s.[3] By automatically restricting imports, it paid tribute to the conception of the balance of trade. By eliminating the cost of foreign freight charges and replacing invisible imports by invisible exports in the shape of English shipping earnings, it recognized the same principle. By canalizing a large volume of English trade with the outside world in English ships and making England its focus, it aimed to create, by legislative compulsion backed by naval force, an entrepôt system such as the Dutch had created by spontaneous effort. And it was able to do this with more confidence because Europe's centre of

---

[1] The registration of English-built ships was not enforced until the 1690s, and thereafter only gradually. The 'statistics' of shipping cannot be regarded as satisfactory until 1785.

[2] See below, p. 187, for the importance of the new colonial dyestuffs to the cloth industry.

[3] See *supra*, chapters III & IV.

economic gravity was shifting westwards. As the settlements spread in North America and the West Indies, and were linked with the growth of trading and slaving ports on the West African coast, England was better placed for strategic control in the unending war of trade. Hence the zeal with which a vociferous section of the merchant community clamoured for a Dutch war in the four years after the Restoration. Its aim was stated simply and brutally by the Duke of Albemarle. 'What we want is more of the trade the Dutch now have.' Neither Charles, nor Clarendon, nor the wiser heads among the royal advisers, like William Coventry, nor, at a humbler level, Pepys, wanted another trial of strength. But by 1664 the war party had its way. New Amsterdam, a notorious loophole in the new navigation system, was captured and converted into New York. The Dutch trading posts in Africa were harassed. This second attack on the Dutch trade ended in disaster and humiliation, with the enemy landing along the Medway and towing away the largest English battleship they could find, the *Royal Charles*. No statistics illustrate the rapidly changing pattern of world trade so well as the difference between the operations of the First and Second Dutch Wars. Where the first had been conducted almost entirely in home waters, the second ramified all over the world — as far as North America, the West Indies, East Indies and West Africa. The prize was larger, and it was more temptingly within the reach of the larger, more powerful and better-manned ships that were becoming available.[1]

Was the System, as Adam Smith said, merely a conspiracy of merchants for their own interests, a plot which sacrificed the interests of consumers to those of producers, replacing 'one fruitless care' (the control of bullion) by another 'much more intricate, much more embarrassing, and equally fruitless' (the balance of trade)?[2] How just was the charge that 'our merchants and manufacturers have been by far the principal architects'? And how did such charges square with the final concession that the Navigation Acts were 'perhaps the wisest of all the commercial regulations of England', which had properly sacrificed opulence to defence? More is known nowadays than was known to Adam Smith about the processes by which private and public interests were blended to issue in legislation.[3] Economic reconstruction

[1] C. Wilson, *Profit and Power*, 1957, ch. VII.

[2] Adam Smith, *The Wealth of Nations*, 1776, bk. IV.

[3] C. M. Andrews, *British Committees Commissions and Councils of Trade and Plantations 1622-75* (Baltimore, 1908); A. P. Thornton, *West India Policy under the Restoration*, esp. ch. I; R. W. K. Hinton, *The Eastland Trade and the Common Weal*.

was the work of Crown and Parliament. But it was only part of the whole task of replacing disorder by order and this was plainly beyond the capacity of the twenty-eight members who comprised the Privy Council. An increased proportion of economic policy-making was therefore entrusted to committees of the Privy Council: the habit of inviting mercantile experts into consultation was an old and familiar one. Many of the same merchants and financiers who had advised Charles's father and even his grandfather, as well as many who had aided Cromwell, were now called in to help. Some were economic Vicars of Bray who had managed to serve all. Yet, except for the great bankers,[1] they were rarely admitted into the innermost counsels of state. Commercial interests were consulted, M.P.s in Parliament and out urged the needs of regions and industries, brains were picked, knighthoods distributed, but the control of policy remained in the hands of the great politicians whose birthright government was. And 'policy' did not consist merely of satisfying the clamour of influential merchants or companies. It had to compass the preservation of public order that might be endangered by large-scale unemployment or food shortages, the yield and collection of tax revenue, and problems of national defence. In the very early days, it did seem possible that two committees — those of Trade and of Foreign Plantations — might prove so heavily weighted by merchant members that the traditional machinery of government might be overwhelmed by sheer numbers. But like all overgrown committees they proved self-defeating. The interests of the members were too diverse to allow them any collective momentum. The conduct of day-to-day business reverted therefore to the great Companies. The Privy Councillors ceased to attend the swollen committees, and after declining into an academic debating society, the Council of Trade died of inanition in 1667. Over the Plantations Committee the Privy Council fairly swiftly re-established its hold. The habitual governing class who comprised it had the habit of command. Merchants had not. When Pepys was called into the Treasury Commission he was received with a characteristic brusquerie. 'I do like the way of these lords [he wrote] that they admit nobody to use many words, nor do they spend many words themselves, but in great state do hear what they see necessary, and say little themselves, but bid withdraw.'[2] Yet the grandees themselves could not manage the whole of public business and its intricate detail. They had their private business and pleasures to manage. They did not always have either

[1] See below, p. 213.   [2] *Diary*, 3 June 1667.

the capacity or the application to endure protracted sessions of intricate discussion of public business, especially of economic affairs. This was doubtless the situation that Adam Smith had in mind when he wrote that between tradesmen who did not understand the principles of national policy and gentlemen who failed to grasp the principles of trade, policy fell into an erroneous obsession with trade balances. But he left out one element of supreme importance in policy-making: the presence of those Crown servants who, after the Restoration, and increasingly in the seventies and eighties, came to exercise a powerful influence on Crown policy. They sat in the Commons and on Privy Council committees, were to be found on the boards of the great Companies, and served in the great departments of state. In all these offices, men like the Coventrys (William and Henry), Sir George Downing, Sir Joseph Williamson, Sir Leoline Jenkins, and later, Sir William Blathwayt acted as interpreters and brokers between the interests of individuals and companies on the one hand, and the Government and the public interest (as they understood it) on the other. After the Revolution, another group of experts was drawn into public affairs. When the Board of Trade was re-created in 1695 it contained not only great merchants like Sir Josiah Child of the East India Company and Gilbert Heathcote, the great banker, but Davenant, the economist, Wren, Newton, and, above all, John Locke, the philosopher. Such men were not yet civil servants in the full, later sense. But they were certainly not mere puppets of tradesmen, whose narrow vision and short-sightedness they often despised. Even the minor ones, like Downing, were men of great ability and independence of mind. Collectively they came to form a 'Third Force' between dynasticism and vested economic interests. In such formidable company, the merchant lobbyer might expect a searching cross-examination before his representations were accepted as conforming to the needs of public policy.[1]

This determination of the Government to retain control of economic policy is a persistent theme of seventeenth-century history. Although that control wavered at times, it was never wholly lost, and of all the diligent royal servants who ensured its continuance, none was more remarkable than Sir George Downing. Personally unattractive, officious, long-winded, two-faced and mean, he had acquired — not least in Holland itself — a grasp of the economic realities of power which made him indispensable. Cynically realistic as usual, Charles had

---

[1] On Locke's appointment, see P. Laslett, 'John Locke, the Great Recoinage and the Origins of the Board of Trade: 1695–1698', *William and Mary Quarterly*, July 1957.

knighted this old enemy even before he returned to claim his throne. Henceforth Downing's hand was to be seen in most of the economic and financial developments of the next decade. If the mercantile system had an architect, it was he. His own hatred of the Dutch and his ability to organize similar hatred in others were prime irritants that led to the Second Dutch War.

The autarchic logic of the balance of trade was fundamental to Downing's economic thought. To a reluctant admiration for Dutch economic skill, he added a venomous jealousy of the success it had brought them, mixed with a contempt for the short-sighted laziness of the average English merchant and a special antipathy for the financiers who, he thought, were fleecing the Crown by charging it exorbitant rates of interest for the loan of money. His letters to his various masters, before and after the Restoration, were filled with schemes to deny raw materials to the Dutch, to entice skilled artisans to emigrate to England, bringing knowledge which would save money spent on unnecessary imports from abroad. 'I have this day', he would write to Clarendon from Holland, 'given a pass to an Englishman to goe for England who is a weaver of camlotts & moohairs.' To Pepys he boasted that he had spent seven years finding a man who could dress sheepskin and thereby save England £100,000 a year spent on imported kid leather. But it was especially his perception of Dutch superiority in shipbuilding and ship management and their concentration on building up trade in bulk cargoes that was most important for practical thought and policy. The Dutch ruled the Baltic by controlling the inward freight of herrings and salt, while the English, having no such cargoes, had to send their ships north in ballast and at a loss. English ships were 'so little in the hold & so big above water' that they were unwieldy to manage and un-economic to run. The Dutch ship only needed half the crew of an English ship. Specialized cargo ships built for cheapness, unarmed, were the secret of Dutch success. 'In this very thinge is the Mystery of their state and by this Meanes doe they gayne all their wealth.' It could be England's secret, too, if English traders could be persuaded or com-pelled to copy Dutch methods. Here was a great potential source of wealth, employment and power to be had by merely keeping at home the money England paid the Dutch for freight and wages. And so to the moral: 'If England were once brought to a Navigation as cheape as this Country [Holland] good night, Amsterdam.' Such ideas, reiter-ated in and out of season, were at this stage the obsession of Downing's life. They found expression in the Navigation Act of 1660 and the

Staple Act of 1663, both of which he helped to pilot through Parliament. Yet Downing, though on occasion a toady to the grandees, was certainly not a lackey of the merchant interest, which he frequently and bitterly opposed. He shared to the full that expansive and brutally realistic view of the ideal economy expressed by Child: that 'Profit and Power ought jointly to be considered'. An overseas trade that depended on a few cargoes of cloth, however valuable, was not enough. There must be bulk cargoes to encourage the growth of England's mercantile marine. Such a fleet must be backed by a powerful navy drawing its crews from the growing pool of tough and experienced deep-sea sailors. By the size and strength of the fleet, and by the condition of the trade balance, all men could measure whether England was or was not great. Downing was not an original thinker: his contribution was to reinforce a trend of thought common to the age from a fund of shrewd observation, common sense and administrative ability that lay buried behind his unengaging front and his prolix and tortuous speeches in Parliament and elsewhere. Few men in this century did more to bring forth practical policy from the clamour of private interests and the fiscal needs of government. It was not inappropriate that he left his name inscribed on the heart of Whitehall.

The growing volume and diversity of England's foreign trade, modest by later standards but dramatic by comparison with what had gone before, can be measured in a number of ways. The most reliable is to analyse the cargoes and ships. Of the new commodities being carried into consumption tobacco, sugar, textiles were the chief. In 1615 England imported some 50,000 lb. of tobacco. In 1700 she imported 38 million lb. Of this 13 million lb. was consumed at home; twice as much was re-exported to Europe and elsewhere. The Virginian and West Indian plantations expanded dramatically. At home, what had been a luxury at threepence a pipeful fell in price until it stood at a shilling a pound in the 1670s. The tobacco habit spread to the middle and even the labouring classes. The western ports drove a thriving trade in importing, packing, refining and reselling it. Similarly with sugar. In 1600 Brazil was still the main producer. From 1640 first Barbados, then Jamaica, poured their production into the market and prices fell by half until the 1680s. West Indian imports into England rose from 150,000 cwt. after the Restoration to over 370,000 cwt. by the end of the century. Again, about two-thirds were consumed at home, one-third was re-exported, and again the western ports appear as centres of sugar boiling, refining and marketing. From the East (via the East India and Levant Companies) came a stream of luxury cargoes – spices, silks and fine fabrics. But there was besides a growing volume of calicoes unknown in earlier times. Between 1600 and 1700 these increased from 240,000 to 861,000 pieces, of which about two-thirds went to the re-export trades. This stream of Indian imports stimulated first a clamour for protection by local textile producers, then a series of violent attacks on the importing companies and finally a revolution in the character of the English textile industry itself.[1] These three trades accounted for two-thirds of colonial imports to England and a similar proportion of English re-exports.

The pattern of steadily diversifying foreign trade was completed by two other trades. One was the trade in cod caught off the rich banks of Newfoundland. Already a motley collection of fishermen much like that cosmopolitan raggle-taggle described later by Kipling in *Captains Courageous* were engaged in a task valued by governments not only for its profit but also for the experience of deep-sea navigation it offered. The product – 'poor John' as it was called – sold well in the Mediter-ranean, and the fishing ships drove a valuable round trip that brought back Mediterranean goods to England. 'Cod from Newfoundland', it has been said, 'was the lever by which she [England] wrested her share of the riches of the New World from Spain.'[2] No wonder the Pope became the toast of the Newfoundland fishermen. In the opposite direction, the mixed cargoes which went to West Africa bought slaves who formed the labour force with which the West Indies and southern plantations built up their exports of sugar, tobacco, and later, cotton, to England and Europe. Finally, the newly protected colonial markets drew an increasing volume of manufactured exports from England; brass, copper, and iron wares, silk and linen, tallow, glass, earthenware, paper, cordage, leather and, of course, woollens. Europe took these things also; and, through the Dutch, a growing volume of English corn and English coal – not cargoes of high value in relation to size, but *bulk* cargoes that demanded shipping tonnage.

The growing variety of cargoes that English merchants could offer their European customers enabled them to make more of their voyages into a profitable two-way traffic where previously they had often had to sail ships one way in ballast. It also eased some of the problems of how to pay for imports from areas that had never been lavish buyers of English cloth. Bulk cargoes demanded more and larger ships. Few

[1] See Wadsworth and Mann, *The Cotton Trade and Industrial Lancashire*, 1931, pp. 117–19.
[2] H. A. Innis, *The Cod Fisheries*, 1940, p. 53.

corners of the murky regions of trade statistics in the seventeenth century
are more obscure than shipping statistics. But all the evidence points
to a remarkable increase. Total tonnage may well have grown from
150,000—200,000 tons in 1660 to 340,000 tons by 1688.[1] Of this
60 per cent was busy in Europe, 35 per cent in the Atlantic, and 5
per cent in the Eastern trades. Yet, quite evidently, all these branches
of trade were interdependent. All in all, shipping was one of the
largest employers of labour by the end of the century. It kept busy
almost as many men as were employed as 'artisans and craftsman' and
perhaps 10 to 20 per cent of the total non-agricultural working population.

All this called for a heavy new investment of capital. And because
the voyages were larger and problems of loading and unloading more
difficult than in the old European trades, new problems of shipbuilding
and ship management proliferated. At first, technology moved slowly,
not least because the English found it easier to put Dutch-built merchant
ships, bought or captured, into service rather than seek out new
methods of construction. Longer voyages brought added risks, too.
Transatlantic transport remained a gamble. The chances of gain
were high: but so, in the seventeenth century, were the chances of
loss.[2]

In these circumstances, the private shipbuilder did not figure
conspicuously as a technical innovator until late in the century. It was
the naval dockyards, building larger ships and disposing larger resources which stood out as leaders in the technology of large-scale
shipbuilding, creating an enormous demand for labour and supplies —
'the most comprehensive and in some respects the largest industry in
the country'.[3] But in 1700, English private shipbuilders were catching
up with the best features of the Dutch flyboats. 'Pinks' built at Whitby
and Scarborough were specialized ships built to carry cargo with
smaller crews and at lower cost. In East Anglian ports, contrariwise,
the industry languished, depressed rather than stimulated by Dutch
competition.

[1] Harper, op. cit., p. 339. Mr Harper's figures are generally lower than those suggested
by Mr Davis (op. cit., ch. II) more recently. I have taken the liberty of doubting Mr
Davis's figure for 1660 on the ground that the war with Spain resulted in heavy losses, as
he himself mentions.

[2] R. Davis, 'Merchant Shipping in the Economy of the late 17th Century', *Econ. Hist.
Rev.*, IX, no. 1, 1956.

[3] J. Ehrman, *The Navy in the War of William III*, 1953, Introduction; also D. C. Coleman
'The Naval Dockyards under the Later Stuarts', *Econ. Hist. Rev.*, VI, no. 2, 1953. R. Davis
op. cit., ch. II *et passim*.

A different, but in some respects less reliable, cross-section of overseas trade may be obtained from the fortunes and misfortunes of the great joint stock companies which were the chosen instrument of colonial expansion between 1660 and 1688. The rise of the most famous companies engaged in long-distance trades, the East India Company (or companies), the Royal African Company, and the Hudson's Bay Company, was accompanied by the decline of the old 'regulated' companies that had formerly conducted the European trades — especially the Merchant Adventurers, the Levant and the Eastland Companies. The clue to this inversion of fortunes lies in the nature of the trades themselves, and in the new relationship of merchant and State brought about by the creation of the navigation code. The European trades did not call for nearly as much in the way of fixed capital as the Indian or African trades with their forts, armaments and large establishments. They were driven in relatively civilized countries and demanded, above all, working capital for stocks of goods. This could now be met without undue difficulty from the resources of private merchants. They might on occasion need the diplomatic aid of Government, but the broad protection of trade was afforded by the legislative regulations enacted by the State–Navigation Acts, tariffs, bounties, etc. The Merchant Adventurers represented a declining phase of trade, in which England had supplied a semi-finished type of cloth to the Dutch entrepôt. Ever since the 1620s they had been harassed, not only by other rivals jealous of their monopoly, but also by the whole tribe of clothiers.

Between the two there was constant conflict of interests, but it was sharpest in depression. For the Adventurers were apt to try to restrict markets and output (so as to raise prices) just when the clothiers were most anxious to expand them. The Merchant Adventurers were therefore unpopular alike in country and Whitehall. The Levant Company felt the competition of its more affluent daughter, the East India Company, and neither it nor the Eastland Company was prosperous in the late seventeenth century. By 1700 the day of the 'regulated' company — a gild of individual merchants without a joint capital — was over.

The new type of company had its origins in the demand of certain colonial trades for large amounts of fixed capital — for forts, warehouse, and great armed ships — and in the added risks of longer voyages and the frequently hostile context in which their trade was conducted; 'private men', said a writer in 1645, 'cannot extend to making such long, adventurous and costly voyages' as those to India.[1] The same was true of the African and Canadian trades. The joint stock companies were, throughout their existence, a regular target for criticism on the grounds of monopoly, and their monopolies were in practice always being invaded by interlopers and rivals. Later on they were to come under heavy fire from doctrinaire *laissez-faire* economists. Adam Smith was to hold it a self-evident truth that no corporate monopoly could manage the business of trade as well as individual merchants. Such criticisms, ranging from the palpably self-interested to the doctrinaire, miss the mark. Without the resources which only a joint stock company could mobilize, the expansion of trade in far-distant and turbulent lands would, at this stage, have been impossible. The obverse of this was equally important, Whereas the regulated company of necessity had to depend on the capital resources of its active merchant members and perhaps their immediate friends or relations, the joint stock company was able to attract the surplus capital of a far wider public, and one that was not limited to the merchant community. There was force in the contention of the East India Company that it represented the willingness to lend of 'noblemen, gentlemen, shopkeepers, widows, orphans and all other subjects'.[2] The same could be argued of the other companies. It was both a source of immediate economic help and ultimate political embarrassment that the African company attracted members of the Court (including the Queen, the Queen Mother, the Duke of York, Prince Rupert, the Duke of Buckingham and many lesser figures) in search of a flutter. About a quarter of the company's stock was held by aristocracy and gentry; the rest by merchants and city men. Most of the holdings were relatively small. In the much more modest affairs of the Hudson's Bay Company, the non-merchants also had a share; its Governor was Prince Rupert.[3]

In 1660 the affairs of the largest joint stock company, the East India, were at a low ebb, and throughout the next forty years they were to be the target for vicious attacks and the rivalry of both Dutch and English competitors. Nevertheless, the continuous growth of business may be assessed very roughly from the facts of capital expansion. In 1660 the paid up capital stood at something over £400,000. On the

[1] *A Discourse consisting of Motives for the Enlargement and Freedom of Trade*, 1645.

[2] *Answer of the East India Company*, 1681. For a general discussion see W. R. Scott, *The Constitution and Finance of English, Scottish and Irish Joint Stock Companies to 1720*, 1912, vol. I, ch. XXII.

[3] Scott, op. cit., vol. II, pp. 229–30.

market its stock stood at a 10 per cent discount. In 1703, this — the 'Old Company' as it was called — had a nominal capital of £1·6 million, standing at a market price of 120 for £100 of stock. There was now also the 'New Company' with a separate capital of £2·3 million, standing on the market at 186. In all, therefore, the India companies alone had a total capital of £3·8 million, with a market value very much higher. The Royal African Company's capital was less than a third as large, the Hudson's Bay only some £32,000.[1]

These figures make it apparent that it is possible to overestimate the many difficulties the companies met in these years, ferocious as some of them were. The immediate post-Restoration years were a time of poor trade, shortage of capital, low dividends, and opposition from the clothiers, who could see nothing to be had from an East India Company that exported so little of their product. To these was added the hostility of all those who objected to that export of silver bullion which seemed to them the company's main preoccupation. But in the 1670s trade improved, and with it the market price of the company's stock rose, touching the very high level of 245 per cent in 1677. Yet this meant that for those who had to buy their way into the stock through the market (as distinct from those who had held on from the start or had bought in the doldrums) the yield on their capital was far from spectacular: for an investment bearing considerable risks 6 per cent was none too high. The long-term investor was enjoying a higher yield — 20 per cent or more on an average. But he could not enjoy both this *and* realize his capital gains (as critics then and since have sometimes suggested). Anyone with a nodding acquaintance with investment will recognize a familiar dilemma. How much movement there was in and out of stock it is not easy to say. In 1681 there were 181 proprietors with £1,000 of stock or more, and a similar number with less. This robs of some of its force the charge of oligarchy made by critics. But there was little doubt where the reality of power lay: it lay with the Governor.

In 1670 Josiah Child was not yet a member of the company. He was a brewer and victualling contractor who numbered the company amongst his customers. By 1673 he had acquired £12,000 in stock and thus became the largest single stockholder. By 1680 his holding had risen to £17,000. From 1674 till 1699, when he died, he was a Director except for one year, and from 1681 till 1690 he was Governor, spokesman and Pooh-Bah of the company. All this in spite of his being

[1] Scott, op cit., vol. I, p. 371.

known and disliked at Court originally as one of several directors 'that have behaved themselves very ill towards His Majesty'.[1] This inauspicious start was followed by a close alliance with the Court based on an exchange of favours. Child became a baronet in 1678, and Charles was from time to time refreshed by *douceurs* in the shape of handsome gifts of money from the company. From 1681 Child had to face the threat of a rival company breaking into his monopoly. But 1686 saw a victory in the shape of a new charter. 1688 brought troubles at home and abroad. While a quarrel with Auringzeb brought expulsion from Bengal, the Revolution at home gave the company's critics their opportunity. For a time Child rode the storm, but by the nineties troubles fell thick and fast. No dividend was paid after 1691, and the price of East India stock had fallen to levels no higher than 67 and as low as 37. In 1698, the quarrels between the company and its Whig opponents led to the formation of a 'New' East India Company. Paradoxically, its appearance was the signal for an improvement in the fortunes of the 'Old Company'. After a long-drawn-out series of negotiations the two companies were to be amalgamated in 1708. By that time Child was dead. He left a large fortune, probably over £200,000, including £50,000 of East India stock, a number of country estates, mainly in Essex, and properties in London. His brother-in-law became Duke of Chandos, his granddaughter was Duchess of Bedford, a grandson the Duke of Beaufort. Too ruthless, too swiftly successful to be popular, he was a remarkably brave and skilful manager of his company. He watched over its affairs with precisely that anxious, sleepless vigilance which to Adam Smith was credible only in a member of a private partnership. Here, indeed, was an early prototype of the professional business manager.[2]

No comparable figure emerges from the history of the Royal African Company which rose in 1663 out of the ashes of the Adventurers to Africa formed in 1660. These in turn were the successors of four previous African companies which stretched back, with many vicissitudes, to 1553. The new company's main business was to sell African gold, ivory, dyewood, hides and wax in England. These it paid for with exports of English goods — textiles, metals, arms. Slaves bought in the Bight of Benin and southwards to Angola were shipped and sold to Barbados, Jamaica and other West Indian islands. A few went to Virginia. By the beginning of the eighteenth century the

1 See W. Letwin, *Sir Josiah Child: Merchant Economist*, Boston 1959, p. 17 *et passim*.
2 For his economic and social ideas see below, p. 233.

Royal African Company had exported goods worth £1½ million, despatched 500 ships to Africa, 100,000 slaves to the plantations, imported 30,000 tons of sugar, coined half a million guineas, and built eight forts on the African coast. Like the East India Company it paid dearly after 1688 for too close an alliance with the Stuart Court and with royal prerogative. In 1698, it lost its monopoly and its most recent authoritative historian has described it as a failure; 'for it failed in the primary duty of a joint-stock Company, the making of profits in a form in which they could be distributed to shareholders'.[1]

It failed in this because its servants were remote, its accounting system and methods of control inadequate. But comparison with the East India Company, which suffered equal drawbacks, prompts one to question whether it did not fail also for lack of leadership: for want, in fact, of a Josiah Child. The Hudson's Bay Company was by the same token relatively successful, but its affairs were only a fraction of the size of those managed by its larger fellows. All three were models of efficiency compared with the Royal Fishery Company of 1664 whose farcical proceedings Pepys could only record in wonder that passed into desperation as he contemplated, 'the loose and base manner' of its management. The history of this, like all the earlier and most of the later attempts to oust the Dutch from the English and Scottish coastal fisheries, ended in dismal failure.[2]

A more impressionistic view of the commercial growth of the period is provided by the physical development of the ports. Exports from the outports were rising as the Devon serge trade, midland metal industries, and northern textiles grew in the hinterland of Exeter, Bristol and Liverpool. Newcastle was busy with the growing coal trade. Smaller ports like King's Lynn were briskly engaged with the growing exports of Norfolk grain. But London still dominated the national scene, and the trade of the other ports remained small in relation to the volume controlled by the metropolis. Between a third and a half of all English ships were owned by London merchants, who controlled more than half the shipping traffic of the country. A quarter of London's population depended on the sea for its living.

After 1660 the development of the areas between the City and Whitehall, temporarily halted by the Civil War, was resumed at a faster tempo. The Great Fire merely sharpened the challenge and the rebuilding was striking proof of London's ability to provide supplies,

[1] K. G. Davies, *The Royal African Company*, 1957, p. 346.
[2] See Wilson, *Profit and Power*, pp. 121-2.

skills and money on an unprecedented scale. The fire started in a bake-house and spread swiftly. The fire precautions were hopelessly inadequate. In three days of pandemonium the Royal Exchange, St Paul's, the Guildhall, Cheapside, Paternoster Row, Old Bailey, Ludgate, Fleet Street were all destroyed. In all, over 13,000 houses, 87 churches, and goods valued at £3½ million were lost. The Stationers' Company alone lost £200,000 of stocks. The country clothiers' stocks at Black-well Hall were burnt. Plate, jewels and money disappeared, not so much in the fire itself as in the widespread looting that followed. Yet, remarkably quickly, a new city rose on the ashes of the old, less picturesque but more elegant and more hygienic.

Instead of the old narrow streets and half-timbered houses there were streets two or three times as wide and modest but capacious houses of stone and brick. Supplies came in by water, and high wages pulled in labour from the countryside into the suburbs. Brickworks were set up by enterprising suburbans. The Navigation Acts were relaxed so that maximum supplies of timber could be let through. Things were never quite the same again. It was not only that the poor stayed where they had been driven by the Fire, herded in huts outside the City wall. The Fire also drove some trades out for good. Paternoster Row lost its luxury shops to Covent Garden, Bedford Street, Henrietta Street and King Street. Displaced tradesmen opened booths on Moorfields and other open spaces.[1] The 'marring of the City' it was said 'was the making of the suburbs'.[2]

In 1675, the Lord Mayor and Aldermen were still petitioning the King to stop building development in the West End until the City had had a chance to catch up with its losses of retail trade. But their problem was Canute's. The Fire had given new impetus to the perpetual west-ward movement based on interests too powerful to be stopped. The growth of population and trade was the opportunity for a new generation of ground landlords to realize their potential assets. It was now the Earl of Southampton in the Bloomsbury area, and the Earl of St Albans, Henry Jermyn, in St James's, who pressed on in alliance with a group of speculative builders to create a series of new 'towns'. Below the ranks of the largest landowners came a group of speculators led by Sir Thomas Bond — Thomas Clarges, Richard Frith, Gregory King[3] — who brought long leases and possessed enough influence to buy

---

[1] T. F. Reddaway, *The Rebuilding of London after the Great Fire*, 1940, passsim.
[2] Brett James, op. cit., p. 503.
[3] For Gregory King as social statistician, etc., see below, p. 228.

licences to build. Their enterprise and sometimes shady talents are perpetuated in London's street names. Bond was the chief of what Evelyn the diarist called a band of 'rich bankers and mechanics' who descended on the site of Clarendon's house north of Piccadilly with 'a little army of labourers and artificers levelling the ground, laying the foundations and contriving great buildings, at an expense of £200,000 if they perfect their design'. An operator on an even larger scale was the fantastic Nicolas Barbon, leatherseller, M.P., economist and demagogue, son of him who had given his name to Barebones Parliament. Barbon's sphere was further east, round the Strand, Fleet Street and the Inns of Court. Bulldozing his way through legal rights and agreements, Barbon pulled down the old decaying palaces of Tudor times like Essex House and York House, filling up the sites with smaller houses, breweries, warehouses and wharves. Bedford Row, Buckingham Street and Red Lion Square were amongst his creations. 'Barbon', said Roger North, 'never failed to satisfy everyone in treaty and discourse, and if he had performed as well, he had been truly a great man.' But having bought and remodelled Osterley Park on a scale to match his pretensions, he became more and more deeply involved in lawsuits and a sea of debts. A few surviving houses and some ingenious tracts written in defence of the speculative builder's contribution to the health and employment of the people are the memorial to this picaresque figure of Restoration London.

Behind the big speculative developers marched an army of small men who ministered to the needs of tradesmen as these replaced the aristocracy in its westwards move. The organizing figure in this type of development was the master builder, himself often a former artisan with enough enterprise to rise from the ranks of the joiners, painters, bricklayers or carpenters.[1] The development of London as a trading city and port is less well documented than is its growth as a centre of fashion and pleasure. But it is clear that in these years, the traditional markets like Billingsgate, Southwark, Leadenhall, Blackwell Hall and the rest were supplemented by a spreading growth of retail shops. While the fairs and markets continued to handle perishable goods – as Covent Garden still does – non-perishable goods like textiles, glass and cutlery were increasingly handled by shopkeepers. As yet the shop remained a general rather than a specialized store, but the principle of display was entering into trade – 'a modern custom', Defoe commented, 'and wholly unknown to our ancestors'. The shopwindow that pushed its

[1] J. Summerson, *Georgian London*, 1945, esp. pp. 4–55.

wares into the street under the eye of the customer and the growing
volume of advertisements in newspapers were beginning to edge the
travelling chapman and pedlar out of business. More and more, the
retail trade was shaking itself free of regulation by town authority or
gild. As it grew, London was assuming more of its modern aspects.

Provincial cities were slower to follow, but Bristol, with 20,000 inhabitants by 1700, was the second largest town and port. In the 1690s,
240 ships were entering and leaving in each year. Bristol's merchants
impressed Pepys by their wealth, hospitality and dignity when he
visited the city in 1668. It was 'in every respect another London', its
quayside 'a large and noble place'. His host, a silver merchant, was
'very good company and so like one of our sober, wealthy London
merchants, as pleased me mightily'. He was charmed by the air of
hospitality — 'good entertainment of strawberries, a whole venison
pasty and plenty of brave wine and above all Bristol milk'.[1] The new
trades that were now joined to the old local trades in salt and dairy
produce were having their effects at Liverpool, still an economic
dependency of Chester in 1600. By the 1660s property values were
rising in the growing port. The merchant community of Liverpool was
still relatively small but amongst it were to be found a few merchant
families of great wealth, the Johnsons, Norrises, Claytons, Clevelands
and Houghtons. Great warehouses and sugar refineries were rising and
in 1694 Thomas Patten of Warrington was busy widening the Mersey.
'Since I made the river navigable to Warrington', he wrote in 1701,
'there have been sent to and from Liverpool, 2,000 tons of goods a
year. . . .' Much more, he added, could be done to ease the flow of
trade, and from 1700 the work of dock building was to go forward
swiftly.[2]

Further north, and growing as vigorously as Liverpool, was Whitehaven. As landowners and coalowners the Lowther family had a strong
stake in Whitehaven's trade. By the 1680s Whitehaven was trading in
tobacco from Virginia. Trading ties with the colonies were strengthened by the marriage of a Lowther into the Penn family and Sir John
Lowther was writing cordial letters about trade connexions to the
founder of Pennsylvania, William Penn.[3]

Glasgow, too, was in contact with the new colonies; in the sixties,

[1] *Diary*, 1668, Everyman Edition, pp. 526–7. According to Macaulay, Bristol milk was
a brew of Spanish wine with which the sugar refiners regaled their visitors along with
West Indian turtle.

[2] H. Fox Bourne, op. cit., ch. XVII.

[3] J. E. Williams, 'Whitehaven in the 18th Century', *Econ. Hist. Rev.*, VIII, no. 3, 1956.

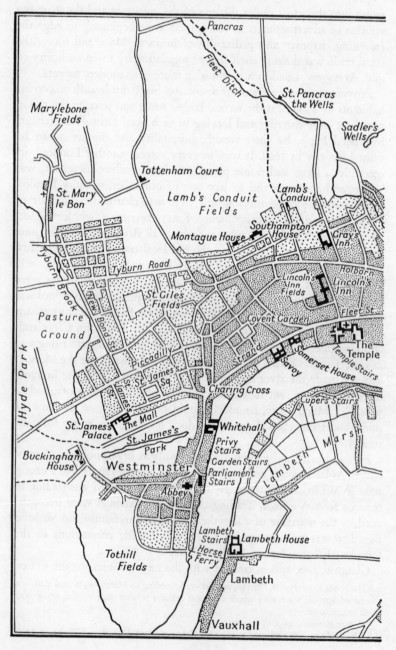

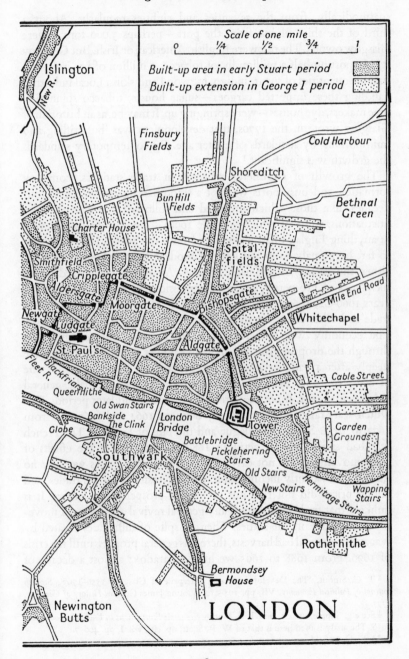

Scale of one mile
0   ¼   ½   ¾   1

Built-up area in early Stuart period
Built-up extension in George I period

Islington

New R.

Finsbury
Fields

Cold Harbour

Shoreditch

Bun Hill
Fields

Bethnal
Green

Charter House

Spital
fields

Smithfield

Cripplegate

Aldersgate

Moorgate

Bishopsgate

Mile End Road

Newgate

Whitechapel

Ludgate

St. Paul's

Aldgate

Blackfriars

Fleet R.

Cable Street

QueenHithe

Old Swan Stairs

Bankside

The Clink

London
Bridge

Tower

Garden
Grounds

Globe

Battlebridge

Southwark

Pickleherring
Stairs

Old Stairs

Hermitage Stairs

New Stairs

Wapping
Stairs

The Borough

Rotherhithe

Newington
Butts

Bermondsey
House

LONDON

spasmodically, from the seventies and eighties regularly. About a third of the ships plying from the port – perhaps 3,000 tons – were Glasgow owned. The rest were English, American or Irish. But Glasgow was importing half a million lb. of tobacco, a million of bar iron, and sizeable quantities of sugar, indigo, logwood and skins. Local industries handling these imported cargoes – sugar houses, tobacco spinneries, pipe makers, dye houses – were springing up. It may be, as an historian of Glasgow wrote in the 1770s, that development was 'but trifling and unimportant' by standards of a later age. By contemporary standards the growth·was significant.[1]

The growth of commerce reflected in trade statistics, company formation and busy ports was not a smooth progression. These four decades, like those which preceded and followed, were marked by fluctuations, some of which – in the 1690s – were probably as severe as anything England had experienced since the 1620s. They have not, so far, been analysed in the light of modern knowledge as closely as either the earlier or the later crises.[2] An earlier analysis detected six phases of prosperity, seven of depression. Prosperity marked the years, 1660–64, 1667–71, 1674–78, 1679–81, 1692–95, 1699–1700: poor trade and crises the years 1664–67, 1672–74, 1678, 1682–90, 1696–97. The economy was vulnerable not only rurally but commercially through the drop in general purchasing power when food prices rose steeply after a bad harvest. Yet, in general, the period was not one of acute or easily definable price movements such as make general judgements easier, if not more reliable, in earlier and later periods. The Dutch wars raised prices markedly between 1664 and 1667 and from 1672 to 1674. So did the Plague and the Fire of London. The French war had similar results between 1689 and 1697.[3] Yet the effects of price movements are not easy to interpret. Rising prices were by no means self-evidently incompatible with adversity for some trades, and falling prices did not rule out periods of prosperity for others. It is unlikely that trade experienced any general revival and forward movement until late in the sixties. Then, in spite of difficulties created by war and occasional bad harvests, there was general progress until the crisis of 1696. From 1688 to 1695 we have a paradox: almost a decade of

---

[1] T. C. Smout, 'The Development and Enterprise of Glasgow 1556–1707', *Scottish Journal of Political Economy*, VII, pp. 194–212, quoting James Gibson, *History of Glasgow*, 1777.

[2] See e.g. Supple, op. cit., and T. S. Ashton, *Economic Fluctuations in England 1700–1800*, 1959. The analysis used here is that of W. R. Scott, op. cit., vol. I, pp. 466–7.

[3] J. K. Horsefield, op. cit., pp. 4–5.

bad summers, unknown since the 1620s,[1] accompanied by an outburst of company promotion and financial speculation likewise unknown since the 1620s, and not paralleled until the boom of the South
Sea Bubble. It began with a successful venture by a syndicate formed
in 1688 to recover bullion from the wreck of a Spanish plate ship at
Hispaniola. Down to 1694 company flotation was encouraged by the
war and the expectation of high profits. Company shares fluctuated
wildly, rose to great heights and then collapsed. Some idea of the boom
and collapse is given by the prices of the shares of the three major
foreign trading companies:

	East India	Royal African	Hudson's Bay
Highest price, 1692–97	200 (1692)	52 (1692)	260 (1692)
Lowest price, 1692–97	37 (1697)	13 (1697)	80 (1697)

Add to war profiteering and food scarcity the crisis of a deteriorating
currency that drove men to hoard good coin and stocks of commodities, and it is not surprising that these years saw the most prolific
economic debate of the century. Bad times were a traditional stimulus
to economic argument: 1695 and 1696 saw more than 250 pamphlets
published on the monetary controversy alone. As the crisis reached its
climax with the usual lament of 'want of money' and the decay of the
cloth trade, it may well have seemed to many that the 1620s had come
again. As in 1622, there were heartsearchings over the balance of trade;
hence the start of systematic analysis of the customs returns and the
establishment of the Board of Trade. Of ninety-three joint stock
companies in business, 1690–95, over two-thirds disappeared in 1698.

Yet there was a fundamental difference between the crisis of the 1620s
and this one. The wealth of England was more broadly based, trade
and industry more widely spread and diversified, and the economy had
a buoyancy lacking in earlier times. Hence recovery was swift and
spectacular. Shipping revived, and foreign trade expanded to a total of
£13½ million by 1700–01, an increase of about 90 per cent over the
1696–97 figure. Although many of the industrial joint stock companies
had disappeared, the new century found the surviving companies with
capital and loan stock of over £10 million – double the figure of ten
years before. Well over half of this represented the assets of the four
great overseas trading companies.[2]

[1] Darby, *Historical Geography*, p. 391.
[2] The two East India Companies, Royal African and Hudson's Bay Companies. This
figure is the nominal value of stock. If market values were adopted the figure would be
higher.

What did this remarkable progress of trade and shipping owe to the system of legislation and control called, by a later and critical age, the mercantile system? Orthodox economists, following Adam Smith, were inclined to condemn it as by definition restrictive, monopolistic, mischievous or at least otiose. More recently, its central core – the Navigation Code – has had a better press. The most careful analysts have concluded that without its protection and stimulus, English trade and shipping would have found it difficult to develop against the greater skill, better technology and entrenched interests of the Dutch.[1] Possibly some of these judgements, in their anxiety to do justice to the Acts, pay too little regard to those other elements of growth in the economy – to developing industries, the removal of internal regulations of medieval ancestry, to social mobility, the release and encouragement of enterprise, to sound government, naval power, natural endowment of material resources and perhaps a growing population. To isolate one chapter of legislation from its economic, social and political context and judge its effect is impossible. But it seems that the laws worked with, rather than against, the forward march of economic forces as a whole. They represented that growing investment of the nation's intelligence and enthusiasm in the cause of material gain. The results do not always bear an aspect pleasing to the liberal mind of a later age. Their logic was often the logic of power, physical force and war, and the increment of wealth did not seem as yet to percolate very far down society. Error, muddle and waste seemed often to be paramount. Yet though some contemporary minds might dissent from their application in particular cases (as the author of *Britannia Languens* or Dudley North did), few dissented from their principles. 'Armed aggression', a modern historian has said of this period, 'was the heart of commerce.'[2] Foreign contemporaries were inclined to think that the difference between the warmongering of the English and of the others was that the English wars represented a material objective broader than mere dynasticism, and one planned with a more cunning regard to the interests of His Majesty's subjects. They may have been right.

[1] The most categorical statement is that of L. A. Harper, op. cit., ch. XXIII. See also R. Davis, *Econ. Hist. Rev.*, IX, no. 1, 1956. On the Baltic trade see also Sven-Erik Åström, 'The English Navigation Laws and the Baltic Trade 1660–1700', *The Scandinavian Econ. Hist. Rev.*, VIII, no. 1, 1960.
[2] G. N. Clark, *The Seventeenth Century*, 2nd edn. 1947, p. 59.

CHAPTER NINE

The Changing Pattern of Manufactures

ECONOMIC conditions during the forty years following the Restoration were not, superficially, particularly favourable to industrial development. The level of prices was at best stable, in some cases falling. Two unsuccessful wars against the Dutch, begun in a spirit of optimistic bravado, proved disastrous for trade. Markets were distorted by Charles's pro-French policy, only to be upset again by the reversal of that policy under William III. In spite of these discouragements, foreign trade increased remarkably. It is true that a large part of that increase was accounted for by the growth of England's entrepôt trade; especially the growth of the import and re-export of colonial goods. Yet there was also an increase in the volume of British manufactures exported and an important change in the pattern of those exports. While the value of cloth exports increased *absolutely* — perhaps nearly doubling between 1660 and 1700 — the most striking feature was the growing *variety* of England's industrial exports. Many of the new export items represented a higher degree of finish and therefore, in general, of profit, than the older primary or semi-finished type of export like wool, tin, lead or white cloth.

Yet it is doubtful whether even these increases in foreign trade reflect anything like the full extent of the industrial change and growth of those years. Indeed, preoccupation with exports may obscure and undervalue the growth of home markets. Several pressures were being applied — some of them the direct consequence of the sagging of prices and profits — which resulted in technical advances in industry. Lower prices led business men to look for means of reducing costs. The obvious way was to get better returns from labour and from invested capital. These are therefore years when the distaff is replaced more quickly than before by the improved 'Saxony wheel' that gave a lighter thread. The design of the loom is bettered. The investigation of new dyes and methods of dyeing goes on steadily. Slowly, and by steps that are often still hidden from us, the use of coal and coke in the smelting side of metallurgical industries quickened. Such changes were not 'revolutionary' in the sense that later applications of power were. Neither the organization of industries, nor the scale of output, nor the social relations of men within industry, underwent a radical upheaval. But scores of minor technical advances went hand in hand with the growth and change of the domestic market for manufactures. Industrial change was closely linked with changes in social habits. These may themselves have been a product of the stagnation or fall in price levels. For the fall in the price of necessities — especially food, drink and clothing — meant that a surplus of purchasing power was released for other, often novel, products. The improvement of the hand-operated stocking frame initiated a phase when, as Sir George Clark has said, 'instead of making silk stockings by the thousand, Nottingham now made worsted stockings by the million'.[1] The falling price level meant that some producers were encouraged to make cheaper articles for wider consumption in the home market. Others, who catered for the more affluent purchaser, decided to concentrate on a better article which cost more, knowing that those who had previously bought cheap kerseys could afford, at the reduced price level, to go in for a serge. Thus two kinds of expansion and change sprang almost automatically from the price depression itself, as entrepreneurs adjusted their methods to the loss of old, congested markets, and sought to replace them by new ones (often at home), and mopped up the purchasing power released by the price fall.[2]

In exploring the new possibilities the industrialists were aided and urged on by a government that inherited all the aggressive, nationalist anti-Dutch, xenophobic ambitions of its predecessors: by the scientists grouped, from 1662, in the Royal Society for whom, in the early years anyway, technological prowess was a prime objective. Of its eight committees, the largest, with sixty-eight members, was the 'Mechanical'. The 'History of Trades' Committee came second with thirty-five. Robert Boyle busied himself with mining and metallurgy, Robert Hooke and William Petty with shipbuilding, pumps, engines of various kinds, and with the enormously important problems

[1] G. N. Clark, op. cit.

[2] It is worth comparing this period of so-called depression with the post-1870 period when depression in prices, profits and foreign trade went along with a rise in new consumption goods industries like soap, patent medicines, chocolates, tobacco, entertainment, etc., often catering for a working-class market.

of dyeing cloth. Here the English manufacturers were very backward. Until 1661 the import of cochineal and logwood was prohibited in the interests of home producers of woad. The Navigation Code reversed this policy by 'enumerating' logwood, an elusive commodity mostly smuggled out of the Caribbean by retired English pirates. It was not accidental that in the next seven years Petty, Boyle and Hooke all presented papers on textile dyeing to the Royal Society. Charles himself did not scorn the idea that the industrial application of science was a prime purpose of the society. The spread of mathematical knowledge was one of the most marked features of the age. That most enchanting of all portrait galleries, John Aubrey's *Brief Lives*, is full of mathematicians. Noblemen like Lord Herbert, second Marquis of Worcester, played with the idea of invention. His own *Century of Inventions*, published in 1663, was compiled when he was a prisoner in the Tower during the Protectorate. Cromwell's brother-in-law, John Wilkins, Warden of Wadham College, Oxford, wrote his *Mathematical Magic* in 1648 and filled it with speculation on submarines, flying machines and perpetual motion as well as with musings on the openings for 'profitable knowledge of those chargeable adventures of draining mines, coalpits, etc'.[1] There were few who did not, for a time at least, in the brave days of gaiety, relief and enthusiasm after the Civil War, share the opinion of 'fat Tom Sprat', the first historian of the Royal Society, that invention was 'an heroic thing'. Yet of its results we cannot be sure, except to note that the enthusiasm of the society flagged after a few years. In industry as a whole, technology was largely then, as occasionally now, a matter of knack, of local knowledge, often inherited and often secret, rather than of scientific reasoning and inquiry. Such were the skills of the brewer, forge master, tanner, dyer, mason and many others. Yet the figures of English patents of invention granted between 1660 and 1699, though subject to many abortions and failures, are not entirely without significance.

1660–69	31
1670–79	51
1680–89	53
1690–99	102

The nineties especially reflect a period of renewed and feverish interest in industrial invention that was not to be repeated until after

[1] G. N. Clark, *Science and Social Welfare in the Age of Newton*, Oxford 1937, pp. 9–11, 31–59 *et passim*.

1760, when another great wave of invention and enterprise swept over England.

Finally, the years after the Revocation of the Edict of Nantes saw the migration to England alone of many thousands of French Huguenot refugees. They included textile workers in wool, linen and silk, printers, paper makers, glass workers and a hundred other kinds of artisan. Ingenious, enterprising and industrious they and their descendants were to find their way into the arcana of English economic life, modifying old methods of manufacture and bringing new skills in trade, industry and finance. A number of the patents granted are in names like Blondeau, Dupin, Le Blon, Ducleu, Pousset, Gastineau, Pasel, etc. Individual inventions, like individual projects of a 'mercantilist' kind, often failed. Drebbel's 'submarine' had no progeny. The Royal Fishery Company was a failure if not a fraud. Wilkins was a visionary. Barbon was a rascal. But taken collectively, these men and their ideas were part of a mass attack against the already crumbling defences of the old society founded on status, custom and an ingrained suspicion of innovation or social change.

New industries, then, were rising: but in spite of its reduced *relative* importance as an export industry, cloth manufacture remained the most widespread industry. It gave employment to more people and accounted for a larger part of national production and national income than any other activity save agriculture, with which it was inextricably entangled. The value of cloth exported, as a proportion of the value of all exports, fell between 1660 and 1700 from some 75 per cent to less than 50 per cent. But since the *total* value of all exported manufactures rose as well, there was room for an absolute increase in the value of the cloth produced. And, with cloth as with other manufactures, it may well be that more was produced for the home market as living standards rose. The process of regional concentration continued therefore, with Devonshire and East Anglia moving into the lead, as the trend away from woollens proper to worsteds and mixed cloths was extended. In the jostling for markets, the products of one region competed strongly with those of other regions, and the English producers as a whole competed, product by product, against those of Holland and, to a lesser extent, of France, Germany, Silesia and Italy.

The Devonshire clothiers had been steadily acquiring a larger share of the home and foreign market with their mixed serges since the middle of the century. In the nineties they were specially vigorous. For their serge manufacture, which was rapidly ousting the older kersey industry, they needed both long and short wool. The long came mainly from Ireland by the nineties and their dependence on it explains the zeal with which they campaigned against the Irish cloth industry which they saw as a dangerous competitor for both raw materials and customers. When John Cary, the Bristol merchant and economic pamphleteer, went to Westminster as an M.P. in 1696, it was to represent the opposition of the south-west to its Irish rivals. The end of the agitation was the Irish Woollen Act of 1698–99. This forbade Ireland to export cloth, and restricted the Irish clothiers to their domestic market. Ireland thus remained a source of long wool. The short came from Kent, Essex, Exmoor and Dartmoor, and, of course, Spain.

The resulting manufacture had carried Exeter into third place (after London and Bristol) amongst the outports by 1700. The serge trade itself had become an elaborate and intricate organization with a wool market in Exeter itself, great areas in the countryside to the west and north of Exeter where the wool was spun in the cottages, and even larger areas where the yarn was woven. They stretched from North Tawton in the west to Taunton in the east, and from Tiverton in the north to Topsham in the south. The largest manufacturing centre was Tiverton, though the bulk of its serges were sold through the Exeter weekly serge market. Serge making employed four out of five of the inhabitants of Exeter by 1700. Serges provided the main prop of a great trade that went coastwise to London and overseas to Holland, Flanders, Germany, Spain and Portugal, bringing back a valuable return trade in German linens bleached in Holland, colonial sugar and tobacco, and wines from Germany and France. Hence the presence in Tiverton and Exeter of a flourishing colony of Dutch merchants (and a few Germans) whose enterprise supplemented that of the local traders and left its mark on the local domestic architecture. Hence came, a little later, the famous Baring family, whose founder was a young German immigrant apprenticed to an Exeter serge maker.

In 1700 Exeter exported well over a quarter of all England's cloth exports. Adding the coastal trade to the trade to London, the annual value of Exeter's seaborne trade was probably a good £½ million. If the ratio of home to foreign trade was the same here as elsewhere – 3 : 1 – the grand total of Exeter's turnover at its peak would be about £2 million a year, or an average weekly turnover on the Exeter market of £40,000. Tiverton and Exeter divided the manufacturing, finishing and trading functions between them. Tiverton's main work was in the manufacturing, Exeter's in the finishing and selling. When Celia Fiennes visited Exeter on her travels in 1699 she left a characteristically gossipy description of the trade. Outside the town she met the carriers bringing in the serges, fresh from the country looms, by packhorse. Before going to the fulling mills, the cloths were cleaned of superfluous oil and grease, soaked in urine and soaped: ' . . . and soe put them into the fulling-mills and soe worke in the mills drye till they are thick enough, then they turne water into them and scower them; the mill does draw out and gather in the serges, its a pretty divertion to see it, a sort of huge notch'd timbers like great teeth, one would think it should impare the serges but it does not.' The serges were then dried on racks on the fields all round the town, then collected, folded in paper ' . . . and so sett them on an iron plaite and screw down the press on them which has another iron plaite on the top under which is a furnace of fire of coales, this is the hot press; then they fold them exceeding exact and then press them in a cold press'.

The serges for London were then ready for despatch, by boat or by packhorse, undyed, but for export they were dyed:

> I saw the several fatts [vats] they were a dying in of black, yellow, blew and green . . . they hang the serges on a great beame or great pole on the top of the fatt and so keep turning it from one to another . . . backwards and forwards till its tinged deep enough of the coullour; their furnace that keeps their dye pans boyling is all under that roome, made of coale fires; there was in a roome by itself a fatt for the scarlet, that being a very chargeable dye noe waste must be allowed in that . . . [1]

Evidently the Devon industry was in a transitional stage: spinning and weaving were still rural cottage occupations; finishing processes like fulling and dyeing concentrated in the town. Marketing seems generally to have been under the hand of a different group of merchants from the clothiers who financed the manufacture. Some of them – the Upcotts and Lewises of Tiverton, the Bidewells, Cocks, Southeys, Heaths and Elwills of Exeter – were men of substance: already a strongly hereditary class. Clearly marked off socially from their inferiors, few were as yet of standing to mingle with the gentry. One or two did. John Elwill, whose letters to his Dutch correspondent have survived,[2] was a shrewd and enterprising Exeter merchant whose Oxford education gave a philosophic edge to his comment on the trends of markets and fashions. A Member of Parliament from 1681,

---

[1] *The Journeys of Celia Fiennes*, ed. C. Morris (1949), pp. 245–249.
[2] Archief Brants. *Gemeente Archief* Amsterdam. See also Hoskins, *Industry Trade & People of Exeter 1688–1800*, 1935, p. 21.

Elwill was knighted in 1696, became Sheriff of Devon in 1699, a baronet in 1709, and married a wife from the Bampfyldes, an old county family. Others were less affluent. George Poe, typical of the smaller Exeter merchant (his letters to Holland also survive), seems to have spent his business life in a state of chronic anxiety, chronic short-age of cash.[1] Most merchants were probably somewhere between the two in wealth and status. Trade was still a highly personal affair, and the wrangling, haggling and continual mutual allegations of bad quality and worse faith that fill the merchant's letters are reminiscent of the oriental bazaar rather than the impersonal flow of mass-produced goods of institutionalized business in the twentieth century. These human frictions were not limited to relations between buyer and seller, Englishmen and Dutchmen. They extended to entire groups. The Exeter merchants watched with jealous eyes the monopoly of the export business enjoyed by Topsham, which stood at the mouth of the barely navigable Exe. Throughout the seventeenth century they at-tempted to cut a channel navigable for lighters as far as Exeter. But Nature worked against the projects, and she was ably assisted (if the men of Exeter are to be believed) by the men of Topsham, who preserved their advantage by pouring stones, bricks, gravel and any rubbish they could find into the channel until it was silted up.

Coming up strongly behind the west were the textile manufactures of Norwich. At the end of the century Celia Fiennes found it 'a rich thriveing industrious place; Saturday is their great market day; they have beside the Town Hall a hall distinct which is the Sealeing Hall where their stuffs are all measured and if they hold their breadth and lengths they are sealed but if they are deffective there is a fine layd on the owner and a private marke on the stuffs which shows deficiency'. Like the Devon industry, the Norfolk industry was also in the transi-tional stage between dispersion and concentration. Norwich drew on neighbouring countries for wool and yarn. Much of the spinning of the worsted yarn was done in Yorkshire or Suffolk. Norwich had come to specialize more and more in 'stuffs', light worsteds, often a mixture of wool with silk or cotton, in bright colours. Finishing was therefore less of a problem than with the heavier serges or broadcloth. Many of the cloths needed no fulling. Some were dyed in the wool or even printed rather than vat-dyed. Like Devon, Norwich had a large stake in the export trade. Norwich stuffs and Exeter serges together comprised some 60 per cent of the trade of the outports. They still went mainly to Europe.

[1] C. Wilson, *Anglo-Dutch Commerce and Finance in the 18th Century*, 1940, pp. 34-5.

The Spanish trade was coveted by both cloth-producing areas, and by the end of the century it is obvious that they had driven out other old rivals – the Colchester bay and say makers and the Suffolk 'callimancoe' makers. Neither was prosperous. The once flourishing Dutch colony in Essex had dwindled into insignificance, its separate identity extinguished partly by intermarriage, partly by the depression in its trade. The centre of gravity in the East Anglian manufacture had moved northwards, and was to move further northwards still in the next century. But as yet, the Norwich clothiers scented danger from the imported calicoes of the East India Company rather than from the manufacturers of Yorkshire.

Here, techniques were still slow to follow the new fashions. The Yorkshire industries did a big trade but it was as yet a cheap trade. The cloths that Hull exported to northern Europe and which reached the rest of England by coastal shipping, the Humber, Trent and Ouse, or by packhorse, were still the kerseys or northern dozens – rough woollens of a sort inferior both to Devonshire serges, Norwich stuffs, or the fine woollens proper of Wiltshire or Gloucestershire. Leeds, Halifax and Wakefield were the markets to which the clothiers brought those goods which were not sent to London.

Events had not treated these older industries kindly. The markets of northern Europe to which the Merchant Adventurers and Eastland Company traders had carried Yorkshire white cloths in earlier years had been upset by war and currency troubles. English markets had been upset by the Civil War. Competition had grown. The Yorkshire industry so far had bred a race of small clothiers who lacked, maybe, the vision, just as they lacked the capital, of their more affluent and powerful neighbours of East Anglia. Was it adversity which turned Yorkshire to manufactures with a more hopeful future? By the 1680s the manufacture of the New Draperies (bays) was taking root. Round Halifax and Wakefield there were signs of a general growth of worsted-type industries, developed and controlled by a larger, more progressive type of merchant clothier than those who organized the cheap woollens industry. None of this had gone far by 1700 but it was important for the future.[1] Even Leeds, though primarily a woollens and finishing centre, shared in the growth of worsteds. By 1700, with large streets 'cleane and well pitch'd and good houses all built of stone' it was a prosperous town – 'the wealthyeast town of its bigness in the Country, its manufacture is the woollen cloth the Yorkshire Cloth in

[1] H. Heaton, *The Yorkshire Woollen & Worsted Industries*, 1920, chs. 3–8 *passim*.

which thay are all employed and are esteemed very rich and proud'
as Celia Fiennes breathlessly reported.

Across the Pennines, specialization of a different kind was taking
place. In the first half of the seventeenth century there had been little
to distinguish the textile manufactures of Lancashire from those of
Yorkshire. Both had produced an assorted mixture of cheap cloths,
'frizes', fustians, linens and so-called 'cottons' that were almost certainly made of wool. 'To cotton' meant to raise the nap of a cloth of
any kind. Certainly textiles made wholly of cotton were rare before
1700. But as early as 1621 a petition to Parliament had described how
'about 20 years past, diverse people in this Kingdom, but chiefly in
the County of Lancaster have found out the Trade of making Fustians,
made of Bombast or Downe, being a fruit of the Earth growing upon
little shrubs or bushes, brought into this kingdom by Turkie merchants
– but commonly called Cotton Wooll . . .' The 'fustian', already well
known in the Low Countries and elsewhere, may have been imported
to England by Flemish immigrants into East Anglia. The 'bombazines'
of Norwich were a branch of the same tree, though finer and more
elegant. In the seventeenth century the Levant continued to be a main
source of the supply of raw cotton. But West Indian cotton was finer,
and as the industry grew and products improved, an increasing proportion of West Indian cotton flowed into Lancashire through Liverpool. By the end of the century Lancashire had three fairly clearly
defined types of manufacture, each with its own area of production.
The linen area stretched round Manchester, westward towards Liverpool, and round Preston in the north. Fustians were made largely in the
middle area between Blackburn, Bolton and Bury. Eastwards lay the
woollen area. Cotton was used in at least three branches – in fustians,
linens and in so-called 'smallwares', which made tapes, ribbons and
garters. In all branches, the need to finance the purchase of raw or
semi-finished materials, and the consequent call for credit and capital,
was bringing the control of the trade more and more into the hands of
merchant capitalists. The linen drapers of Manchester were rising fast
in the world by the 1690s, accumulating capital and living in style. A
description of 1686 explains that the draper's business was 'buying and
selling, putting out linen yarn [and] cotton wool to the spinning, winding, warping, weaving'.[1]

Joshua Browne (1651–93), who rose from apprentice boy to great
wealth that enabled him to keep a private chapel as if he were a landed

[1] Wadsworth and Mann, op. cit., p. 78 *et passim*.

magnate, was typical of the big merchant capitalists. He is commemorated in Brown Street, Manchester, still. Browne went further than many for he also controlled the finishing and dyeing processes at his dye house, just off St Ann's Square. Thomas Marsden and Edmund Brooks were fustian drapers at Bolton, doing a similar business. Many of the drapers were Dissenters descended from those 'elders' who had actively forwarded the Puritan cause during the Commonwealth period. While the same factors that were present in the textile industries at large were leading in Lancashire also to the dominance of the merchant capitalist, one feature peculiar to the 'small ware' industry created an added need for capital. This was the 'engine-loom', or what in Lancashire was called the 'Dutch loom', or inkle-loom. With this machine, it was claimed, one man could make twelve pieces of ribbon 432 yards long in two days. On the old 'narrow loom' the same task would have occupied four men.[1] Its merits had not endeared it to the organized weavers of London or even of Leiden, its place of origin. They had managed to suppress it for nearly three-quarters of a century. In 1675 Cockney weavers were still rioting against it, smashing looms and burning them in the streets. Lancashire had no such well organized crafts. The looms had slipped into use soon after the Restoration and by the 1680s they were a common sight in Manchester. Grouped in batches of half a dozen to a dozen in a suitably sized workshop, they were often owned by a substantial master weaver who received work from the merchant and employer. Here was a kind of miniature factory, though without power.

What the Dutch loom was to Lancashire, another hand-operated knitting machine, the stocking frame, was to the Midlands — Nottingham and Leicester especially. Neither town held more than a few thousand people in 1700 but both were growing steadily. As an industry, hosiery came from humble origins. It was often developed as a means of 'setting the poor to work'. Yet out of what was sometimes called 'the leavings of the woollen trade', those 'descenters' whom Celia Fiennes remarked there in considerable numbers, were to make a substantial industry.

After, as before, the Restoration, England's debt to Europe in matters of technology and business organization is incalculable. In many branches of manufacture, Englishmen continued to go to school to the Dutch. They still did — in spite of some progress — in cloth dyeing. There was, however, one major contribution to English

[1] Wadsworth and Mann, op. cit., p. 103.

advance in the second half of the seventeenth century which came from Europe and was of a somewhat different kind. Industry was only one of the facets of national life which reflected, after 1685, the influence of the Huguenots, but it was not the least important. Of the 15,000 immigrants reported in the records of the French Relief Committee in December 1687, the overwhelming majority were described as artisans or workmen. This was only the start of a process which did not end until the middle of the eighteenth century. A high proportion settled in Spitalfields, Soho and Bethnal Green, some in the City itself. Fewer went to the provinces, though twelve of the fifteen French churches built for the refugees were outside London and their influence was larger than the numbers might suggest. Endowed with all the rational intelligence, enterprise and economy of their race, they brought their talents to bear most of all on those industries with which they had been most familiar at home; what may be called superior consumption industries — precision instruments, watches, cutlery, fine textiles, glass and paper. Many of these articles had previously helped to swell the adverse balance of trade with France which England had uneasily contemplated earlier in the century. The English market for such products was not simply a luxury market limited to the aristocracy. It included also an expanding proportion of country gentlemen, city merchants and professional men and their wives. The rising tide of trade, the demands of shopkeepers and counting houses, and the needs of literacy itself swelled the demand for a commodity like paper. Into this world of economic opportunity the Huguenots swiftly and dexterously fitted their technical and business talents.

Apart from the instrument makers who worked chiefly on and around the Strand, the London Huguenots went mainly into fine textiles or clothing of one sort or another. The beaver hats that had come from Caudebec were now made in Southwark and Wandsworth, whence came (it was said) even Roman cardinals for their caps. Calicoes were printed at Richmond and Bromley in Essex. The old Walloon tapestry works at Fulham was taken over by a Huguenot, who removed it to Exeter and staffed it with workers from the Gobelins. Far outstripping all these was the silk manufacture which settled at Spitalfields, henceforward the home of velvets, satins, brocades, lustrings, the so-called 'English taffeties', and silk stockings. How much the Huguenots contributed to glass technology is less clear. England had already by this time a glass industry on a considerable scale, in London, Newcastle, Liverpool, Bristol and Stourbridge, and important basic progress was being made in the eighty or ninety 'glass houses' in these areas.[1] It may well be that French workmen were able to focus the attention of manufacturers on finer glass for making mirrors and crystal. But St Gobain was to remain unchallenged for the finest glass for nearly another century.[2]

The paper industry, like glass, was already well established before the French refugees took a hand in it.[3] The material requirements of the paper maker were two: plenty of suitable, e.g. linen, rags, and plenty of clear water and rapid streams. With its widespread textile industries, England was well placed for raw materials. Water of the right kind was abundant in Hampshire, Kent and Somerset where the paper mills sprang up. The progress of the industry through two phases can be observed from the change in paper imports in the seventeenth century. In 1600, England still imported most of the coarse and fine paper she needed. The import of the blue paper that grocers used for wrapping sugar and the brown paper that all tradesmen used reached its peak in the 1630s and then declined as local manufacture increased. Imports of white paper went on growing till about 1700 and then declined. It was with this second change and the rise of a fine paper industry that the Huguenots, amongst others, were associated. Dupin, de Vaux and above all de Portal were a few of the famous names. When the 'Governor & Company of White Paper Makers' were incorporated with a monopoly in 1686, its Board included many French names. It was less successful than the de Portal business. Henry de Portal of Bordeaux, a victim of the Dragonnades, fled first to Holland, then to England. His paper mill at Laverstoke in Hampshire quickly acquired a high reputation for quality. In 1825 Cobbett, Radical hater of paper money, was to sit in contemplation beside 'the stream which turns the mill of Squire Portal which mill makes the Bank of England notepaper' and reflect characteristically that 'this river has produced a greater effect on the condition of men than has been produced by all the other rivers, all the seas, all the mines, and all the continents in the world'. Altogether six new companies were formed in the thirty years after the Fire of

[1] See below, p. 302.

[2] See Nef, Clowes, op cit. Also T. C. Barker, *Pilkington Brothers and the Glass Industry*, 1960, p. 44. Samuel Smiles (*The Huguenots*, 1868, p. 330) speaks of Abraham Thévenart as a refugee setting up the glass manufacture in England after the Revolution. This seems suspect in the light of Mr Barker's description of Abraham Thévart's experiments in casting glass in France at the same period (op. cit., p. 43).

[3] For the most modern account see D. C. Coleman, *The British Paper Industry 1495–1860*, 1958.

London. They were medium-sized enterprises. The paper mill was one of the family that included the corn mill, fulling mill, slitting mill; all powered by water. Its products were needed in larger quantities by a growing population that was wrapping more goods, reading more newspapers and writing more letters. The man who could supply such needs was a social asset. If he could improve the balance of payments, an economic and political one too. The prospects for paper were good.

So they were for another industry to which the Huguenots contributed much, though in Ireland and Scotland more than in England. Linen was made everywhere in Europe. England was peculiar in producing more woollens than linens. Indeed, just as Englishmen prided themselves on wearing leather where others wore wooden shoes, they might take equal pride in weaving wool where others wove flax. Fine linen, gentleman's ware, was still imported in the late seventeenth century. Merchants like Sir John Elwill at Exeter bought German linens fine-bleached in Haarlem in return for the serges they sold to their Dutch correspondents. English linen was still, for the most part, bumpkin ware. This situation was to change in the eighteenth century, and the change came from two Huguenot settlements. The first was that of a colony of weavers from Picardy in an Edinburgh suburb which became known as Picardy Place. More important still was the arrival in the ruined village of Lishgarvey, later called Lisburn, ten miles south-west of Belfast, of Louis Crommelin. His was not the first attempt to promote the linen industry in Ireland. Others, including Strafford, had tried and failed. But now the need to provide a substitute for the woollen cloth manufacture with which the Irish threatened the Devon clothiers gave a fillip to William III's scheme. Dublin already had linen weavers in plenty. Huguenots had come from London, bringing London street names with them, so that Dublin already had its Pimlico and Spitalfields. Crommelin was no ordinary martyr to his faith. A native of Picardy, he had foreseen the troubles long before 1685 and sold a prosperous linen business at St Quentin before leaving France. Until 1698 he lived in Holland, which possessed, round Haarlem, the most expert linen-bleaching industry in Europe. Crommelin possessed therefore a full knowledge of those finishing processes which, with linen as with other fabrics, provided the key to progress and profit. His Irish bargain was a good one. He put down £10,000 of his own money and was guaranteed a return of 8 per cent per annum on it by the Government, together with a life annuity of £200 and enough to pay two assistants. Their function was to travel round superintending the flax cultivation, the bleaching grounds and finishing processes. The subsequent expansion of the Irish linen trade forms a remarkable chapter in the economic history of the eighteenth century.[1]

Finally, there was a complex of industries which needed fuel, and whose rate of expansion depended on whether coal could be substituted successfully for the wood which was getting scarcer and dearer. The more closely one looks at the relative rates of growth of different industries, and the reciprocal effect of one industry on another that was to become more pervasively characteristic of the economy, the more central does the fuel problem become. The industries may be divided into three groups. The first was composed of those industries like soap or sugar boiling which simply required heat for boiling liquids or melting solids. No chemical reactions were involved and therefore there was no problem. The second group of industries used fuel in such a way that a chemical problem, but not too intractable a one, was created. Such were malting and brewing, salt and alum refining and glass making. A third group were the tin, lead, copper, brass and iron industries where the smelting of the ore created difficult problems of industrial chemistry. The seventeenth century saw continual experiment on industrial fuel problems. Soap boilers, sugar boilers, maltsters, brewers, salt refiners, tin and lead miners and metal workers were all using coal. In every industry save one – iron – substantial progress had been made towards a solution of the technical problems created by the use of coal instead of wood.

It is impossible to estimate what proportion of the rapidly rising coal output went to industrial uses, but it may be safely inferred that it was increasing. The coalfields that were being exploited most rapidly were those of the Midlands, with Wales and Scotland following close behind in *rate* of growth. It seems probable that it was in this period and about 1700 that the Midlands first began to catch up with the north-eastern coalfield. This may well have reflected the growing saturation of the London coal market. By the end of the century, as the rate of growth of the London population slackened, the market for household coal levelled off. So did some important industrial uses which had sprung up earlier – brewing, for example. Contrariwise, industrial uses elsewhere were increasing – in brewing, brick making, malting, sugar and soap boiling and in many branches of metallurgy

[1] S. Smiles, op. cit., pp. 356–64. See also Conrad Gill, *The Rise of the Irish Linen Industry* (1925). S. C. Regtdoorzee Greup-Roldanus, *Geschiedenis der Haarlemmer Bleekerijen*, p. 324.

and metal working. Brewers and maltsters were among the largest non-domestic users of coal, benefiting from those technical improvements which accounted for a number of patent applications of the seventeenth century. They had aimed principally to eliminate that 'unsavoury and unwholesome taste' which might spoil the consumers' pleasure when wood was replaced by 'seacoal' or other cheap fuels. Since the mid-century the substitution had been successfully effected. John Houghton, the news-sheet proprietor, wrote that the excellent flavour of Derby malts was due to the way they used 'coales' in its manufacture. ''Tis not above half a century of years since they dryed their malt with straw (as other places now do) before they used cowkes, which has made that alteration since that all England admires.'[1] It was no accident that Abraham Darby, who was to be responsible for a major break-through in iron technology by converting coal into coke for the blast furnace, was apprenticed in the malt trade where he is said to have become familiar with the merits of coke. The brewing side of the industry, as distinct from malting, suffered no problems. The effects of abundant coal in the industry were twofold. It enabled it to expand its output, and it increased the size of the unit of production, not only in London but elsewhere. A visitor to Edinburgh earlier in the century noticed:

> ... that common brewhouse which supplieth the whole city with beer & ale, and observed there the greatest, vastest, leads, boiling keeres, cisterns and combes [wooden tubs] that ever I saw: the leads to cool the liquor in were as large as a whole house, which was as long as my court.[2]

Many factors had favoured the concentration of the brewing industry in towns in the course of the seventeenth century. Demand was high and steady, the growing use of hops preserved the beer and made it less perishable and more transportable. There was little competition as yet from tea or coffee. Wine sold to a different kind of customer. With the substitution of coal for wood, the advantages of large-scale production became more evident. London, with its growing population, not only had a large brewery industry. It already had large breweries. The cockney of Elizabeth's day had had his beer from the small publican-brewer. By 1700 he had it from one of 200-odd 'Common Brewers' who had, in the interval, come to control the London industry. They brewed, all told, about a million barrels of strong ale and nearly three-quarters of a million barrels of 'small' beer. Although

---

[1] P. Mathias, *The Brewing Industry in England 1700–1830*, 1959, p. 412.
[2] William Brereton, *Travels 1634–5*, p. 104.

modest in size compared with the great porter breweries of the eighteenth century[1] these London concerns were already industrial establishments on a recognizably modern scale, using centralized plant and machinery, as well as great stocks of malt and hops that flowed in from Hertfordshire and Kent respectively. In its scale of production and the size of its fixed capital, brewing was an exceptionally advanced industry for the times. Some of London's brewers were already men of wealth, influence and social standing. Josiah Child, later Governor of the East India Company and one of the richest men in England, had risen through the ranks of the brewers, having bought a brewery in Southwark about the time of the Fire to enable him to supply the navy and the East India Company.[2] Byde, whose ale Pepys particularly admired, was an Alderman. Others were M.P.s and knights. One brewer's daughter had already married a peer. Several of the breweries where the great brewers of the eighteenth century – the Thrales and Trumans – were to learn their trade, were already large businesses.[3] Few industries can show such continuity.

Raw material supply was the other main factor influencing the location and growth of industries. In general, industries tended to grow up in and around ports because water transport was cheaper and easier than overland transport before the coming of railways. Most industries that used bulk materials, including coal, were strongly influenced by transport. In turn, their growth gave rise to further demand for bulk transport. Cloth making was the conspicuous exception. Its location was less radically influenced because wool could be carried overland relatively easily. Nor did the cloth export business call for much bulk shipping. Raw cotton, on the other hand, had to come long distances from overseas and the superiority of West Indian cotton pointed to the western ports as the natural reception point for it. Another industry that was springing out of the transatlantic trades was sugar boiling. This, too, centred round the ports where the raw sugar was entered and where coal could be bought: Bristol, Liverpool and Glasgow. When the great Liverpool property owner, Edward Moore, drew up a statement of the family lands for the guidance of his son and heir in 1665, he described Sugar House Close.

> This croft . . . fronts the street for some 27 yards. I call it the Sugar House Close because one Mr Smith, a great sugar baker of London, a man, as report

[1] See below, p. 308.
[2] William Letwin, *Sir J. Child, Merchant Economist*, 1959.
[3] Mathias, op. cit., ch. I.

says, worth £40,000, came from London on purpose to treat with me, and accor ling to agreement he is to build all the front, twenty seven yards, a stat ly house of good hewn stone, four storeys high, and then to go through the same building with a large entry, and there, on the back side, to erect a house for boiling and drying sugar, otherwise called a sugar baker's house ... If this is done, it will bring a trade of at least £40,000 a year from the Barbadoes, which formerly this town never knew. This house, it is thought, will cost at least £1,400.[1]

Glasgow, like Liverpool, had West Indian sugar and local coal. While the Forth boiled salt, the Clyde boiled sugar. From the mid-seventeenth century, Gallowgate, where the wholesale traders gathered, began to fill up with manufacturers of woollens, linen, hardware, soap and refined sugar. The raw sugar had begun to flow in soon after the culture was introduced into the West Indies between about 1630 and 1640. Quickly the complex of interrelated trades had grown – sugar, cotton, rum, tobacco, slaves. In 1669, John Cross and four other Glasgow tradesmen clubbed together to build the East Sugar House and operate it under a Dutch master boiler. Later in the century the North, South and West Sugar Houses followed. Other sugar houses sprang up in Bristol. Sugar boiling was one of the few manufactures that Bristol merchants invested in, and sugar was to be the main pivot of Bristol's prosperity in the eighteenth century. In the seventeenth its importance was growing, but it remained only one source of wealth among many.[2]

From the early Middle Ages, salt had been a vital article of trade. Even that model of self-sufficiency, the Arab, had had to depend on the caravan for salt. Likewise the English villager. In the 1670s and 1680s the salt industry was on the move technically and geographically. The one serious technical alteration that was necessary when coal replaced wood in the boiling of the brine was in the pans themselves. Lead was replaced by iron which stood up better to the high temperatures: hence on the shore near Edinburgh those 'iron pans, eighteen feet long, nine feet broad ... larger pans and houses than those at the Shields ...'.[3]

A number of salt works provided for purely local needs, as did the Derbyshire and Lymington works. But the Scottish and Tyneside industries were much more than that. It was not only to remote hamlets that the travelling salt man brought his monthly supply of salt from Salt Preston (the old name for Prestonpans). The coal-fired salt pans of

---

1 *The Moore Rental*, ed. T. Heywood (Chetham Society), pp. 57–78.
2 See P. McGrath, *Merchants and Merchandize in 17th-century Bristol*, 1955, Introduction, esp. pp. x–xxix.
3 Brereton, op. cit., p. 98.

the Forth area — maybe a hundred or so of them — exported on a large scale to Holland. So did the lesser producers of Ayrshire and Sutherland. The Tyneside salt industry was feeling the competition not only of Scottish producers but of the new brine pits sunk at Droitwich by Robert Steynor in 1692. These added to the output of the ancient *wiches* of the area — twenty-seven at Nantwitch, twelve at Northwich. The town of Northwich was 'full of smoak from the salterns on all sides'.[1] More important was William Marbury's recent discovery of rock salt on his land in Cheshire, which was in due time to add to the trials of the Tyne industry and provide another valuable export trade for near-by Liverpool. The brine pits in Cheshire had been found to contain 'a hard rocky salt that lookes cleer like sugar candy, and its taste shows it to be salt, they call this Rock Salt, it will make very good brine with fresh water to use quickly ... and soe they boile these pieces of rock or some of the salt water when the tydes in which produces as strong and good salt as the others ....'.[2] The rock-salt solution yielded, in fact, about ten times as much salt as the natural brine solution, and expanding production set up an increased demand for both coal and iron.

Salt refining was not the only industry where technological advance was drawing productive processes together and inaugurating the phase of reciprocal demand for coal and iron that was to characterize the Industrial Revolution itself. The quest to protect material burned with coal from the noxious elements in coal had had its first victory in the 'closed pits' for melting glass. This was followed by the development of the reverberatory furnace between the 1670s and 1690s. By the end of the century the problem of smelting lead, tin and copper with coal was solved and the production of all these metals was rising. The Cornish tin mines were a scene of vigorous activity. In one concentration of twenty or so miles, Celia Fiennes estimated about 1,000 men to be employed. The importance of coal is clear from her description:

... they take the oar and pound it in a stamping mill which resembles the paper mills, and when its pure as the purest sand ... this they fling into a furnace and with it coal to make the fire, so it burns together and makes a violent heate and fierce flame, the wattle by the fire being separated from the coale and its own drosse, being heavy falls down to a trench made to receive it, at the furnace hole below: this liquid mettle I saw them shovel up with an iron shovel and soe pour it into moulds in which it cooles and soe they take it thence in sort of wedges or piggs I think they call them; its a fine mettle thus on its first melting looks like silver.

[1] C. Fiennes, op. cit., pp. 224–5.   [2] Ibid.

The workmen, she noticed, laboured Lord's Days as well as week-days to keep the mines from flooding. The danger from water and the expense of drainage were the permanent nightmare of the mine owners. As output increased and mines deepened, the problem attracted the attention of inventors, including Thomas Savery. Savery was a Devon man who had spent his childhood near the mines. He became a military engineer with a number of inventions to his credit. In a work called *The Miners Friend* (1698) he described an engine for pumping water out of a mine. It consisted of a boiler and condenser. As the steam condensed, a vacuum was created and water was sucked from the sump by a pipe up to ground level. The idea was not novel. A French inventor, Papin, claimed that it was copied from him. The Marquis of Worcester[1] had adumbrated something very like it much earlier. But Savery was the first to produce a working model. We know little of the detail of his engine except that its defects encouraged Savery to cooperate with Newcomen a few years later to produce an improved 'atmospheric' engine. It was still prodigal of coal and of iron. Yet even its faults were a stimulus to other industries and to further experiment.

Even though the improved technology they sought repeatedly and obstinately eluded them, the ironmasters of the west were certainly increasing their output under the later Stuarts. And though methods of production had not yet changed much, capital investment was evidently becoming more concentrated in those new areas. Three partnerships controlled about half the old charcoal iron industry that was scattered from North to South Wales and throughout Cheshire, Lancashire, Nottinghamshire, Staffordshire, Worcestershire and Gloucestershire. One was concerned principally with the Forest of Dean and the Stour Valley; a second with north Staffordshire and a third with Cheshire and North Wales. Money belonging to various members of the Foley family were in all three, and the managing director, John Wheeler of Wollaston Hall near Stourbridge, was common to all. The group controlled the major processes — furnaces for smelting the ore, forges for refining the pig iron produced by the furnaces, and slitting mills for rolling and cutting the iron bars from the forges into rods, which then went on to the nailers. It was the midland iron users above all who created the demand for the varied output of the Foley businesses.

[1] See above, p. 187.

By sea and river, by road and bridlepath, raw materials and iron of various qualities and in its several stages of manufacture, moved towards this hub of the finished iron trades, where swarmed the blacksmiths and whitesmiths, locksmiths, edge tool makers and gunsmiths, and out numbering them all, the nailers.[1]

Another use for iron was as a base for tin plating. The Foleys were amongst a group of midland iron masters who commissioned that lively jack-of-all-trades, Andrew Yarranton, to visit Saxony and bring back the secrets of the tinplate process. But the industry that arose is part of the eighteenth- rather than the seventeenth-century story.

The pattern of industry in later Stuart Britain was changing perceptibly. Inventive talent, immigrant skill and a reservoir of enterprise had already by 1700 made good the loss of markets sustained by the old woollen industries. New and varied textile industries — wool, part wool, linen, silk and lace — had grown up. Industries known for centuries as household processes, like brewing and soap boiling, had become specialized industries operating on a considerable scale, with large investment in building, plant and raw material stocks; all this in response to a growing demand that came first from towndwellers and then spilt over into country markets. If Leland could have retravelled his sixteenth-century itinerary, he would have seen some striking changes. Along the Tyne and the Weir, in the West Riding and in Lancashire, new towns had appeared. In East Anglia and in Devon, villages had become towns. In a steady process of urbanization, coal had played its part by making town life possible. Here and there, by turning cottages into workshops, it sometimes made them almost uninhabitable with the reek of fumes from the stove that heated combs and cards. Yet, save for glass making and brewing, few industries showed much sign yet of radical reorganization of production. The great textile industries, which contributed so much to the nation's income and exports, were still, broadly, 'domestic' industries working under the direction of merchant organizers. Great variety of production, and great increase in production, had been achieved; but so far it had been achieved within a framework of industrial arrangements long familiar. Modified it had certainly been, but not revolutionized. And this was true also of the forges where a growing army of gunsmiths, cutlery makers and metal workers of many kinds was changing the rural scene round Sheffield and Birmingham.

Change of a different kind was visible where the salt boilers of the

---

[1] B. L. C. Johnson, 'The Foley Partnerships', *Econ. Hist. Rev.*, IV, no. 3, 1952.

Tyne and of Cheshire, the lead miners of Derbyshire, the tin and copper miners of Cornwall, and — parent to all these — the coal miners of north-east, Midlands, Scotland and west were creating a new kind of industrialized, or semi-industrialized society. The contribution to the national income and trade of such industries was as yet limited by comparison with, say, the textile industries. Yet they had already made their presence felt, not always happily. Salt works were early offenders, and round Newcastle the sulphur tainted the air. The local inhabitants were already used to it but it smelled 'strongly to strangers'. The holdings and privileges of villagers in mining areas were falling victim to manorial lords who enclosed land just as much to control and lease out the coal, mineral or clay under the soil as to improve the agriculture on the surface. It was such industrial spectacles that caught the eye of an uninstructed lay chatterbox like Celia Fiennes. She took it for granted that cloth of some sort would everywhere be made. Tin mines, copper mines, salt pits — she herself had a mortgage on a Cheshire salt estate — and iron mines were different. They were interesting, exciting even. In one respect, her eye was a more faithful guide than even she realized. For though iron technology was the will-o'-the-wisp of the seventeenth century, the iron masters were on the brink of their great discovery which would ultimately release their manufacture from its medieval shackles. Like most scientific discoveries, this one had a long history. Within the industries that had, in their different ways, adapted their technologies to meet the problems of using coal — the salt, malt, brewing, soap, glass, tin, lead and copper industries — was contained a growing reservoir of observation and experience. The seventeenth century had already listened to a number of claims to smelt iron with sea coal. So far they had been proved false. But some of the basic principles had been grasped. It seems, in retrospect, to have been only a matter of time before this problem, too, was solved.

CHAPTER TEN

The Pyramid of Debt and Credit

To speak of a 'money market' in the seventeenth century is to suggest a refinement in contemporary financial arrangements that did not exist. The bulk of economic transactions was settled locally in hard money — mostly in silver coins. 'The common payment', it was said, 'is more in silver ... payments run betwixt merchant and merchant in silver; in the Customs House in silver; and all petty payments throughout the kingdom in silver.' Gold might be used in great capital deals or as a means of holding wealth, but silver, less precious, was more convenient. 'The silver coins do rule the market in all places, because of the abundance thereof, being 500 to one of gold.'[1] The coinage, increasingly in need of reform and renewal, was to be supplemented as the century progressed by various forms of paper monetary substitutes and forms of credit. But outside London the dominance of hard money was only very gradually disturbed. Other means of payment were still subject to serious disadvantages. Even by the end of the century, it was still difficult to transmit funds from the country to London. One writer said in 1697 that such payments were still made in specie. Whether this was wholly true or not, there appears to have been only one provincial 'bank' in the seventeenth century — Thomas Smith's at Nottingham. Most writers on finance agreed that some means of transferring capital, the proceeds of taxation, and of settling commercial debts across country, was still urgently needed. Financial institutions were still largely metropolitan affairs. Contemporaries deplored this as draining ready money from the rest of the kingdom to London. At best, the circulatory system was imperfect and full of lesions. Yet there had been important advances since the beginning of the century in the techniques and mechanisms by which money was lent and borrowed. Funds were lent by those with money over and above

[1] Supple, op. cit., p. 173, quoting Malynes.

what they needed for their immediate or foreseeable needs. Funds were borrowed by those who had less than they needed, and the borrowers now regularly included not only private individuals but Government, which needed to borrow on the scale that dwarfed all private borrowings. These abnormal needs of Government played a major part in bringing into existence a class of men who increasingly acted as intermediaries between lenders and borrowers; for they were so large that no one lender could possibly satisfy them out of his own resources. The rudimentary character of government financial machinery and the generally low estimation in which government credit was held by the public combined to bring to the fore this class of financial middlemen — 'bankers' as they came to be called — who were trusted by lenders with their funds. These were then re-lent to Government. A major theme of the financial history of the times is the rise of these 'banker' middlemen, mostly goldsmiths by origin, and their subsequent decline and replacement by financial institutions which enabled the State to raise its capital funds more directly from the lending public.

Much of the machinery for private lending and borrowing in operation after the Restoration was a legacy from early Stuart times. Merchants had become familiar with the convenient practice of raising money on bills of exchange due to be paid to them at a later date. A lender who wanted to invest cash for a short period could buy such a bill. He might even realize his cash by reselling it. But there were legal difficulties about recovering his cash if the transaction went wrong. And bills were often for relatively small and inconvenient amounts. For an investor who wanted to place his cash more safely and for a longer period, the bond was a better vehicle. It ran usually for six to twelve months and the penalties for a defaulting debtor were more severe and more easily enforceable. The cautious lender was even better off with a pledge than with a bond. For here he had the security not only of the borrower's credit but the assurance that if the borrower defaulted, he would become the owner of whatever piece of real or personal property was pledged as security for the loan. Jewels, plate, even a peer's robes, might be used in this way, but the most common was the mortgaging of land. Down to the third and fourth decades of the century, the mortgage remained a desperate expedient, for the penalty on default was harsh: immediate foreclosure. By the 1640s, the law was less severe. Defaulters could, and did, apply to keep their lands, provided interest payments were made promptly. Such changes made matters easier for the borrower and stimulated the needy landowner especially to look for a mortgagee to help him over his shortage of capital. They did not necessarily work to the disadvantage of lenders provided they could realize their capital claim if necessary. But for this, financial middlemen were necessary. Hence the growing business of the scriveners and goldsmiths. Lenders would deposit their cash with a scrivener or goldsmith who made it part of his business – not yet a major part perhaps – to relend these deposits to selected borrowers. Neither the terms nor the extent of such transactions are by any means clear. All we know is that they were common, and growing, by the 1630s and 1640s and thereafter. 'Bankers', Clarendon wrote, 'were a tribe that had risen and grown up in Cromwell's time, and never even heard of before the late troubles, till when the whole trade of money had passed through the hands of the scriveners; they were for the most part Goldsmiths.'[1]

Why should the scriveners or the goldsmiths have become the progenitors of the banker? Partly, no doubt, because they dealt, in the course of their ordinary professional or commercial dealings, with men who were either affluent enough to have surplus cash to place out at interest, or enterprising or extravagant enough to need more capital than they could raise from their own resources. Also because they were compelled to provide for their everyday business a safe repository where money, bullion, plate and jewellery could be stored. After Charles I closed the Mint in 1640 and seized the bullion in it, such private treasures found their way to the goldsmiths for safe deposit. Until it was wanted, the money could be used for 'running cash', or lent out, or used to buy bills of exchange at a profitable discount. As the bills were realized, the cash could be used to meet the demands of those depositors who needed their cash back. Finally, the receipt which the goldsmiths normally gave the depositor came to be used in a new way: initially, the bank note was merely a promise to pay the depositor his rights, and this in turn passed from hand to hand as a substitute for hard cash. A different form of money was provided by the order which a depositor sometimes gave the banker to pay one of his creditors – the forerunner of the modern cheque. Somewhere between 1640 and 1675, the City of London came to know the three essential functions of the banker as a later age recognizes them; to take deposits, to discount bills and to issue notes.

To issue notes: strictly, the note required the banker to repay the

[1] Clarendon's *Life*, 1872, vol. III, p. 7. And see R. Ashton, *The Crown and the Money Market 1603–1640*, 1960, esp. ch. I.

depositor his deposit. But experience soon showed that depositors did not all come back to claim their rights at one time. It was therefore possible for the banker to issue a volume of notes larger than the volume of cash deposited with him. This took the banker's function a step beyond the provision of amenities and credits for individuals with property to pledge. It associated the banker with the supply of additional money for the community at large. From 1650 onwards, writers on economic problems focused their attention increasingly on this aspect of banking: as a means of enlarging trade and releasing the nation from that nightmare of 'a scarcity of money' by which it was always haunted. Most of them were interested in easing methods of payment between business men – in the same way as the Bank of Amsterdam enabled their Dutch contemporaries to settle mutual obligations by transferring amounts from one merchant's account to another. The easier transmission of money from one part of the country to another, and easier ways of raising money on the security of property were other popular topics of debate. Samuel Hartlib believed that 'there be no way to raise this Credit in Banks but by mortgage of lands'. Here was the germ of the later fashion for land banks which came to fruition in 1695. All in some degree shared the belief that William Petty expressed in a dialogue in an essay of 1682:

Qu. 26. What Remedy is there if we have too little money?
Answer: We must erect a Bank.

The general drift of the pamphleteers was plain. Banks would benefit private individuals by offering a secure placing for funds that might otherwise be hoarded, and by providing more generous credit for merchants and manufacturers wanting to expand. They would also assist the Crown by making it easier to transmit funds – the produce of taxes especially – from place to place. They would promote employment, especially of the poor, by new enterprises founded from larger credits. They would, specifically, benefit the landowning classes by enhancing the value of land, because more money meant cheaper money and a reduced rate of interest. For was not the price of land closely linked to the rate of interest? Child, for example, argued that as the rate of interest had fallen during the seventeenth century, the number of years' 'purchase' had risen. In earlier times, land was selling for ten or twelve years' purchase; now it sold for at least twenty. If the rate of interest was now to be reduced from 6 to 3 per cent the purchase period used would rise to at least thirty years. Child's arguments were powerfully countered by Locke, who argued that the price of land was largely independent of the general rate of interest. Both agreed, nevertheless, that as an investment land had several advantages. Its relatively stable value made it a secure investment. It could always be used as security for mortgage. It had snob as well as economic appeal.[1] Both were also correct in believing that the rate of interest was falling. The imperfections of the money market meant that there was not always and in every case a rate of interest that everybody could confidently expect to enjoy. Local conditions and special risks were always blurring the picture; but the general trend was a falling one and towards this the growing volume of paper instruments and credit transactions contributed. The preoccupation with a reduced rate of interest was almost universal in the years after the Restoration. In one sense, it was yet another reflection of the belief, half admiring, half jealous, that the Dutch held the secret key to all the principles of economic advancement. In his *Brief Observations* (1668) Josiah Child listed fifteen points wherein the English should observe and follow Dutch economic practice. But the keystone of the Dutch arch he found in the low rate of interest prevailing there. This enabled entrepreneurs of every kind to borrow capital for expansion cheaply and easily. This was 'the CAUSA CAUSANS of all other causes of the Riches of that people': lower the rate in England and all else would follow. The rate of interest, in fact, was already invested with some of the qualities of a sort of economic phlogiston, capable of imparting its inflammability to a still soggy economy.

In another sense the clamour for a lower rate of interest was merely one facet of an immediate economic and political controversy that raged throughout the sixties and seventies and was to continue, though in rather different forms, thereafter. This controversy centred not primarily upon private but upon public finance – specifically upon the needs of the King's Government for resources larger than could be provided from the income at its disposal. This need for money, mostly to fight the wars against the Dutch, was being met – many would have said shamelessly exploited – by a handful of large 'bankers', mostly goldsmiths, and the immediate target of the most powerful critics was the apparently extortionate rate of interest which they managed to screw out of the Exchequer. Like most of the fruitful economic debates of the century, then, this one was not abstract but concrete. It

---

[1] For a full discussion see H. J. Habakkuk, 'The Rate of Interest and the Price of Land', *Econ. Hist. Rev.*, V, no. 1, 1952.

arose from a specific situation. The key to its understanding lies in the relationship between government income and expenditure.

When Charles II came to the throne, a bargain was struck with Parliament by which the King was given an hereditary revenue calculated at £1·2 million: in return he gave up those ancient feudal dues like wardship and knight service which had caused so much trouble before the Civil War. The Court of Wards had been estimated to be worth £100,000 even at the time of the abortive Great Contract; its abolition by statute in 1660 was a wise move — 'possibly the most important single event in the history of English landholding'.[1] The three main sources of permanent revenue under the new arrangements were the Customs, as of old; to these were now added the Excise, whose parentage men were apt to attribute alternately to Pym, the Devil and the Dutch; and the almost equally unpopular Hearth Tax introduced in 1662. The Customs were estimated (on the experience of the Interregnum) to contribute £400,000 a year, but during the first four years after the Restoration yielded barely £300,000 and fell below this during the Dutch wars. Only after 1674 did the yield rise to £500,000 and more. The Excise — on ale, beer, cider, spirits, tea and coffee — yielded at first less than the Customs — about £268,000 in 1662–63.[2] Here again wars and economic difficulties kept the yield down until after the end of the Third Dutch War in 1674. Thereafter it rose to an average of over £400,000 a year — another pointer to a rise in general standards of consumption. By comparison with these, the Hearth Tax was of minor importance. The first collection brought in a mere £37,000. This rose to £200,000 when it, too — like the Customs and Excise — was handed over to the customs farmers in 1667 and thereafter produced an average of £170,000 a year. Its yield was low, its vexations were notorious. To establish whether a house had a fire hearth or a stove falling within the definition of the Act an offensively inquisitorial system was necessary. Poor men without votes complained they had to pay two shillings a year for a stove 'not worth two-pence, which the chimney villains call a hearth'. Evaders walled up their chimneys or gave false returns or bribed the collector. It was dropped in 1689. Unpopular as the Excise was it had its supporters — landed gentry who thought that a consumption tax spread the load more

---

[1] D. Ogg, *England in the Reigns of James II and William III*, p. 55. For earlier history see above, p. 93.
[2] *A State of the Revenue of Excise since Michaelmas 1662*, H.M. Customs and Excise Department Library.

widely over the nation, tax reformers (like Petty) who thought it both desirable and just, and bureaucrats and devout Royalists who thought it convenient.

To the hereditary revenues had to be added numerous other sources of income and special parliamentary grants for extraordinary expenditure. Again, the most usual form was the Assessment, a legacy (like the Excise) from the Commonwealth. Theoretically, the yield from the Assessment was fixed – usually at a rate of £70,000 for one to eighteen months. The total was spread over the counties and cities, each being rated for a specific quota. Local commissioners then reallocated the load over parishes, until each victim's real or personal property was assessed for tax. The special aids to support the Dutch wars in 1664–65 and 1666 were similar in character, and from this type of tax came the later so-called Land Tax of 1677.

The parliamentary revenues were in large measure a recognition that wars could only be financed by extraordinary taxation. But, as we have seen, the hereditary revenues anyway fell a long way short of what they were supposed to provide for normal expenses, at any rate in the early years of the Restoration. Charles II, like his predecessors royal and republican, faced the same disadvantages of a growing reliance on taxation as his main source of income. It was irregular, it was too little and it was always too late. Like them, therefore, he was thrown into the hands of moneyed men who would help him put right these deficiencies. The problem of timing the royal income was largely the business of the tax farmer. Down to 1671, the Customs were farmed; so till 1683 was the Excise, and from 1667 to 1684 the Hearth Tax also. Through the farmers, the Government anticipated an irregular and tardy income – also, to some extent, supplemented it from time to time by loans. They functioned (to use the language of a later age) as a form of deficit, as well as anticipatory, public finance. In the early years after the Restoration, the customs farms went back to the old stalwarts as a reward for faithful service. When Pepys visited the customs offices[1] he found the representatives of families that would have been familiar to Cranfield four decades and more earlier in the same office: Sir John Wolstenholme, Sir Nicolas Crisp, Sir John Jacobs, Sir John Shaw. But on the very same day, he recorded an interesting event: the knighting of Martin Noell by the King – 'which I much wonder at; but yet he certainly is a very useful man'. The incident was important. Noell was a Cromwell supporter[2] but he was very useful: so were the

[1] 5 September 1662. *Diary*, p. 284.   [2] See above, p. 130.

other goldsmith bankers – Backwell, Vyner, Meynell, Duncomb and the rest. Once again the royal need for funds on a scale far exceeding any one man's pocket was to invest such men with a unique importance. Their private banking business was founded on good will. Surplus cash from merchants and gentry alike flowed into their coffers. Here as nowhere else was a repository of wealth large enough to mitigate the royal poverty. Thus the goldsmith bankers came to occupy a position of unique power in the economy, advancing money not only on the hereditary revenues but also upon the extraordinary grants made by Parliament from time to time for the war. Clarendon describes the way they worked. As soon as an Act of Parliament was passed authorizing a tax, the King sent for the bankers. These were not 'above the number of five or six . . . some whereof were aldermen and had been Lord Mayors of London.' The Lord Treasurer then declared the need for cash. 'Thereupon one said "he would within such a time pay one hundred thousand pounds, another more, and another less . . .".' Then came the haggling over the rate of interest to be paid. The bankers then asked for specific revenues to be assigned to them as security and the contract was made and sealed in the King's presence.[1]

His Majesty, Clarendon added, 'always treated those men very graciously, as his very good servants, and all his Ministers looked upon them as very honest and very valuable men'. Charles certainly knew their value. Very special measures were taken under the Privy Seal in 1664–65 to make a free gift of additional interest of £8,000 – over and above the normal 6 per cent – on the loans which Backwell alone had made to the King of over £280,000.[2] Clarendon was probably right to defend their personal honour, and to add that the system worked satisfactorily until the multiple disasters of war, plague and the Great Fire made it impossible to collect taxes. Thereafter the principal of the debt grew, interest payments lagged. The bankers became indispensable: but they did not become more popular. No one could doubt who was their chief enemy. It was George Downing. In earlier years Downing had worked in the office of one of the tellers of the Exchequer and observed how much that office lost by reliance on the bankers. Hence (says Clarendon) it was he who took the initiative in forming a parliamentary claque against the bankers, calling them 'cheats, bloodsuckers, extortioners . . .

[1] Selections from the *Life*, pp. 450–3.
[2] I am indebted for this and other references in this section to Mr. H. Roseveare. They are taken from his unpublished thesis on 'The Advancement of the King's Credit 1660–1672'.

the causes of all the King's necessities'. Yet there was more behind Downing's antipathy than personal malice. Odious though his methods frequently were, Downing was inbued with a passion for economic efficiency. That the royal finances stood in desperate need of reform needs no elaborate proof. It was not that Charles was particularly profligate as such things were managed at the time. But his generosity, like that of his father and grandfather, was secret and unregulated. The Lord Treasurer, as administrative head of the Exchequer, was virtually powerless to carry out his duties as head of the national accounts so long as each compartment was kept entirely separate and each source of revenue reserved to a separate commitment. He could not prevent the King from charging a new pension for a favourite as a priority on a revenue fund already burdened with debt. Except for the first incumbent of the office (the Earl of Southampton) the Treasurers – Clifford, Danby, Rochester and Godolphin – were all hard workers. When the Treasury was put into commision, as it most often was in this period, its members were likewise zealous and efficient – no one more so than Downing who was Secretary to the Treasury Commissioners from 1667 to 1672. But the Treasury's task remained unsolved. Taxpayers were reluctant and hostile, methods of collection and accounting rudimentary, the influence of politicians, favourites and sinecurists powerful; above all expenditure was always outrunning funds.[1]

Downing's plans were adumbrated in 1665–66; when the Additional Aid was voted for the Dutch War, he succeeded, against Clarendon, in getting parliamentary authority for four innovations. First, that all money raised by the Bill should be appropriated to a specific purpose, i.e. the war. Second, that a direct appeal should be made to the country at large to lend *directly* to the Exchequer on the product of the Aid. Third, that those who lent should be repaid by a regular chronology – first in, first out. Fourth, that these repayment orders could be 'assigned'. A creditor could therefore take his order to a banker and have it cashed – at an appropriate discount – if he needed ready money before his repayment fell due. There followed a long period in office at the Treasury for Downing and the first real attempt to make the Exchequer master of its business of controlling receipts and issues. Even the great Backwell would be peremptorily summoned to come to Downing's house at 8 a.m. 'without faile'.[2] In January 1671 Downing even succeeded in persuading the House to impose a tax of fifteen

---

[1] See S. B. Baxter, *The Development of the Treasury 1660–1702*, 1957, *passim*.
[2] Roseveare, op. cit.

shillings on every £100 lent by the bankers that carried over 6 per cent interest. The aim was clear: to encourage lenders to place their funds directly with the Exchequer instead of *via* the bankers. Contemporary events seemed to support his belief that the money was there if only means could be found of tapping the resources that the goldsmiths managed to tap. Why, otherwise, was it easy for the Royal African Company to open its subscription books for £100,000 in November 1671 and exceed its target by £10,000 in less than a month?[1] In his campaign against the bankers, Downing had the powerful support of the East India group, led by Josiah Child, who appeared before the Lords in 1669–70 to deplore, *inter alia*, 'The late innovated Trade by the Bankers in London'.[2]

Downing's dream of a national Exchequer 'bank', drawing loans directly from the investing public, was based, like most of his ideas, on his observation of the Dutch system. But it was not to be realized – in his lifetime, anyway. The bankers retained their power, in spite of his efforts and in spite of individual bankruptcies. It was to take a revolution in financial methods to make government loans competitive with commercial investment in the eye of the ordinary lender. During the first twelve years of his reign, Charles's debts rose to more than £2 million. In 1672 capital bankruptcy was only staved off by suspending the repayment of loans to the lenders. And when this was done – by the famous 'Stop of the Exchequer' – the truth emerged; most of the repayment orders issued to individuals had already been discounted by the bankers, in whose hands they now stood. The burden of the 'Stop', therefore, fell mainly on them – nearly £1 million. The Government was enabled to spend its revenues on the Dutch war instead of on repaying its debts. But the effect on the bankers was dire. Five large ones went bankrupt. The largest survived, but precariously. Backwell crashed later in 1682; Vyner followed in 1684. The bankers' grip was broken, and England had stumbled, as it transpired, into the device of a funded debt; for in due course, arrangements were made to pay to the bankers annual disbursements large enough to cover 'annuities' to them and their stricken clients. The principal of the loans thus remained unpaid, but interest of 6 per cent was forthcoming on the capital. Downing's ambitious schemes remained unfulfilled at his death in 1684. But Pepys, to whom he had confided so many of his hopes, lived to see the national finances transformed in the 1690s upon principles that bore Downing's stamp: statutory guarantees of

[1] Davies, op. cit., p. 66.   [2] Roseveare, op., cit.

appropriation and interest, and assignability under Treasury control. Under Downing, the country had taken a major step forward to a modern system of public finance.

After the comparative lull of the eighties – comparative peace, comparative prosperity – the chronic malady of the public finances attacked again in 1689. In January of that year William entered upon eight years of war, beginning with a succession of disastrous blunders and reverses. But these, as Montagu observed with truth as well as felicity, had the effect not of frightening Englishmen out of their wits but into them.[1] Again, as in the days of the Dutch war, a wave of pamphlets and projects welled up from merchants, bureaucrats, publicists and cranks. Once again the talk was all of banks and of credit. Yet the situation was now fundamentally changed in several respects. The political basis of public credit had been transformed by a revolution which had altered the relationship of King, Parliament and people. The country was, for the time being, politically unanimous as it had not been since the days of the Spanish menace. A more buoyant economy was capable of bearing an increased load of taxation. The tax system was now better administered by a direct system of collection through the commissioners who had largely replaced the old tax farmers. Though far from perfect, this improved system of revenue collection formed (as a recent authority has said) 'the first condition of success of the new funding devices'.[2] Through the new funding devices, supported after 1696 by a reformed coinage and a revivified administrative system, the Government was able to take immediate command of economic and financial resources that far exceeded its income from taxation.

The yield of taxes from November 1688 to March 1702 and the expenses to be met were broadly as shown in the Table on opposite page. The deficit, of just over £13½ million, was left to be raised by loans.[3]

---

[1] D. Ogg, op. cit., p. 355.

[2] E. Hughes, *Studies in Administration and Finance, 1558–1825*, 1934, p. 167.

[3] 1. Including such items as fines on smugglers, licences to hawkers and pedlars, fines on Hackney coaches.

2. Including 'the late Queen's coffin and mourning and funeral expenses of nearly £50,000: subscription to the French Protestants £75,000; cost of royal jewels and plate £170,000; bounties "for apprehending" Highwaymen, Tratitors and Libellers and very many other accidental Payments'.

3. The gross figure was largely the cost of servicing debts.

In printing the accounts in the Appendix to his *History of the Public Revenue* (1789), Sir John Sinclair commented on the accuracy of the national bookkeeping at the time which drew attention 'to the error of a single farthing' and contrasted this with the complexity and confusion of the public accounts of his own time. He might have added that it contrasted also with the much worse confusion of the decade before the Revolution.

Government Income and Expenditure 1688–1702

Income	£ million	Expenditure	£ million
Customs	13·3	Navy	19·9
Excise	13·6	Army	22·0
Hearth Money	0·2	Ordnance	3·0
Letter Money	2·0	Civil List	8·9[2]
Land Tax	19·1	Divers Issues	18·4[3]
		Less Repayments	14·0
			4·4
Poll Tax	2·6		
Promiscuous Taxes	3·9[1]		
Divers Receipts	4·0		
Total	£58·7 m		£72·0 m

The main burden of cost emerges plainly enough: the war. So does the largest single source of revenue. Although the yield of the Customs and Excise had risen as the rates of duty on old items of consumption were increased and new ones, like salt, added, neither of these equalled the yield of the Land Tax. In the years after the Revolution the rate varied from one shilling to four shillings in the £. Early in Anne's reign it was to be standardized at four shillings, with a yield of some £2 million a year. While the majority of the revenue came from the pockets of consumers in general — more than half the Excise, for example, fell in one way or another on the national beverage, beer — the landed gentry as a class formed the largest single source of one tax. Some observers have seen the Corn Bounty as a *quid pro quo* designed to persuade the squirearchy to acquiesce more readily in the Land Tax. Be that as it may, its burdens increased the problems of the small squire. Living in increased isolation from their greater neighbours with more ample resources, and bitterly critical of City finance and government influence, they made up the strength of the Tory Party. Their suspicions fell most on that Whig or 'Dutch' finance, as they called it, which taxed them in order to pay interest to the affluent investor in such mysteries as the trading and industrial companies, the Bank of England and the new government annuities and lotteries.

217

The Act of January 1693 is usually taken as the founding of the National Debt, and in so far as it represented a new blend of several older elements, its title need not be disputed. Its principles were simple enough. A million pounds was to be borrowed. Each subscriber had a choice. He could either take a straightforward annuity of 14 per cent per annum for his life, tax free, or he could gamble, by accepting 10 per cent until 1700 and thereafter a presumably growing share in a fund that would have fewer calls to meet as the annuitants died off. Those who lived longest benefited most. (The last died in 1783, enjoying a pension of over £1,000 a year on his original investment of £100!) The fund of income to pay the annuities was provided by new excise duties on beer and other liquors, placed in a special and separate fund at the Exchequer. Two principles were thus firmly established. The annuitant was not to see his capital again. And the creditor lent not upon the security of the King's word but on the security of an Act of a sovereign Parliament which included provision for severe penalties against any servant of the Crown who disobeyed the terms of the Act. What had happened by accident in 1672 was now established as an accepted principle of public finance. Again, although the King had been compelled on several occasions since 1678 to agree that loans be secured on 'a good fund of credit', based on specific duties allocated by Act of Parliament, this was the first time the two principles had been combined. From this device of allocating specific duties for the payment of perpetual but theoretically redeemable annuities, repeated over and over again, came the National Debt. In return for a statutory promise to pay interest on a long-term basis, the Government secured a large volume of spending power to tide it over its immediate emergency.

Of the many other schemes of the nineties for providing credit for the war, most foundered, amongst them the so-called Million Lottery of the same year, which was run as a sweepstake. Its failure discredited for the moment this method of raising money. A large number of projects for land banks likewise came to nothing. The essence of this proposal was the idea that land, rather than cash, could be made the reserve against which notes and credit could be issued. It was therefore somewhat in the manner of the modern building society. But its sponsors were men of imagination rather than reputation, and investors preferred something more in line with earlier forms of banking.[1]

The acrimonious debates of the sixties and seventies had in general

[1] For a full discussion of the schemes of the nineties see Horsefield, op. cit., esp. Part IV.

indicated not so much a fundamental disbelief in banking principles as a disbelief in individual bankers. Doubts centred not on the fact that there were too many bankers, but too few. And the few there were operated too much in secret and under too little public discipline. The Bank of England emerged in 1694 from a jumble of schemes, one of which at least proposed to connect a settlement of the still unrepudiated debt to the goldsmiths of 1672 with the issue of a new loan. But the goldsmiths themselves did not like the idea that their debt should be permanently funded, and therein lies perhaps one explanation of the alleged hostility of the goldsmiths to the new Bank. Another scheme proposed that Parliament should assign a yearly rent to pay interest on a new loan of £1 million. And this may have stimulated Montagu to launch the annuity scheme already described. The moving spirit behind both proposals was a much-travelled Scottish pedlar turned merchant, William Paterson. What finally emerged in 1694, with the backing of more powerful and reliable City men, was a scheme which grafted a system of commercial banking on to an orthodox plan for lending money to the Government. Against formidable opposition in the Lords (which included all the bishops except the Archbishop of Canterbury) an Act of Parliament allocated certain duties to cover the payment of interest at 8 per cent on a loan of £1,200,000. They included duties on ships' tunnage, which caused the new Bank to be know popularly as the Tunnage Bank. But besides interest on their capital, the subscribers obtained other privileges – and responsibilities. Under a charter of incorporation, they were empowered to borrow money on parliamentary security, to deal in bullion and bills of exchange and act as a pawnbroker. The Bank's powers in regard to the issue of notes was left strangely obscure.

That did not prevent the subscription being made an immediate and resounding success. By the end of 1694 the Bank had advanced the whole of its capital to the State, mostly in the form of bills. These were taken by the Exchequer in return for tallies and used to pay government creditors. The creditors could either cash them at the Bank, leave them on deposit, or, most important, they could accept a bank note. For, having parted with much of its capital, the Bank could only carry on by issuing an equivalent amount of paper money, on the security of the tallies received from the Exchequer. The position looked – and for some time was – risky. But with Montagu and a group of City men of integrity behind it, the Bank survived a succession of early crises. It was already indispensable to the Government, not only as a source of credit but as a channel through which remittances were made to the armed forces overseas. And it attracted the support not only of English investors but of foreigners too. Dutch investors, those resident in England not least, had been in the habit of leaving their surplus capital on deposit with goldsmith bankers. Others had invested more recently in annuities.[1] The presence of men like the great Houblons and Gilbert Heathcote in the direction of the Bank encouraged them from the start to buy Bank shares. For long the Dutch were to remain supporters of the Bank. Even in the twentieth century a chair of Divinity in Utrecht University still counted original Bank stock amongst its endowments.

The Bank survived the perils of the nineties — even of the recoinage which despatched all its rivals except the Bank of Scotland founded a year after itself. There was general agreement that the currency was urgently in need of reform. The old silver coin had been clipped until its uncertainties were wreaking havoc with trade and prices, 'people being cautious in setting a price on their goods, without knowing in what money they would be paid'. As the Mint price undervalued silver against gold, there was a regular export of the further clippings of silver coins. Although ranking as petty treason, clipping and melting were becoming minor industries. Between 1672 and 1696 about £2 million of silver coin had been exported in this way. Everybody agreed that currency reform was overdue. There was less agreement about how it should proceed. In a classic controversy, one school of thought, led by the Secretary of the Treasury, William Lowndes, proposed that silver coins should be devalued by 20 per cent. The other, led by John Locke, argued that the silver coin should be restored to the nominal weights fixed at the recoinage of Elizabeth. This latter view carried the day. But the immediate result was an extreme shortage of currency which placed all bankers in a serious predicament. It was fortunate for the Bank of England that its Directors were not only men of integrity but of great personal wealth and credit. Gilbert Heathcote might be litigious, parsimonious and unpopular, but he was reputed 'the richest commoner in England', and such reputations made all the difference in a crisis of credit. As it was, the recoinage pricked the bubble of inflation that had grown since early in 1695. From the spring to the autumn of 1696 prices fell rapidly. They would certainly have fallen more if the Bank had failed, for the volume of coinage in circulation after the reforms remained smaller than before by £1 million.

[1] See C. Wilson, *Anglo-Dutch Commerce and Finance in the 18th Century*, 1941, pp. 90–7.

Notes, on the other hand, were playing a larger role in the economy. More than a half were private bankers' issues but rather less than a half came from the Bank of England.[1] Having survived the ordeal, the Bank emerged stronger than before. From 1697 its ties with Government were more intimate. Its note issue grew and became increasingly standardized. Its discount business flourished, and its bullion trade was buoyant. These hopeful signs were reflected in the price of bank stock which rose from $51\frac{1}{2}$ in February 1697 to 98 on 15 September 1697.[2]

An eighteenth-century historian, Anderson, 'often heard it said by persons who lived at this time that Sir Gilbert Heathcoat gained by that rise of the price above sixty thousand pounds'.[3] If Heathcote really did realize capital gains of this magnitude (as distinct from enjoying the thought of an improved valuation of his estate) he can only have done so by selling his stock. This he may well have done. For at this point in our financial history, something like a national – indeed an international – market in securities is becoming apparent. Once again the model was Dutch. Since 1609 Amsterdam had had a Bourse and Dutch investors and speculators had not only bought and sold the shares of the great trading companies but had developed a lively speculative market in them. Gamblers with little or no cash could bet on a future price of shares even when they had no intention of buying or selling them.[4] Since the Restoration a similar market had been growing up in the stock of the great trading companies and of the industrial companies that proliferated in the nineties. Not unnaturally, some of the unwise or unlucky lost money. In the chagrin and confusion of the deflation of 1696–97 much of the blame for the losses by investors was attributed to 'the pernicious art of stock jobbing' and its practitioners. The goldsmith-bankers, practising in larger numbers than before, seem to have achieved comparative respectability. The odium they had sometimes had to bear was now transferred to the stock-jobber; occasionally it fell on those 'monied men' and promoters who used them as agents. Josiah Child was said to have established a private express service from the south of Ireland which gave him advance information of the arrival of the East India Company ships. Bank of England

[1] See Horsefield, op. cit., p. 14, for figures. Circulation of coins in 1693 came to £20 million, in 1698 to £18·5 million. Notes in 1693 totalled £2 million, in 1698 £4·3 million.
[2] Scott, op. cit., vol. I, p. 350. Clapham, *The Bank of England*, 1944, vol. I, p. 51.
[3] Anderson, *History of Commerce*, vol. II, p. 631.
[4] See C. Wilson, op. cit., p. 81. The fullest description of a modern Stock Exchange by Joseph de la Vega, *Confusion de Confusiones* (1688), is now available in translation, ed. H. Kellenbenz, 1957.

Directors were also said to have a private news service from the Continent which guided their investments or speculations in the market.[1]

In November 1696 the Trade Commissioners themselves entered the lists against the bogus company promoters and their stock-jobbing agents. 'Ignorant men', they said, had been 'drawn in by the reputation, falsely raised and artfully spread, concerning the thriving state of their stock.' The promoters then sold what was in fact worthless stock to the gullible. The brokers' share in this was said to be their venal willingness to act as tools of the bogus promoters – that 'they confederated themselves together' either to raise or depress prices as suited their interests.[2] The charge had often been made on the Amsterdam Exchange. It was to be made many times afterwards, wherever stocks and shares were marketed.

The immediate outcome was an Act of 1697 'to restrain the number and ill-practice of brokers and stock-jobbers'. Not more than 100 were to be allowed. A broker needed a licence and badge from the City authority, was required to keep books, and was made liable to heavy fines for transgressing these rules. An unauthorized broker might be fined £500 and thrice pilloried. The following year the brokers were expelled from the Royal Exchange, migrating to a near-by coffee house in 'Change Alley'. The importance of these allegations lies less in their truth or falsehood[3] than in the light they throw on the development of an investment market. The dealings in the stock of the East India Company, the Hudson's Bay and Royal Africa Companies, often at prices double that at which they had been issued, indicated a buoyant supply of capital. New companies evoked a lively response from City investors. Yet, before the nineties, the issue of stock and subsequent dealings in it were relatively unorganized. Government borrowing was, as we have seen, even worse organized, unsatisfactory to borrowers and lenders alike until after the Revolution. Subscribers had little idea when they would get their capital back and tallies circulating at a 40 per cent discount still bore witness to the lack of confidence in government credit.

In the nineties this situation was changing fast, and the appearance of the stockbroker and stock-jobber is one evidence of it. Another is the appearance (in John Houghton's *Collection for Improvement of Husbandry*

---

[1] John Francis, *Chronicles and Characters of the Stock Exchange*, 1849, pp. 23, 365.

[2] Scott, op. cit., vol. I, p. 357.

[3] For a reasoned case that the charges were exaggerated see Scott, op. cit., pp. 359–61.

and Trade, 1692) of quotations of stocks and shares, or 'Actions'[1] as he called them. His early lists contained only eight quotations, including the East India, Africa and Hudson's Bay Companies. By 1694, the list had increased to over fifty quotations. The stock of the Bank of England and a large number of industrial companies now came in; most of the 'industrials' only to be ousted (in deference to the outcry against stock-jobbing) by 1698. In 1700, a much-abbreviated list testified to the slaughter of the mid-nineties. But as well as the four great trading companies, Houghton did quote one or two semi-public stocks, like those of the Million Bank. Government annuities he could hardly as yet quote. The annuity was not yet a freely transferable thing. But it would not be long before it was. Bank of England stock, which was more than half way to being a government issue, was already a familiar quotation. The market in company stocks was a pointer to what could be done once confidence could be established in government credit. Bank stock illustrated the possibilities clearly. The Government had borrowed from the public. But the investor who wanted to realize his investment in cash no longer needed to worry about selling his tally or order-to-pay at a heavy discount by a cumbrous process. Bank stock now circulated from hand to hand on a recognizable (if still imperfect) market at published prices which could be watched from week to week. If need be, it could be sold by a relatively simple transfer procedure at the Bank.

If the workings of this embryonic Stock Exchange seemed to some (especially to those who lost by them) to bring new perils, it also brought considerable benefits, both to borrowers and lenders. It did not, of course, eliminate risk. No investment method since has done so either. The fluctuations between the highest and lowest quotations within a single year remained very wide by later standards. For a cool-headed investor with plenty of resources and patience, or for the shrewd speculator, such large margins could promise large gains. They could mean ruin for a small investor who, having bought at the top of the market, lost his nerve and tried to get out at the bottom. The bulk of the securities offered on the market were therefore unsuited to the investor in search of security for his *capital*. The annuity only offered him an assured *income*. The ordinary stock of the great trading companies offered him the certainty of neither. Their bonds, however, did. By 1685, the East India and Royal African Companies had both issued a considerable amount of bonds, redeemable at par and carrying a

---

[1] The usage underlines Tory gibes about 'Dutch finance'. The Dutch word was 'actiën'.

fixed rate of interest. They were therefore an admirable repository for the investor who knew that he might want his capital back, perhaps at short notice, and wished to avoid the risk of getting it back only at a depreciated figure.

Under the pressure of war economics, the England of the nineties had transformed its financial institutions. The new complex embodied much of the experience of earlier decades. Its workings were far from perfect, far from complete, and there were crises yet to come. But a series of incentives had now been designed to draw out the savings of investors of all types, from those of small means who took life annuities, those of moderate means who took the bonds of the trading companies, to the affluent or speculative who could afford the luxury of high risks in the fluctuating stocks of the great companies. The growing market in such securities was a natural, but far from inevitable, development from the restricted and precarious assignment system that had broken down in 1672. Relations between Government and the great companies with the investor were slowly achieving new standards of probity; this was not because morality was improved, but because experience had repeatedly shown that the failure to honour obligations ricocheted on the borrower. While the interest on these invested savings flowed back to a widening class of investors, a large part of the product of taxation and loans was redistributed to government contractors supplying munitions, ships, naval stores, iron, timber, uniforms, boots, ordnance, paper, sailcloth, biscuits, beer, pork and victuals of all kinds to the armed forces. A sizeable share was redistributed in pensions, sinecures, rewards and bribes of all kinds so that politicians and Crown servants even of the second order, like Downing and Blathwayt, could end as landed gentry with large fortunes. Even the squires and farmers reaped their modest harvest from the Corn Bounty. So, in one way and another, the new financial institutions helped to redistribute wealth and stimulate the growth of trade, industry and even agriculture, though the mobility of money left much to be desired. All this was a far cry from the days, still within the memories of those living in 1700, when land had been virtually the sole, and certainly the best, investment for a man with surplus income. The reform of the coinage was a necessary condition of continued progress. The economy survived the drastic blood-letting operation so 1696 the more easily because paper substitutes for money of all kinds had grown steadily since the Restoration. All these innovations combined to create something that can fairly be called a financial revolution.

Probably nothing comparable was to happen until the introduction of inconvertible currencies in the twentieth century.

This structure of public finance was only possible because it was accompanied by a fiscal system that was, by contemporary standards, remarkably well devised and administered. Taxation was drawn from two main sources: direct taxation of the propertied classes, indirect taxation of trade, manufactures and consumption (through customs and excise duties). Thus all classes of society contributed. All grumbled and cursed – but all paid. The burden was therefore spread between propertied and non-propertied, producers and consumers. It did not fall so heavily on industry (as it did in Holland) that production costs, wages especially, were raised to levels that priced its products out of the market. It did not fall (as it did in France) on the non-privileged classes so as to create deep and permanent grievances. For all its faults, the system provided a steady flow of revenue without destroying the economic and social conditions within which trade, industry and agriculture could expand. Many eighteenth-century writers were to believe that this was the greatest single achievement made possible by the English constitutional settlement worked out between 1660 and 1702.

CHAPTER ELEVEN

Political Arithmetic and Social Welfare

'HE was in those days very mathematical, and I have heard him say his genius lay more to mathematics than chymestry.' So wrote John Aubrey of Thomas Willis the physician. And of William Harvey, who discovered the principle of circulation of the blood: 'He was pretty well versed in the Mathematiques.' Observations such as these recur frequently throughout the gallery of seventeenth-century portraits he called *Brief Lives*. The striking fact is not merely that mathematical aptitude was diffused amongst large numbers of the dons, divines, physicians, antiquaries and gentry of Aubrey's world: but that it had become with many of them a passion, a supposed key to the knowledge of man, society and the universe. The sixteenth century had witnessed a renaissance in mathematical knowledge, especially of algebra, in Italy and the Low Countries. This was developed in the seventeenth century by Napier and Briggs with their invention and perfection of logarithms, by Descartes in the field of geometry, by Fermat and Pascal in the theory of numbers and probability, and crowned by Newton and Leibniz with the invention of the calculus. Applied mathematics became a new science with the appearance of the *Principia* in 1687. Our immediate concern is with the social uses of mathematical knowledge; but in the unspecialized imagination of the seventeenth century, the key that unlocked the secrets of the universe was essentially the same as that which might unlock the vaults of social wealth. Oxford dons and dilettante noblemen like Lord Herbert played with the mathematical principles of invention. The Royal Society's experiments brought forth improved clocks and optical instruments. The appointment of the first Astronomer Royal and the founding of Greenwich Observatory by Charles II were closely linked with problems of navigation, especially that of discovering longitude at sea. This is not to say that science was merely a product of social or economic development, nor could it yet afford adequate guidance for the understanding of the movements of society. But, as always, the independent logic of thinkers interacted with social needs, fundamental and applied science overlapped generously, and the greatest scientific minds of the day like Boyle, Hooke and Newton did not disdain the practical conundrums of invention and technology. Isaac Newton was from 1699 a diligent and successful Master of the Mint who raised it to new standards of accuracy and precision.[1]

The use of mathematics for social and economic purposes crystallized in what the seventeenth century called 'political arithmetic'; what a later age would call statistics. These in turn were polarized round two related concepts: the measurement and social distribution of wealth, and the balance of trade, by which it was thought the economic health of the nation might be judged. In Charles II's England, neither concept was new but each was given a new and sharper definition by more accurate and refined statistical methods.

Attempts to compute the wealth of the nation derived primarily from the *Observations on the London Bills of Mortality*, published in 1662, which seem to have been the joint work of John Graunt and William Petty. Petty, later a Fellow of the Royal Society, made his mark on contemporary society in many ways. He was doctor, public servant, surveyor and geographer, statistician and political economist, an astute business man who amassed a great fortune and founded a noble family. The governing passion of his life was his belief that quantitative measurement was the key to the understanding of social facts, and that inductive reasoning must be based on statistical data.[2] Politics, whose end was 'to preserve the subject in *Peace* and *Plenty*', could only be founded on such knowledge of 'the lands and the hands of the territory'. Such knowledge was indispensable 'in order to get good, certain and easy Government'. These doctrines from the *Observations* almost certainly represent Petty's contribution. His central idea was an imaginative marriage between medicine and mathematics, his subject for anatomy being the body politic, his surgeon's knife the 'algorithm'. Five years later, at the end of the disastrous Dutch war, he wrote his *Verbum Sapienti*, an essay in which he applied his ideas of quantitative measurement. His immediate object was to influence tax policy by showing that property could with advantage be taxed less heavily and

---

[1] Sir John Craig, *The Mint*, 1953, ch. XII.
[2] E. Strauss, *Sir William Petty: Portrait of a Genius*, 1954, esp. ch. 16; also G. N. Clark, *Science and Social Welfare in the Age of Newton*, 1937.

the people more heavily: perhaps also to justify a further dose of that most unpopular of all taxes, the Excise. But it was essential to his purpose to place his convictions on a statistical base. Accordingly this has been called the first serious attempt at a calculation of the national income. Six million inhabitants, he believed, spent an average of £6 13s. 4d. a year. Out of the resulting total of £40 million, about £15 million could be identified as deriving from property in all forms – rent, shipping, investment, etc. – so that the rest must be the reward of labour. In other writings he puts the fashionable faith in trade as a source of wealth on a statistical basis. Agriculture was a relatively unrewarding form of economic activity. A husbandman could earn only a quarter of the wages of a seaman. This reflected their respective economic and social values. Enrichment therefore lay in an increased population increasingly engaged in trade, industry and shipping.[1] Like many of his contemporaries Petty had lived and studied in Leiden and other Dutch universities. The influence of his long residence there emerges not only in his statistical convictions but particularly in his repeated disbelief that territorial size was necessarily related to national wealth. Holland was small, but she was rich. Hands, not acres, were the key to riches.

The natural heir to Petty's methods and ideas was Gregory King, whose *Naturall and Political Observations* (1696) carried the scientific observation of social facts a stage further. King, like Petty, combined practical ability with great powers of logical argument and method. The son of a land surveyor, he became assistant to the Royal Cosmographer, drew up the plans for the development of King (now Soho) Square, held the office of Lancaster Herald (which gave him access to the records of the great landed estates) and ended as Secretary to the Commissioners of the Public Accounts.[2] King did not publish any of his works on political arithmetic, but his findings were quoted by Charles Davenant in his economic *Discourses* in 1698. Like Petty, King aspired in time of war and desperate need for larger public revenues to measure the means by which the nation could sustain a protracted struggle. 'If to be well apprized of the true state and Condition of a Nation, Especially in the Two maine Articles of its People, and Wealth, be a Piece of Politicall Knowledge, of all others, and at all times, the

[1] In his *Conditions of Economic Progress*, (1951) Mr Colin Clark describes the persistent tendency for labour to move from agriculture into commerce and industry as 'Petty's Law'.

[2] See *Two Tracts, by Gregory King*, ed. G. E. Barnett, 1936; also Colin Clark, *National Income and Outlay*, 1937, ch. 10. On his activities as speculative developer in London see above, p. 177.

most usefull, and Necessary; Then surely at a Time when a long and very Expensive Warr . . . seems to be at its Crisis, Such a Knowledge of our own Nation must be of the Highest Concern. . . .'

There follows a calculation of the population, divided into their social groups and credited with the proportion of the national income they represented, from the King and Royal Family down to the humblest of the poor and vagrant. Like his contemporaries, King was still trying to reconcile his scientific outlook with an imagination and a set of beliefs essentially traditional and medieval. He is therefore encouraged to discover that his population estimates are consonant with the repeopling of the world by eight persons after the Flood in 2300 B.C. Some of his countings (like his million rabbits and 24,000 hares and leverets) are less reliable than others. But in general his work is a meticulous product of the technique of 'sampling' of tax records. His final figure of 5·4 million for the population of England and Wales and his conclusions as to its age distribution have been reckoned by modern experts to be not far from the truth.[1] London, he thought, held 530,000 people, other cities 850,000, villages and hamlets the rest. Over 3 million earned or drew their living from the land, and a total national income of over £49 million was attributable to agriculture and to industry and trade in the proportions of about 2·5:1. Three million persons in agriculture therefore earned some £25 million while about one-tenth of that number earned over £10 million by trade and industry. Here again, as in Petty's work, statistics appeared to confirm that there was more wealth to be got out of trade than out of agriculture.

Coming as it did in the midst of the economic and financial crisis of 1696–97, King's other work, *Of the Naval Trade of England a.*[0] 1688, links up directly with the second and related preoccupation of the statisticians; the balance of trade. This was the essay on which Davenant based his famous work of 1699: *An Essay upon the Probable Methods of Making a People Gainers on the Ballance of Trade*. The idea of the balance had been a long time a-growing. Double-entry book-keeping in counting-house and farm accounts may well have generated the idea that Leviathan itself might have its own balance of account that showed either profit or loss. In several economic crises – in the 1620s, in 1650, in 1669 – successive governments had directed that this balance

---

[1] D. V. Glass, 'Gregory King's Estimate of the Population of England and Wales 1695', *Population Studies*, 1949–50; P. E. Jones and A. V. Judges, 'London Population', *Econ. Hist. Rev.*, 1935.

should be calculated, so that they could not only assess the probable yield of taxes but better understand the sources of national wealth and devise policies to husband and expand it. The obvious point at which the flow of wealth was observable was the Customs House. After 1671, when customs were collected by the State (instead of the farmers), it became easier to obtain information. In 1673, in the middle of the Third Dutch War, the Council of Trade and Plantations once again resolved that 'a motion be made . . . about putting the account of the Ballance of our Trade into some method of Inquiry and satisfaction'.[1] But it was not until the next great economic crisis of 1696 that much was done. In the commission of the Board of Trade, dated 15 May 1696, the Board was directed to survey economic conditions and 'to enquire into and examine what trades are or may prove hurtful, or are or may be made beneficial to our Realm of England . . .'. But when the Board asked the Customs Commissioners for the necessary facts, they were told that the answers were simply not available. The Board therefore recorded its opinion: ' . . . it may be necessary to have an officer of skill and Experience in the Customes to collect from every day Entrys in the Custome House such a distribution Accompt . . . and also to Digest the Books of the Out Ports with the same Distribution and method.' The Treasury agreed, Edward Culliford was appointed the first Inspector-General of Exports and Imports, and the continuous history of English trade statistics began. Culliford and his four clerks were instructed 'to make and keep a particular, distinct and true account of this importaciouns and exportaciouns of all commodities into and out of this kingdome and to and from what places the same are exported and imported . . . and to present a faire and exact Scheme of the Ballance of Trade . . . between England and any other part of the world'. They discharged their duties methodically and faithfully.

That England was ahead of France and Holland in attempting to coordinate her national trade statistics was probably because she had been more successful in unifying her tariff system and bringing provincial administration under central surveillance. But, ironically, it was only when the idea of striking the balance was put into practice that the intricacy of the task was fully realized. How relevant were the summaries of Culliford and his successors to the actual movements of goods and money? Did the official values given to goods for purposes of taxation represent their real value? How far did smuggling falsify the picture? How much English coin was illegally smuggled out or melted

[1] G. N. Clark, *Guide to English Commercial Statistics 1696–1782*, 1938, pp. xiv et seq.

down in addition to the foreign coin and bullion which could (since 1663) be legally exported? Finally, what of those invisible exports and imports which were not anywhere recorded – payments for freight, commissions, insurance, armies and navies victualled abroad, embassies in foreign countries, and the costs of travellers abroad?[1]

It became increasingly clear that the 'statistics' were very imperfect. Yet the intellectual ferment generated by the socio-economic problems of the time was not to be stilled because one concept showed signs of coming to grief. The simplest view of the balance of trade had been to equate surplus of exports over imports with a net gain of treasure to the nation. This view – essentially that of Mun's writings – was by no means extinguished even much later in the eighteenth century. But from the Restoration, trade balance theory began to undergo a subtle change as it merged with other concepts, especially those concerned with the role of labour in society. These in turn reflected a growing preoccupation with the greatest social problem of the day: the poor. We need look no further than Gregory King's statistics for striking evidence of the magnitude of this problem at the end of the seventeenth century. Out of his total population of 5·5 million, 1·3 million – nearly a quarter – are described baldly as 'cottagers and paupers'. Another 30,000 were 'vagrants, or gipsies, thieves, beggars &c'. 'Labouring people and out-servants' accounted for another 1¼ million. At a conservative estimate, a quarter of the population could be regarded as permanently in a state of poverty and underemployment, if not of total unemployment. This was their chronic condition. But when bouts of economic depression descended, the proportion might rise to something nearer a half of the population.[2]

Writers – especially the statistically minded concerned with population and its employment – could hardly avoid reflecting on the waste of human energy that might with thought and effort be fruitfully employed. The same thought had occurred to some of those unsophisticated benefactors who made provision in their charitable trusts for the teaching of new skills to the children of the poor. When such

[1] For a critique of the value of the Inspector-General's statistics see G. N. Clark, *English Commercial Statistics*, pp. 33–42.

[2] See D. C. Coleman, 'Labour in the English Economy of the 17th Century', *Econ. Hist. Rev.*, VIII, no. 3, 1956. I entirely agree with the contention of this stimulating article that seventeenth-century attitudes to labour were rooted in economic conditions of the time but Mr Coleman seems to me to underestimate the theoretical links forged by writers between balance of trade theory and employment proposals. See my 'Other Face of Mercantilism', *Tr. R.H.S.*, fifth series, vol. 9, 1959.

ideas appeared in a writer like Petty in the form (as has been said) of a 'labour theory of value in its embryonic stage',[1] it was not merely the result of abstract speculation. It was a logical deduction from his statistical analysis of society; so that, as Petty said, 'the whole stress (of production) lies upon the equivalent of 1,800,000 labourmen'. Hence his favourite epigram that 'labour is the Father and active principle of wealth, as Lands are the Mother', and the starting point for later theorists of labour value from Adam Smith to Karl Marx.

Such ideas, logical, statistical, deductive, blended with another stream of humanitarian and remedial proposals for employing the poor. The incidence of these was often closely related to the onset of acute depressions in trade and employment. For example, 1649, a year of regicide, mutiny and disorder was also afflicted by a disastrous harvest that drove grain prices up to famine levels and added to the prevailing depression in the cloth industry. Hence a crop of proposals for social and economic reform by writers including Samuel Hartlib, Rice Bush, Peter Chamberlain and William Goffe. These men were not Utopians or radical reformers, as the Levellers and Diggers were. They were anxious to come to terms with the existing social system, not to transform its character in a revolutionary way. Hartlib outlined in numerous pamphlets a scheme of workhouses, to be financed by Parliament, for employing the poor and educating their children. In *The Poor Man's Friend* Bush described the efforts of 'eleven gentlemen' (Hartlib being one) who actively promoted such an institution in London. Chamberlain and Goffe, both strongly influenced by the charitable schemes common in Holland, likewise urged ambitious projects of public works to stimulate employment. The note of compassion struck by these writers was genuine, 'The poor', wrote Goffe, 'ought to be encouraged and mercifully dealt with and kindly used, until their slow hands be brought to ready working . . .'

The recognition that the problems of poverty, employment and national welfare were all intimately connected was common to many of these writings. It was to recur whenever, as in 1659, 1668 and especially in the 1690s, chronic underemployment became acute and men were provoked to ponder social remedies. The idea of public workhouses and charity schools was mooted in many of the pamphlets of the nineties. John Bellers, the Quaker clothier, published his *Proposals for a College of Industry* in 1695; in 1697 his *Epistle to Friends concerning the Education of Children*. John Cary, the wealthy Bristol sugar

[1] Strauss, op. cit., p. 214.

merchant, touches on similar proposals in his *Essay* (1696). All these writers were 'mercantilist'. They believed firmly in state regulation of trade. None departed from the basic principles of the balance of trade. Yet their conception of the balance was changing, and the change is nowhere more clearly visible than in the writings of the great London merchant and Governor of the East India Company, Josiah Child. Child first set down his ideas on economic policy in the Plague year — only one year after Mun's *England's Treasure by fforraign Trade* was first printed. The first edition, called *Brief Observations*, dealt mainly with problems of interest and usury but it had an appendix containing an earlier essay by Culpeper which included a plea for the relief of the poor. Child's work went into five editions between 1668 and his death in 1696. As edition succeeded edition the problem of the poor occupied more space. From the text that it is man's 'Duty to God and Nature to provide for and employ the poor, whose condition is sad and wretched, diseased, impotent, useless' he developed his proposal for an assembly of 'Fathers of the Poor'. These should have power to buy land, build workhouses and hospitals, set the poor on work. Simultaneously, Child modified the conception of the balance of trade. Sharing the doubts of those who despaired of measuring accurately the volume of imports and exports, Child concluded that the balance might be better judged by assessing 'the number of hands' any economic project seemed likely to employ. This juxtaposition of organized charities with a theory that came near to equating national prosperity with the value of the nation's labour might seem suspiciously like a marriage of convenience for the benefit of a sectional interest. Yet what emerges, rather surprisingly, is not an argument for low wages but for high. Pointing to the Dutch example, Child concludes: 'Wherever wages are high, universally throughout the whole world, it is an infallible evidence of the riches of that country: and wherever wages for labour run low it is proof of the poverty of that place.'

Child was not, as used to be maintained, a precocious forerunner of of the *laissez-faire* school.[1] He was simply a more enlightened mercantilist who believed firmly in all the fundamental principles of that school. But he saw no reason why these, and the balance of trade principle in particular, should not be reconciled with a more generous social theory designed to spread the benefits of an expanding economy downwards through all the ranks of society. On both counts — the new conception of the trade balance and the treatment of the poor — his works were to

[1] For an extensive discussion of this see Letwin, op. cit., *passim.*

be a matrix of opinion and policy, not only in England but in Europe. Charles Davenant, who succeeded Culliford as Inspector-General, was writing in terms remarkably similar to Child's in his essay on the trade balance in 1698. Brewster's *Fifth Essay: That the Full Employment of All Hands in the Nation is the Surest Way and Means to bring Bullion into the Kingdom* (1702) tried to juxtapose and reconcile the old theory and the new. A dispassionate reading of these and many other writings on the trade-and-employment theme does nothing to support the theory, long maintained, that Restoration society was dominated by the commercial classes 'whose temper was a ruthless materialism, determined at all costs to conquer world markets from France and Holland and prepared to sacrifice every other consideration to their economic ambitions'.[1] The rhetorical image becomes even less convincing in the light of recent evidence concerning the extensive philanthopy of the seventeenth-century merchant class as a whole and of men like Cary the Bristol sugar merchant, Child the East India Director, Firmin the London mercer, who founded movements and institutions to help and educate the poor.

The flow of charity has not been analysed for this period so thoroughly as for the earlier period. But different evidence suggests that the movement continued, with a growing emphasis on the endowment of active apprenticeship and instruction for the juvenile poor.[2] The later years of the century saw the beginnings of that remarkable institution, the Charity School, to teach the rudiments of education to poor children and enable them to earn their living. At Norwich, one-third of the 160-odd charities created in the city date from this period. At Bristol, and above all in London, benefactions continued and may have increased proportionately in the barren years of the mid-nineties. If anything, the conscience of the merchant was more tender than that of his feudal predecessors in social office; for his status was less secure and he did not always move in the world with the unselfconscious ease

[1] R. H. Tawney, *Religion and the Rise of Capitalism* (1921) p. 268. This theory was adopted in other studies, See e.g. M. Beloff, *Public Order and Popular Disturbance 1660–1714*, 1938, p. 18. M. James, *Social Policy during the Puritan Revolution*, 1930, pp. 334–5, E. Roll, *A History of Economic Thought*, 1939, p. 99, holds that mercantilists 'if they held any wage theory at all, believed in an economy of low wages'. Such *dicta* seem to me, to say the least of it, exaggerated.

[2] Under Gilbert's Act (1782) parishes were required to make returns of all the charitable trusts under their jurisdiction. An *Abstract* of this information was printed, by order of the House of Commons, in 1816. But, so far as I am aware, the contents have never been systematically analysed. See my communication to the Royal Hist. Soc. 1959.

of the landed gentlemen nor speak with the authority of the learned clerk. Thus charity kept breaking in.

Yet it is fair to ask what the practical effects of this growing concern for the poor were. Plainly it could not, as yet, provide more than emergency aid of a marginal kind. The opinion was widely held in the later years of the seventeenth century (by Child amongst others) that 'our charity is decreased'. How accurate this was we do not know, but it seems probable that private donations would fall off as *public* provision for the poor increased: and the yield of the poor rate rose from £665,000 to £900,000 between 1685 and 1701.[1] Nearly a century later the total capital assets of all the charities amounted to about £5 million, the annual income to £259,000. It would be reasonable to assume that in the late seventeenth century the income could hardly have exceeded £200,000 a year. The total of poor rate and private charities could hardly therefore have yielded £1 a head *per annum* for the needy poor: enough, perhaps, to stave off the worst of the immediate hunger and cold but little more. The educational and training schemes, on the other hand, had a real value, but their effects were slower to make themselves felt.

Even the poor stood to gain something from the improved prospects of trade, manufactures and farming. As described elsewhere[2] this period saw a diversification and spread of manufactures in London, the Midlands, and the north. The woollen cloth industry itself was changing its nature and shifting from its old locations. The new products of Norfolk and Devon, Yorkshire and Lancashire — stuffs, serges, and cheap worsted mixtures — were cheaper than the old and were competing vigorously in world markets. This trend towards cheaper and more varied articles for wider consumption, in home as well as in foreign markets, was itself a kind of expansion generated in part by the depression or stagnation of prices, an escape from the overcrowded markets for older products.[3] Stable, even sagging, prices and mercantilist policy alike stimulated the search for invention, creating a new rhythm of innovation that was to reach its climax in the mechanical inventions of the Industrial Revolution. The invention of the stocking frame brought the opportunity of employment to thousands of cottage workers in and around Nottingham, Derby and Leicester. Somewhere about the middle of the seventeenth century, England managed to convert her marginal deficit of grain supplies into first a marginal, and

---

[1] Figures from Beloff, *op. cit.*, *passim.* [2] See ch. Nine.
[3] G. N. Clark, *Science and Social Welfare in the Age of Newton* (1937), pp. 57–9.

later a substantial, surplus. Supplies of coal were more abundant, prices pretty stable. Colonial imports like sugar and tobacco expanded in volume and fell dramatically in price.

Such developments offered the labouring poor prospects a shade less gloomy, provided no spectacular disaster overtook the nation's trade or agriculture. But the social situation remained precarious. Dramatic economic expansion so far was limited to overseas commerce and the measurable profit from this went in the first instance to the middle and upper classes. The instinct, based partly on observation, that 'employment' was the main social *desideratum*, was sound. The increase of population in the sixteenth and earlier decades of the seventeenth century had created a labour surplus. To absorb this gainfully into an economy still in many respects inflexible was a process that could only advance when the economy itself advanced. But this was a slow, almost imperceptible process. Often, the poor could only look for their immediate salvation to the voluntary redistribution of income through charity and poor relief.

CONCLUSION: THE 'MERCANTILE' AGE

All boundaries in economic history are disputable. The frontier between the Middle Ages and modern times is no exception: it has been placed at many points. The Restoration has a better claim than most dates to be regarded as the economic exit from medievalism. The material basis of medieval economic policy – and of much medieval economic thought – was scarcity and the fear of scarcity. This lay behind the policy of 'provision' which Heckscher saw as typifying official attitudes towards economic life in the Middle Ages everywhere: its object was to try 'to ensure the greatest possible supplies for native consumption'.[1] After 1660, this policy of 'provision' (essentially a concern for distribution) gave way at point after point to the conscious encouragement and protection of home *production*. Instead of relying on legislation and penalties aimed at the exploiters of scarcity, the authorities now adopted a new strategy designed to increase output: from this the consumer would benefit – so the argument ran – in the long run. In the primary matter of food production, the Corn Laws of 1663, 1670 and 1689 devised an ingenious system of regulations designed to encourage the producer of corn. The consumer was not abandoned, but plainly the emphasis of favour was on the producer. The effects have been infinitely

[1] E. Heckscher, *Mercantilism*, rev. ed., 1955, vol. II, pp. 80 et seq.

debated: by those who (like Arthur Young) believed that the system had brought prosperity, bigger output and stable prices to agriculture generally, and those (like Charles Townshend and Adam Smith) who (for different reasons) believed the system did not encourage the growth of corn. The only incontrovertible fact, one historian has said, 'is that between 1689 and 1765 English agriculture underwent a vast improvement'.[1] This was England's contribution to the process of agrarian change that was going on everywhere in western and southern Europe after the mid-seventeenth century. The increase in population that had marked the previous century and a half seems to have stopped, or at least slowed down. The former gaps in the European food supply opened up had been filled by Dutch shipping enterprise exploring Baltic sources. This had been one of the foundations of Dutch economic expansion before 1650. Now local supplies were catching up with the rise of population. The consequences for local economies like that of England and the universal middlemen, the Dutch, were considerable.[2]

Increased local, national production was the object also of the numerous Acts of Parliament and regulations made under them for stimulating, protecting and subsidizing other forms of trade and industry, including the cloth industry, and of the great Navigation Laws themselves. Later economists, of whom Adam Smith was the greatest, came to regard the whole system as a mischievous and corrupt distortion of the economy in the interests of private individuals. Such measures as comprised 'the mercantile system' constructed in these years subordinated 'consumption' to production and to the interests of producers, wrote Adam Smith. By Adam Smith's day, the criticisms of the system had some force, though they reflected, besides rational criticisms, some imagined and exaggerated ones. A century or so earlier, when the system was fashioned, it is arguable that it was the necessary matrix within which the infant economy had to be coaxed into growth. Of the economy as a whole, as of agriculture, the only incontrovertible fact is that it did improve and did grow. Trade, industry, agriculture, exports, ports, shipping all showed abundant evidence of vigour and enterprise in an age that lacked the convenient explanatory apparatus – spectacular price rises, population increase or revolutionary inventions – available in previous and subsequent periods of growth. While

---

[1] D. G. Barnes, op. cit., p. 29.

[2] See J. A. Faber, 'Het Probleem van den dalende graanaanvoer uit de Oostzeelanden in de tweede helft van den zeventiende eeuw', *Afdeling Agrarische Geschiedenis Bijdragen*, 9, Wageningen, 1963.

it may be conceded that the most obvious beneficiaries of the new policies *were* the 'producers' — landlords, farmers, manufacturers, merchants, shipowners — it can hardly be doubted that a rising volume of employment followed in the wake of their enterprise. Standards of living for the people at large might not yet show any spectacular or measurable rise, but certainly a larger population was living at standards that were not falling and were in some respects tending to improve. The expanding market for New Draperies, especially for the cheaper varieties like fustians, must have included a sizeable proportion of customers from the lower half of society. Even the luxuries of early Stuart times were now selling at prices poorer people could afford. Tobacco, which legend said was worth its weight in silver earlier in the century, could be had for 3½d. a pound by 1680. The brewers were worried by the competition of coffee. Clothiers were feeling the effects of imported calicoes. And so on. Plainly, habits of consumption were changing, and not only among the rich. For all save the 'Poor' — and their numbers remained very large — life was a little more varied, a little less primitive. Most remarkable of all was the co-existence of real economic expansion with a long period — over a century — of stable prices that lasted from the 1620s to the 1750s.[1]

---

[1] As Professor E. H. Phelps Brown and Miss S. Hopkins point out, the general stability of price levels survived the short-term upheavals that afflicted society at intervals. See their article, 'Seven Centuries of the Price of Consumables', *Economica*, 1956.

Political Arithmetic and Social Welfare

GREGORY KING (1648–1712), herald, genealogist, engraver and statistician compiled a series of 'Natural and Political Observations and Conclusions upon the State and Condition of England' which he completed in 1696. It was 'received' by the Board of Trade on 27 September 1697, but was not printed until 1801 when George Chalmers appended it to the second edition of his *An Estimate of the Comparative Strength of Great Britain.* Though Harley commented that 'these assessments are of no good foundation', they are nevertheless the best surviving account of the economic state of Britain towards the end of the seventeenth century. King had ample opportunity during tours of England undertaken in the course of his genealogical and heraldic researches, to record at first hand. The table given here is taken from the 1804 edition of Chalmers's *Estimate.* The column 'Heads per family' should be read in the sense of 'heads per household'.

Number of families	RANKS, DEGREES, TITLES AND QUALIFICATIONS	Heads per family	Number of persons	Yearly income per family	
160	Temporal Lords	40	6,400	2,800	
26	Spiritual Lords	20	520	1,300	
800	Baronets	16	12,800	800	
600	Knights	13	7,800	650	
3,000	Esquires	10	30,000	450	
12,000	Gentlemen	8	96,000	280	
5,000	Persons in Offices	8	40,000	240	
5,000	Persons in Offices	6	30,000	120	
2,000	Merchants and Traders by Sea	8	16,000	400	
8,000	Merchants and Traders by Land	6	48,000	200	
10,000	Persons in the Law	7	70,000	140	
2,000	Clergymen	6	12,000	60	
8,000	Clergymen	5	40,000	45	
40,000	Freeholders	7	280,000	84	
140,000	Freeholders	5	700,000	50	
150,000	Farmers	5	750,000	44	
16,000	Persons in Sciences and Liberal Arts	5	80,000	60	
40,000	Shopkeepers and Tradesmen	4½	180,000	45	
60,000	Artizans and Handicrafts	4	240,000	40	
5,000	Naval Officers	4	20,000	80	
4,000	Military Officers	4	16,000	60	
511,586		5¼	2,675,520	67	
50,000	Common Seamen	3	150,000	20	
364,000	Labouring People and Out Servants	3½	1,275,000	15	
400,000	Cottagers and Paupers	3¼	1,300,000	6	10
35,000	Common Soldiers	2	70,000	14	
849,000		3¼	2,795,000	10	10
	Vagrants		30,000		
849,000		3¼	2,825,000	10	10
SO THE GENERAL ACCOUNT IS:					
511,586 Families	Increasing the Wealth of the Kingdom	5¼	2,675,520	67	
849,000 Families	Decreasing the Wealth of the Kingdom	3¼	2,825,000	10	10
1,360,586	Nett Totals	1 1/20	5,500,520	32	

PART THREE

The Wealth and Poverty of England
1700 to 1763

CHAPTER TWELVE

Rural Change. The Uses of Adversity

IF grain prices are any criterion, the first half of the eighteenth century had even less natural comfort to offer the farmer and landowner than the preceding half century. In the early 1700s, corn prices were as low as in the bad years of the 1680s. After a better showing in the second decade they slumped again in the mid-twenties, and again between 1730 and 1745. Meat prices were steadier, and by-products like tallow even rose, but in the early thirties everything fell – beef, mutton, tallow, butter, cheese and wool – and recovered only in the late thirties and early forties. To deepen the gloom, the farming world was harassed by what might be called acts of God in unusual number – bad winters, bad droughts, bad harvests. In many a year cattle and sheep had to be killed off because fodder was short after a poor harvest. After 1744 the cattle plague took heavy toll of the herds. There was, wrote Horace Walpole in 1745, a murrain among the cows: 'we dare not eat milk, butter, beef nor anything from that species'. It was all as distressing as the '45 itself. The beginning and end of the period compete in gloom. One historian has written of the period 1680 to 1710 as having the strongest claim of the whole century after the Restoration to be regarded as 'critical' for the farming community, because its wide fluctuations of price forced critical changes of crop and method on to farmers. The farmer's world had become a place in which only those with stamina, skill or capital could survive.[1]

The twenty years from 1730 to 1750 constitute a virtually continuous agricultural depression when rents fell and tenants were unwilling and unable to offer as good payment as before. '. . . tenants were never so backward in paying, nor so much in Arrears with their Rents as they are now . . . several Gentlemen have forgiven their Tenants in general

[1] A. H. John, 'The course of Agricultural Change 1660–1760', in *Studies in the Industrial Revolution. Essays presented to T. S. Ashton*, ed. L. S. Pressnell, 1960, p. 151.

a Great Part of their Arrears to induce them to hold their Farms at the same Rents, and to try a little longer'.[1] Here was a duke (in the mid-thirties) who would have lost his tenants if he had insisted on his rents; there another whose tenants owed him three years' arrears of rent. Three years later another writer alleged that there were many farmers who could not maintain their families – 'not even in a Mean way'. Sympathy with the necessitous husbandman vied with gloom over the untenanted farms amongst writers on rural affairs. Heavy arrears of rent throughout the widespread estates of the Duke of Kingston, a landowner with property extending throughout the midland counties, testified to the reality of the distress. In Nottinghamshire in 1741, substantial arrears were written off as irrecoverable. Sometimes, the tenants were sold up 'for the Duke's benefit'. In Lincolnshire, the Duke's steward noted: 'Arrears Desperate.' Some tenants were insolvent. 'Smith and Carr are run away, and Connywell very poor.' Widow Thacker was insolvent. Throughout the depression, some £1,400 in rents was 'forgiven' or written off. The Duke of Kingston was not exceptional. The same phenomena of distress – arrears, bankruptcies and fleeing tenants – were reported by his neighbours, Lord Monson and Lord Ancaster, from their estates in Lincolnshire and Rutland. The Earl of Westmorland was having trouble in finding tenants and letting farms.[2]

Much of the land worst hit was the heavy land of the Midlands, and much of it was still open-field country. Here, amongst the arable farmers, the distress was worse than it was in the pasturelands by the Trent, the mixed farming areas of east Derbyshire, or, of course, the light soils of East Anglia. Those who depended on dairy produce for their income seem to have escaped its worst effects. As in the early seventeenth century, the really large landowner – no doubt with non-agriculture sources of income to help him – survived the rigours of the time better than the smaller gentry. Oxfordshire, once a county of small squires, was dominated by the Marlboroughs by the mid-century.

The immediate result of bad times was to increase the financial burdens of the landlord as well as the misery of the tenants. Faced with the threat of empty farms, landlords were compelled to concede reductions, or more often temporary abatements, of rent. Other costs that in

[1] Quoted by G. E. Mingay, 'The Agricultural Depression 1730–1750', *Econ. Hist. Rev.*, VIII, no. 3, 1956. For a regional survey revealing similar cycles see J. D. Chambers, '*The Vale of Trent 1670–1800* (*Econ. Hist.* Supplement).
[2] Mingay, op. cit.

palmier days fell on the tenant had to be taken over by the landlord —
new buildings, fences, the cost of sowing crops, liming, marling and
manuring, as well as the payment of the land tax and poor rates. Paradoxically (at first sight), improvements went ahead at an increased pace
in the midst of depression. Contrariwise, as the outlook gradually
improved from the mid-1740s down to 1760, the landowners restored
the stiffer conditions of their leases and the proportion of rents ploughed
back into estates fell from the high levels of the thirties. These phenomena were not as strange as they might seem. The effect of falling and
fluctuating prices was to compel lords and tenants to adjust their production to the needs of the markets and gear their costs to lower prices;
in short, to improve the efficiency of agriculture by getting more output for less outlay. The first decade of the eighteenth century therefore
continued the work of the late seventeenth century. Wastes and fallows
on the arable clays were put to better use, strips in the open fields were
consolidated, attention focused on more profitable crops. The process
of adjustment is reflected in the growing number of Acts of Parliament
for enclosure. The committee that reported in 1797 put the rate of enclosure by Act of Parliament — some was still going forward by local
agreements enrolled in Chancery — at:

Under Queen Anne	(1702–14)	1,439 acres
Under George I	(1714–27)	17,960 acres
Under George II	(1727–60)	318,778 acres

Obviously the tide was rising, though even the acreage enclosed under
George II was only a fraction — roughly one-ninth — of the area that
was to be enclosed in a similar period under his son.

The different regions continued to adjust themselves to changing
conditions as convenience and profit suggested. The graziers, who had
been active in converting arable to grass in Leicestershire and in an area
of similar soil between the Chilterns and the Trent, slowed down their
operations after 1710, as meat became comparatively less profitable.
Elsewhere, on the lighter soils of East Anglia and of Wiltshire, the process was reversed and grassland was converted to arable. Defoe saw
'many thousand acres of carpet ground [that were] of late years turned
into arable land and sowed with wheat'. The process continued into the
fifties. Thus the first relatively intense phase of agricultural improvement culminated in a remarkable increase of output of grain, meat and
other agricultural produce. The animal population on the farms was
growing everywhere. Although the clothiers were demanding more

wool to support their still growing industry, falling wool prices show that supply was more than keeping up with demand. Finally, under the stimulus of the Corn Bounty, England was becoming a major exporter of grain. Cargoes of all kinds of grain which were running at the rate of between $2\frac{1}{2}$ and 3 million quarters in the first decade, had risen to more than $6\frac{1}{2}$ million in the forties and fifties, with malt and barley for the Dutch brewers and distillers playing a major part. All in all, it seems that the supply of foodstuffs (except dairy produce) had, for a variety of reasons, temporarily overtaken the demand in a period when the population was growing only relatively slowly. Even the allegedly high standards of the working classes – their habit of eating meat and drinking beer recorded by Defoe and others – were not enough to raise agricultural prices, which were said between 1730 and 1750 to have been 'the lowest ever known'.[1]

Norfolk and Suffolk, with their easy access to the London and Continental markets, their deep soil of lightish loam, and a nucleus of improving landlords, were furthest forward in the new husbandry. Two names are traditionally associated with this phase, Jethro Tull and Charles, second Viscount Townshend. Here, as so often, it is the lot of research to blur the clear outlines drawn by the historical pioneers, to make history more complicated and maybe duller in the process of getting it right. In this instance, the mighty must be pulled down a little from their seats. Neither Tull nor Townshend stands quite where he did. Tull, after being trained as a lawyer, went back to his home farm in Oxfordshire in 1699 and for the next forty years preached his doctrine that good husbandry was rooted in tillage. In 1701, inspired by the ingenious mechanism of the tracker-action that controlled the speaking of the organ pipe, he invented his seed drill, which still stands with the later threshing machine and combine harvester as one of the major steps towards a scientific, mechanized agriculture. His specifications ranged from one for a simple wheat drill to another which would sow barley and undersow clover and sainfoin at the same time. Its purpose was two-fold. Following in the steps of earlier inventors like Platte and Worlidge, Tull wanted to save the waste of seed involved in broadcasting it. Secondly, he wanted his rows of plants evenly spaced and at an even depth. This was the necessary corollary to his scheme for hoeing the ground between the growing plants by means of a horse-drawn hoe. This was in fact a wooden plough. The mould board was removed and the draught animal (or animals – for he contem-

---

[1] J. Wimpey, *Rural Improvements*, 1775, pp. 492–3.

plated oxen as well as horses) muzzled to prevent it eating the growing crop. The object was to cultivate and pulverize the soil in depth, and this in turn was based on Tull's pseudo-scientific theory about plant nourishment. A plant received its nourishment, Tull argued, through its roots, and its source was earth, divided into particles as fine as could be achieved. The division could be achieved by dung, but dung also tainted the earth, and Tull allowed it little virtue. That reduced him to tillage – deep and continuous – as the basis of good farming. The truths of his doctrine, as he believed them, were set out in full in his *Horse Houghing Husbandry* of 1731. It was a strange mixture of truth and fantasy, often viciously attacked by farmers in his own day and by writers since. Yet it led, almost in spite of itself, to results of great value – most of all, to the substitution of root crops for the hitherto unavoidable but wasteful tradition of fallowing. His fanatical insistence on the importance of tillage could have been dangerous to the evolution of a balanced husbandry. Yet in practice his disciples winnowed out what was absurd and exaggerated amongst his ideas. Slowly his implements were improved and made more practicable. Fanatic he may have been; fraud he was not.

The name that is always bracketed with that of Tull is Lord Townshend – Turnip Townshend. His Raynham estates in Norfolk had already for at least half a century been associated with the new methods of convertible husbandry – manures, rootcrops, long leases – when the second Viscount quarrelled with Walpole and left politics for ever to devote himself to the improvement of agriculture and especially to the advocacy of root crops. Hence his nickname. His conversation, they said, was of turnips, turnips and nothing but turnips. Just as Tull must share his claims to originality with earlier writers like Worlidge, so Townshend must lose some of his reputation as a pioneer of the Norfolk husbandry. He may have popularized the Norfolk rotation, turnips barley or oats, clover or rye, and wheat, feeding sheep on the roots and clover. This in conjunction with Tull's practice of planting in straight rows, wide apart and mechanically hoed, achieved great economies of cost and great increases in yield. Hence larger margins of profit for the farmer and larger rents for the landlord. But none of this was really new. Much of what Townshend publicized (and much of the improved organization of estates later associated with his neighbour Coke of Holkham) had been established on the great estates of Norfolk and Suffolk for some time. Houghton, the Walpole estate, was already the scene of a vigorous modern commerical agriculture even before Robert inherited it at the turn of the century. Turnips, clover, enclosure, long leases were already common form. Walpole's steward was already fattening up Scotch bullocks, selling to the Norwich butchers and reaping good profits from the taste of fashionable London for Scotch beef. Similarly at Holkham, great improvements took place in the half century that separates the inheritance of Thomas Coke, Lord Lovell, (later Lord Leicester, the friend of Lord Burlington and of William Kent, creator of Holkham Hall) from that of his more famous improving kinsman. The great rise in Holkham rents was not a sudden revolutionary achievement of Coke of Holkham himself after he succeeded to the estates in 1776. Rents had been rising steadily ever since the early years of the century; remarkable as it may seem, even through the times of falling prices in the first half of the century. How had this been done? By gradually grafting on to the holdings of the tenant farmers (some of which might be as large as a thousand acres) new methods and crops pioneered on the home farm. Here the landlord could only work through the instrument of the lease granted to the tenant; and the longer the lease the better, for both lord and tenant stood to gain from the security a long lease gave a good tenant. The long lease did not have to await Coke of Holkham as used to be thought. As early as the 1720s, leases for twenty-one years were in operation and seven- to fourteen-year leases were probably to be found earlier still. Even in times that were poor for farmers in general, the Holkham stewards had little difficulty in finding tenants willing to contract for a long lease. As early as the 1720s, their leases prescribed in detail the practices essential for good husbandry. Too many straws crops in succession are ruled out. Grass or turnips are to be interspersed after three white straw crops. Marling[1] is to be carried out to prevent erosion of the sandy soil. Manure is not to be sold off the holding. By such devices, the Holkham management wrote their own best practices into the many thousand acres held by tenants, ploughing back nearly a quarter of their rents into farm buildings and improvements.[2] Coke of Holkham was later able to build on the solid foundations of well established practices.

... it is in these two Counties [Norfolk and Suffolk] beyond all others in *England* [wrote an intelligent observer in the 1740s] that some fine improvements in husbandry may be seen, to the infinite Profit of both Landlords and Tenants which have been brought to pass within these fifty Years, ever since

---

[1] Marl was a mixture of clay and carbonate of lime dug from underlying beds.

[2] Parker, 'Coke of Norfolk and the Agrarian Revolution', *Econ. Hist. Rev.*, Vol. VIII, No. 2, 1955.

they learned the way of sowing and houghing Turnips in their open, common, sandy Fields, which has not only proved a Preparation to their succeeding crops of Barley, but such Turnip-Crops give them a vast Profit besides, by feeding their horned Beasts with them to the Degree of Fatting; so as to fit them in a compleat manner for a *Smithfield* market, where Thousands of them are sold in a Year, and by their cooling, Fat Dung and fertile Urine, that their Runts, Oxen or cows leave behind them in the Land, they so dress and prepare their dry husky hungry warm sandy grounds, as to cause them to retain more plentiful crops of barley of late years than they had formerly.[1]

It was especially in the fourth and fifth decades – the era of low prices – that yields had increased most rapidly under the stimulus of these new methods. On a single Norfolk farm, the value of the crops in the market went up from £144 to £505, the weight from 1,768 bushels to 6,592. Away in the west, on the Chilterns, farmers were experiencing similar improvements, and on the Lincolnshire wolds, the turnip brought up the value of the hill country as against the marsh. It was no longer necessary, a steward on a Lincolnshire estate explained in 1726, to rent land in the marsh. You could feed the sheep off turnips, and 30,000 lusty Scotch cattle testified each year to the rich goodness of the wolds after the rigours of their native pasture. Even on the northeast coast, where customary tenants (their palms itching perhaps for the bonus promised by the Corn Bounty) were apt to bleed the soil white by growing corn upon corn, the voice of improvement was making itself heard. William Cotesworth, a new self-made man of the kind found in the rising coal, iron and salt industries on Tyneside, was experimenting with clover and grasses on a farm of 500 acres near Gateshead after 1718. By the 1730s, farms in this area were fetching extraordinary rents – £2 an acre for dairy farms, £3 an acre for market gardening.

From what has been said about prices and markets and the relation between these and the movement of population, it is evident that the spring and source of all this improvement of agriculture is not to be sought simply in the pursuit of easy profits on a rising market. On the contrary, the times were difficult and profits low. So that only improved efficiency and a willingness to lay out capital in achieving it could save the landowner and his tenants from the bankruptcy which threatened equally from the scarcity prices of the 'barren years' or the embarrassments of plenty in the thirties and forties. The little man, the peasant, probably did best when prices were stable. He was hit worst by extremes. In years of bountiful harvests he was only paid starvation prices

[1] *The Modern Husbandman*, 1750, quoted by A. H. John, op. cit., p. 146, note 1.

for his crop. When prices ruled high after a bad harvest, his surplus was too small to make up his loss by a good year. Like all farmers, he was at the mercy of the weather, but he was much more at its mercy than his more progressive and larger neighbours. As they increased their output, and as the increase was reflected in a larger national output, it was their prices that ruled the market. Quite apart from the short-term fluctuations caused by the weather, the price structure of an increasingly commercial, capitalistic market for agricultural produce was shaping against the small peasant farmer. Here and there the surviving peasantry were helped by local circumstances; where the potato could be grown, as it was in the Isle of Axholme from the late seventeenth century, it provided a prop for the peasant as surely as it did in Ireland. On twenty acres in north Lincolnshire a peasant could do pretty well. After the end of our period Arthur Young noticed even smaller holdings of four and five acres which were 'cultivated with all that [sic] *minutiae* of care and anxiety in the hands of the family which are found abroad in France and Flanders. They are very poor respecting money but very happy respecting their mode of existence.' In some of the often still unenclosed villages of the Midlands, too, life continued without any revolutionary disturbance. There were still many owner-occupiers of small holdings of ten acres or less who could still borrow, free of charge, the 'town plow'. They survived bad times by simply pulling in their belts. The old familiar way of life had not entirely gone by the mid-century; but it was fading. Bigger farms of 100 to 200 acres and more were being formed by the 'engrossing' of smaller holdings. At Wigston near Leicester, which Dr Hoskins has investigated in detail,[1] two-thirds of the land was now farmed (1765) by the tenants of absentee landlords — large institutions, wool dealers, graziers, butchers and the like.

Why was the peasant in decline? Was he, as older writers often suggested, driven out by a ruthless process of expropriation against which he was now no longer protected by a paternal central autocracy as (theoretically) he had been in previous centuries? Certainly, instances of 'arbitrary' enclosure of the kind that Stuart favourites had been permitted to impose on Wiltshire a century before could still be found. Such was the enclosure of Benefield in Northamptonshire by the Marquis of Powys in 1712 which even the local gentry thought imposed great injustices on the poor.[2]

---

[1] W. G. Hoskins, *The Midland Peasant.*
[2] W. E. Tate, 'Inclosure Movement in Northamptonshire', *Northampton Past and Present* I, no. 2, 1949.

But such examples were not common. More of the enclosure that was taking place was carried out by private Acts of Parliament, instead of by agreements enrolled in Chancery. Perhaps the objector got shorter shrift under the new procedure. Certainly 'the poor', that vast and growing class of rural England who lived at the very edge of subsistence, felt keenly the loss of common pastures and waste where they could graze a cow or fatten a pig. Certainly, here and there, the stewards of a large landlord could be found acting with officious zeal to extinguish by fair means or foul the rights of copyholders. Yet, in general, the amount of evidence of deliberate and calculated expropriation is small. If a landlord or his agent could sometimes hold a villager to ransom, there is plenty of evidence that villagers often conspired to do down their landlord. Peasant owners were not always the innocent rustic clowns that urban sympathizers have sometimes supposed. Cumberland juries called to determine disputes between landlord and tenant could always (it was said) be relied on to find for the tenant. There was 'a kind of conspiracy', and the lord who was not on the watch would find himself cheated of his rights. And where the gentry wanted to buy a copyholder out of his rights by purchase, they often fell into competitive bidding from which the vendor emerged triumphant with a good price for his land.[1]

Yet, justly or unjustly, voluntarily or under pressure, there can be little doubt that the small landowner and semi-landowner – the copyholder of qualified ownership – was slowly but surely drifting out. The author of *Advice to the Stewards of Estates* (1731) urged that as well as keeping his eyes open for any freehold land going for sale and promoting enclosure, the steward should convert copyhold to leasehold wherever it was legally possible. The small man would, under an enclosure award, normally be allocated a share in the redesigned village fields which was apparently equitable and based strictly on a calculation of his existing rights by the commissioners. Yet he could rarely afford to provide it with the fences, hedges and drains that the enclosed farming required. He was therefore under strong temptation to accept a good offer from a larger landowner for his share. Freeholders, and even some of the smaller squires, found that the new husbandry and the larger fixed and working capital it demanded put it beyond their means to continue. Some of these joined the ranks of the wage labourers and the landless poor as 'engrossing' went on and the optimum size of farms tended to increase.

[1] See e.g., E. Hughes, *North Country Life in the 18th Century*, 1952, pp. 121, 129.

It is tempting to overdramatize the picture. Not all the increase in
the numbers of 'the poor' can be ascribed to the expulsion or attraction
of the less enterprising or less lucky from their land. Even the long,
slow increase of population placed a necessary strain on the framework
of village society which could not maintain anything beyond a modest
increase in the numbers of people on the land. The surplus, younger
brothers and sisters mostly, drifted away to the nearest towns. Those
who stayed were not always materially worse off than they had been.
If the small owner was particularly lucky, shrewd or enterprising, he
might turn the situation very much to his own advantage by selling his
land and getting reasonable security of tenure in return. If; it was an
important condition and not always fulfilled. There is no doubt that the
cost of preserving his rights was a heavy one. The new farming needed
capital, above all working capital. The freeholder or copyholder who
could realize the value of his land and transmute it into stock, seed,
manure and the like was certainly at an advantage compared with his
capital-starved customary neighbour. It is doubtful, one authority on
farming history has said, 'whether since the early part of the eighteenth
century it has profited the man of middle acres to own the land he
farms'.[1]

The peasant who was ingenious enough to drive a shrewd bargain
with the squire, and thrifty and enterprising enough to keep himself
afloat as a tenant farmer in the new husbandry, might look to a better
future. There were many such in East Anglia and the West Country.
Tenant farmers in Devon with leases for three lives or 99 years had good
security and made excellent use of it, though by the eighteenth century
they were apt to take on too much land and run themselves short of
cash. But it was on the light lands and enclosed farms that the new
tenant farmer was most in evidence. In the eye of his contemporaries,
the tenant of the Chiltern 'turnip-farm' was synonymous with the new
husbandry; but he was only kept in business by adhering to good pre-
cepts: 'if such a Farmer does not sow clover, he cannot pay his rent, as
Times now go in the Farming Business; meaning that as many large
Downs on the *West* and Commons elsewhere, are of late plowed up
and converted into Arable land, and by the new Improvement of
Husbandry in many Places carried on with great success, grain is now
become very plenty and cheap and like to continue so'.[2] In short, only
the efficient producer could survive these testing times. He did so by

[1] R. Trow-Smith, op. cit., p. 128.
[2] Ellis, quoted by A. H. John, op. cit., p. 147.

keeping his costs down and increasing his production: more grain at lower prices. As the *Gentleman's Magazine* remarked in 1752, Norfolk farmers could make money when wheat stood at prices which were putting the farmers on the midland clays and open fields out of business. They were not land *owners*. But the advantages of ownership can be overvalued. It brought burdens as well as security. Hundreds of seventeenth- and eighteenth-century farm houses testify to the solid prosperity of the new tenant-farmer class. And the Norfolk farmer was a by-word for independence.

Contemporaries were often puzzled by a question that has been much debated by later historians. Was a bountiful harvest a blessing or a curse? Did high prices or low prices bring most benefit to the community? There was little agreement in the eighteenth century, and modern historians are still far from unanimous. Some writers of the day, as we have seen, blamed a succession of good harvests for the plenty of corn and the low prices of the thirties and forties. But, more generally, opinion seems to have supported the view that a bountiful harvest made for general prosperity. '... A fine harvest has afforded both work and plenty', said the *Gentleman's Magazine* after the harvest of 1756. Certainly those who had to buy corn in the market, whether for human or animal food, could pray for good corn crops. And if the price of necessities fell, more money was freed in the people's pockets for the purchase of other things. The sales of cloth, boots and shoes, sugar, tobacco, tea, etc., rose when corn was plentiful and cheap. Thus the non-agrarian part of the economy prospered. So did those farmers who were in the market for fodder – dairy farmers, and stock breeders especially. What of those unfortunates, then, who were fleeing their stewards and bailiffs in the 1730s? They were, evidently, the representatives of the old-fashioned farming. Their output was low, their costs high. Their case was quite different from that of the Norfolk or Wiltshire farmers whose efficient methods enabled them to rejoice with the others, including their landlords and their customers, who welcomed a good harvest as a general blessing. On balance, the traditional view that the good harvest favoured the economy at large seems to have been reasonable enough.

Increasingly, the tenant farmer was to be the human pivot on whom the new rural arrangements turned. He was the symbol of a new society that no longer relied on customary relationships based on the ownership or part-ownership of land, but on legal and contractual relationships designed for a world of commerce. He survived so long as he could honour his contract and pay his rent. In practice, the landlord-and-tenant system was not as hard or inhuman as it has sometimes been made out to be. Landlords – the bigger ones especially – had a reputation for dealing fairly and reasonably with their tenants. They seem to have preferred (as any sensible landlord still does) a reliable and reasonably contented tenant at a fair rent to a precarious or mutinous one at an extortionate rent. ('Rack rent' is one of those rare instances of a word that began as a synonym for injustice and oppression and ended as a neutral description of an ordinary process of negotiation.) The tenant-newcomers to rural society were established economically long before they were accepted socially. In Henry Fielding's novel *Amelia*, published in 1751, Amelia's husband, Captain Booth, is so rash and ambitious as to rent several farms and then buy himself a coach.

> Before this [he says] as my wife and I had very little distinguished ourselves from the other farmers and their wives, either in our dress or our way of living, they treated us as their equals: but now they began to consider us as elevating ourselves into a state of superiority, and immediately began to envy, hate and declare war against us. The neighbouring little squires, too, were uneasy to see a poor *renter* become their equal in a matter in which they placed so much dignity . . . they began to hate me likewise . . . my neighbours now began to conspire against me. They nicknamed me, in derision, the SQUIRE FARMER.

The end, naturally, is bankruptcy and social degradation. Yet in real life the working farmer proper was frequently a man of means, who considered himself, in Norfolk anyway, the natural equal of the free-holder, or even of the small squire or parson, and was certainly often a person of more substance than they. Nothing illustrates the changing social values of the time more vividly than the appearance in Wiltshire (Booth's own country!) of a class of so-called 'gentleman farmers'. The 'gentleman farmer', and *a fortiori*, the 'gentleman clothier' over the border in Gloucestershire, were not the simple contradiction in terms that they would have been at an earlier date. They symbolized society's acceptance that social standing could be bought by money earned by a sort of trade: a trade, nevertheless, still associated with land. A good tenant, especially one with some capital of his own, was a treasure to be prized by a sensible landowner or his agent. They naturally tended to favour the larger tenant. The more efficient and well-found, the less vulnerable he would be to depression. Hence a tendency towards larger farms. A tendency: no more. Early Victorian England was still to be a land of small farmers. But the proportion of bigger ones was going up.[1]

The new agrarian system was operated not by the lord or squire but by the tenant farmer. Yet behind the farmer stood the squire or his bailiff or steward, and behind them there stood not infrequently the figure of the banker, or scrivener, or moneylender or mortgagee or whoever happened to have advanced the means necessary for the land-owner to live, as they said, 'like a lord'. Even upon the squire who lived thriftily, the rising expectations of living among his own kind pressed hard. Social status meant social responsibilities. The local Bench had to be filled, the local Member returned to Parliament. By tradition the squire kept open house, responded suitably when subscriptions were called up for local charities, schools and medical aids, church repairs, pensions and almshouses, and comforts for the old and sick. It was often a less formal, organized type of charity than the urban trusts set up by the great merchants of London, Bristol or Norwich, but it was con-tinuous, and it was costly. Less costly, however, than the agreeable exigencies of fashion which now faced the heir to the landed estate. If he survived the peculiar combination of savagery and neglect that marked life at the public school, he might pass on to the expensive delights of Oxford or Cambridge:

> Half seven years spent on Billiards, Cards and Tippling,
> And growing every day a lovelier stripling,
> Half clowne, half prig, half pedant, half sot,
> Having done all that ought to be undone,
> Furnish'd those studies which were ne'er begun,
> To foreign climes my lord must take his flight.[2]

Moralists, poets and philosophers might differ as to the educational merits of the Grand Tour. There was no disagreement on its cost. When Thomas Coke landed at Dover in 1718, 'accompanied by his friend Lord Burlington and by Mr Kent' it was the beginning of a chapter which was to end with the building of the great Hall at Holk-ham, 'according to Palladio', based on his plans of an Italian villa and built in brick because the Romans used brick. When finished, Holkham was furnished with treasures from Italy – tapestries and velvets from Genoa, statues that had belonged (so it was said) to Cicero, pictures by Titian, Veronese and Holbein. Other graduates of the Grand Tour

---

[1] See G. Mingay, 'The Size of Farms in the Eighteenth Century', *Econ. Hist. Rev.*, April 1962.

[2] James Miller, *On Politeness*, 1738.

were agreed to be less cultivated: Lord Chesterfield thought they returned with manners of footmen and grooms, dirty in person, fit only to disturb playhouses, break the windows of taverns where they drank, and in general act as 'the support, the terror and the victims of the brandy-houses they frequent'.[1]

The Grand Tour was inordinately expensive. The total cost of the second Duke of Kingston's Grand Tour was £20,000. By the mid-century the entire paraphernalia of the aristocratic tourist industry had come into being. The proprietor of the Hotel d'Angleterre at Calais was said to have made a fortune in ten years. Coaches and guide books, like Nugent's *Grand Tour*, containing all the information needed by travellers, ran into many editions. In the two years after the Peace of Paris in 1763, it was said that 40,000 English travellers passed through Calais.[2] If each spent £100 on his tour, the annual cost of this invisible import to the country was some £2 million.

Meanwhile, the London season, with its round of balls at the great houses, the masquerades at Vauxhall and Ranelagh Gardens (rebuilt in 1749 as 'an immense amphitheatre with balconies full of little ale-houses' for £16,000), the gaming houses, the parties, the theatres, clubs and the opera, beckoned seductively to the aspiring young man of fashion. So did the more specialized pleasures of the provinces at Bath, Newmarket, Nottingham, Bristol and many others. Gaming debts were enormous. In one evening, at Kew Palace, the Prince of Wales would win £1,100 of Lord Granby and £800 of Dick Lyttleton. Duke Hamilton lost £1,000 in a night at Lord Chesterfield's. Captain Scott would take £2,300 off Sir John Bland at Whites – more than half the value of a sizeable country mansion. Lord Rockingham and Lord Oxford wagered £500 between five turkeys and five geese to run from Norwich to London. In 1753, if Horace Walpole is to be believed, £100,000 of coin was carried to Newmarket to cover betting debts for a single week's racing. It is not the least probable of his anecdotes.

The largest single expense that fell on landed incomes was building. In the first half of the century Vanbrugh, stepping down dramatically from the theatre to his new profession of architect, rang up the curtain on an age of magnificence such as only Italy had ever witnessed. Creators followed one another in rapid succession – Vanbrugh and Hawksmoor, the masters of Palladianism, Burlington, Colin Campbell, William Kent, Giacomo Leoni (a Venetian brought to England by Burlington),

[1] *Lord Chesterfield's Letters to his Son*, ed. C. Strachey, 1932, vol. I, p. 330.
[2] J. A. R. Pimlott, *The Englishman's Holiday*, 1947, p. 68.

James Gibbs, Henry Flitcroft and a score of lesser men. Tastes acquired by patrons on the Grand Tour mingled with the researches of architects themselves to steer building fashions towards the antique. While the antiquaries were busy in the fifties at Athens and Baalbek, Robert Adam was exploring the ruins at Spoleto. The result was, as Horace Walpole observed, that England became filled with noble houses 'dispersed like great rarity plums in a vast pudding of country'. And all the time, alongside the vast and barely habitable palaces such as Vanbrugh's Seaton Delaval and Blenheim, or Flitcroft's Wentworth Woodhouse, scores of smaller manor houses by unknown artists were added to the existing collection of those vaguely known to later generations as 'Wren', or 'Queen Anne'.

The origins, motives and economic consequences of this passion for building houses are even now only partially explored. It went naturally with the desire to found a great and famous family. The fashion for country life was rooted in the quite natural conviction that country life was one of the most agreeable of pleasures, especially when it could be alternated with spells of more sophisticated entertainment in London or Bath. 'I much long to be in the country', wrote Daniel Finch, second Earl of Nottingham, while his great house at Burley-on-the-Hill was a-building in Rutland. 'I am resolved to go into the country, even though I live in the stables at Burley.' To such natural feelings was added increasingly the need to live grandly and to prove to one's self and others that one was as grand as one's neighbour by being palpably more grand. Fashion and expense became competitive and the age entered upon a series of disastrously costly building contests like the one which eventually reduced the Earl of Verney to bankruptcy at Claydon House near Buckingham. Here, to outface the family rivals, the Temples, the Earl rebuilt the house in 1752 to Adam's design adding 'a hall with a great dome and a lofty Ball-room' all at a cost of some £50,000.[1] Others amongst the builders were relatively new to the country, like Daniel Finch's neighbour at Normanton, Sir Gilbert Heathcote, East Indies merchant, Governor of the Bank of England, Lord Mayor of London, reputed the richest commoner of England. 'The selected walk of Heathcote's leisure' (as Dyer calls it in his poem *The Fleece*), was bought from its previous owners, the Mackworths. Its prime object was social status and the pleasures of the countryside, with income as a secondary motive. Others of the new landowners were not unmindful that land was the best security for borrowing money

[1] See below, p. 259.

and still the safest investment for a man seeking to maintain the value of his capital rather than to maximize his income. Such considerations were reinforced in 1711, when Parliament passed the Act which made ownership of an estate worth £300 a year an indispensable qualification for sitting in Parliament. Yet when due allowance has been made for the influx of money from trade or politics into rural life, it remains true that much of the cost of building and upkeep fell on incomes that came from rent rolls.

The cost of building a country mansion in the first half of the eighteenth century was upwards of £3,000–£4,000. A modest country house of the less grandiose kind, like Hinwick Hall in Bedfordshire, a model of its kind, would be of that order. The larger house of the secondary kind cost ten times as much; the grandest, twenty or thirty times. Blenheim cost a quarter of a million. In the twenties and thirties Houghton Hall was transformed by Walpole from a modest country gentleman's house to a small palace at a cost nobody will ever know. Walpole's biographer puts it at 'tens upon tens of thousands'. Similarly at Holkham, the cost of the first Earl of Leicester's building of the Hall is unknown. But we know that when he died in 1759 he was reserving £2,000 a year for finishing off the work begun a quarter of a century before. The alterations to Audley End cost the Nevilles £100,000. Even the rich were under relentless pressure created by their own aspirations to high living in this age of elegance.

The great house, it is true, was not always built out of normal income from rents. Sometimes it represented the fruits of place or office. Blenheim was largely paid for out of state funds gratefully granted to a victorious hero. Walpole, it has been said, was 'one of the last of the King's servants to make a great fortune from politics'.[1] Daniel Finch's gains from his incumbency as Secretary of State between 1689 and 1716 may have been round about £40,000–£50,000. The cost of buying the land and building the house at Burley was nearer £80,000, and Finch was an unusually prudent man for his time and station in life with all 'the exterior airs of Business and application enough to make him very capable'.[2]

These were the able and the fortunate ones. But most were neither particularly able nor fortunate. A speaker in the Commons in 1737 remarked on 'the great numbers of borrowers who borrow only for

---

[1] J. H. Plumb, op. cit., p. 196.

[2] See 'Daniel Finch, 2nd Earl of Nottingham: His House and Estate', by H. J. Habakkuk in *Studies in Social History* (ed. J. H. Plumb) (1955), p. 168.

supplying their own extravagance or for the atoning of the extravagance of their ancestors'.[1] The building mania, coming on top of social responsibilities and high living, ran many into a state of chronic indebtedness. Unless he were saved by a felicitous windfall in the shape of a legacy, a rich heiress, a government job or the timely discovery of assets such as coal or iron under his estates, the landowner would find himself, sooner or later, a suppliant to the banker, the moneylender or the affluent friend. The money for the Verney schemes already described came from a large mortgage for nearly £50,000 negotiated by the Earl with an Amsterdam merchant and secured on the Verney estates and the timber growing on them (a frequent object for security). A quarter of a century later, more than half the loan was still unpaid. When Robert Walpole died in April 1745, Horace reported him 'dead very poor: his debts amount to £50,000. His estate much mortgaged. In short his fondness for Houghton has endangered Houghton'. This was an exaggeration. Walpole had accumulated assets of far greater value than his debts, and in the end the beneficiaries did well enough. But the situation illustrates vividly what may be called the 'liquidity crisis' brought on by profuse expenditure. The experience was a common one: that a man was in debt did not necessarily mean that he was bankrupt. But it did mean that out of his income he had to provide for a number of new and unavoidable expenses. Like a modern building society's dependent client, he had to pay regular interest on his debt. Like him, he had to honour whatever obligation he had accepted to pay off the capital of the debt by instalments. All this on top of the increased costs of running and maintaining a larger and more luxurious establishment. The task proved too much for the abilities and self control of many. They fell by the wayside. Those who survived did so by assiduity in the scramble for lucrative government jobs, or the diligent pursuit of desirable heiresses which occupied a considerable part of the time of the ruling class in the eighteenth century. Debt explains the importance of both games. It seems likely that fewer landowners had to sell their land because of debt than in the previous century. But this was not because their debts were smaller: on the contrary. It was because legal and financial changes had made bankers and other moneyed men readier to lend on the security of land.[2] Debt, life in the grand manner, and the consequential need for ever-growing income also help to explain

---

[1] *Hansard, Parliamentary History*, vol. X, pp. 111–12.
[2] See H. J. Habakkuk, in *Britain and the Netherlands*, ed. J. S. Bromley and E. H. Kossmann (1960).

the steady interest in agricultural improvement. For only through improved husbandry, larger output and relatively lower costs could a better income be squeezed out of the home farm and a bigger rent roll be squeezed out of the tenants.

Central to the whole process of agricultural management, therefore, stood the lord's steward. For the greater part, the steward's labours went unrecorded but a few have survived in the portrait gallery of the eighteenth century — John Spedding, agent to the Lowthers of White-haven, Thomas Sisson, agent for the Cotesworth estates at Gateshead, Dan Eaton, the faithful steward of the Brudenells of Northamptonshire, or Bulmer of Ashridge wielding *plena potestas* for the Earl of Bridge-water. They were cast in the same mould as the old steward of the Norths — prudently managing the household expenses with one hand and the rent roll with the other. They surveyed the estates, drew up leases and enforced them, managed everything large and small, from enclosure agreements to replenishing the coverts and pheasantries. As estates tended to grow larger and the problems of management more complex, a good steward became ever more necessary. The fortunes of the whole estate turned upon his vigilance and fidelity. He was in a unique position to speed the rate of rural change and agrarian progress.[1]

Agricultural progress by the mid-eighteenth century has been both overestimated and underestimated; overestimated statistically, under-estimated qualitatively. Even in the 1790s when the Board of Agriculture made their surveys, there were still nearly 8 million acres of waste, especially north of a line from Derbyshire to Northumberland. A quarter of a million acres of Yorkshire was still waste and swamp. Between Sleaford and Brigg lay the great wild expanse of Lincoln Heath, a barren wilderness with only Dunston Pillar, a land lighthouse, to guide travellers. The Fens were still only partially drained. Indeed, they were in danger of regressing as the outfalls silted up and the levels fell with the shrinkage of the peat. Round Sedgemoor, the Mendips and Quantocks, and through Devon and Cornwall, lay great tracts of waste land. London itself was surrounded by woods and wastes like Hounslow Heath, Epping Forest and Finchley Common that were 'only fit for Cherokees and savages', sheltering hardened criminals on the run. 'Improvement' tended to be restricted as yet to lighter soils. The clays of the Midlands had to await the coming of efficient land drainage and heavier ploughs. Improvement was therefore still on a local rather than a national scale. Pressure to accelerate the process —

[1] See E. Hughes, op. cit., Joan Wake, *The Brudenells of Deene*, 1953, pp. 210–22.

whether generated by heavier consumer demand or the needs of land-owners for bigger incomes – was building up steadily: but it still faced major obstacles of ignorance and inertia.

Total corn production probably went up by 15 per cent or there-abouts between 1700 and 1760. This larger output was achieved at lower cost and with less human labour. Agricultural efficiency had increased substantially.[1] To expect that Tull or Townshend should have changed all in the twinkling of an eye is absurd. But there was hardly an area where an observer could not see some evidence of the methods by which the vicious circle of agrarian stagnation and poverty could now be broken. Not sesame, but turnips, were the key that opened the door to prosperity. How many of the improvers who financed enclo-sures and wrote turnips and clovers into longer leases were making a net profit cannot yet be known. It may never be. Too many drew their wealth from a variety of sources – offices of state, legacies, dowries, urban properties, mineral rights, speculative finance – to make gen-eralizations easy. But on the best-managed estates rents were moving up, even though prices were only stable or even falling. And this pointed a moral which even less-enterprising landowners were in time to grasp. Succeeding generations had only to imitate and extend the best practices adumbrated by 1760.

Socially, the changes entailed losses and sacrifices as well as gains. Ideally, widespread freehold ought to have meant security and stability and there was unquestionably some conscious loss of both to free-holders and copyholders who were victims of depression and the new commercial farming. It was a Mediterranean experience that large capital schemes of drainage and improvement tended to drive out the peasants who could not contribute to them. It was in part true of England. The new farming encouraged the enterprising who gave it birth. The poor were sometimes submerged by it. Yet the ideal picture of the landowning peasantry had not by any means been typical. Peasant ownership had often meant stagnation, poverty, ignorance. By the mid-eighteenth century England was well set towards its twentieth-century rural framework of a general landlord-and-tenant relationship. The system has been much criticized by agrarian reformers. It was capable of abuse and injustice. Yet, on its average showing, and certainly at its best, it had much to recommend it. It relieved tenant farmers of the need to lock up their limited capital in land. It freed them from burdensome financial responsibilities so that they could concentrate

[1] See Deane and Cole, *British Economic Growth*, pp. 65–75.

their capital and intelligence on their husbandry. The landlord got a return on his capital. If he or his agent had the sense to follow his best interests, and appreciate the value of a good tenant – as many did – the tenant did not need to fear insecurity or extortion nearly as often as is sometimes assumed. The tenant farmer was neither less independent nor less self-reliant than the yeoman, but his fortunes were subject to contract. This fact alone made him aware of the need for effort. It has been said that in the home of intensified husbandry, the Low Countries, the origins of innovation are to be found not in wealth but in poverty; in the need to make a living for a growing and dense population out of relatively low incomes.[1] Something of the same kind happened in England, too, though here the pressure of the rising costs of high living on the landowners introduces a uniquely English factor into rural improvement.

[1] Professor Slicher van Bath in *Britain and the Netherlands*, 1960 p. 153.

CHAPTER THIRTEEN

Trade, Policy and War

In the first half of the eighteenth century, Britain moved into the second of the three phases by which she was to achieve her domination of the world's markets between 1660 and 1815. In the previous half century she had elaborated a code of legislative regulation which aimed at securing, by policy and by the exercise of strategic power, a position similar to that enjoyed by her then major rival, Holland. Holland's strength and prosperity rested on her entrepôt trade with a growing proportion of the known world. This in turn was secured by her large and efficient merchant fleet and by her technological prowess. These gave her merchants and manufacturers command not only of raw material supplies but of a range of semi-finished manufactures like English white cloth and unbleached German linens. These were finished off in Holland and resold at large profit margins. To all this was added a command of the techniques of banking, credit and investment unique in the contemporary world. By 1700, Britain had learned many of these techniques. The Navigation Acts had created a major obstacle to further Dutch advance. Improved ship designs based partly on Dutch models helped British shipbuilders. Foreign trade expanded, notably to and from the colonies, within the protective framework of the Acts. Britain now possessed the naval power and the administrative corps of waterside officials necessary to enforce the Acts. Industrial processes such as dyeing, bleaching and metallurgy were improved, and new industries like silk, linen and paper making introduced.

The new century was marked by further growth and diversification on the lines already begun. This was reflected in the figures for foreign trade shown overleaf.

These figures are not 'statistics' in the modern sense. They were not, *ab initio*, measurements of trade volume or value. They were a by-product of tax records and they were from the beginning known to

TOTAL IMPORTS AND EXPORTS 1700–63[1]

	Imports (£m)	Exports (£m)
1700	6·0	6·5
1710	4·0	6·3
1720	6·1	6·9
1730	7·8	8·5
1740	6·7	8·2
1750	7·8	12·7
1760	9·8	14·7
1763	11·2	14·7

embody errors which distort their statistical value when used for measuring either economic growth or the balance of trade.[2] The major weakness was that the 'values' of trade were official, not real or market values. This error is less serious than it was to become later and it does not rob the series of all value as a means of measuring growth. Moreover, the general trend of prices in these years was, if anything, downwards. The increases do not therefore represent inflated prices. After a downward trend from 1700 to the 1730s, prices were generally stable until about 1760, only rising gently for the next few years. It is safe to conclude that the broad impression of growth in these sixty-three years — ±100 per cent — is genuine and, in the later years of the period anyway, impressive. This growth of foreign trade seems to have been at a higher rate than that of domestic trade during the same period when the excise figures suggest that the increase in home consumption was much smaller.[3] It was somewhat slower than in the preceding forty years, especially down to the mid-century, and a mere crawl compared with the later gallop of the Industrial Revolution;[4] but it was remarkable evidence of the vitality of the economy that it could bear the strain of costly wars and continue to expand at all.[5]

As a guide to the balance of payments — and this was their main

[1] Figures from Mrs E. B. Schumpeter, printed in Ashton, *The 18th Century*, Table XIV, p. 252.
[2] For a full discussion see G. N. Clark, *Guide to English Commercial Statistics*, esp. pp. 33–42; also T. S. Ashton's Introduction to E. B. Schumpeter, *English Overseas Trade Statistics 1697–1808*, 1960.
[3] See *An Account of the Quantities of the General Articles which have been charged with Excise Duties etc.* H.M. Customs and Excise Dept. Library. The trend seems common to beer, salt, soap, starch, candles.
[4] See R. Davis, 'English Foreign Trade 1700–1774', *Econ. Hist. Rev.*, XV, no. 2, 1900.
[5] For an admirable account of the general deceleration between the 1720s and the 1750s see J. D. Chambers, *The Vale of Trent 1670–1800*. (*Econ. Hist. Rev.* Supplement).

interest to those who had established the systematic collection of data —
the customs figures were more disputable. Joshua Gee represented an
increasing body of doubters when he wrote in 1729: 'It is a matter of
great difficulty to know the true balance of trade: some expect the
custom-house accounts will set us to rights, but there may be a great
many fallacies in those accounts.'[1] The main difficulty was that imports
were regularly undervalued, and to a much greater extent than exports.
As duties increased, so did smuggling. Even in 1746 a witness before a
Commons' committee thought over £1 million was exported annually
in specie to pay for smuggled imports. Later on, the amount was probably double or treble that figure.[2] If these suspicions were correct, the
apparently 'favourable' margin on visible trade was partly mythical.
There remained the profits and losses on 'invisible' payments which
were unrecorded in the customs figures: on one hand, the income from
a growing merchant fleet; on the other, payments to foreign shippers
for freights, to foreign investors for their dividends on holdings in the
British National Debt, for war debts on the Continent and elsewhere,
for the upkeep of embassies abroad, and — not least — for private travel
abroad. The Grand Tour was increasingly an indispensable part of a
gentleman's education. The cost of these sentimental journeys can no
more be accurately calculated than those of the other invisibles.

In this, as in most attempts at measurement, we must be content with
impressions. In reality the apparently favourable balance was evidently
charged with heavy calls. Wars and international crises like those of
1720, 1745, 1763 and 1773 put it under strain, and reserves of bullion
and coin at the Bank fell. It was impressive evidence of underlying
strength and good administration that the Bank did not need to suspend
cash payments for the century from 1696 to 1797. But it had some
shaky moments. It was not yet unreasonable that statesmen and writers
should continue to be exercised by concern for the balance of payments
and by attempts to improve it. Here and there voices were raised to
suggest that no man or government could see with God's eye, that the
operations of the economy were best left to look after themselves. In
his *Discourses* of 1691, Dudley North had written that 'the whole
world as to Trade is but as one Nation or People, and therein Nations
are as Persons'. One nation's loss, he went on, was not another's gain;
it was the loss of all, 'for all is combined together'. There were no
'unprofitable trades'. Therefore there was no point in forcing com-

1 Quoted, G. N. Clark, op. cit., p. 26.
2 W. A. Cole, op. cit., *Econ. Hist. Rev.*, X, no. 3, 1958.

pulsions on trade by law. No laws could 'set Prices in Trade, the Rates of which must and will make themselves'. Money was 'a Merchandize'; exported in the course of trade it increased the national wealth; spent in war or 'Payments abroad' it was 'so much impoverishment'. North's general view that economic regulation entailed an illogical and damaging discrimination of 'one Trade or Interest against another' made him a great favourite with Victorian economists. To McCulloch he was an 'Achilles without a heel'. But he was also a swallow that made no summer. Most economic writers of the first half of the eighteenth century refined the cruder ideas of the seventeenth century on the balance of trade but they did not yet reject the concept itself.[1] Others continued to express themselves in phrases little changed since the days of Mun. Matthew Decker, a typical pragmatist, began his *Essay on the Decline of Foreign Trade* (1739) by repeating the argument that nations without mines of gold and silver could only obtain supplies through foreign trade:

> Therefore, if the Exports of *Britain* exceed its imports, Foreigners must pay the Balance in Treasure, and the Nation grow Rich.
> But if the Imports of *Britain* exceed its Exports, we must pay Foreigners the Balance in Treasure, and the Nation grow poor.[2]

Put in such crude terms, the monetary argument was beginning to wear thin, for an increasing proportion of international transactions was settled without the transfer of bullion or coin. The East India trade and some others remained an exception to this trend. Between 1700 and 1720 the East India Company annually exported coin and bullion on a large scale – often between £½ million and £1 million a year – and in the early years of the eighteenth century William Culliford, the Inspector-General of Customs, believed that the large deficits on England's trade with the Baltic were paid for by the illegal smuggling out of English coin.[3] Meanwhile, the balance of trade argument had drawn added force from a different consideration: the need to create employment. Latter day mercantilists like Child and the Bristol merchant, John Cary, were accustomed to divide trades into harmful and beneficial trades by a new criterion. The beneficial ones were those which created most employment and helped to solve the problem of the poor. Thus the concept of the balance of trade as a Midas agency slowly gave

---

[1] See Supple, op. cit., pp. 219–21, for example, for a valuable analysis of the work of Rice Vaughan in the 1670s in elaborating and refining Mun's theories.
[2] Decker, op. cit., p. 7.
[3] *House of Lords MSS*, second series, vol. IV, pp. 1699–1702.

way to another: it was now envisaged as an agency of social welfare. In this form it was to be adopted and developed by the German Cameralist school of mercantilists and by Italian economists like the Neapolitan Genovesi.[1] In this form, too — as a means principally of industrial encouragement — mercantilist ideas now reached their final stage in Walpole's fiscal reforms. In Walpole's scheme there was characteristically little room for fantasy. His plan was clear, practical, direct, hard-headed; yet it was not merely a fiscal trick. In it were embodied ideas of national economic development, matured and purged of mystique over two centuries. The patterns of policy, clearing since the mid-seventeenth century, now assumed their final form. They were to survive until the coming of Free Trade in the nineteenth century. Even before 1691 duties on exports — cereals, meat, beer and metals — had been reduced. Many went altogether before 1699. In that year, the duties on the export of cloth, corn, meal and bread were abolished. The export duty on coal was retained and even increased after 1714: the foreigner needed our coal, therefore he must pay, being the motto. There was a particularly swingeing duty on coal exported in foreign ships. This, as much as the Navigation Acts, spelt the end of Dutch competition. Walpole's reforms in 1721 and later years completed a long process. To the abolition of export duties was added a series of bounties to stimulate industry positively: on whale fishing, linen, sail cloth, paper, etc. Protective duties on competing manufactured imports were multiplied. The pattern was consistent. 'Primary' materials produced at home were reserved for the benefit of home industry. Wool remained the most important instance, the regulations against export being rigorously though not always successfully enforced. An export duty on the unfinished — 'white' — cloth was also retained. The motive was that advertised by Alderman Cokayne a century earlier: to encourage the local dyeing and finishing of all woollen cloth. The apparent exceptions — coal and grain — showed how governments tried to balance fiscal claims and the interests of one industry against the possible interests of other industries. Coal and grain, like wool, might be held to be raw materials. Did not a rise in their price threaten those industries — brewing, for example — which used them extensively? Possibly. But against any such risk had to be placed the stimulus to mining and agriculture afforded by larger markets; above all, to the shipping industry, which gained thereby valuable business in bulk freights. These two commodities had already made a valuable contribution to the rise of the English

[1] See Wilson, 'The Other Face of Mercantilism', *Tr. R.H.S.* 9, 1959.

mercantile marine. So had the Newfoundland and Greenland fisheries which entered their great phase of prosperity from 1729 to 1763. By the mid-eighteenth century, these ventures, often precarious in the past, were a well-established business.[1] The surveyor of Newfoundland calculated in 1740 that 20,000 tons of shipping and 8,000 people were employed. A high proportion came from the West Country, London and Irish ports. The ships — snows, brigs, brigantines, schooners, sloops galleys, pinks, ketches — carried fish to Bilbao, Corunna and beyond into the Mediterranean. The worst enemy of the trade was war, which brought (especially in the Seven Years War) captures, impressments, high insurance charges. All these hit the West Country hard.

The growth of shipping reinforces the impression derived from the customs figures that the major advance of the period was in overseas trade, even though the fluctuations were wider and the average rate of increase was slower than in the forty years before 1700, certainly until the mid-century when it accelerated notably. Mr Davis has recently estimated the increase of shipping as follows;

	(000 tons)
1702	323
1751	421
1763	496[2]

Seventeenth-century writers like Petty, Child and Downing had seized firmly on the economic as well as the strategic value of shipping. Child had summarized it thus:

> No trades deserve so much ... as those that employ most shipping, altho' the Commodities transported be of small value in themselves; for *First* they are certainly the most profitable; for besides the gain accrewing by the goods, the *Freights*, which is in such trades often more than the value of the goods, is all *Profit to the Nation*. Besides they bring with them a great access of *Power* (Hands as well as Money). Many Ships and seamen being justly the Strength and Safety of England.

[1] R. G. Lounsbury, *British Fishery at Newfoundland 1634–1763*, 1934, p. 311.
[2] Another estimate is that of Professor Harper, op. cit., p. 339.

	Total	Colliers	Coastal	Newfoundland and Greenland Fisheries	Other Fisheries	Foreign trade
1702	267,444	78,212	41,454	16,157	8,763	122,858
1773	581,000	125,346	89,631	38,585	23,646	303,792

For Professor Harper's justification of admittedly questionable figures see ibid, pp. 339–40 and 340n.

Put in terms of the balance of payments, the growth of the mercantile marine meant that what had often been an invisible import item was turning perceptibly into a profitable item of invisible export. While inland transport might remain poor, the British economy was being provided with an increasingly efficient system of external transport, exploiting an ingeniously protected market.

The relatively ordered framework of duties and laws called by Adam Smith 'the mercantile system' provided the matrix within which continued economic expansion went forward. It was not without anomalies, even scandals, and in due time it would outlive its usefulness. But that it did in time do so does not destroy its claim to have been effective in the early stages of growth. It did not differ in essentials from systems of economic protection, stimulus, even autarky, frequently adopted by later nations, especially in the stage of nascent growth. Its fundamental assumption — that the economic plant may be induced to grow in apparently infertile soil — embodied a truly dynamic view of economic growth. This contravened later ideas that a nation was best advised to adopt industries for which it was 'naturally' suited. But this is of less importance than the fact that Britain had to spend many years painfully learning from foreigners most of the industrial and commercial skills that formed the basis of her later pre-eminence. In any event, the system represented an ordered balance between the claims of fiscal need and economic interest that contrasted strikingly with the topsy-turvy chaos of, say, the Spanish economy, where exported manufactures were heavily taxed and local raw materials freely sold abroad — even with subsidy payments.[1]

As the changing conditions of international trade enabled the State to undertake a comprehensive economic policy, the agencies which had earlier controlled economic life lost their utility, dwindled and fell away. London mercantile interests had thwarted the restrictive attempts of the industrial gilds to enforce the regulation of industry. An attempt in 1690 by the Leeds clothworkers to stop cloth leaving Leeds until it had been dyed and dressed likewise failed. By 1720 the Leeds company was a dead letter. Similarly, but more slowly, many of the great trading corporations which had been, or claimed to have been, the instruments of earlier commercial policy and expansion were now falling into decay. In part, their demise was due to the more abundant supply of capital

---

[1] See, for example, G. de Uztariz, *The Theory and Practice of Commerce and Maritime Affairs*, trans. J. Kippax, (London 1757), for an eighteenth-century critique by a Spanish writer of Spanish policy.

now available to individual merchants or partnerships. In part, also, to the growth of conventions governing the conduct of business amongst those nations which regularly traded together. As the responsibility for diplomatic negotiations passed increasingly to the appropriate depart-ments of states and their envoys accredited to foreign Powers, it was no longer necessary for merchants in strange lands to live under corpor-ate rule as the Italian 'nations' had once lived in Bruges, the Merchant Adventurers in Dordrecht or the Eastland merchants at Elbing. The cus-tom of appointing state envoys had been growing since the end of the fifteenth century amongst the European States. But it was some time before satisfactory and unanimous agreement could be obtained on protocol, even on the fundamental question of legal diplomatic im-munity. It marks a decisive phase in this process of civility that in the eighteenth century envoys first felt sufficient assurance to take their wives and families abroad on duty.

At the Restoration, the idea that trade could best be conducted through the grant of monopolistic powers to chartered companies was still at full strength. But thereafter it weakened rapidly. The Merchant Adventurers were the first to go: in any event, their main business in exporting unfinished cloth was out of harmony with current economic aspirations. Another 'regulated' company, the Eastland, had its privi-leges abruptly curtailed in 1673; thereafter it became increasingly nominal. It admitted a new member hopefully in 1713. But by 1728 it had become reduced to a dining club.[1] The Russia company survived longer (and it still survives) no doubt because of the peculiar difficulties of trading in its area. So did the Levant Company, partly because of the pressure of French rivalry in the eastern Mediterranean, even more because the caprices of a succession of Grand Viziers at Constantinople and the depredations of Mediterranean pirates made trade in this area a costly and trying business. But in 1754 this trade was also thrown open. Even in the extra-European trades, where the financial, political and military problems involved in trade were obstinate and formidable, the monopoly system came under heavy attack after the Revolution of 1688. The Royal Africa Company, tarred with the brush of Stuart favouritism, lost its monopoly in 1698 after a contest with interlopers that lasted nearly half a century. The 'old' East India Company had a similar battle with interlopers, and later with a rival organization that called itself the New East India Company. It survived only at the cost of amalgamating, in 1708, with its rival. The case for corporate trading

[1] Hinton, *The Eastland Trade and the Common Weal*, p. 161.

and capital in India in the conditions of the eighteenth century was really irrefutable. Much of the jousting against the old company came from disaffected outsiders who wanted to get inside. No one seriously disputed the need in India for a permanent apparatus of defence that was clearly beyond the resources of any but a powerful corporate body. The trades to America and the West Indies were free and individual.

These pressures towards greater liberty in trade were important; but their object was 'freer trade' and not, as has often been suggested, 'free trade' in its later doctrinal sense. They came from the empirical, self-interested demands of particular merchant or industrial groups, not from philosophy or doctrine. Those who supplied goods for export felt that they might get better prices for what they sold if the purchasers were many rather than few. Thus the West Country clothiers wanted the African trade freed, just as their grandfathers had wanted European trade freed from the Merchant Adventurers' monopoly.[1] So did those colonists who bought slaves from the Africa Company for their plantations, suspecting that the supply was restricted to keep prices high. In France the corresponding French companies came under similar fire. It was the common and justifiable fate of monopolies. In England especially, monopoly was still associated in the popular mind with the danger that London mercantile cliques might acquire a dangerous hold over Government. The most striking consequence of the movement for freer trade was the ending of the dominion of London and the rise of the west coast ports.[2] The doctrinal attack on the regulation of foreign trade that was designed to secure a favourable balance of trade came later. As yet relatively few shared in a view that derived essentially from philosophy and logic: at this stage the facts, rivalries and experience of commerce were still paramount in shaping opinion.

The increasingly positive role played by Britain in world trade was bound up with physical changes in the volume and direction of business: especially with the receding role of the Dutch. In the earlier seventeenth century, Holland had been the main source of British imports, the principal market, finishing depot and retail centre for British exports, and a main supplier of shipping services. In 1700 Holland still came high on the list, but as a source of imports she was now second to the Plantations, and seven-eighths of what they sent was tobacco and sugar. As a market for British exports Holland still retained first place. Sixty years later, Holland had fallen to tenth place as a source of British

1 Davies, op. cit., p. 133.
2 Davies, op. cit., p. 152. See below, p. 274.

imports. British colonial imports had grown most rapidly of all. As a market for British exports Holland's share had fallen proportionately to one third of what it had been. The change may be summarized as follows:

	1696–97 (£m)	1772–73 (£m)
Total *Imports* to Britain	3·5	11·4
From Holland	0·5	0·4
Total *Exports* from Britain	3·5	14·8
To Holland	1·5	1·9

In other words, Holland's trade remained about the same, in absolute figures, in a world where the *total* flow of trade had enormously increased. Her share in British trade therefore fell from 14·6 to 3·6 per cent in imports and from 41·5 to 12·7 per cent in exports.[1] In both directions, British merchants were increasingly by-passing the Dutch entrepôt, taking imports directly from suppliers and selling a larger range of (mainly) finished manufactures directly to their final purchasers. The trends emerge very clearly from the surviving evidence about particular Anglo-Dutch trades. Exeter and London merchants who had formerly sold serges to Amsterdam middlemen were exporting directly to markets in Spain, Hamburg and Bremen by 1716. In 1733 Bosanquets, a London firm that had traded heavily with the Dutch, sent a young family cadet, Jacob, to Hamburg to learn the trade with the idea that henceforth they would trade directly to north Germany. In the opposite direction, English merchants who had formerly bought German linens, sailcloth and Russian hemp through Dutch middlemen were looking for their supplies either to Ireland or Scotland, and buying directly from Archangel.[2]

The trend was persistent and widespread. It was not easy for the Dutch, with their essentially middleman functions, to resist the tide of economic nationalism that was eroding the very foundations of their business. But the process was not universal or complete. While Britain managed to get a firm hold on the market for American *leaf* tobacco in France, Holland and Germany, her attempts to conquer the northern markets for *treated* tobacco in Scandinavia and Russia from the Dutch were a comparative failure. The petition of the English tobacco manufacturers for special regulations which would encourage the export

---

[1] T. P. van der Kooy, *Hollands Stapelmarket en haar Verval*, Amsterdam, 1936, p. 36.
[2] See C. Wilson, *Anglo-Dutch Commerce and Finance in the Eighteenth Century*, 1948, part I, ch. 2.

of their products cut little ice. Not all their claims to be creators of employment for thousands of 'poor People' could induce successive governments to risk the loss of the great trade in untreated tobacco which was of such consequence to the powerful colonial lobby and to the planters. Anxious as governments were to promote manufactures, here was a case where the facts were against the petitioners. It was too easy, presumably, for importing countries to cut and roll their own leaf. No government wanted to risk another Cokayne fiasco.[1]

With such changes in the nature of British foreign trade went a marked change in the location of the new trades and those who handled them. If London was still growing, its increase was now slower than that of the western ports and of the northern and midland towns which were supplying them with manufactures for export. The population of London's central areas remained pretty steady – between 670,000 and 680,000 – in the first half of the century. What growth there was went on in the suburbs and the final merging of the 'Two Cities' into one was symbolized in 1760. The City gates were in that year dismantled, chopped up and made into souvenirs by ingenious contractors who made small fortunes out of their enterprise. There was still only one public dock east of London Bridge, the Howland Wet Dock of 1660 named after the Director whose daughter married the Earl of Bedford's heir. Large ships found it difficult to snatch berths on the quayside. Their valuable cargoes were transhipped in mid-stream on to open lighters, vulnerable to weather and pilferers, while they awaited the attentions of an inadequate and ill-organized customs service. Into the nineteenth century the river was to remain a hazardous jumble of ocean-going ships jostled on all sides by lighters, punts, barges, lugger-boats, sloops, cutters and hoys all needed to help in handling cargoes from ship to shore. This congestion of the port helps to explain the marked slowing down of London's growth in the eighteenth century; just as the deceleration may help to explain the growing political disgruntlement of the City after 1763. More characteristic of this phase of politics and fashion in London history was the development of the great Mayfair estates between 1713 and 1730: of Hanover Square and George Street by the Whig nobility, of the Cavendish-Harley estate north of Oxford Street by the Tories. Behind Piccadilly, the Burlington estates were taking shape and the Grosvenor estates were developed between 1725 and 1735. Thereafter little was done till after 1763.

1 See J. M. Price, 'The Tobacco Adventure to Russia', *Trans. of the American Philosophical Society*, March 1961.

While London's commercial growth marked time there was brisk activity in the western ports. In the first half of the eighteenth century the population of Bristol doubled, from 48,000 to 100,000: Liverpool increased from some 6,000 to 35,000; Whitehaven and Glasgow were growing fast. Similar rates of growth could be registered in the towns where the new industries were developing. Manchester, Sheffield and Birmingham all had populations of between 30,000 and 50,000 by 1750, and while none yet reached Norwich's figure of 56,000 they were all growing at a faster rate.[1]

The striking growth of the western ports was confirmed by the figure of the outward clearances of ships from British ports in the twenty years after the mid-century.

	1750 (tons)	1770 (tons)
London	180,000	245,000
Whitehaven	100,000	192,000
Liverpool	40,000	87,000
Bristol	28,000	35,000

The figures for the ownership of shipping tonnage tells a similar tale.[2]

	Shipping owned in	
	London	Outports
	(000 tons)	
1702	140	183
1751	119	302
1763	139	357

The older ports were growing more slowly than the new, perhaps because of the growing congestion of ships, perhaps because – at Bristol, for example, which was a long way up a tidal river – the problems of adapting the port to a larger volume of shipping were considerable. In all the western ports, the largest trade was tobacco. Liverpool in the first decade of the century imported about 13,000 tons, half for home use, half for export. In 1745, Whitehaven was said to be 'deem'd the 3rd if not the 2nd port in the Kingdom on the Tob.º way'.[3] Perhaps because its communications with the industrial hinterland were poor, its fall was to be as rapid as its rise. Liverpool on the other hand

[1] Westerfield, op. cit., pp. 423–6.
[2] Figures from Davis, op. cit., p. 27.
[3] J. E. Williams, 'Whitehaven in the 18th Century', *Econ. Hist. Rev.*, VIII, no. 3, 1956.

was rapidly diversifying its growing trade until by 1760 it was doing a varied trade with Africa, America and the West Indies, exporting cloth, cottons, Midland metal wares. These were exchanged on the Guinea coast against slaves, gold dust and ivory which were in turn sold against the sugar, rum and tobacco of Jamaica, Barbados and the southern plantations. By the mid-century Liverpool had become the chief slaving port. The enterprise of the Aspinalls and Cunliffes, Leylands and Fildarts might be a 'horrid traffic' to Horace Walpole. More probably regarded it as 'an inexhaustible Fund of Wealth and Naval Power' (1749).

Cotton imports grew rapidly after the end of the Austrian Succession War, but they remained a long way below the older import cargoes in value. Here is a first-hand glimpse of colonial business from the instructions to a Liverpool slaving captain in 1762. He was told to load his ship in the Leeward Islands with 'about One Hundred Cask good Muscovado Sugars for the ground tier, the remainder with first and second white sugars, and betwixt Decks with good Cotton and Coffee'. And 'At Jamaica' with 'as much Broad Sound Mahogany as will serve for Dunnage, the hold filled with the very best Musc. sugar and ginger and betwixt Decks with good cotton and Pimento and about Ten Puncheons Rum'.[1] All the Colonial trades were increasing rapidly after 1748, and with them the wealth and importance of the provincial merchant communities. Markets were not always stable. Tobacco in particular was easily overdone. Of sugar it was said by a dealer in 1745: 'Nothing can be more fluctuating than the Market for sugar, the Continuance of an Easterly Wind for a few weeks shall raise it, and a Westerly Wind with the bare expectation of the arrival of Ships shall lower it again.'[2] Such vicissitudes called for resource and ingenuity in the merchants. Not all who attempted succeeded, but new aspirants were never lacking. 'The true-bred Merchant', wrote Defoe, 'is the most intelligent Man in the World and consequently the most capable, when urged by necessity, to contrive new ways to live.' The hazards of the markets were merely one of the challenges he met, and usually conquered.

The principal changes in the character of the nation's trade and industry may be illustrated by three facts: London's share in foreign trade — imports, exports and re-exports — fell markedly between 1700 and

[1] Wadsworth and Mann, *The Cotton Trade and Industrial Lancashire, 1600–1780*, p. 187, n. 3. See also graph of cotton imports, p. 184.
[2] R. Pares, 'The London Sugar Market', *Econ. Hist. Rev.*, IX, no. 2, 1956.

1750. The value of British produce and manufactures exported rose in the same period by about two and half times. And direct trade with other countries — the colonies especially — dwarfed the shrinking volume of trade with the Dutch entrepôt. The swift rise of the western ports was matched by an equally swift rise in the volume and value of trade with America and the West Indies. Between 1700 and the end of the period, the value of English exports to these areas increased five-fold. Imports increased about fourfold. By the 1760s, the transatlantic trades probably employed about a third of the total English shipping engaged in overseas trade. The centre of gravity of the entire economy was shifting.[1]

The statistics of economic growth of the period will mislead us if they are taken to suggest a steady, unbroken climb towards affluence. They were, on the contrary, interrupted by wars, bad harvests, failures of confidence, and overproduction. These brought bankruptcies or hard-ships to individuals and widespread misery, sometimes culminating in riot and bloodshed, to whole sections of society.[2] One student after another has revealed the ebb and flow of economic life in these years. Almost all sectors — agriculture, trade (home and foreign), industry, population growth — show a weaker momentum from the twenties to the fifties, when the forward movement was strongly resumed.[3] So that though here and there voices might be heard quoting philosophical arguments in favour of something like policies of *laissez-faire*, things were not so settled or secure that opinion in general was prepared to contemplate abandoning either economic development or social wel-fare to the free play of market forces.

Since the onslaught of Adam Smith and others on the eighteenth-century conception of trade and empire, and the loss of the American colonies, the debate has raged on the wars of the earlier decades. Did they, as some historians have argued, distort the natural patterns of the economy, diverting labour, capital and economic effort from produc-tive and peaceful investment in such urgent enterprises as transport, building and more consumer goods to the more immediate but socially wasteful needs for war? They involved (Professor Ashton has written) 'many losses in men and ships, and in intangible human qualities. If there had been no wars the English people would have been better fed,

---

[1] See E. B. Schumpeter, in *English Overseas Trade Statistics 1697-1808*, ed. T. S. Ashton, 1960, p. 9, and Tables II-VI, Harper, op. cit., pp. 271-2.

[2] See e.g. T. S. Ashton, *Economic Fluctuations in England 1700-1800* (1959), p. 177.

[3] See R. Davis, op. cit.; G. Mingay, J. D. Chambers, op. cit.

better clad, certainly better housed, than they were. War deflected energies from the course along which — so it seems in retrospect — the permanent interests of England lay'.[1] Others have doubted whether this is supported by the facts. They submit that these wars 'exerted, on the whole, a beneficial influence on the development of the English economy'.[2]

That the wars of these years did divert and absorb a substantial part of the economic resources of Britain there can be no doubt. Specific as well as general instances of this can be quoted. The depressions in the building trades in 1709–12, 1716–17 and, most obviously, 1739–48 were in large measure attributable to the shortage of shipping and the cutting off of those timber supplies which were a vital element in building. Demands of war led, as we shall see,[3] to heavy demands for capital which pushed up the price at which money could be borrowed for ordinary business development. But it does not seem that this was in itself the cause of those recurrent depressions which marked the economy between 1713 and 1760. The major depression of 1761–62 may have been so caused, for the capital needs of those war years were quite unprecedented.[4] While the higher cost of borrowing in wartime did not in general rule out business investment altogether, it may have helped to reduce some business men's profits and thereby have made investment of certain types less attractive. Higher taxation, by reducing purchasing power amongst consumers, and by raising labour costs, may have worked in the same direction. There is no need to dispute the general contention that Britain's crying need in this stage of growth was for more and better transport. But it was not altogether denied by war. Coastal shipping especially went on growing. The collier fleet rose from 78,000 tons in 1702 to 125,000 tons by 1773 and other coast-wise tonnage more than doubled — from 41,000 to 90,000 tons — in the same period. Internal transport, though not entirely stagnant, was slower to grow. The age of canals was not yet come. James Brindley managed to build his first canal for the Duke of Bridgewater — from Worsley to Manchester — in 1759–61, but this seems to be one of those exceptions that prove the rule. The characteristic method of the age was to ease the flow of river traffic. Heavy goods — corn, coal, bricks, stone, iron, salt — moved more easily and cheaply where rivers like the

[1] T. S. Ashton, op. cit., p. 83, see also J. U. Nef, *War and Human Progress*, 1950.

[2] A. H. John, 'War and the English Economy 1700–1763', *Econ. Hist. Rev.*, VII, no. 3, 1955.

[3] Below, p. 313.

[4] T. S. Ashton, op. cit., p. 105.

Don, Aire and Calder, Weaver and Mersey, were made more navigable. Such improvements helped to open up the industrial regions of the north and link east England with west. They provided valuable experience also of the problems of financial organization from which canals, in their turn, were to benefit. In such joint stock companies as the 'Company of the Proprietors of the River Medway' the 'undertakers' were authorized to borrow capital on the security of tolls which they were empowered to levy on traffic. Technically, too, valuable experience was gained. John Hore of Newbury, the engineer of the Kennet improvements of 1715, was the father of the engineer who later designed the Kennet-Avon Canal. Similarly, the turnpike trusts nibbled at the problems of road construction, and earned a return on their capital by levying tolls on traffic other than foot passengers. The first Turnpike Act was as old as 1663. Each short stretch of road needed a separate Act, and they were common enough after 1700. Yet progress was fractional. How far were such delays the result of war and the competing demands it exerted for capital and labour?

Certainly shortage of capital and labour was not the only obstacle. Even in peace, opposition to river and road improvement was formidable. Farmers and others feared the competition from the outside world which such new channels might bring to their secluded local markets. Turnpikes met ferocious obstruction from local interests between 1730 and 1750. Contrariwise, Professor Chambers finds that in the Vale of Trent, turnpikes 'forged ahead' during the Seven Years War.[1] No less formidable was the more anonymous complex mass of laws and regulations, product of centuries of chaotic legislation, which faced the river improver. War was far from being the only begetter of bottlenecks in transport.

The figures of foreign trade seem to afford better evidence of the interference of war. At the Treaty of Utrecht in 1713, exports (£6·9 million) stood precisely where they stood in 1701. Imports (£5·8 million) were £100,000 lower than they had been at that date. The war of the Austrian succession likewise brought down the figures of exports and imports. The Seven Years War affected foreign trade much less.[2] On the face of it, industries like cloth making might expect to be seriously deranged by the interference with those foreign markets on which they depended so heavily. (It was said in the 1770s that 90 per cent of the

---

[1] C. R. Fay, *Great Britain from Adam Smith to the Present Day*, 1932, p. 177; Chambers, op. cit., p. 13.

[2] T. S. Ashton, *An Economic History of England: the 18th Century*, 1955, Table XIV.

Berwick

Parts of river navigable
in 1600–1660

Further stretches navigable
in 1724–1727

Newcastle
Tyne

Carlisle
Cockermouth
Derwent

York
Leeds
Beverley
Hull
Wakefield
Aire
Ouse
Idle
Warrington
Bawtry
Foss
Mersey
Dyke
Lincoln
Chester
Dee
Dane
Derwent
Boston
Weaver
Derby
Trent
Burton
Nottingham
Shrewsbury
Stamford
King's Lynn
Welland
Norwich
Yare
Welshpool
Peterborough
Nen
Beccles
Thetford
Gt. Ouse
Little Ouse
Woveney
Leominster
Severn
Stratford
Lark
Bury St. Edmunds
Cambridge
Ipswich
Bedford
Avon
Sudbury
Wye
Stour
Hertford
Colchester
Towy
Carmarthen
Oxford
London
Lea
Lechlade
Kennet
Thames
Bristol
Wey
Medway
Stour
Guildford
Fordwick
Maidstone
Bridgwater
Tone
Salisbury
Parret
Taunton
Avon
Exeter
Poole
Chichester

Plymouth

0   50   100 miles

Based on Willan, *River Navigation in England*, Oxford University Press.

Yorkshire broadcloths were sold abroad.) We know that the Devon serge manufacture took a hard knock from the Spanish and Austrian Succession Wars. Yet much depended on the flexibility and enterprise with which local merchants and makers faced such crises. Some clothiers, in Yorkshire and the West Country especially, moved swiftly into army contracts. We do not know how far the temporary loss of foreign markets may have been offset by the expansion of such wartime demand for uniforms. Other industries, like Spitalfields silks and Irish and Scotch linens, benefited positively from the disappearance of competitive imports in wartime. War demand stimulated the heavy metal industries and led to the search for more efficient technologies. Cheaper copper and brass were the foundations on which the 'new trades' of the Midlands – guns, toys, buttons and brass goods – were to rise. Similarly with the iron trades. Naval shipbuilding itself acted as a 'multiplier', creating a complex of demands for coal, metals, tar, ropes, as well as for the skilled and semi-skilled labour of carpenters, sailmakers, anchor makers and the like. Did these demands delay the expansion of consumer goods industries? If they did, one might expect the results to be reflected in enhanced prices and scarcities of such goods. Yet these are not easily observed. Prices remained pretty stable, consumer goods falling from 100 (in 1700) to 81 (in 1735–36), rising only to 90 in 1761–62.[1]

The British economy in the first half of the eighteenth century was more complex, more diversified, more broadly based, than at any previous time in its history. But its stability was still exposed to some major threats from Nature and from man. A bad harvest was still a potent source of trouble. Corn exports disappeared. Imports of grain had to be paid for, and the higher prices of essential goods reduced the demand for semi-necessities and luxuries like sugar, clothes and footwear.[2] Such conditions were to be seen after the bad harvests of 1709, 1725, 1728–29, 1740 and 1756. War added to this kind of instability. It may, therefore, have helped to *postpone* progress by creating immediate shortages and uncertainties. But it was only one factor amongst many. And against such short-term results must be placed the undoubted stimulus it afforded to certain types of industrial development, where it was responsible for technological innovations. These had permanent effects that were passed on to peace-time production. And if, as many

---

[1] T. S. Ashton, *Economic History*, p. 199, using Dr E. Gilboy's figures in her *Wages in Eighteenth-Century England*, 1934, 1700–1701 = 100.

[2] T. S. Ashton, *Economic Fluctuations in England, 1700–1800* (1959), p. 44.

men believed, the most fundamental need of the time was for a greater volume of more varied employments, the demands of war may have helped by developing new technologies.

There remains a more fundamental, and even more impalpable, problem. The wars of the eighteenth century are generally agreed to have led to the acquisition of new territories and new markets.[1] Yet, in retrospect, we often view the problem from the vantage point of a century where in spite of war the small and pacific nation is often able to maintain and expand its economy. We therefore assume that the same economic opportunities were open to all nations, strong or weak, in earlier times: that but for wars, of our own wilful making, available resources 'wasted' on war could have been turned to better social account. Such views may or may not be correct. They cannot, in the nature of things, be more than speculative. What is certain is that few statesmen, politicians, philosophers, merchants or manufacturers of the day believed this to be so. There were, to be sure, sharp differences of opinion on the merits of particular wars. Walpole was content with unenterprising peace because, unlike his jingo opponents who shouted for war with the Bourbons and simultaneously moved for a reduction of the army, he saw clearly the immediate consequences. War meant, for the time being and probably longer, heavier taxation; most probably heavier taxation of his own class. In 1742, the general appetite for more aggressive war forced even Walpole to resign. Amongst the majority who opposed him, most still held to the view propounded by Albermarle (Pepys's 'stout blockhead') on the eve of the Second Dutch War: that there was only so much international trade to go round and that England's share would be determined in proportion to her power to grasp and hold it against powerful competitors. The case was crudely put: it did not differ essentially from what has been described as Pitt's system in a nutshell: 'Our trade depends upon a proper exertion of our maritime strength: that trade and maritime force depend upon each other ... that riches, which are the true resources of the country, depend upon commerce'. Nor, in its turn, was this far from the text of Josiah Child in the previous century: that 'Profit and Power ought jointly to be considered'. Because the wars of the eighteenth century are now commonly (and rightly) considered to have been 'wars of limited liability'; because they were, providentially, waged almost everywhere except on English soil, it is tempting to regard them as the extravagant frills of policy, external to the broad and inevitable process of economic

[1] Ibid., p. 83.

expansion, producing a temporary bonus here or a temporary deprivation there, but hardly central to the national destiny, Rightly or wrongly, such views were alien to the general opinions of the day and would have been incomprehensible to the vast majority of contemporaries. For them, trade and sea power were inextricably bound together. The task of sea power was in essence defensive, but defence could often only be secured by attack. Without it, not only the expansion of trade but the maintenance of what trade the nation possessed would have been endangered. Such views may have been erroneous. They need to be more carefully examined than they sometimes are.

From 1689 Britain was faced by a hostile power far more formidable than Spain or Holland had ever been. France had a population some three to four times the size of that of Britain. She was rich in natural resources. She possessed a ring of excellent ports and potential naval bases. Where the exposed lifelines and precarious economy of the Dutch had invited plunder and blockade, France seemed almost impregnable. The only defence against her attempted hegemony was attack. The Anglo-Dutch strategical situation was now reversed. The penalty of English economic expansion was self-imposed. It was now England's communications with her growing markets and colonies overseas that were threatened by France. English defence must consist (as it had seemed earlier to de Ruyter that Dutch defence against England must consist) in striking out of the opponent's hand his most powerful weapon of attack — the French Fleet. Alternatively, in diverting his energies away from maritime war to a land war fought on the Continent. To the threat to trade should also be added recurrent threats of cross-Channel invasion by a power upon which had fallen the mantle of absolutism and (since the Revocation of the Edict of Nantes in 1685) of intolerance and persecution; and whose policy combined the dynastic ambitions of the Bourbons with the central principle of Colbert that trade was only another form of warfare.

The burden of protracted war against France had become plain in the fighting that ended, with both sides exhausted, at the Treaty of Ryswick. The Spanish succession question, which cropped up immediately after the peace, raised a much more serious threat. If Spain were to become a satellite of France, or even if (as the Second Partition Treaty envisaged) the Two Sicilies, with Naples and the Sicilian bases, were to fall to France, two major areas of British trade would be at once exposed to attack. The Mediterranean and Levant trade would be indefensible. Worse still, the Spanish American and West Indian Empire with all its rich resources of trade and treasure, would be at the disposal of France. The British settlements on the eastern American seaboard might be ringed by a great arc of French influence curving down from French Canada west and south down through Louisiana to the mouth of the Mississippi. These were the main preoccupations of British policy from 'Queen Anne's War' which broke out in 1701, down to 1763. To these were added others – the threat from the French in India, and the subsidiary but vital need to keep our Baltic trade – essential if the fleet was to get the timber and naval stores it needed – flowing freely in face of the threat of domination by Sweden or Russia.

Peripheral though the Baltic incidents may appear, they were crucial to British maritime supremacy. Although alternative supplies from our North American colonies were being stimulated, the total demand was now so enormously increased that the building not only of the Royal Navy but of the mercantile fleet depended more than ever on Baltic supplies. The government's instructions to Carteret in 1719 regarding the threat of domination by the Czar made the current view clear: the freedom of the Baltic was 'a consideration of such importance to the commerce of our subjects, and even to their safety, which could not be so well provided for without the naval stores we draw from these parts . . .'.[1] This was only enlarging upon something the British envoy in Stockholm had said earlier when the King of Sweden was proving difficult: 'how much it was in the power of the King of Sweden either to forward the fitting out of the Royal Navy or to keep it in harbour'. If safer supplies could be got from North America, well and good. Meanwhile, the balance of power on the Baltic must be preserved. With this in mind, the British Government despatched a fleet to the Baltic nine times between 1715 and 1727.

In the early years of the century, the centre of strategic gravity remained in Europe. Fleets were despatched from time to time to interfere with the Spanish trade in the West Indies – especially the movement of the treasure fleet which Swift, for example, saw as the prime mover of enemy effort. The permanent problem for strategists was whether to rely on sea power or on military power to reduce the enemy. By and large, the Tories formed the main support of the 'maritime' policy, the Whigs that of the 'continental' policy. At sea, strategy was focused on the reduction of Toulon, the main French Mediterranean base. When peace came, the English took no territory in Europe, contenting themselves with securing the Mediterranean position by

[1] *Diplomatic Instructions (Sweden), 1689–1727*, p. 109.

taking Gibraltar and Minorca. Overseas, the economic element in policy remained strong. Nova Scotia was secured, together with a share of Newfoundland and the overvalued Asiento to supply slaves to the Spanish colonies from British West African slavery ports.

A strong case can be made out for the basically defensive character of the strategy of these years. Along with measures designed to limit the offensive power of France, Spain, Russia and Sweden went others designed specifically to protect trade: notably the 'Cruisers and Convoys' Act of 1708 which allocated a naval force to trade protection and probably accounted for the improvement of the trade figures by 1712. Thereafter, in this part of the eighteenth century, losses due to enemy capture were probably less than in the previous century.[1] In 1725, in a period of nominal peace, the Government despatched a strong squadron to blockade the Spanish American ports from which the Austro-Spanish coalition hoped to finance an attack on Gibraltar. A contemporary, Bishop Hoadley, could write that the move prevented a European war by 'depriving the Courts of Vienna and Madrid of the means of putting into effect the dangerous course which they had projected'.[2]

In 1739 the merchant community, especially the powerful West India lobby, were in a bellicose mood. The war with Spain that began in that year was a protest against Spanish interference with what the Spaniards regarded as smuggling and the English regarded as legitimate trade with the Spanish colonies. The enthusiasm for war swiftly turned (as Walpole had predicted) to lamentation as one disaster succeeded another. The British were thrown back on defensive methods – convoys in the manner of 1708 – until 1746. Thereafter, British naval supremacy was re-established, French trade was brought to a standstill and France was compelled at the peace of 1748 to restore all her continental conquests in exchange for Cape Breton, the key to Canada, which she had lost to the British.

The Seven Years War began with an irritation of the North American wound. The French hope was to unite Quebec and Louisiana. A French invading force from Canada overwhelmed a local Virginian militia force in Ohio. Then Minorca was attacked and lost. No government could have ignored two such deliberate challenges and survived in authority. From these two events followed the most expensive war of the century. Commercial aims were a powerful component in Pitt's strategic thinking. It was not for nothing that he was descended from a

---

[1] See Davis, *The Rise of the British Merchant Shipping Industry*, ch. xv, *passim*.
[2] *An Enquiry into the Reasons for the Conduct of Great Britain*, Dublin, 1727.

grandfather – 'Diamond Pitt – who had made his fortune as an inter-loper in the East Indian trade. His close study of the French economy had reinforced his passionate conviction that the greatest danger to England's power and prosperity came from France, in association with Spain. In the war strategy which he personally directed his main instrument was sea power, his main objective the reduction of French trade. Hawke at Quiberon Bay brilliantly smashed the French Fleet, Wolfe at Quebec secured the great trades in fish and fur and cut off the French West Indies from their access to North American timber. The British colonists were secured from attack. The French saw their forces driven from India, their sugar trade in the West Indies strangled. Pitt's City supporters and advisers could apparently rejoice in utter victory. They did not rejoice for long. The peace of 1763 gave back to France the West Indian 'sugar bowl', her fishing rights off Newfoundland, Dakar and the gum trade. Pitt out of office might denounce all this as treachery which gave France 'the means of recovering her prodigious losses and of becoming once more formidable to us at sea'. But for the first time doubts seem to have assailed the merchant community. Could they any longer put their confidence in war – even maritime war – as an instrument of commercial policy? In their chagrin they forgot that the grand strategy had in fact achieved its object: the com-mand of the sea. The City merchants had been traditionally a centre of opposition to the Government – especially the smaller, newer men. But their leaders so far – Sir John Barnard and William Beckford in particular – had limited their aims to economic problems. Now the leadership was to pass to a more dangerous demagogue – John Wilkes. Wilkes drew his support from many sources but amongst them frustra-tion of the merchants in a city no longer growing at its former pace was certainly a powerful source of the new radicalism.

There is no lack of examples of stupidity, greed, waste and ineptitude in the economic and strategic policies of this period. Yet their ultimate achievement was this naval predominance which gave effective control of the seas to Britain. Here, on the high seas, was created a great web of ocean trade routes at least as vital to trade as the roads and inland water-ways of Britain. Under the protection of this shield of real or potential force came and went the export and import trade of Britain. British textiles, iron, coal and a growing variety of manufactures streamed out to pay for the raw cotton from the West Indies and American colonies which supplied the growing industry of Lancashire, the lumber from the Baltic and America that kept the shipyards busy, the dyewoods that supplied the clothier's vats in Yorkshire, Norwich and the west, the Swedish iron so necessary for the fine steel industry, the sugar, tea, tobacco, spices and calicoes that supplied scores of secondary industries, wholesalers and retailers and formed the basis of re-exports of enormous value. The contribution made to Britain's economic progress by the various elements in its motive power – natural resources, political order, social mobility, sound credit, legislative controls, naval power – cannot be apportioned. To the final historical reality, all these, and many more, contributed. No one component can be subtracted from the historical whole without distorting the reality that is the historian's only evidence. It may be speculated that if men had been more pacific, more rational, social progress would have been faster, welfare more abundantly spread. It may be true that if 'England had enjoyed un-broken peace, the Industrial Revolution might have come earlier'.[1] But such hypotheses must remain hypotheses. In the historical reality, the British conquest of the seas played its role. Its function has never been very clearly understood, even by those who benefited from it. Vol-taire thought that England's good fortune rested on her toleration. Montesquieu attributed supreme virtue to her constitution. Yet, as a maritime historian has written: 'Philosophers left out of account the Navy, for there were no books to tell them about it, and in peace its ships were laid up and its men scattered over the trade routes.'[2] The most recent historian of the shipping industry has added this: 'If, in the century after the Dutch War, it was the English rather than the French or Dutch shipping industry which became the greatest trans-atlantic carrier, this was in large part the result of success in war, trans-lated into the maintenance and extension of an area within which Englishmen had a monopoly of trade and transport.'[3] It is easy, in retro-spect, to take the results of wars for granted because the wars were conceived in rashness, wastefully or incompetently directed and by later standards motivated by material greed. Yet they were also the product of a vigour and enterprise the fruits of which we still enjoy. In a world of absolutism, dynasticism, persecution and matching national-isms, contemporaries saw them as wars for liberty as well as for gain. When the authors of 'Rule, Britannia' (1740) proclaimed that Britons never, never should be slaves, they were saying something that thous-ands of Britons believed to be real, as well as something rhetorically

---

[1] T. S. Ashton, op. cit., p. 83.
[2] J. A. Williamson, *Great Britain and the Empire*, 1944, p. 42.
[3] Davis, op. cit., pp. 336–7.

popular. Whatever the merits of this view — and there is still something to be said for it — they cannot, historically, be regarded as irrelevant to the main course of British history. The rise of the British economy was based, historically, on the conscious and successful application of strength; just as the decline of the Dutch economy was based on the inability of a small and politically weak state to maintain its position against stronger states. Without the wars, the entire course of world history might have been different. The Bourbons might have triumphed and survived, neither learning nor forgetting. New France might have gone on, authoritarian, bureaucratic, orthodox, neo-feudal. The United States might never have emerged, and Britain herself might have declined into the economic lethargy of Sweden or Holland.

CHAPTER FOURTEEN

Concentration and Diversification of Manufactures

THE nature of English industrial development in the sixty years that preceded the beginnings of 'industrial revolution' is not to be divined by any single or simple analysis. Industry did not stand still, but neither did it everywhere or in all respects go forward. Some industries progressed faster than others. Some like the 'Old Draperies', foundered altogether. Some like brewing underwent technological change: but that did not always go hand in hand with 'growth'. Other industries, like the worsted industry, grew without undergoing technological change. Contraction or concentration in some industries was associated with increased efficiency. Each industry has its own story. Statistics of production, investment, profits or turnover are rare and frequently unreliable. But the churning vitality of industry was widely visible. Mining, salt refining, nail making, silk throwing, linen weaving, sugar refining, pottery and glass making and a score of others were growing up, to diversify or enrich society and embellish its civilization. The scars inflicted on Cornwall by the tin and copper miners are still visible. Bristol or Lowestoft 'Delft' may still be bought. 'Social' history consists to a large extent of the record of the consumption or use of the new or growing products of such industries. Yet the consumption was often too small to have left any mark capable of being recorded statistically on, say, the national income, or on the average income enjoyed by Englishmen of the early eighteenth century. Only over pretty long periods can it be said that 'the standard of living' has risen; the manner of its rising is not infrequently obscure. The use of glass, or silk, or iron, or coal becomes, one is aware, more common than it has been. A new or improved commodity increasingly enters into consumption. But the general improvement is at first too slow and too slight to show through the crude arithmetical apparatus we use to measure these things. There is no statistical X-ray camera to penetrate the minute and subtle changes in the socio-economic process. We must do our best with imperfect evidence that often only masquerades as statistics. For the rest we have to rely on observed fact and on impressions handled as carefully as possible.

The significance of a change should not be underestimated because it was slow to gestate or small in result. The spread of invention, whether it be root crops, coke smelting or mechanical spinning, was necessarily slow to affect aggregate output. But to read the statistical expectations and standards of the twentieth or even the nineteenth century back into the pre-Industrial Revolution world is to misread and misunderstand the nature of economic history. The economic historian must never cease to try to measure sizes and quantities: but he must also remember that

> Large streams from little fountains flow
> Tall oaks from little acorns grow.

England's industries in the early eighteenth century were to be found at every stage of development: some were only germinating, some had reached maturity, some had even passed it.

Without any question, cloth remained far and away the nation's most important manufacture, even though its *relative* importance as an export industry had declined from the monolithic status of earlier times. In 1740, cloth still represented about one-third of the net value of the output of all manufacturing industry.[1] Whatever yardstick of measurement is used – capital, or labour employed, or value of production – cloth was still the first manufacture. Although a considerable measure of geographical concentration had taken place, it was still manufactured over a very wide area of country in the west, in East Anglia, in Yorkshire, in Lancashire. The welfare of the industry remained a major national concern and its wool supply from home sources was still reserved by scores of Acts of Parliament to the local manufacturers. From the late seventeenth century, surveyors had patrolled the coasts to check smuggling. Yorkshire had a surveyor and eighteen 'riding officers'. How effective the legislation and enforcement was is still a matter of debate. In 1732 witnesses complained that smuggling was rife. Why should the State not purchase wool in bulk at fixed prices and put an end to 'owling' (as wool smuggling was called)? It was difficult to prevent illicit export from the Kent marshes to France. There was probably a trickle of wool stowed away in holds and labelled 'hops' till the end of the century. But by and large there can be little doubt that this

---

[1] Hoffmann, *British Industry 1700–1950*, trans. Henderson and Chaloner, 1955, pp.18–19.

strong home supply, supplemented by a sizeable import of Irish, Scotch, Spanish and Saxon wool gave the English clothier a ponderable advantage over foreign competitors.

Within a framework of slowly expanding markets, the period saw a further extension of the trend in textiles already plainly observable in the seventeenth century: rising living standards, urban growth, more elegant houses more graciously furnished, the examples of oriental manufacture, and technological improvements – all pointed to a demand for lighter, more elegant, more highly finished textiles. Hence also a shift of location, uncompleted in our period but already strongly marked enough to create grave economic and social problems, as custom deserted first Devonshire and Somerset, then East Anglia, for Yorkshire and Lancashire.

Devonshire was the first to feel the keen wind of change. The Treaty of Utrecht was followed by a severe and prolonged slump. Exports to Holland were badly hit, and Exeter's share fell by more than two-thirds (from £386,000 to £111,000) between 1710 and 1721. The collapse seems to have been due to two principal factors. The first was the weakening of the Dutch entrepôt trade. Dutch merchants had previously bought large quantities of Devon serges for re-export in other countries. These former customers were now beginning to trade directly with producers, eliminating the need for the middleman's services of the Dutch. Although individual Devon merchants like the Lewises of Tiverton, Edmund Cock and Benjamin Heath of Exeter, were doing a rising business to Hamburg and Cadiz, the disruption of the Dutch intermediary trade seems to have hit the Exeter serge trade hard. Anglo-Dutch trade was made no easier by the rising competition of Irish linens. For Exeter had imported German linens, Dutch-bleached, against the sale of Devon serges. The growing sale of high-quality Irish linens was already beginning to eat into the profits of this trade. Simultaneously, there was one of those striking changes of fashion which from time to time stretch the ingenuity of the manufacturer and consign the unenterprising to perdition. A shrewd Exeter merchant, Sir John Elwill, wrote to his Dutch correspondent in 1714:

> I judge that Mixt Serges are not worn by Many Sort of People as formerly, and that the Trade will never flourish as heretofore. The Trade of Serges is indifferent: the Serge makers hoped great Advances in Price on the Peace, But are disappointed. Many have discontinued these Trades and others make but half the Quantity they made some years past.[1]

---

[1] C. Wilson, *Anglo-Dutch Commerce and Finance* . . ., p. 37.

There were, he added, some 'new sorts of Drapery invented . . . which are used by many that formerly used Serge'. They came from Norwich.

Just as serges had swept the board in the 1670s, so now Norwich 'stuffes' carried all before them once the peace was signed and trade returned to normal. (It may be that war conditions had made it difficult for new fabrics to establish themselves and had thus given an automatic protection to Devon which lapsed with the peace.)[1] For the rest of our period, the export of Norwich 'stuffes' rose steadily to all markets, while Devon's trade fell away. After 1748, it is true, there was some recovery of foreign markets. A new one – Italy – was added, but the American rebellion and the revolutionary wars finally inaugurated the decline and collapse of this remarkable industry. The causes seem to lie in high labour costs, a certain reluctance or inability to follow changes of fashion, and perhaps – though such impressions are difficult to substantiate fully – a certain lack of enterprise on the part of the organizing capitalists. As to costs, it was said in 1760 that weavers' wages were 40 per cent lower at Norwich than in the West Country, reducing *total* costs by 8–10 per cent. This may have been the result of those early workmen's clubs – precocious trade unions – which were prominent at Tiverton and other manufacturing towns from 1700 to 1725 when they were declared illegal. Labour relations were difficult and embittered through all this period of export depression. Led by the combers, the most militant branch, strikers destroyed serges and looms in 1717 and 1724 and the Mayor of Bradninch, attempting to put down a riot, narrowly escaped being killed.[2] Such troubles made it difficult for the Tiverton clothiers to succeed in their attempts to improve methods of manufacture, to reduce costs by importing Irish worsted ready spun and combed, and to introduce fabrics with more of the attractions of the Norwich 'stuffes'. Was control by the Company of Weavers, Fullers and Shearmen at Exeter another brake on enterprise? Regulating as it did all branches of the industry except the recent one of dyeing, its influence seems to have been conservative and oligarchic; the company stood for quality, it is true – so did Colbert's *réglements* – but many argued that 'the narrow door of apprenticeship' which restricted the trade to a relatively small circle was bad for the welfare of the industry. New names in the trade were rare. The masters were virtually an hereditary clique, shielded from the rivalry of quicker wits that might have come up from the journeymen class.

The collapse of the Devon industry was not sudden: but the signs of

[1] See Hoskins, *Exeter*, p. 75. [2] Ibid., p. 59.

decay multiplied from the 1720s onwards. The twenties were full of bankruptcies. By the forties it was a common saying on the Exeter cloth market that 'we have a trade but no profit'. 1743 was a particularly bad year, when the gloom of the cloth trade, prevalent unemployment, bankruptcies and crowded workhouses of the towns and villages were equalled in the countryside. Record numbers of estates were up for sale. Record numbers of farms to be let. Yet observers noticed that the cloth industry elsewhere did not share these burdens. One writer with a more than usually prophetic eye thought it was because 'the woollen trade in the west has removed into other parts of the Kingdom, especially to Halifax and the western parts of Yorkshire'.[1] By 1760, this impression had spread widely. The importance of wages as the predominant element in production costs makes plausible the contemporary preoccupation with wage differences as between the different cloth areas. The cloth trade, said one writer, was travelling 'Northward where greater Plenty of Firing, and Cheaper Rates of other Common Necessaries of Life, or very small Taxes, favour their Increase much more than in our Southern Counties'.[2]

Exeter's other sources of income — its function as a market and regional centre — did something to mitigate the decline of the serge trade. Exeter did not grow much but it did not decline like Tiverton. Workmen and small masters drifted into shopkeeping and a variety of other occupations. A few men of great wealth continued to flourish in spite of the times. Elwill has been mentioned. Robert Burridge, George Osmond, Oliver Peard, Charles Baring, John Duntze, were all wealthy men by any contemporary standard, merchants of outstanding ability and enterprise. But it is not accidental that they all kept a due proportion of their eggs in baskets labelled finance and politics. All of them bid for and most secured that plum of local influence, the office of Receiver-General of the Land Tax. It gave them the disposal of very large sums of public money in days when the public and private weal was not as strictly separated as later. For twenty years, Oliver Peard had a stranglehold on the trade and politics of Tiverton, and his death in 1764 came as a release from tyranny. When Charles Baring bid for the succession the Mayor spoke feelingly against the risks of a monopoly that would put Tiverton back into a state of dependence comparable to that it had suffered under Peard.[3] Yet Charles and his brothers John and Francis

---

[1] Quoted Hoskins, op. cit., p. 76.
[2] Massey, *Observations upon the Cider Tax*, 1760, p. 4.
[3] Hoskins, op. cit., p. 45.

inexorably rose to power and wealth. Long before John Baring founded his first Plymouth bank in 1770, he had seized firmly on the advantages of the higher profits and greater flexibility of general trade as compared with manufacture. The Barings, like the Duntzes, the Katenkamps and Hirtzels, were part of that foreign colony which in Devon as in East Anglia (and later in northern England) linked local trade to the technology and markets of Europe. Married into local money, they were above all merchants of the entrepreneur type, opportunist but methodical, international rather than parochial. Long training in accountancy, currency problems and economic fluctuations had widened their horizons and sharpened their wits to profit where others lost.

In East Anglia, the Colchester and Essex New Draperies were fast going the way of the Suffolk Old Draperies. The colony of Dutch immigrants who had introduced them was slowly losing its identity and, apparently, its mercantile enterprise. Increasingly the 'stuffs' manufacture became focused on Norwich. Even the Norwich makers were facing serious competition after 1700 from local cotton goods and from the imported textiles of the East India Company. In 1709 they were petitioning the House of Commons. An address to George I in 1718 lamented the loss of markets in France, Spain and Turkey. 'The poor increase and the rich forsake us.' Such lobbyings were amongst the pressures that brought about the Act of 1721 to forbid the weaving of cotton goods. Yet, like business men before and since, the Norfolk merchant clothiers were doubtless hypersensitive to competition. Every breeze felt like a gale. Poor relief, though increasing, was not abnormally burdensome until after 1760. Competition from Yorkshire was felt after 1740, but generally the first half of the century was a good time. The Norwich that Defoe found when he visited there in the twenties was 'an ancient, rich and populous city'. The fifties and early sixties saw the Norwich 'stuffs' industry at its peak. Basing themselves on yarn brought from Suffolk and Yorkshire, the Norwich stuff makers built up a position of great strength in export markets. Their home position was more vulnerable to the new machine-made cottons and to the coarse worsteds of Yorkshire. The slow decline of the worsted industries of Holland[1] left them with few competitors in European markets, especially in the warmer zones that looked for lighter fabrics. Between 1700 and 1721, Norwich exports to Spain rose from £23,000 to £112,000. By 1750 Norwich merchants were selling six times as much

[1] See C. Wilson, 'International Competition in Cloth', *Econ. Hist. Rev.*, XIII, no. 200, 1960.

by value as the Exeter merchants to Spain. In output of worsteds, they were probably not outpaced by the West Riding until after the Seven Years War. At its height the Norfolk industry commanded some 12,000 looms. They worked to the orders of some thirty very large clothier-dyers, and kept 72,000 workers – six to a loom – busy in and around Norwich. The annual output of a loom was valued at about £100.

The collapse of Norwich textiles was to come only in the early nineteenth century, and its causes are complex and not well understood.[1] But signs of weakness were apparent in the eighteenth century. Supplies of water and coal were difficult. Norwich constantly protested against Yarmouth dues on imported coal, which caused losses to 'householders, dyers, hotpressers, lime burners, brewers, maltsters, iron smiths etc by the high price of coals . . .'. Most dangerous, Norwich imported much of its yarn from the West Riding and elsewhere. Norfolk wool was too short to be combed for worsted manufacture.[2] Arthur Young, writing in the seventies, could muster little sympathy for Norwich. The workers, he thought, were idle, the masters unenterprising and bad employers. 'Examine the trade and you will look in vain for that ardour of enterprise, that activity of pursuit, that spirit of invention which has so nobly distinguished the efforts of British industry, when exerted on iron, cotton, porcelain, glass etc . . . all is sluggish, dead.' By contrast, Yorkshire manufactures were increasing – 'pushed with vigour'.

The West Riding, as we have seen, had been trying its hand at worsteds during the seventeenth century. Its worsted yarn export to Norfolk was a standing invitation to local enterprise to try its hand at full manufacture. In 1700 its manufactures were still mainly the cheaper, coarse woollens – 'Northern Dozens' and kerseys. In the next sixty years, the worsted industry made prodigious progress, stealing markets formerly held by Devon or East Anglian clothiers. By the seventies Yorkshire worsted manufacture was valued at just under £1·4 million, its woollens at just short of £2 million, and Yorkshire was exporting nearly £2½ millions of textiles a year. The total *national* production had increased at a relatively slower rate – perhaps some 50 per cent between 1700 and 1760. Plainly, Yorkshire was winning trade partly at

[1] The account here owes much to M. F. Lloyd Prichard's article 'The Decline of Norwich' in *Econ. Hist. Rev.*, III, no. 3, 1951. J. H. Clapham's much earlier study – 'The Transference of the Worsted Industry' (*Economic Journal*, 1910) is still valuable. But the industry still awaits a full investigation.

[2] Lloyd Prichard, ibid.

the expense of other cloth areas — especially in worsteds. Her advantages were both physical and psychological. There was water in plenty to operate fulling mills, to grind log wood for the dye vats, coal to heat combs and vats. An ample supply of wool — especially long wool for worsteds — was available from the Lincolnshire wold country. Halifax worsted makers sent their buyers regularly to the Lincolnshire wool fairs. Abundant labour was available in this county of small holders accustomed to hard work, long hours and small rewards. Wages were lower than elsewhere: in 1700 perhaps 50 per cent of London averages and 75 per cent of western averages. But they were *rising* faster here in the next half century than anywhere. Yorkshire was becoming a prosperous place. Clothiers were rich, workers relatively well cushioned against adversity.[1] Its spacious countryside still contained fewer people to the square mile than Norfolk or Devon, the Midlands or Home Counties. No weaver was far from his allotment and its frugal harvest of oats and potatoes. The alliance of land and loom gave Yorkshire industry a stable, if austere, social foundation. There was an air of bustle, enterprise and hard, shrewd bargaining about its rising manufactures.

The entry to the woollen cloth industry was open to any weaver who could save or borrow a capital of, say, £100–150. The class of small clothiers grew accordingly. Round Leeds a few big clothiers employed up to twenty looms. But they were not typical of the woollen side. The clothiers who frequented the Leeds cloth halls were nearly all small men. The worsted industry, west of Bradford and north of Halifax, was entirely different in its organization. This was the preserve of the big clothier, increasingly identified with the big merchant. These were the men upon whose capital and enterprise the worsted industry was established and who were to provide the later capitalist system of the Victorian age. Sam Hill, the Halifax clothier whose enterprise, brash and indomitable, lives on in the pages of his surviving letter books, was a typical example of his race. By 1737 Sam Hill was deeply involved in the worsted trade. Since 1700, the weavers round Halifax had been making coverlets — chalons or 'shaloons' as they were called. Evidence of the manufacture of serges and bays multiplied in the twenties. When Defoe visited Halifax a few years later he estimated that the parish made 100,000 shaloons a year and strong blue 'says' for the African trade, wrapped 'in an oilcloth painted with negroes and elephants to captivate the natives [of Guinea]'. Wakefield specialized in 'tammies', a thin worsted used glazed for window blinds and curtains. From 1699 the

[1] E. Gilboy, op. cit.

Aire and Calder Navigation brought Wakefield the long wool from Lincolnshire. Slowly it appropriated the monopoly of tammy manufacture formerly owned by Coventry. In explaining such commercial victories by which Yorkshire ate into the markets – especially the home markets – of Devon and East Anglia, we must not leave out the dogged, pushful spirit of pioneers like Sam Hill who toiled ceaselessly to thrust the new makes on customers at home and abroad. 'I am studying to outdo all England with the sort Sam Hill [shaloons] if quality and price will do it . . . but must earnestly beg of you to lett them go for a small profit however till they be known.' A little later: 'I like to make [shaloons and Long Ells] and fancy I shall in time doe it well.' So he hung on, through bad times, defying his rivals to undersell him, until in the end the daylight grew. 'I think it now evident these manufactures will come in spite of fate into these Northern Countreys.' If they had not, it would not have been Sam Hill's fault. But they did. By 1750 shaloons, calimancoes, tammies, camlets, bays and says were made all the way to Leeds and Wakefield. Twenty years later the Yorkshire worsted industry had overtopped Norwich by a quarter of a million pounds.[1] Halifax, Wakefield, Huddersfield, even Leeds, had been invaded by the newcomers, finishing, dyeing and selling worsteds. Bradford alone languished. To Defoe, it was 'of no other note than having been the birthplace of Dr. Sharp, the good Archbishop of York'. The thirty-eighth verse (out of 104) in a Methodist hymn of 1757 issued a respectful invitation to the Almighty:

> On Bradford likewise Look Thou down
> Where Satan Keeps his seat.

Westwards, the growth of the Lancashire textile industries showed again how lighter and finer fabrics could rise out of a heterogeneous local peasant industry. In this instance a principal model to be followed was the oriental printed fabric. Down to the mid-century progress was not spectacular, but it was steady. By then, the consumption of raw cotton was roughly twice what it had been in the first decade of the century. Cotton manufacture was fast becoming localized in Lancashire and round Glasgow. It may be significant that these were the two areas where linen manufacture flourished before the age of cotton. Cotton manufacture was grafted on to the earlier technology. Secondly, both were well placed for the import of supplies of raw West Indian cotton,

[1] For the Yorkshire woollen and worsted industries see H. Heaton, *The Yorkshire Woollen and Worsted Industries*, 1920, chs. VIII and IX.

and of Irish linen yarn. Local coal stimulated a general expansion of industry and population. Finally, the growing skill of local spinners reduced the price of yarn to the local weavers and made it difficult for other areas to compete with Lancashire prices.[1]

By the mid-century Lancashire had enormously extended the range of cottons and semi-cottons made locally. Stripes — part of the maid-servant's wardrobe — checks for clothing and furnishings, fustians, velvets and muslins were all growing fast. A large part of the ordinary cottons or mixed cotton-linens went to the printers to be finished in decorative imitation of those Indian fabrics imported by the East India Company. These were a prime source of anxiety to the woollen clothiers who feared their erosive competition. A trial of strength between the company and the woollen interests ended in the Act of 1701. This forbade the use or wear of Indian and Chinese silks and Indian prints or printed calicoes and striped or checked cottons. The consequential growth of a successful local imitative industry did not please the promoters of the earlier Act any more than Indian competition itself. An Act of 1721 attempted to enforce the earlier prohibition but to allow a place to local or even imported cotton-printed fabrics provided they did not compete with woollen goods. Protection, it has been said, 'was almost entirely responsible for the use of English-made cottons by the printers'.[2] The fabrics so made filled a particularly important place in the textiles market; for although experiments with dyeing cottons were in progress in the forties and fifties progress was slow. John Wilson, an enterprising manufacturer of Ainsworth, 'sent a young man to Turkey' and spent a good deal of money trying to discover the secret of 'Turkey Red'. In 1756 the Royal Society of Arts offered a reward for a solution of the same problem. But little progress was made until the eighties.

Nor, outside the ribbon industry,[3] did progress as yet owe much to mechanization. There was already a lively interest in mechanical improvements. A clockmaker, John Kay — Lancashire clockmakers had been famous for their ingenuity since the sixteenth century — contrived a flying shuttle in 1730 which enabled one weaver to do the work of two. Lewis Paul of Birmingham made a machine which produced a similar improvement in spinning. But neither invention, it seems, was of much practical effect until several generations later, and they

[1] Wadsworth and Mann, op. cit., ch. ix.
[2] Ibid., p. 144.
[3] See above, pp. 193–4.

encountered either technical teething troubles or fierce opposition from those handworkers who feared for their livelihood.

Manchester, already the centre of the merchanting side of the industry, was a wealthy and expanding town. Pamphleteers were eloquent, and even accurate, in observing the growth there of large fortunes that seemed to spring from nothing more than enterprise. A congratulatory fanfare of 1756 has a prophetic ring of John Bright. 'See, as the Owners of old Family Estates in Our Neighbourhood are selling off their Patrimonies, how your Townsmen are constantly purchasing; and thereby laying the Foundation of a new Roll of Gentry! Not adorned, it's true, with Coats of Arms and a long Parchment Pedigree of useless Members of Society, but decked with Virtue and Frugality . . .'[1] These Manchester capitalists were manufacturers as well as merchants, often finishers and dealers in raw materials as well. Check making was handed out to weavers in the villages round Manchester, Oldham and Ashton. Fustians were the speciality of workers further west, round Bolton and Blackburn. The general trend was for fustians, and later cotton velvets, to replace checks, as their popularity grew with European buyers. Some of the Manchester men were capitalists on a large scale. Samuel Touchet, son of a migrant Dissenting pinmaker of Warrington, inherited a sizeable fortune made in the cotton trade. By the fifties Samuel was the leading Lancashire man in London. By 1761 he was an M.P., adding moneylending to hard-up nobility and government loan contracting to his wide mercantile activities. But he swerved too far from that world of trade he knew well. In 1763 he was bankrupt – 'a broken merchant of a very bad character' as Horace Walpole severely remarked – and never recovered. His brothers were wiser to stick to their last. Touchets were still in business, respected Dissenters, in the nineteenth century.

The Lancashire industry, like the Yorkshire worsteds, was focused and guided by sizeable capitalists, though men of Touchet's standing and ambitions were, perhaps fortunately, not common. When Josiah Tucker, future Dean of Gloucester, compared the woes that had overtaken the West Country cloth industry in the late fifties with the continuing vigour of the northern industries, his explanation hinged in large measure on what he believed was the narrower gap between master and man in the north. Although the northern workman – spinner, weaver, dyer, dresser – was employed by the capitalist or his

---

[1] *A Sequel to the Friendly Advice to the Poor*, 1756, p. 19, quoted in Wadsworth and Mann, op. cit., p. 242.

agent, he still felt a kind of independence of his master. He was still ambitious to do well for himself. Hence a sober and industrious people, little inclined to riots. In the west (Tucker thought) the relationship was more akin to the planter-slave relationship of a colonial society. Industrial relations were bad because the gap between classes was too large. Others felt there was little to choose between the drunken hopelessness that Tucker thought characteristic of the West Country weavers, and the bull-baiting, cock-fighting and contests between naked men shod in iron-tipped clogs which the magistrates deplored in Lancashire.[1] The truth lies hidden amidst a welter of moral sentiment and embryonic economic doctrine. Perhaps the social ladder was a little more accessible in the north, incentives larger and more common, the field for enterprise wider. All we can say is that everywhere the 'domestic' organization of industry pressed hard on the worker, affording him an uncertain employment in squalid surroundings that tended to destroy health and decency. We need waste no tears on its later disappearance.

The same process of concentration of industry and population that was beginning to be apparent in the textile industries of Yorkshire and Lancashire, the same tendency towards specialized and improved techniques of manufacture, was also visible in the Midlands. At Derby, the Lombe silk factory was in full production by 1724; the harbinger of revolutionary change in textile manufacture. Its story was truly spectacular. Like many innovations, it was not original but borrowed — more bluntly, purloined — this time from Italy. John Lombe came from Norwich, of a family of master weavers of silk. Working in an Italian mill that made thrown silk, Lombe made drawings of the local machines. With the aid of a royal patent (1718) the technical help of George Sorocold, a Derby engineer, and finance from a London half-brother, Thomas Lombe, the mill was built. It employed machinery that was said to embody '97,746 wheels, movements and parts'. Power came from a water wheel on the Derwent. More than 300 women and children were working a 24-hour day of two shifts by 1724, and the mill was underselling the imported Italian organzine by 30 per cent. In the thirties, the Lombe mill faltered and failed: but its successors in Derby and Stockport were a microcosm of the Industrial Revolution. Amongst the non-woollen textile industries, silk remained pre-eminent till the 1740s. Thereafter it was to be overtaken by linens and cottons. But it had set an example of what could be done to concentrate production in a mechanized, power-driven factory.

[1] For a full account see Wadsworth and Mann, op. cit., ch. xx.

The location chosen by the Lombes was not accidental. Everywhere in the Midlands, highly skilled craftsmanship was going into partnership with merchant capital and enterprise to lay the foundations of the later *congeries* of skills called engineering. By the early eighteenth century the Midlands were beginning to fill up with people. In Stuart times Worcestershire had been about as densely populated as Suffolk – about 100 persons per square mile – less populous than Essex, more populous than Norfolk. By 1700 it had increased its density by nearly 50 per cent, but the growth of population in and around Birmingham was soon to cause Worcestershire to yield to Warwickshire. And Coventry was to fall behind Birmingham as the trickle of immigrants from near-by counties was swelled round 1700 by more distant travellers from Wales.[1]

Neither Birmingham nor Wolverhampton was hampered by those remnants of medieval gild control that lingered at Coventry or Lichfield. (When Boswell taxed Dr. Johnson with the idleness of Lichfield, Johnson defended his native city. 'Sir, we are a city of philosophers; we work with our heads and make the boobies of Birmingham work for us with their hands.') Freedom from economic controls is, indisputably, an important factor in the economic progress of these rapidly growing midland towns and the surrounding countryside. The distinction between the two was not as yet easy to draw. The nailers, spinners and swordmakers and the whole army of metal workers were still recruited from small tenant farmers and freeholders of the country. The nailers – perhaps 10,000 of them – were said later in the century to consume half the iron output of the Midlands. Certainly they were the most numerous type of metal worker. The nailers' craft was easy to learn: hence, like weaving, it became a part-time job for cottagers, traditionally associated with indigence and the misery of a life that fluctuated between slack time of unemployment and starvation and booms that demanded grinding, unbroken toil by day and night. More and more, the nailer was falling under the economic control of capitalists (as the weaver had long ago fallen under the control of the clothier) as the need for capital to buy equipment and fuel and raw material grew. The slitting mill and its machinery had everywhere become necessary to supply the rod-iron to the nailers by the end of the seventeenth century. All along the Stour and Tame a visitor could see a growing cluster of furnaces, forges, rod mills and blade mills. But the capitalists were not yet urban industrialists of the kind that was to be familiar later. Families

[1] The best account of the midland economy is by W. H. B. Court, *The Rise of Midland Industry*, 1953.

like the Wyvleys of Handsworth were of yeoman stock. Their stake in
the iron industry — their blade and slitting mills — still went along with
a paper mill, a flour mill and landholding.

As in the cloth industry the source of power was still water. But the
forges, anvils, smithies and glass works used prodigious amounts of
coal for heating. In 1709 came the discovery by Abraham Darby, a
Shropshire Quaker iron master, of a method of smelting iron ore with
coke, which was later to revolutionize the technique, organization and
output of the entire industry. Not at once. Quaker reticence, fear of
competition too, kept the secret within Quaker circles for some time.
Nor was the product pure enough to serve the forge masters who
wanted a high-grade, malleable iron: and it was in forge work that the
midland iron masters excelled. So, eighty years after Darby's discovery,
there were still large furnaces in Shropshire that smelted with charcoal.
Total iron production down to the mid-century probably stayed fairly
steady. In the Midlands, however, it almost certainly rose, as the demand
of tool makers, locksmiths, chainmakers, nail masters, gunsmiths, sword-
smiths, and saddlers grew. Nevertheless it was not so much the iron
master as the smith in his many guises who, along with the brewer, the
glass maker, the dyer and the soap boiler, created the expanding market
for coal as an industrial fuel that is a striking feature of the times.

In the century between the 1680s and 1780s, coal production in
England, Scotland and Wales rose by 300 per cent: from just under 3
million tons to about $10\frac{1}{4}$ million tons.[1] Even allowing that the rate of
increase was probably accelerating in the later years, an increase of
100–150 per cent for the period 1700 to 1760 does not seem an unreasonable estimate. Within the total English coal industry, the midland
coalfield (including Yorkshire, Lancashire, Cheshire, Derbyshire, Shropshire, Staffordshire, Nottinghamshire, Warwickshire, Leicestershire and
Worcestershire) had emerged as far the largest producer, with a production
that rose from 850,000 to 4 million tons between 1690 and 1790. Again,
in the years 1700–60 it may have risen from 1 million to $2\frac{1}{2}$ million tons
And the demand was industrial as well as — maybe more than — domestic. Thus while many of the industries that had risen in response to the
demands of the expanding London market in the seventeenth century
were levelling off, and others were growing more slowly, the midland
coal and metal-fashioning industries were expanding at a rate unique
for the times.

Already by the 1760s we may see the shape of things to come. New

---

[1] Nef, *Rise of the British Coal Industry*, vol. I, pp. 19–20.

men were devising new methods of organizing industrial production and employing new capital goods in the process. In an old industry like nailing we have seen the new man of substance, the nailmonger or nail master, emerge, as the capital cost of slitting and rod mills rose far beyond the means of the hand worker. Glass making, too, was naturally capitalistic, from the outlay on furnaces, pots and buildings it needed. 'Glass houses' were rising at Stourbridge, Dudley and Birmingham in this period. Glass men, like paper men, had 'an affluent air and country complexion; their property was a curious mixture of rural estate with industrial enterprise'.[1] One glass-making family married into another. Here, as in brewing, personal connexions were close. Like the glass industries at Newcastle and St Helens, the midland glass works were showing the common tendency towards concentration. It was a Stourbridge firm which bought the Prescot bottle glass works near St Helens in 1751 'in order to shut it up'.[2]

The portents of large-scale industrial capitalism were visible in other Birmingham industries, where already hopeful business men were dabbling in science in the expectation that the new knowledge could be profitably applied. By the sixties, Birmingham had one or two really large manufacturers. Biggest was John Taylor, said to have begun his business life as an artisan and to have risen swiftly by a shrewd grasp of how to combine design and high profits in such matters as japanning tin-plate and button making. From 1766 Taylor's most formidable competitor was Matthew Boulton whose Soho works were completed in that year to become the wonder of Georgian enterprise. When James Boswell visited Soho a few years later he marvelled at the 'vastness and contrivance' of the machinery. Under Boulton's able leadership, the factory had grown until it employed about 700 people. 'An *iron chieftain*', Boswell remarked, 'and a father to his tribe.' By that time Boulton was in partnership with Watt to exploit the steam engine.

Observant visitors noted two special features in factories such as Taylor's or Boulton's. One was the way the division of labour was applied to speed up production. 'Thus', Lord Shelbourne noted on a visit in 1766, 'a button passes through fifty hands, and each hand perhaps passes a thousand on a day; likewise, by this means, the work becomes so simple that, five times in six, children of six or eight years old do it as well as men, and earn from tenpence to eight shillings a

---

[1] Court, op. cit., p. 220.

[2] T. C. Barker, *Pilkington Brothers and the Glass Industry*, p. 40.

week.'[1] The other feature was the employment of machinery — stamping machines, dies and presses which replaced the need for laborious craftsmanship in the manufacture of standardized candlesticks, coffee pots, cream jugs and similar articles for a mass market.

Similar tendencies towards more capitalistic types of production could be discerned, though perhaps less overtly, in other areas, like Sheffield and Newcastle upon Tyne, where metal working was developing. High-quality Swedish iron suitable for steel making was imported at Newcastle. Hence the growth there of a highly specialized industry that made tools, swords, guns and wheels for clocks and watches. It was a Quaker clockmaker at Sheffield, Benjamin Huntsman, who discovered a method of making high-quality cast steel in small crucibles: an important step but only one of many towards precision engineering. Sheffield, wrote Horace Walpole in 1750 was 'one of the foulest towns in England in the most charming situation; there are two-and-twenty thousand inhabitants making knives and scissors; they remit eleven thousand pounds a week to London'.[2] Neither of these areas was forward in producing large capitalists before the second half of the century. The largest exception to the rule in the north was Ambrose Crowley, the great iron master of Winlaton and Swalwell near Newcastle who developed a series of varied but related enterprises in the north-east, London and the Midlands. Originally a Stourbridge boy, Crowley was apprenticed to an ironmonger in London, set up a nail factory in Durham in 1684, developed slitting mills, furnaces and forges at Swalwell and Winlaton, warehouses in and round London and in the Midlands, to say nothing of a fleet of ships that sailed between Tyne and Thames. In 1728 the Crowley estate was valued at a quarter of a million. But in these years Crowley was only the shape of things to come, an intruder into the economy of the north. The important point was that while the output of the raw material with which all these manufacturers worked — iron — was limited by technological weakness greater skill was everywhere increasing the refinement and therefore value of the articles fashioned out of it. A Birmingham gun was economically as well as technically a spectacular advance over a Sussex cannon.

Change of a different kind was taking place in the mining industries. The output of lead, mainly in Derbyshire, was increasing slowly. Various attempts to develop the industry in Scotland included an ambitious

---

[1] Court, op. cit., p. 240.
[2] A. B. Mason, ed., *Horace Walpole's England*, 1930, p. 143.

failure by the York Building Company in the 1720s. Cornish tin output was still rising towards its mid-eighteenth-century peak. Here, as in the coal mines, problems of drainage drove the entrepreneur to explore any hopeful means of pumping out flood water. Savery's clumsy monster of 1698 was followed by an improved engine for raising water, again the work of a Devonian, Thomas Newcomen. When a company was formed in 1715 to exploit the new invention it claimed that steam-engines of the Newcomen type were already at work in pits in Stafford-shire and Warwickshire, as well as Cornwall and Flint. Ten years later there were certainly at least three in the Midlands and possibly more. The number was to grow steadily, hauling up first water and later coal. To a well-placed pit, with good resources and good management, a steam engine could be a valuable, if expensive asset. It might kill a weak mine. The capital outlay was large: the consumption of coal very heavy and wasteful. The broader significance of these early prodigals was, first, that they themselves were amongst the growing collection of items that called not only for capital but for iron and for skill in manufacture. With the different kinds of 'mill' that were invading and modifying industry, they represented the tendency, growing with each year that passed, for industry itself to become a great consumer, a customer to other industries; that process of interlocking growth that can best be understood as a sort of economic counterpoint. Secondly, these primitive engines were a stage in the exploration of the problem of power. Like all pits, Midland pits had water where it was not wanted. But as an area the Midlands was short of water where it was needed for driving power. Hence a powerful incentive to that search which created engines of improved design and efficiency, and which could provide a mobile source of power wherever it was needed. Watt's engine initiated a new era in the history of *production*, but it was itself the crowning glory of a long period of technological experiment.

Here was a radical development, truly new. Not all were so. Many of the 'mills' that helped to expand and refine the ouput of, e.g. iron, were essentially borrowings or modifications of foreign inventions, usually from that nursery of modern technology now called Belgium, or from Germany. The effect, as with tin-plate, was to replace an earlier imported supply by a domestic supply, not to create an entirely new product. South Wales was to be the largest residuary legatee of Andrew Yarranton and his visit to Saxony after the Restoration: but his sponsors were mainly midland iron masters (including the ubiquitous Foleys).[1] The

[1] See above, p. 203.

intended beneficiaries were the distressed Cornish tin miners. Yarranton's object was to find out how to manufacture a non-rusting iron sheet, covered with tin, which could then be fashioned into canisters, saucepans, lamps and similar articles. The problems were to get the iron sufficiently smooth and the tin properly applied. It seems to have been a Pontypool iron master, John Hanbury, who first solved the problem satisfactorily by the use of rollers to flatten the plates. Energetic and enterprising, Hanbury went on improving his process. The Subsidy Acts of 1703 and 1704 increased the duty on foreign plate massively to assist the infant industry. After reaching a peak in 1710, imports fell away to nothing by the mid-century, as the home-produced article became cheaper and better than its foreign rivals. The largest concentration of the industry was in South Wales, within reach of Cardiff coal and Cornish tin.[1] Local landowners had often supplied the money for iron works, as Lord Mansel did at Aberavon. Tin-plate works were sometimes financed in the same way. The Kidwelly mill was erected by a local gentleman, Roger Lewis. But increasingly South Wales was being invaded by midland iron masters in the thirties and forties, and the ranks of the invaders were swollen by merchants from Bristol – 'the Welsh metropolis' – from which the South Welsh procured 'every article of consumption'.[2]

Another industry that won official support and protection by its promise to reduce a manufactured import was paper. It had already progressed to a point at which home needs of brown paper were now supplied by local industry. From 1700, the imports of the finer white paper began to decline as the English industry improved its technique of manufacture. The natural stimulus to greater output was a steadily rising demand from a large population that transacted more business and was starting to read more newspapers. The first provincial newspaper, the *Norwich Post*, appeared in 1710, and newspapers, journals, broadsheets and books proliferated rapidly thereafter. The growing towns threw up an increasing quantity of rags and to them was applied, from the 1730s, a new machine (called 'the Hollander') which reduced them to pulp. By 1720, England was producing about two-thirds of her needs, and by 1742 a former London paper importer could write to his Dutch supplier: 'We are pretty much out of Business and entirely discouraged out of the Paper Trade, which is brought here

[1] For a full and modern account see W. E. Minchinton, *The British Tinplate Industry. A History*, 1957; also J. C. Westermann, *Blik in het Verleden*, 1939, Introduction and chs. I and II, *passim*.

[2] A. H. John, *The Industrial Development of South Wales, 1750–1850*, 1950, ch. I, p. 14 and *passim*.

to a very low Ebb, and will decrease more and more, by reason of the great Quantitys made in England, which manufactory encreases every day.'[1] Paper was an industry of high costs and conservative habits. How did it succeed in establishing itself over foreign competitors? Good supplies of raw material, fuel and, above all, water, helped. So did concentration in fewer hands, casualties amongst the less efficient producers, and larger mills. But none of these would have sufficed without the duties against imports provided by Government. Immediately, consumers paid higher prices for their paper, but England got a new industry. As the historian of the paper industry has said, this is a classic case of an infant industry brought to maturity under the shelter of a protective tariff.[2]

The linen importer was to be no more happily placed than the paper importer. The optimism of William III and of Crommelin was justified by the progress of the linen industry in Northern Ireland. By 1750 it was 'a populous scene of improvement, traffic, wealth and plenty . . . a well-planted district, considerable for numbers of well affected and industrious subjects'.[3] Hardly less satisfactory it was no longer a threat to English woollen cloth producers. Exports of linen cloth rose prodigiously:

1710	1·7 million yards
1730	4·1 million yards
1750	11·2 million yards.

In Scotland, too, linen production was growing. In 1746, the British Linen Company was created, partly to enable Scotland to avail itself of the bounty on exported linens, partly to allay the agitation of the '45. By 1760, about 12 million yards were stamped for sale. The combined sale of Irish and Scottish linens in England in that year was about 20 million yards. Although the value of imported German linens bleached in Holland remained high, the new industries were competing fiercely. A London importer wrote in 1738 to Holland: 'The Sales of Holland's [linens] begin to prove very slowly, and if the Fabrik of Irish linens continues to improve 'tis probable there will be little else wore in England.'[4] Three years later, another importer thought that 'Scotch and Irish Linnens . . . are improved to a great perfection and if linnens

---

[1] Archief Brants, Amsterdam, quoted C. Wilson, *Anglo-Dutch Commerce*, p. 61.
[2] Coleman, *The British Paper Industry*, p. 145.
[3] Macpherson, *Annals of Commerce*, vol. III, p. 318.
[4] Gilbert Allix, Archief Brants, Amsterdam, quoted C. Wilson, op, cit., p. 57.

from your part [Holland] are not sent on much cheaper Terms than heretofore, [they] will not do for our markett'.[1] Other textile industries were given similar official encouragement, which discouraged former import trades. Foreign-made cambrics were prohibited in 1750. Sail cloth, formerly imported on a large scale from Holland, was protected by the Act of 1736 which obliged all English-built ships to carry one whole suit of sails of English cloth; 'which', as a London importer wrote, 'will of consequence lower the price of Holland's Duck'.[2]

While new and youthful industries like these were growing at a perceptible rate, older industries that made articlès of common consumption were in general levelling off and even dropping. There is one exception to this: starch manufacture (of which little is known) increased in general proportion with the increase in the textiles on which it was used. Consumption rose from 2·5 million lb in 1714 to 3·6 million lb in 1763 – another of those symptoms of civility in a changing society. The candle manufacture similarly grew, in response to the increase in the numbers of town dwellers who perhaps sat up in artificial light longer than countryfolk. But the production of urban industries like brewing and soap making was little more than stable.[3] In London, production actually fell, probably through the competition of other beverages. Restoration brewers had feared the threat of coffee and had deployed every possible argument, including the balance of payments and the threat of impotency, against 'that Drying, Enfeebling Liquor'. The women of England were represented as petitioning their men to reject a poison which would make them 'as unfruitful as those Desarts whence that unhappy Berry is said to be brought' and to forbear 'to trifle away their time, scald their chops and spend their money, all for a little base, black, thick, nasty, bitter, stinking, nauseous Puddle Water'.[4] As it happened the brewers were aiming at the wrong target. After a century of vigorous life, during which it rivalled the tavern as a social institution and cradled Lloyds and the Stock Exchange, the coffee house died. The English were to become a

1 Ibid., Leon Bowles, 21 March 1741, C. Wilson, p. 58.

2 C. Wilson, op. cit., p. 61.

3 These statements are based on the excise figures. According to the *Account of Quantities* (Custom and Excise Library) 'Sope' rose from 24·4 million lb in 1712–13 to 29·6 million lb in 1763. Beer from 3·2 million strong and 2 million small barrels in 1700 to 3·8 million strong and 1·8 million small in 1763. See Deane and Cole, op. cit., for comments on the statistical value of the figures. They do not seriously affect the argument here.

4 '*The Women's Petition Against Coffee, Representing to Publick Consideration the Grand Inconveniences accruing to their Sex from the Excessive Use of that Drying, Enfeebling Liquor*, 1678.

nation of tea drinkers, not coffee drinkers, and the rivalry of tea was stronger in town than in country. The annual consumption per head of the population rose by six-or sevenfold between 1725 and 1760 as the price fell. Imports, legal and illegal, created a problem for the brewer larger than that posed by his enemy, the distiller. The gin menace like the coffee menace was temporary. The tea problem was permanent.

The answer offered to such competition by the brewers was the common one: a cheaper and more marketable product, more efficient production and a larger unit of production. The new product was 'porter', a black, thick, bitter, strong beer, first brewed in Shoreditch in 1722. Wartime taxation of malt may have been an added spur to its appearance. For porter used more hops and less malt than ordinary beer. It could therefore be kept longer (and indeed gained in quality by keeping). It sold for threepence a quart — a penny a quart cheaper than pale ale. 'Porter' was the first beer suitable for mass production. It ranks therefore as an invention comparable to coke-smelted iron or machine-spun yarn, for it was the vehicle upon which some of the largest industrialists in London were to ride to affluence in the following decades. From the thirties, porter brewing was an increasingly scientific and rational affair, demanding knowledge as well as capital and enterprise to control its growing complex of buildings, offices, labourers, vats, stocks, barrels, drays and horses. By the 1740s, the twelve leading porter brewers controlled a third of London's output of beer. By the sixties their share was nearer a half and among them were several names still famous — Whitbread, Barclays, Trumans. All three were expanding rapidly. Benjamin Truman's business was valued at £23,000 in 1740. Twenty years later it was worth £92,000.[1] He it was who in extreme old age explained the secrets of the mass market to his grandson: '. . . there can be no other way of raising a great fortune but by carrying on an extensive Trade. I must tell you, young man, this is not to be obtained without Spirit and great Application.'[2]

The great London brewers certainly were men of spirit and application, comparable with the Boultons, Arkwrights and Wedgwoods as pioneers in the science of large-scale business. They rose, besides, to social and political eminence. Ralph Thrale of Barclays, father of Dr Johnson's friend, was a Member of Parliament and High Sheriff of Surrey. Samuel Whitbread, industrious and abstemious, stuck more closely to business but managed to marry an earl's daughter. Ben

[1] Mathias, op. cit., ch. 1.
[2] Quoted, ibid., p. 265.

Truman achieved a knighthood and a Gainsborough portrait as impressive as it was large. A major source of taxation (in the shape of excise), brewing felt the need of a voice in politics and saw to it that it never lacked able spokesmen in Parliament and on the local Bench. It needed capital, too, and therefore strengthened its ties, not least by marriage, with the bankers and the gentry. It needed barley and for reasons of business as well as pleasure the great brewers bought large estates in the barley country of Norfolk and elsewhere. Finally, as the brewer turned into the public figure – M.P., J.P., philanthropist, knight and peer – he looked increasingly for an able manager to conduct his purely business affairs. Brewing was therefore at an early stage a 'managed' industry. John Perkins, Thrale's partner in Barclays, was one of many who rose from comparatively humble status to riches by personal ability and astuteness. Finally, because the brewer was accustomed to having to grant credit to his raw material suppliers, he was amongst those business men who tended to move, a little later, into banking.

The hundred and seventy odd brewers of London produced about a quarter of the national output. But substantial brewers were to be found all over England. The other area of concentrated production was the Trent Valley, where Nottingham, Derby, and Newark and Burton all enjoyed the advantages of local well-water with high mineral content, plenty of river water for cooling and cleansing, and excellent barley land. The age of the great Burton breweries was to come later. But in 1744 one famous firm was founded – Worthington – and in the second half of the century Burton began to take that precedence over its neighbours it was long to enjoy.

An observer in 1720 (in the pre-porter age) might have been forgiven for supposing that the brewing industry in England had reached a static and unpromising condition. He might, equally justifiably, have supposed that the English pottery industry was of relatively small importance, actual or potential. He would have been wrong on both counts, and south and north Staffordshire were to prove it. In north Staffordshire, in a narrow belt of country about nine miles long and three or four miles broad, lay, and in large measure still lies, the most concentrated area of English pottery manufacture. Its location originally depended on the presence of pottery clays and shallow coal beds. Although 'slipware' – dishes, loving-cups, tankards, etc., of earthenware lead-glazed in 'toffee and treacle' tones – was a local craft in several other parts of England in the seventeenth century, this was its chief home. The later seventeenth century saw innovations from abroad. A Dutch immigrant began to make red, unglazed ware in delicate and more precise shapes than his local neighbours and salt-glazed 'stoneware' for portraits and busts. Already London and Bristol potters had come under the influence of Dutch models in their so-called 'Delft' ware: tin-enamelled pottery painted in colours in imitation of oriental wares. But it was not until the 1750s that there occurred that remarkable efflorescence which finally took the industry out of the peasant phase into one of expensive elegance which at the same time opened up an avenue to the age of mass production. At Chelsea and Bow the first English porcelain figures were made, often in imitation of those of the Meissen industry. French and Belgian influence was strong in the management – Nicolas Sprimont, the first manager, is still commemorated in Sprimont Place, Chelsea – and the custom was aristocratic. Other porcelain 'factories' followed at Langton Hall, Staffordshire, Lowestoft, Derby, Worcester and Liverpool.[1] Although the workshops where pots and porcelain were made were called 'factories', the industry remained for the most part a series of local handicrafts working on a smallish scale. Middle- and upper-class Englishmen, it was said, still ate their meat off plates made at Delft, while Meissen still supplied the decorative porcelain market. In the fifties, a number of straws in the wind suggested that the time was ripe for a major change. Sprimont was pleading 'The Case of the Undertaker of the Chelsea Manufacture of Porcelain Ware' for heavier duties on imported German porcelain. At Liverpool, in 1756, local makers of English 'Delft' ware were said to have reached an output of 200 printed wall tiles an hour, using a variant of a process of transfer-printing invented three years earlier at Battersea. In the fifties, too, William Cookworthy, a Quaker chemist from Plymouth, discovered the deposits of Cornish china clay. And in 1759 Josiah Wedgwood, who was to revolutionize the industry, started work on his own at Burslem. His contribution was to draw together the varied threads of experience of his predecessors and contemporaries, to seize firmly on the principle of economic organization known as the division of labour, and to put his business at the head of the entire industry by a peculiar mixture of enterprise, an opportunist sense of taste, shrewd intelligence and a genuine if somewhat self-righteous public spirit. The fifties had given him his raw materials.

By 1760, no other country could claim to command as wide a range

[1] For a full account see W. B. Honey, *English Pottery and Porcelain*, 1949.

of industrial activities and skills — many of them imported from abroad — as Britain. After three decades when the economy had tended to mark time, the fifties and sixties brought (in Professor Chambers's phrase) 'a new surge of energy, moving forward with all the greater force, it would seem, for the long period of waiting that preceded it'.[1] The 'improving spirit' of an age that was rapidly adopting mechanical labour-saving and cost-reducing devices was described by a keen observer in 1757:

> Few countries are equal, perhaps none excel, the English in the number of contrivances of their Machines to abridge labour. Indeed the Dutch are superior to them in the use and application of Wind Mills for sawing Timber, expressing Oil, making Paper and the like. But in regard to Mines and Metals of all sorts, the English are uncommonly dexterous in their contrivance of the mechanic Powers; some being calculated for landing the Ores out of the Pits, such as Cranes and Horse Engines; others for draining off superfluous Water, such as Water Wheels and Steam Engines; others again for easing the Expense of Carriage such as Machines to run on inclined Planes or Roads downhill with wooden frames, in order to carry many Tons of Material at a Time. And to these must be added the various sorts of Levers used in different processes; also the Brass Battery works, the Slitting Mills, Plate and Flatting Mills, and those for making Wire of different Fineness. Yet all these, curious as they may seem, are little more than Preparations or Introductions for further Operations. Therefore, when we still consider that at Birmingham, Wolverhampton, Sheffield and other manufacturing Places, almost every Master Manufacturer hath a new Invention of his own, and is daily improving on those of others; we may aver with some confidence that those parts of England in which these things are seen exhibit a specimen of practical mechanics scarce to be paralleled in any part of the world.[2]

Already there was more than a touch of that spirit in the air, later evoked by Macaulay: the idea of progress that was enshrined in the mastery of nature by human intelligence and capacity. 'The age', Dr Johnson declared, 'is running mad after innovation.' Rarely in English history has the poetic muse been invoked so frequently (or to such dire effect) in praise of the economic arts. Round the mid-century minor bards were celebrating not only the general triumphs of trade, manufactures and navigation, but the particular beauties of the Leeds cloth warehouses, imparting poetic hints on slave-breeding, hop growing and sugar planting and apostrophizing the virtues of workhouse discipline.[3]

---

[1] Chambers, *'Vale of Trent'*, p. 15.

[2] J. Tucker, *Instructions to Travellers*, p. 20.

[3] For a convenient if unflattering selection see *The Stuffed Owl, An Anthology of Bad Verse*, selected by D. B. Wyndham Lewis and Charles Lee, 1930, esp. pp. 5–98.

Of one – the fashionable parson-poet Edward Young (1683–1765) – it has been said he was 'the Kipling of his time, trumpeting in addition the glories of Big Business like a poetic Callisthenes'.[1] As yet 'industry' did not mean industrialization as a later age was to understand it. The manufacturing part of the economy was like the components of a watch ready for assembly but not yet interacting with each other. There were already urban industries (like brewing, soap boiling, sugar refining, etc.) but industry as a whole was far from urbanized. The greater part of the expanding export trade was sustained by rural and semi-rural industries organized on a 'domestic' basis. 'Factories' there were, but few of them were mechanized on the scale of Lombe's Derby mill. Many a cottage, on the other hand, employed a machine, sometimes of considerable value. Everywhere the need for capital for machinery, plant, buildings, stocks, was promoting the capitalist to a position of control and initiative. The technology of coal had advanced steadily, the smelting of ore and pig might still be in the future, but its principles had long been investigated and in part mastered. Power was everywhere still sought from the water wheel or the horse. The steam engine remained a clumsy and extravagant monster of uncertain temper and limited utility. Yet throughout the economy pressures were being applied which would shortly push all these disparate components into place and into action. Of the great men this age was prepared to praise (and reward) not the least was the entrepreneur through whom the pressures were brought to bear. As yet, social acclaim went to him in his capacity as merchant-capitalist-organizer, rather than as manufacturer. And in most industries the manufacturer was still a subordinate of the merchant-capitalist. Economic initiative – decisions about when and where to buy materials, what designs and types of manufacture to pursue, when and where to sell them – all this came mostly within the province of the merchant-entrepreneur. It was his opportunistic sense of the market that counted. But, again, the time was not far off when the balance of advantage would swing to the manufacturer-organizer – the Wedgwood, Crowley, Boulton, Whitbread – whose knowledge of technology was as important as his flair for buying and selling. This change awaited the spread of the factory system and the rationalization of production.[2]

[1] *The Stuffed Owl, An Anthology of Bad Verse*, selected by D. B. Wyndham Lewis and Charles Lee, 1930 pp. 64–5.

[2] See C. Wilson, 'The Entrepreneur in the Industrial Revolution in Britain', first published in *Entrepreneurship and Economic Growth*, 1954, reprinted in *History*, XLII, 1957, and in *The Experience of Economic Growth*, ed. B. E. Supple, 1963.

CHAPTER FIFTEEN

An Age of Debts and Taxes

Of the non-economic factors that shaped Britain's economic destinies in the eighteenth century, the most potent was war. During the period 1700 to 1763, some thirty years were years of declared war, to say nothing of other years when war measures were being prepared or tailed off. In all, perhaps half the whole period could be regarded as a time when war exercised a dominant influence on economic development. About the effects of this on industry, trade, employment and general welfare there may well be different opinions.[1] There can be none about its effects on financial institutions, and especially on what men called the public credit. Between the Restoration and the end of the seventeenth century, the Government's *net* borrowings, largely for war, had totalled £14 to £15 million.[2] In 1702 the National Debt owed by the Government to the public stood at £12·8 million. Its subsequent growth and purpose may be summarized as follows:

	£ million	
1702	12·8	} War
1714	36·1	
1739	46·4	} War
1748	75·4	
1757	77·8	} War
1763	132·1	

'Queen Anne's war' – as it was called – cost over £50 million, of which £23 million was added to the National Debt. The wars of Jenkins's Ear and the Austrian Succession cost £43 million of which £30 million were added to the Debt. The Seven Years War was far

[1] See above, p. 277.
[2] Horsefield, *British Monetary Experiments, 1650–1710* (1960), p. 245, following the figures of Dr Chandaman.

the most costly. The total bill was £82 million. About £60 million of this was added to the Debt. At the end of the Seven Years War the Debt was more than ten times its size in 1700, and its growth had profound effects on every aspect of the nation's economy. For much of what was borrowed found its way into the pockets of war contractors and suppliers who were thereby encouraged to invest more capital in expanding their business. Yet it was not merely the growth of the Debt that was important but the reorganization and consequent change in the character of the lending process itself: above all the division of the Debt into funded debt and floating debt, and new methods of mobilizing and managing both types of debt. Already before the end of the seventeenth century, the principle of such a division had been firmly established. Successive administrations had struggled with the problem of living beyond their means. The result was that expenditure exceeded the tax yield until, in the 1690s, there was, on the one hand, a floating mass of short-term debts due sooner or later to be repaid from taxation; on the other, a growing proportion of long-term debts which came to be recognized as virtually permanent liabilities on which interest was paid from taxation, though in theory they were redeemable if and when a future administration felt itself able to wipe them off. It was this quality of *permanence* in the public debt, to which governments now became resigned, that distinguishes the period after 1692.

In the last few years of the seventeenth century, the most urgent problem was the floating debt. In 1696 there was some £5 million of debt for which no proper provision had been made. This was the situation in which the Exchequer Bill was devised. At first circulating only slowly and on a small scale, it was to become, in the eighteenth century, the principal instrument for providing the Government with short-term credit. By the time the Bank of England's charter was renewed in 1707, the Bank had come to regard the handling of Exchequer bills as a major part of its responsibilities. In succession to the departmental tally and the old repayment orders of the Exchequer, the Exchequer bill was now a negotiable security bearing interest. It could be proffered in payment of taxes by the holder, or cashed at the Bank. In this way the Bank itself became the principal agent for providing temporary loans and advances to the Government.

As events were to prove, the permanent debt was to become a matter of far greater consequence. In 1700 the National Debt consisted for the larger part of floating obligations. By 1714 the funded debt, perpetual but redeemable, was predominant. So far, it was still largely made up of loans from the three great trading or finance corporations. Even in the 1730s this remained so. Between then and the end of the Seven Years War, a fundamental change occurred. In the 1660s Downing had sown the seed of the idea that Government might borrow directly from the public. Nurtured by his successors, the seed became Montagu's plant of 1693.[1] Thereafter it grew but the growth was slow. When the old middlemen of Stuart finance, the goldsmiths, were ousted, new ones took their place. It was so convenient to use the existing channels of credit and good will in the shape of the great companies rather than saddle an overworked Exchequer with the complex business of public borrowing. Lenders were more likely to trust the merchant companies with their money than civil servants and politicians – just as earlier they had once trusted goldsmiths rather than kings. Thus, in return for trading favours and monopolies, the Bank and the United East India Company had accepted responsibility for making long-term loans to the Government. The South Sea Company of 1710 owed its existence to the optimistic belief that the chronic disease of the floating debt, much of which was circulating at a heavy discount, might be solved by the old medicine in a new bottle. 'The Governor and Company of the merchants of Great Britain trading to the South Seas and other Parts of America and for the Encouragement of the Fishery' (as their charter of incorporation described them) were to lend their capital to the State as a 'fund of credit' and raise loans on their commercial prospects. Behind this lay the hope that the unprovided-for floating debt would thus be converted into one which ranked for interest paid out of specific taxes. It was not, perhaps, a much wilder speculation than the original proposal for the Bank of England had seemed to many contemporaries, though large areas of the trade envisaged belonged, in fact, to Spain and were held under a rigidly exclusive system of control. Still, the South Sea Company caught the imagination of thousands, and inaugurated a new phase of speculation.

During the rising boom of the years of peace after 1713, the share capital of the twelve largest joint stock companies rose rapidly. By 1717 it totalled over £20 million. Half of this was South Sea capital. Yet the hollowness of the boom was evident. The South Sea Company had virtually no trade, and while the market price of company stocks was rising, the volume of trade was actually falling after 1718. By 1720, amidst a host of newly promoted companies – insurance, industrial, trading – the South Sea Company fought with every weapon at its

[1] See above, p. 218.

disposal to secure a monopoly hold on the National Debt. Rationality evaporated (as it had already evaporated in France under the heat of Law's scheme for a company to carry on the whole of French foreign trade). The idea of a 'fund of credit' became a mystery, a miracle, a 'realized alchemy'. In April a Dutch attorney who went to see for himself wrote back to a Dutch client that it was 'as if all the Lunatics had escaped out of the madhouse at once. I don't know what to make of it all'. In June 1720 the total capital of the companies floated in a single week totalled £224 million. Later that month South Sea stock reached its peak of 1050. One of the less lunatic projects of the month was a company (popularly known as the Fishpool) proposed by Steele, the essayist, for conveying live fish from the fisheries to the market in tanks. It succeeded in raising a premium of £160 a share before any call for capital was made! The lunacy could not last. In August it began to abate. In September, corresponding panic ensued. South Sea stock fell to 180. Money became unobtainable. 'Every note and bill', wrote a contemporary, 'except those of the Bank and a few others, is now become as mere pieces of waste paper, as if a prayer or creed was writ on it instead of money.' Bankruptcies abounded.

From the aftermath of recrimination, inquiry and reconstruction, few men or institutions emerged with credit. The creditors — mainly annuitants and holders of redeemable stock — had clear grounds of grievance against the Government (which had appointed the South Sea Company its agent) and against the directors themselves. Of the ministers, Walpole alone retained public confidence. Although he too had speculated in South Sea stock, he had retired from any public connexion with it at a shrewdly early moment and managed to create at any rate an illusion that he stood aloof from the hysteria. Hence a reputation which made him the chosen instrument for rehabilitating the public credit.[1] The Bank itself had not escaped infection from the fever. Two of its directors — Janssen and Bateman, prominent men both — were also directors of the South Sea Company. In 1717 it had been tempted into close relations lending money and extending an overdraft to the company. But from the lunacy of 1720 it had the sense to stand aside — 'like the Capitol of Old Rome' as a contemporary put it.

When the dust was settled, the crimes and follies expiated and the fines paid, financial reconstruction went ahead. The creditors got South Sea stock on terms better than might at one time have seemed possible, though the company's capital was reduced by £20 million

[1] J. H. Plumb, *Sir Robert Walpole*, 1956, vol. I, ch. 8.

from its former figure of £37 million. The Bank took up £4 million. £2 million was written off. The East India Company declined the invitation to take part. Thus ended what one authority has called 'a predestined failure', and the wildest manifestation of half a century during which the idea of 'a fund of credit' had become a nostrum for every economic ill. Of the companies which survived the Bubble, the insurance ventures – the London, Royal Exchange and the Sun – were scarred; but fundamentally sound. They still are. So were the great trading companies. The legacy of mistrust left behind – mistrust of speculation and the joint stock companies – is considered elsewhere. It is enough to say here that the effects were on balance salutary.[1]

Henceforth the South Sea Company made no pretence to be a trading company – it had in all two voyages to its credit so far. Its function was to act as a holding company for government stock, and its stock-holders and annuitants were only paid out by Mr Gladstone in 1854. Thus the situation that had grown up in Queen Anne's war that more than half the funded debt was owed to the great corporations was perpetuated into the 1730s and later. The individual public creditor, or fundholder as he was called, who was to be typical later on, was still dwarfed by these great corporate investors. This meant that the financial policies of governments might occasionally be swayed by these corporate bodies. The traders, bankers, and shipping agents who had votes in city elections were long referred to as the 'household troops' of the East India Company. Its directors sat in the Commons and ministers exploited their connexions with them in favour of their political supporters. Yet the importance of the financiers should not be exaggerated. It was the politicians who had the power to make or break the merchants, not *vice-versa*. The 'bankers' ramp' was a myth. Defoe was nearer the mark when he argued that not 'They that have the money must have the management' but 'They that have the management will have the money.'[2]

The financial power of the corporations rested upon a bargain with the State. In their favour it was argued, with some justice, that the floating of public loans was a dangerous business full of risk. Those who carried the risk were entitled to adequate return in the shape of income plus commercial privilege. The argument of the new establishment did not go unchallenged. Those interests excluded from the arcana of policy by the entrenched company interests formed a kind of

[1] See below, p. 372, for the effects on company organization.
[2] Lucy Sutherland in *Essays presented by Sir Lewis Namier* (1956), pp. 50–53.

parliamentary financial opposition. At its head in the 1730s and 1740s stood a Quaker underwriter (formerly a corn merchant) Sir John Barnard. Always a vigorous opponent of stock-jobbing, high interest rates and monopolies, Barnard was a natural forerunner of the City radicals of the late eighteenth century. In 1737 he turned his attention to the reduction of the interest on the National Debt to 3 per cent. That he failed is of less importance historically than that the controversy he aroused illuminates the state of the money market at the time. He was, naturally, opposed by the great corporations. Worse still, Walpole, who had earlier been with him, turned the full weight of his oratory against his scheme and in favour of the creditors. On these twin rocks the Barnard conversion scheme foundered. Yet he had succeeded in doing one thing: he had focused attention on the division of interests the funded debt had introduced into the nation. 'To speak properly', he wrote, 'the Publick Funds divide the Nation into *two* Ranks of Men, of which one are *Creditors* and the other *Debtors*. The *Creditors* are the *Three Great Corporations* and others, made up of *Natives* and *Foreigners*; the *Debtors* are the *Landholders*, the *Merchants*, the *Shopkeepers* and all *Ranks* and *Degrees* of Men throughout the Kingdom.'[1]

Criticism of 'Dutch Finance', as it was called, had often been the theme of Tory malcontents, echoing the frustration of hard-pressed country squires. The novel spectacle of the precocious City radical attacking the whole edifice of the public credit suggests that its supposed victims included many who were not landowners. A glance at the changing structures of the tax system as it responded to the pressures of war confirms that this was indeed true. In the early years of the century the largest single source of revenue was the land tax which fell, for the most part, on landlords. As the century went on, war necessities, mercantilist policy and administrative convenience, and Walpole's own fiscal principles and social prejudices combined to turn the excise into far the most important form of taxation. Hence Barnard's theme was to recur whenever excises were raised during the wars of the eighteenth century. Even more when peace came and the excises were not lowered. For this was the monotonous tale of the times – familiar today, novel then. Indirect taxation initiated in wartime tended to stick long after the war was over, for the interest on war debts still had to be paid in perpetuity unless later governments could pay off the capital. And, in our period, governments rarely managed to do more

[1] *Reasons for the Representatives of the People of Great Britain to take Advantage of the Present Rate of Interest for the More Speedy lessening the National Debt*, 1737.

than scratch at the problem. Invariably the land tax went up when war was declared, from one or two shillings in the £ to three or four shillings. When peace came it reverted to its former level. The landed classes were providing a rather smaller share of total taxation than in Marlborough's wars. But nobody could grumble at the £2 million that was the yield of the increased land tax in the first year of the Seven Years War. The squire was still doing his duty. He could not be squeezed much more. The customs were limited as a source of revenue for two reasons. First, because excessive or indiscriminate duties encouraged smuggling and defeated the prime object of raising maximum revenue. Second, there was general agreement with the mercantilist principle that imported raw materials needed by industry should be taxed as little as possible. So should exported British manufactures. Any demand for a substantially increased yield of tax tended, therefore, to draw attention to the attractions of the excise. The pincers of this logic were fully operative in Walpole's financial policy. As a squire and no lover of tradesmen, Walpole wanted to reduce the land tax. As an adminis-trator and a conventional mercantilist balance-of-trader, he modified and reduced tariffs from 1721 to 1724. But his proposal of 1732 to increase the excise roused the mob and set up the cry of 'excise, wooden shoes and no jury'. Walpole, the most skilful tactician ever, had to beat a planned retreat. The truth was that the excise fell — as even Petty would hardly have wished in his wildest dreams[1] — on the consumption of the ordinary people. Powerful interests might divert the attention of the Exchequer from particular commodities particularly profitable to particular individuals. In the Seven Years War Alderman Beckford, supported by the powerful West India lobby, largely defeated a proposed tax on sugar. Beckford's fortune came from Jamaica: as Horace Walpole remarked: 'A tax on sugar touched his vitals.' Taxation had therefore increasingly fallen on objects of popular consumption — soap, candles, spirits, calicoes, drugs, tea, coffee, pepper, tobacco, etc. But above all, on malt and beer, the national drink. For the first time for forty years the price of a quart of porter went up: from threepence to threepence halfpenny.

The net yield of the excise in 1700 was £849,000, of which the malt excise was roughly half. The fact reflected the part beer played in the lives of Englishmen. By 1760 it was £1·6 million. It paid for many things including — illegally and under duress — the costs of Bonnie Prince Charlie's troops as they marched south to Derby. They

[1] See above, pp. 227, 228.

were paid for out of the rifled cash boxes of the excise offices *en route*. That was why the Jacobite army did not otherwise find it neccessary to loot and plunder. Rather less than a half of the excise still came from malt. But the yield from tea was rising fast, and salt, another necessity, accounted for about 10 per cent of the total excise yield. Yet no article of consumption besides beer, except perhaps bread, could be expected to bear an additional load of taxation in the wartime stress of 1760 without being forced into a decline of sales — and therefore, eventually, of tax yield. Pitt, like Walpole, came round ineluctably to view excise as the best source of revenue. The yield of the malt and beer taxes was by 1763 the main pillar of the national tax system. There was, therefore, an increasing measure of truth in the argument that the ordinary people at large were taxed in their necessities in order that a small minority who were fundholders might receive the interest on the capital they invested in the funded debt.

Paradoxically, the force of this criticism became less as the debt became larger; for it also became more widely held in the country at large. It was not accidental that Walpole, in opposing Barnard's proposal to reduce the rate of interest on the funded debt in 1737, deployed as his main argument the burden that would fall on the small investor. According to his figures more than 17,000 annuitants held £1,000 or less in South Sea Annuities, amongst them those widows and orphans whose case was to be a regular standby in such arguments. Their total investment was £5·8 millions. Another 5,000 executors of estates and trustees of charities held £8·4 million in the same funds. Walpole was probably not unaware that ever since Downing's appeal to the country in the 1660s, the Norfolk squires — the Pastons, Townshends, Cokes, Cremers, Knyverts, Spelmans and many others — had been active investors, along with his own family.[1] Against the interest of the tax-payers had to be set this growing vested interest of the public creditors. Yet as the great corporations were edged out of their dominant position as lenders to the State, it became more difficult for a more amorphous body of investors to lobby their case against reductions in the rate of interest. One focus did still remain in the 1740s–1750s. Just as the corporations had replaced the goldsmiths, so now the corporations were replaced by the underwriters. The risks of flotation were still too heavy to be left to chance. Successive governments therefore cultivated relations with a group of moneyed men who formed an indispensable link with the investing public, and often

[1] Roseveare, op. cit. See E. L. Hargreaves, *The National Debt*, ch. III, for a full discussion.

spoke in their behalf. The biggest fortunes in the City were made out of this business of supplying money to the Government.

The underwriter's job, in the recurrent emergencies of war finance in the mid-century, was to take upon himself a block of stock in the new loan and siphon it off to his clients. Each underwriter seems to have represented a more or less coherent investing 'interest'. When Samson Gideon, one of the leading underwriters of the forties and a skilled financier and speculator, came to present his claim for a peerage to the Duke of Newcastle in 1758 he included amongst his claims to recognition that in 1742: 'After a declaration of War with Spain Mr Gideon delivered a scheme for raising of Three Million at Three p.cent, and made himself answereable for the first Payment upon upwards of £600,000, and otherwise assisted to compleat the whole. . . .'[1] Gideon, whose father was a member of the Sephardim, by name Abudiente, did not get his peerage but his son inherited a fortune of £300,000 (made, his enemies said, by financial manipulations of a sharpish kind) and was created Lord Eardley. Gideon's system represented the so-called 'closed subscription' at its closest: the special *bête noire* of Barnard and the financial outsiders. It was not the least merit of Henry Pelham as First Lord of the Treasury that he managed, by uniting Gideon and Barnard in agreement, to supplant the underwriters and raise the 1747 loan by 'open subscription'. Two years later, he succeeded in his ambition of reducing 'the vast load of debt' by converting £59 million of 4 per cent loan into 3 per cent — what Walpole and Barnard had both aspired to do in their time.

Pelham's success was at least partially due to the changes that had at once enlarged the number of creditors and atomized their political influence. Yet though the connexion between subscriber and Government was becoming more direct, the middleman was not eliminated for good. In the crisis of credit in 1758 Newcastle was compelled to talk (as he said) to 'the most knowing people in the city'. As a result the great loan of £8 million of that year was underwritten by twenty-two city financiers. They included the Governors of the Bank, East India and South Sea Companies whose function was not now to undertake a corporate subscription for their institutions but to tap the resources of their business friends and acquaintances. Of the others fifteen were M.P.s, seven were of foreign origin — Dutch, Jewish or Huguenot and represented to some extent the social connexion of their nation,

[1] L. S. Sutherland, 'Samson Gideon and the Reduction of Interest 1749–50', *Econ. Hist. Rev.*, XII, no. 1, 1946.

race or religion. The largest of all – responsible for £1·2 million – was Sir Joshua Van Neck.[1] Van Neck and his brother Gerard were Dutch, the sons of the Paymaster to William III's army, prominent in the East India and West India trades and the leaders of an entire colony of Dutch merchants and financiers which played a not unimportant role in the economic and financial life of England in the eighteenth century.[2] Every Friday night Gerard entertained a number of his Dutch and Huguenot friends at his great house at Putney. It is difficult to think they did not talk financial shop. He died in 1750 leaving a fortune of over a quarter of a million. Joshua survived to serve successive administrations as an underwriter and adviser on public finance and to draw on his friends – the Van Nottens, Muilmans, Bosanquets, Deckers, Crayesteyns and the rest – in the Whig interest. His son was to become Baron Huntingfield in 1796.

Vanneck and the other Christian Dutch merchants had their social centre round the Dutch church in Austin Friars (close by the Bank), of which many of them were deacons or elders. A different Dutch connexion was tapped through Joseph Salvador and a corresponding group of Sephardic Jews closely connected with the synagogue at Bevis Marks in the City. Both groups were closely linked with potential Dutch investors – individuals and institutions – through a group of Dutch attorneys, Christian and Jewish, who acted as London agents for their clients. The size of this foreign stake in the National Debt is uncertain.[3] Contemporaries, in their anxiety at English reliance on alien money, were apt to exaggerate. One report put it at over a third of the National Debt. Another Dutch report assessed it at three-sevenths. More reliable estimates suggest that it may have been as high as a quarter of the whole. What is more certain is that it grew, with fluctuations depending on the attractions or otherwise of the market, from the late seventeenth century until the late 1770s. This, the largest experiment so far in international investment, was made possible by legal and technical changes which from early in the century made investment in the Funded Debt relatively easy and increasingly reliable. From 1714, a buyer or seller of Bank, East India or South Sea stock had only to register his transaction at the Bank or (in a few cases) at East India

---

[1] L. B. Namier, *The Structure of Politics at the Accession of George III*, 1929, vol. I, pp. 67–9.

[2] For a full account see C. Wilson, *Anglo-Dutch Commerce and Finance*, ch. IV.

[3] See C. Wilson, 'Dutch investment in Eighteenth-Century England: a Note on Yardsticks', and Mrs A. C. Carter, 'Note on A Note on Yardsticks', *Econ. Hist. Rev.*, XII, no. 3, 1960.

House or South Sea House. Dutch investors could do this through a London attorney who, armed with an authorization, could transfer stock and collect dividends. To supply their clients with intelligence about market conditions, some stockbrokers issued regular *courants* which the attorney could send to his client by the regular packet boats sailing between Harwich and Helvoetsluys. By this network of communications, a growing volume of savings of Dutch merchants, widows, orphans, pensioners, and the endowed funds of Dutch schools, orphanages, universities and churches flowed into England in support of the public credit.

In all this there was nothing of sentiment or sympathy, even less of political alliance. It was a straightforward business arrangement. The Dutch investor could usually obtain a return on his capital somewhat higher than he could get at home and at times (when the English were hard pressed for money) a good deal higher. If he chose, and was shrewd, he had the opportunity of substantial capital gains on a fluctuating market; the less shrewd no doubt suffered equivalent losses. The British Government needed foreign capital for several reasons. Dutch investment was regarded as a support for the public credit; in other words it supplied capital which kept down the costs of borrowing. Popular and informed opinion agreed on this. A satirical article in the *Gentleman's Magazine* for 1762 on how to send down the price of the Funds remarked: 'Two or three hints from Holland that the Dutch are going to join our enemies and will take their money out of our stocks may also be of service, and I think will easily gain credit, as anything treacherous or base in a Dutchman will be at once believed.' Within the Treasury, the knowledgeable were equally exercised during the Seven Years War about methods of inducing the Dutch to maintain their interest in the Funds. When the Duke of Newcastle consulted his advisers amongst the underwriters, Joseph Salvador explained the difficulties of offering better terms to attract new Dutch capital without causing the older (Dutch) investors to feel 'a diffidence of the *Security* of their Capital'.[1] Antony Chamier, Under Secretary for War and a member of a well-known Huguenot family with large financial interests, thought that an offer of life annuities would help to attract Dutch funds and keep them intact after the war. The Dutch, he thought, would be tempted to 'withdraw large sums from their trade, that can never yield them a profit equal to that that is to be made in our funds'.

[1] Quoted Wilson, *Anglo-Dutch Commerce*, pp. 164–5.

The impression such comments leave is that of an active and mobile group of Dutch investors, shifting their capital spontaneously in search of the best yields. How far were these typical? It is difficult to know. Some certainly followed staider policies. One prosperous Dutch merchant, David Leeuw, whose books have been investigated, built up steadily over a quarter of a century a stake of about £40,000 on the British Funds.[1] The records of the Bank and the East India Company stock suggest that there were many such. But the more active investor who played the market was certainly regarded as important, especially in wartime. It was then that the Government's anxiety over two other related aspects of the economy became acute. 'Public Credit' became essentially tied to the problem of the balance of payments and the condition of the exchanges.

Britain's balance of payments was probably never more than precarious in this period. 'Invisible' income (from shipping, insurance, etc.) was probably barely enough to balance those 'invisible' costs about which we know even less – the costs of the Grand Tour, of embassies abroad, of shipping and commission services provided by foreigners. In wartime, the Government was in special need of money to finance the heavy costs of military expeditions abroad. There was therefore a heavy outflow of funds – much of it in the first instance to Holland, and handled by the same men who organized the inflow of Dutch investment. Such payments pressed heavily on Britain's rate of exchange with foreign countries. The problem was therefore to keep the two movements in equilibrium. Explaining to Newcastle in 1761 how he transmitted funds to the Deputy Paymaster in Amsterdam for paying the army in Europe. Joshua van Neck concluded: '. . . I do not well conceive how such large sums could be remitted quicker consistent with the interest of Government in the support of the Exchange.'[2] The willingness of the Dutch to invest in the funds created for Britain an asset similar to an additional branch of export trade, helping to keep up not only the market price of the Funds but the exchange itself.

By the mid-century, the buying and selling of government stock has been reduced to a routine. The investor or his agent went to the offices of the Bank or East Indian or South Sea Houses of the Exchequer to sign the transfer. The offices were normally open all the morning on three days a week and in the afternoons until three o'clock. The counters were arranged under the letters of the alphabet. You attended at the counter labelled with the first letter of your surname, being

[1] C. Wilson, ch. IV.   [2] C. Wilson, op. cit., pp. 159–60.

careful not to call on any of the forty-nine bank holidays which included, ironically, the celebration of the death of King Charles the Martyr, when the offices were shut.[1] Callers included investors collecting their dividends – those members of 'the public in general, whose principal concern is that the payment of the interest on the money borrowed of them is regular and at the same time well secured'.[2] If this had been the end of the story, no more would need to be said of the origins of one of the most important financial institutions of the modern world. But it was not. An observer could remark that 'two thirds of the people that are constant attenders at the books on the transfer days . . . are known to be jobbers'.[3] That is, part of the buying and selling was transacted by agents of various kinds acting on behalf of others. Obscure as the process of investment proper remains, it is less obscure than the speculation which accompanied it and which cannot entirely be dissociated from it. A proportion of investors, English and Dutch, always kept a vigilant eye on the market movements of stocks, increasingly circulated by brokers for their clients' information. Their hope was to buy when prices were low and realize when they were high. The yield on stocks was controlled, broadly, by two considerations. The stocks of the companies were influenced by both political and trade prospects. The Government issues proper depended more exclusively on political factors. In peacetime when the Government's need for money slackened, the yield dropped and prices hardened. In 1750, for example, 4 per cent annuities stood well above par, reflecting the plenty of money and reduced rates of interest obtainable. War, or threat of war, brought the prospect of new loans at higher rates. The price of the existing Funds therefore dropped in expectation of higher yields on new issues. There was a spectacular example of this from January 1755: 3 per cents fell from 100 to 62 by January 1762. Bank Stock from 130 to 94, East India from 180 to 115. Such fluctuations affected only marginally the investor who was prepared to let his money lie and draw his dividends. They could make or break the speculator looking for capital gains. It was not least of the misfortunes of the injudicious which had, since the 1690s, brought down the curses of reformers on the heads of the speculative element, called collectively the brokers and jobbers, whose malpractices now vied with those

---

[1] T. Mortimer, *Every Man His Own Broker*, edn. of 1769, pp. 143–4. (First published 1761.)
[2] Ibid., p. viii.
[3] Ibid., p. viii.

previously detected in the goldsmiths. Their fundamental crime lay, according to their critics, in their habit of buying, fictitiously and purely for the sake of speculative gain, stock for which they had no capital to pay.

Ejected from the Royal Exchange, they had taken up a new abode in 'Change Alley', midway between the Bank of England and the later site of Lloyds Exchange. Here, in canyons now clothed in white and shining sanitary brick and unrecorded by even such a cultural plaque as nowadays celebrates the birthplace of a minor sculptor or poetaster stood Jonathan's Coffee House, the original of the modern Stock Exchange. Burnt down in 1748, it was replaced by 'New Jonathans', officially called the Stock Exchange from 1773. From these days of the Coffee House derives, no doubt, the traditional title of the Stock Exchange as 'The House'. The essence of the speculative system was the contract to buy or sell *at a future date*. This was fully developed at Amsterdam in the seventeenth century – the so-called *termijnhandel*. It was often believed that the mechanics of speculation, like many other financial techniques, were imitated from Dutch precedents. In some degree this was probably true. It is unlikely, on the other hand, that the interval between purchase and sale itself sprang from the participation of absentee Dutchmen who needed time to complete their bargains, as some believed.[1] The name for the quarterly settlement day when transactions were completed and mutual debts discharged – Rescontre or Contango – was certainly in use in Holland at a much earlier date. The basic method of gambling, apart from lotteries and insurance against speculative losses, was fictitious buying or selling by 'Bears' and 'Bulls'. Briefly, a 'Bear' was an operator who 'sold short', i.e. sold stock he did not own in order to buy it back at a profit.

> A Bear [wrote an eighteenth-century observer] in the language of Change Alley is a person who has agreed to sell any quantity of the public funds more than he is possessed of, and often without being possessed of any at all, which, nevertheless, he is obliged to deliver against a certain time: before this time arrives, he is continually going up and down selling ... whose property he can devour ... rejoicing in mischief at any misfortune that may bring about the wished-for change or falling the stocks, that he may buy in low and so settle his account to advantage.

Contrariwise, a 'Bull' was

> the name by which the gentlemen of Change Alley choose to call all persons who contract to buy any quantity of government securities, without any intention or ability to pay for it and who consequently are obliged to sell it

[1] See Mortimer, op. cit., p. 29.

again, either at a profit or loss, before the time comes when they have contracted to take it.[1]

Alongside the Bulls who gambled on a rise in prices and the Bears who gambled on a fall, were the option holders who insured themselves against loss by agreeing to buy or sell at a future date while at the same time taking up the optional right to pay a fine for not doing so. Probably most of these types of transactions were in existence before the eighteenth century. In the hysteria of the South Sea Bubble, much of the apparent investment must have been in reality dealings 'on the margin' by speculators with little or no cash. By 1730, brokers were circulating lists of stock prices and the costs of options to buy or sell a wide range of stocks. Amongst them was Joshua van Neck's father-in-law, the Huguenot merchant Stephen Daubuz. Critics alleged that Dutch speculators, Christians and Jews, were prominent amongst the sharp characters of Change Alley who swindled each other by inventing false rumours of war or peace (as suited their book) and battened on the hopes of the ignorant or gullible. Such were 'the Professors, Doctors and Tutors of the Sacred College of Stockjobbers' who whiled away 'vacations' when the markets were idle by 'fiddling' (i.e. gambling) on the prices of green peas or mackerel.[2]

Modern opinion might be kinder to the ancestors of the Stock Exchange. Their activities had little to do with the steady flow of capital into the Funds from investors, English or foreign, in search of a reliable income. In the short term they were sometimes responsible for booms or panics that involved the unwary in catastrophe. For good or for ill they probably influenced the *price* of stocks, and thereby the cost of borrowing, to the Government. But by advertising the opportunities of the stock market they helped in the long-run to widen the circle of investors and speculators, to create habits of investing instead of hoarding, and even to level out fluctuations by increasing competitive bidding for stock.

The effects of these developments in public finance may be summarized by saying that London had become a centre to which surplus capital could be attracted not only from the rest of the country but also from abroad. What was drawn in was redistributed, either in London — where the army and navy was often fitted out, armed and

[1] Ibid., pp. 46n and 49n.
[2] Ibid., pp. 74–80, 92, for an entertaining if unedifying picture of Change Alley. It should be remembered that the author's avowed intention was to discredit 'the artful combinations' of the speculators whom he credited with the fall of the market in 1755 which had personally cost him dear.

victualled – or in the provinces, where troops and ships might occasionally be stationed. From the north and Midlands too came a stream of
manufactures from contractors for iron, timber, uniforms, ammuni-
tion and ordnance and stores of all kinds often paid for, in the last
analysis, out of loans. Beyond this were the payments which had to be
made in wartime, usually through Amsterdam agents, to the forces in
Europe. None of this spreading network of payments for goods,
services and investment could have worked without a corresponding
expansion of the mechanism of payment and of credit. The great
recoinage 1696–98 had failed to solve the problems of the metallic
currency. Silver remained undervalued in England in terms of gold.
There was, for this reason and because of the reluctance or inability of
the traders in those countries to buy English goods, a drain of silver
on a large scale to India, to Holland, and to Scandinavia and the Baltic
countries.[1] Very little silver was therefore offered to the Mint for
coining and silver coins became scarce. So, later on, in the Seven Years
War, did gold. Even copper coins – halfpennies and farthings – deter-
iorated until tradesmen would only accept them by weight. The silver
coinage relapsed into chaos, and clipping and export combined to
decimate it.

The deficiencies of the metallic currency were mitigated (not
remedied) by the growing varieties of paper instruments which helped
men and institutions to settle their obligations with less resort to coins.
The National Debt itself was partly recorded in the form of certificates
– exchequer bills, navy and army bills and East India bonds – which
holders could use to pay their debts and taxes. Even the stock of the
trading companies and long-term annuities could be realized in time of
need for the same purpose, though it might prove at a loss if the market
happened to be slack. More important as a new form of money were
the notes issued by the banks and the cheques which their customers
could draw against their deposits or against the overdraft or loan
which the banker might, on suitable security in the shape of land or
valuables, allow his client.

In London, the monopoly of joint stock banking belonged – a
little dubiously after 1694, more precisely after the renewal of its
charter in 1708 – to the Bank of England. From 1708 to 1825 other
bankers could accept deposits, make loans, discount bills, issue notes
and transfer money by cheques, but the scope of their business was
limited by the resources that could be mobilized within the limits of a

[1] For details see Clark, *Guide*, pp. 77–9.

business partnership. The maximum number of partners allowed to a
banking concern was six. The note issue of the private bankers was
never more, therefore, than a fraction of that of the Bank of England.
Rebuilt in 1734 on the site of a house in Threadneedle Street formerly
occupied by its first Governor, Sir John Houblon, it developed mainly
as a government bank and as 'the Bank of London' — as it was often
called in the eighteenth century. Four-fifths of its business, and of its
profits, came from its government connexion by the end of the Seven
Years War; but it it also provided credit for other companies — the
East India, Royal Africa and assurance companies. It discounted bills
for these companies and for individuals, and its notes circulated in
London and occasionally in Bristol and other large towns.

The Bank of England was the prime London bank: it was far from
being the only one. Descended lineally from the goldsmith bankers of
the Restoration was a nucleus of private bankers, outside the City now
as well as within it, who provided important facilities for clients, from
the country as well as from town. The Bubble made a hole in their
numbers in 1720. Nearly a third of the 'goldsmiths keeping running
cashes', it was said, disappeared. In 1725 there were twenty-five of them,
so that before the Bubble there may have been thirty to forty. Their
numbers grew fairly steadily again down to the 1760s. The London
bankers tended to fall into two groups, the character of their clients
and business dividing along the geographical, social and economic line
that separated the 'West End' of high politics and high fashion from
the mercantile world of the 'City' proper.'[1] Writing in the 1720s,
Richard Cantillon, himself a London banker, said of the banking
business: 'Some trust one banker, some another. The most fortunate
is the banker who has for clients rich gentlemen who are always looking
out for safe employment for their money without wishing to invest
it at interest while they wait'.[2] It was out of this situation that such
famous 'West End' banks as Hoares, Childs, Goslings, and, after the
mid-century, Coutts, Drummonds and Herries, fashioned their reputation and their profits. Their business was not (as one of them said)
'with mercantile men' but with the gentry and aristocracy. Hoares in
Fleet Street had moved away from their original goldsmithing, pawn-
broking and trading interests. By 1720 they were a focus for aristocratic
finance, cautious and well-conducted, a sound bank where the stewards
for great estates sent their rents, and lords in need of capital borrowed

[1] D. M. Joslin, 'London Private Bankers 1720–85', *Econ. Hist. Rev.*, VII, no. 2, 1954.
[2] R. Cantillon, *Essay on Commerce*, ed. H. Higgs, 1931, quoted by Joslin, op. cit.

on mortgage. In the seventeenth century a landowner in heavy debt often had to sell out. Now he could turn to the banker for a loan. Childs, also in Fleet Street, were likewise bankers to royalty and the nobility, closely connected too with the East India Company. A third Fleet Street bank was Goslings. Unlike Hoares and Childs, who had developed from goldsmiths, Goslings were originally printers and booksellers and their clients – including Longmans, Rivingtons and Edward Gibbon – reflected the early character of their trade. But they too developed connexions with the gentry and did a growing business with returned nabobs. Clive, Wedderburn and Hastings were to figure among their later customers. Herries, in St James's Street, specialized in providing travellers cheques for gentlemen on the Grand Tour. Wrights in Covent Garden were intimately connected with the Papist gentry. It was all very gentlemanly, intimate, secretive, and was to continue so. Already before 1750 the bankers were indistinguishable socially from their customers. A Hoare was Lord Mayor in 1754. By 1714 one partner had bought a large estate at Stourhead in Wiltshire and employed Colin Campbell to build him a Palladian mansion. Thirty years later the vast landscape garden, mindful of Poussin with classical temples and romantic grottoes, was taking shape. It remains one of the most spectacular pieces of contrived scenery in England. About the same time the descendants of the original Francis Child, goldsmith, were converting the Tudor mansion at Osterley Park which he had bought from Barbon's executors into a model of classical elegance. Another family in the Child partnership, the Morses, born yeomen, had moved into an Oxfordshire mansion at Woodperry. There was no shorter cut from trade to gentility than via the bankers' parlour.

The Lombard Street banks did business of a different kind. Some, like Surman and Stone, had dropped their goldsmith business and turned to discounting, investment and note issue. Their connexion was especially with the merchants and great financiers, with a special emphasis on the foreigners. Van Neck, van Notten, Sir Matthew Decker[1] and Samson Gideon all appear in their books. It was no accident that they helped in floating loans for the Seven Years War. Others, like Vere, Glyn and Hallifax, came from trade – Glyn being a drysalter who joined partnership with Joseph Vere, a banker. Some, like Smith Payne Smith, were really country bankers who set up a London branch to manage their metropolitan business.

[1] See above, p. 266.

In 1750, when Edmund Burke left Ireland for England, he thought there were not more than a dozen 'bankers shops' outside London. Twelve years later a well-informed observer guessed that the number was 400–500.[1] Burke may have omitted those considerable numbers of provincial tradesmen who already did banking as a part-time occupation. (The miscreant with whom the Vicar of Wakefield lodged his capital and who ran off with it was plainly a 'banker'. Goldsmith calls him a 'merchant'.) Even so, the discrepancy probably reflects the great banking expansion that took place in these years. Bristol and Norwich each acquired two banks. But at Norwich the Gurneys, ultimately to be the largest and most famous, were still characteristically only part-time bankers. Their bank proper was only separated out from their trade as wool merchants in 1775. Cambridge had Mortlocks, Birmingham Lloyds (bankers but still in trade partnership with a button manufacturer); the Stuckeys served Somerset as Bolithos served Cornwall. This proliferating 'banking' system reflected in part the growth of local trade but it gained momentum from one source in particular — the growing balances of local tax collectors. The collection of the land tax brought into being some fifty receivers (with numerous deputies and a tribe of parish collectors). Of these about half were local gentry, like the Blofelds in Norfolk. The rest were merchants, like Sir John Elwill in Devon or the Geldart family at Liverpool. One or two — like Cromptons at Derby — were themselves bankers. Thomas Marsden at Bolton was a fustian maker who turned banker. Receivers were apt to hang on to the proceeds of their collections for a long time, partly because they could — with profit to themselves and their local banker — deposit their cash in the bank, partly because they could argue with some force that moving large quantities of coin about the country in the teeth of thieves and highwaymen was not a risk to be taken lightly.[2] Unquestionably these very large deposits helped to profit local bankers. But they did not always save them. When Tozer's Bank at Bristol failed in 1761 they held £1,750 belonging to Daniel Harson, the local tax collector.

The relationship between government borrowing and taxation and the growth of private agencies for the creation and transfer of money and credit was a mutual one of crucial importance. Country bankers helped to remit savings and tax proceeds to London, normally to a

[1] Clapham, op. cit., vol. I, p. 157.
[2] See W. R. Ward, op. cit., p. 107, also L. S. Pressnell, 'Public Monies and the Development of English banking', *Econ. Hist. Rev.*, III, 1953.

private banker in the West End or, more often, in Lombard Street. Both London and country banks invested a proportion of their deposits in government securities, either long or short term. A big London bank would, in addition to its reserve of cash, keep a good proportion of its assets in annuities, Bank stock, navy bills, exchequer bills and company bonds. If it was wise, it would remember that some of these were liable to wide fluctuations of price and keep such investments in a safe relationship to their note issue and loans to customers. Not all were so prudent. The sudden failure of confidence and the consequent run on the bank was a commonplace of eighteenth-century life which only the sound survived. In spite of frequent failures, the services of the banks — lending to the creditworthy client in need, providing working capital for trade and industry by discounting bills and giving occasional loans, remitting funds to and from the capital — enormously eased the mobility of capital and stimulated the flow of money through the country. At the head of the banking system stood the Bank of England. It was not yet 'the bankers' bank' with that general control of credit it was later to assume. Some London bankers kept an account with it but by no means all. It remained primarily a bank for Government and for London but already it was beginning to bear some of the aspects of a central bank.

While Government borrowing and the growth of banks combined to make the internal movement of capital more fluid, complementary techniques were developed to settle obligations arising out of foreign trade and the very large expenditure abroad for naval and military operations. Such payments influenced, and in turn were influenced by, the rate of exchange between Britain and foreign countries. Rates of exchange in sixteen European countries were being printed and circulated by an exchange broker in 1697. The growth of payments for external transactions caused a corresponding growth of business in foreign exchange and the discounting of bills of exchange. Just as some merchants evolved into bankers, others specialized in foreign exchange. In some circumstances, payment was still made in coin or bullion. The export of foreign coin and bullion was legal, the export of English coin was not, but, as we have seen, it still took place.[1] Increasingly, however, international obligations were settled by bill of exchange. If the exchange brokers found that the demand for bills to pay debts abroad was larger than the supply (if, in other words, the balance of trade was adverse) the pound lost value in terms of foreign

[1] See above, p. 266.

currency. The rate turned against England. If the balance of payments was in England's favour, the pound appreciated. When the rate of exchange fell beyond a certain point it might become profitable to export bullion. Whether remittance was by bill or by metal, that is to say, it usually depended on the rate of exchange. But, contrariwise, a low rate of exchange might in turn stimulate exports and restore the equilibrium of the exchange.[1] The balance of visible trade was not the only factor affecting the rate of exchange. The approach of war invariably sent down the rate because it opened up the prospect of large overseas payments. The subsequent flow of Dutch capital into the Funds might in turn raise the rates; but if war was protracted it might well fall again. So long as England was frequently a net borrower of capital Amsterdam retained its position as a financial centre, and the bill on Amsterdam continued to be the main international currency, especially in wartime. But it was, in the long run, more significant that throughout these years of costly military operations, with expenditure running at an unprecedented level, successive governments managed to maintain the reputation of the public credit. Between 1698 and 1797 there was no suspension of cash payments by the Bank of England. The evolution of the financial techniques sketched above was steadily making London a centre not only of local finance but of European finance also.

One other type of financial business, insurance, was likewise growing, but it was connected more loosely with the other financial institutions. None of its branches was in essence new. Insurance of ships and cargoes was well known in the Middle Ages. The earliest Italian 'policy' (the word itself derives from *polizza*, a promise) afforded cover against 'sea, fire, and jettison, reprisals or robberies of friends and foes and all other cases, perils, tempests, disasters, impediments and misfortune, even such as cannot be thought of, that may happen . . .'.[2] In modern jargon a comprehensive policy. In the later seventeenth century, the main branches of insurance – fire, marine and life – all developed into a more or less specialized type of business. All three were in some degree the fruit of a marriage – often an eccentric and unstable union – between business enterprise and mathematics. The essence was that the insuring party paid a premium against some kind of risk – loss by fire, or shipwreck, or death. Business could only develop if the degree of

---

[1] See below, p. 353, for Hume's exposition of the theory of exchange.
[2] Reproduced by Nicholas Magens, *Essay on Insurances*, 1755.

probability of losses over a period could be calculated in advance, and if the statistics of such losses could be collated with sufficient precision to form a basis for the future. Hence insurance business as a merchant's sideline soon gave way to specialized insurance offices employing professional actuaries.

The Great Fire of London did not originate fire insurance but it gave it a special impetus. Fire insurance was felt to be a more urgent need. With the rebuilding of the City in brick it was also less risky. By the 1690s the 'Hand-in-Hand' Fire Office — it took its title from the badge it pinned on policy-holders' houses — was in business, first in Tom's Coffee House in St Martin's Lane, later in Angel Court on Snow Hill. A fire office established by Nicolas Barbon, the greatest speculative builder of the times, was still in business and known after 1705 as 'The Phenix Office'. It disappeared about 1720, but in its place rose another, which was to survive and flourish down to the present day. This was the Sun Fire Office, again known by a badge of the smiling sun. It may still occasionally be found on old houses identifying those originally entitled to the services of its fire brigade. The 'Sun' was the creation of a former coal merchant, Charles Povey, an aggressive, speculative, litigious innovator, prolific of pamphlets on all kinds of economic, social, moral and religious problems, whose restless imagination was stirred by the financial possibilities of fire insurance.[1] Fortunately, no doubt, for his office, Povey was bought out by his colleagues and the 'Sun' went on from strength to strength.

The Bubble mania gave a further twist to insurance history. 'Policies and Premiums', wrote a contemporary, 'were in the mouths of all. It was the El-Dorado of the London Craftsman, the alchymy of the needy tradesman.' Some of the more ambitious joint stock insurance projects became entangled, in the fashion of the times, with ideas of enlarging the public credit through loans secured on the grant of monopoly privileges. Out of the wreckage, two survived: the Royal Exchange and the London Assurance Companies. The Bubble Act left the business of marine assurance to them and to the private underwriters. In the end, these joint stock companies turned to fire insurance and left marine business largely to the private underwriters. Seventeenth-century shipowners and freighters had often insured at Amsterdam. Now a growing share of this business moved to London. From 1686, the underwriters' social and business headquarters had been at Edward Lloyd's coffee house in Tower Street which served as a club where they

[1] See P. G. M. Dickson, *The Sun Insurance Office 1710–1960*, 1960, chs. I–V.

could collect shipping news for their clients. Lloyd himself had issued the first *Lloyd's News* in 1696. The steady growth of business encouraged a successor to publish *Lloyd's List* in 1734 and from the fifties *Lloyd's Register of Shipping* was published regularly. It was through Lloyds that Walpole first had the news of Vernon's capture of Portobello in 1740. Lloyd's was not, and never has been, an insuring institution itself. Its function, like that of the Stock Exchange, was to provide a forum with rules of conduct for private brokers and underwriters.[1]

Life insurance was, in the end, to be the most widespread and popular of all types of insurance and it drew most directly on the actuarial work of the statisticians in computing tables of mortality. In Holland, both life annuities (an annual payment for life) and life insurance (the payment of a lump sum at death) had been purchasable since the mid-seventeenth century. Even Johan de Witt, the Grand Pensionary himself, had helped to produce actuarial calculations upon which the terms of policies might be based.[2] Graunt, Petty and Halley, the Astronomer Royal, all did similar work in England. The Government itself entered the life annuity field in 1693. But it may be doubted whether governments, hard pressed for cash on almost any terms, were ever in a strong position to pay much heed to actuarial factors in calculating their terms. The private companies which took over the life insurance business could not afford to neglect them. The earliest specialized office of life insurance was the Society for Assurance of Widows and Orphans of 1699. The Amicable followed in 1705 and was the only life office to survive the Bubble.[3] The Equitable followed in 1762 and remains prosperous still.

None of these insurances against the hazards of fate was new. Precedents can be found for most of them in the Middle Ages. But their emergence as specialized types of business testifies to a new and more conscious form of social — mainly urban — organization. Within the old framework of rural life, peasants had sometimes insured against old age and infirmity by conveying their small capital to a friend or neighbour in return for an undertaking to care for them. Such agreements were still occasionally to be found in the late seventeenth century. A Leicestershire peasant, Thomas Cleye, and his wife Joan, had such an understanding with a neighbour who was 'to provide for,

---

[1] See D. E. W. Gibb, *Lloyds of London*, 1957.

[2] D. Houtzager, *Hollands Lijf- en Losrenteleningen Voor 1672*, Schiedam, 1951.

[3] It merged in 1866 with the Norwich Union and may thus claim a continuous history down to the present.

mentayne & keepe . . . with good wholsom meat & drinke, lodginge, fyre washinge starchinge cloathes both Lyninge & Woollinge hoose shooes & all othe nesessaryes & thinges Convenient & fitting for people of their quallatys & Condicion'.[1] How commonly rural people could thus cushion themselves comfortably against the fears of old age is not known. But plainly it became more difficult for the growing population of the cities. Working men in the towns sought insurance of a sort against illness and unemployment through their friendly societies, even through savings banks maintained in public houses by the big breweries.[2] Increasingly, the middling and trading classes looked to those who insured as a business, substituting for the neighbourly offices of the village the anonymous aids of social and commercial insurance that were to reach full maturity in the Beveridge scheme of our own century.

---

[1] See W. G. Hoskins, *The Midland Peasant*.
[2] See Mathias, op. cit., pp. 277–8.

CHAPTER SIXTEEN

Towards a Concept of Social Welfare

FEW historical problems resist generalization so effectively as that of
social welfare. What benefits, what burdens did the economic changes
described in earlier pages bring to the people of England? Facts and
prejudices conspire against any complete answer. The 'people' were
grouped, but very loosely grouped, into what the writers of the next
century would call 'classes'. These plainly gained unequally by an
economic progress heavily weighted in the direction of foreign trade,
unequal as between one region and another, and between one type of
farming and another. Even within these 'classes' some men gained
more, by luck or enterprise, than others. Nor were men only divided by
'class'. Each region had its own story, often distinct from that of other
regions. While Yorkshire and Lancashire were enjoying a growing
trade in textiles, the West Country and East Anglia were on the brink
of a decline as industrial areas. Nor does the yardstick that can usefully
be applied to the later stages of national economic development –
the measurement and distribution *per capita* of national income –
offer much help in these early stages. To divide the estimated wealth
of the nation by the numbers of its people gives us another dimension,
but an abstract one. Where growth is slow by modern standards,
statistics of output and population scant and imperfect, the artificial
distribution of the social dividend into infinitesimal fractions can throw
little light on the real changes in distribution of wealth. It seems best,
therefore, to concentrate on such social trends as can be verified by
observed fact. Briefly, to note that the economic advances of the age
added generously to the wealth of many that already had wealth; they
also enabled those who chose to get rid of it by spending more easily
and lavishly than ever before; that they offered special advantages to
those who were so placed as to benefit naturally by the tides of wealth
and fashion – Norfolk squires and farmers well placed for the London

and Dutch markets, London men of money conveniently placed for investment and speculation in government finance and foreign trade, textile manufacturers with an eye to the new luxury fashions or the mass markets, Bristol and Liverpool merchants on the doorstep of colonies needing slaves and offering sugar, tobacco and cotton, and so on. Yet everywhere, as by universal rule, the pattern was only suggested by events. Its final definition rested with those individuals who could assess and seize the opportunity of the market, moulding it to their convenience by the curious mixture of skill, daring and intuition we call enterprise.

At the top, political and social life was still dominated by a relatively small group of the real aristocracy. The great houses of the Whig oligarchy – Houghton, Holkham, Castle Howard, Wentworth Woodhouse and the rest – were the arcana of political and social life where the great decisions were made. Immensely rich, the great families were getting richer, their estates bigger. After the 1720s less land was sold and what was sold made high prices. The plums of patronage still fell copiously into their laps. The new structures of investment, banking and credit opened up new opportunities of fructifying their surplus wealth and transferring their rentals to pay their bills for London life and luxuries. The legal devices of the later seventeenth century stabilized their estates and made it more difficult for the spendthrift heir to disperse them, while the desire of the first two Georges to protect the peerage from dilution meant that the additions to their numbers were few. From time to time, an agricultural depression hit even the big landlord, as the slump of 1702 left Lord Stanhope hard pressed. But times had changed since the Tudor age when a writer could note of a great lord that he was 'in the year 1575 rated at 12,000 a year sterlinge, within 2 following was vanished and no name of him founde, haveing in that time prodigally spent and consumed all even to the selling of the stones, timber and lead of his Castles and howses . . .'.[1] The eighteenth-century nobility might individually be spendthrift, wild, prodigal. As an institution they were remarkably stable. The few additions to this central group were a handful of politicians like Walpole and Onslow, lawyers like Lord Macclesfield, soldiers and sailors like Cadogan and Rodney. This was the last age when men made large fortunes out of political office. But there was an outer ring of men who, while missing the highest social rewards,

[1] T. Wilson, *The State of England, Anno Domini 1600*, ed. F. J. Fisher, Camden Miscellany, vol. LXVI, 1936, p. 22.

bought their way into baronetcies or even Irish peerages and founded or bought imposing estates or great houses from the profits of office or trade. Within thirty years of the Glorious Revolution London was ringed by the 'Citizens' Country Houses' as Defoe called them. The great City men no longer lived in the City but at Putney, Chiswick and Kew, or Wimbledon. Sir James Bateman, of the Bank and South Sea Company, could leave great estates in Herefordshire, Essex and Kent. His son became an Irish peer and married the daughter of an earl. Sir Charles Duncombe, the goldsmith banker, like Bateman of humble origins, could buy the Duke of Buckingham's Helmsley estate in Yorkshire for £90,000 and from his heir was descended the Earl of Feversham. Sir Josiah Child, the East India merchant, died enormously wealthy. His grand-daughter became the Duchess of Bedford, her grandson the Duke of Beaufort. Sir Gilbert Heathcote, Governor of the Bank and a colonial and export trader on a vast scale, bought a large Rutland estate, left a vast fortune, said to be the largest left by a commoner, and descendants who became peers. Joshua van Neck, the underwriter of Dutch origins who served successive governments well in channelling Dutch money into the Funds, ended as a baronet, his son as an Irish peer, with a Suffolk mansion and estate. Sir William Blathwayt, Secretary of State for War, built the great house at Dyrham Park, Gloucestershire, from the profits of office and was at one time tipped for the earldom of Bristol. He did not get it. The times were against him. For the time being, the caste system was hardening.

Squires from Norfolk prosperous on barley and the Corn Bounty, and from elsewhere if they had made good marriages for their daughters or squared their consciences with the Whigs, could afford to risk a town season. Those who shared none of these benefits were falling in social esteem, especially in the bad times of the 1720s, 30s and 40s. In the pages of the social satirists busily making London respectable, they are caricatured as Squire Western or, more kindly, as Sir Roger de Coverley. Lower still, the Squire-yeoman lives on in the person of Tony Lumpkin. 'Taken together', as G. M. Young has written, 'they form the bulk of the Stupid Old Tory Party.'[1] More characteristic of the new social order, and profiting more from its commercial, competitive methods, were the tenant farmers – 'equal strangers', as Oliver Goldsmith wrote, 'to opulence and poverty'. Their social obligations were small, their tastes simple. What capital they could accumulate they

[1] In 'Domus Optima', *Last Essays*, 1950.

could put into their farming operations. Debt did not pursue them as it did their social superiors.

> As they had all the conveniences of life within themselves, they seldom visited the towns or cities in search of superfluities. Remote from the polite, they still retained the primeval simplicity of manners; and frugal by habit, they scarcely knew that temperance was a virtue. They wrought with cheerfulness on days of labour, but observed festivals as intervals of idleness and pleasure. They kept up the Christmas carol, sent true love-knots on Valentine morning, ate pancakes on Shrovetide, showed their wit on the 1st of April, and religiously cracked nuts on Michaelmas eve.[1]

The Provinces could show few mercantile fortunes to compare with those that grew in the metropolis from the conjunction of trade and influence. Bristol, Liverpool, Manchester, Birmingham, had plenty of merchants and an increasing number of merchant-manufacturers of comfortable affluence, but very few of wealth comparable to the great City fortunes. Where great fortunes were found, as with the Lowthers of Whitehaven, the Moores of Liverpool or the Delavals of Northumberland, they were the joint product of land ownership and the enterprising exploitation of mineral rights or trade that arose from it. Few of the provincial merchants before the Civil War seem to have been Calvinists, and by no means all of them were in later decades. But after the Restoration Settlement deprived the Dissenters of their full status of citizenship, many of them were driven into economic enterprise, not so much 'from any (supposed) emphasis on usury and profit-making, such as writers nowadays attribute to Calvinist and Puritan ethics, as for a simpler or better reason, namely, because trade and industry provided practically the only outlet for their activities'.[2] This practical interpretation of the link between Calvinism and economic development is supported by the social trends of Dissent. In the sixteenth and early seventeenth centuries, the ruling Saints were drawn from the ranks of the penurious and discontented gentry, the rank and file from the artisanate and peasantry. Neither in England nor in New England (nor in Holland) was the much-discussed connexion with merchant capitalists much in evidence. More often there was conflict between the medieval asceticism of the Saints and what they took to be the acquisitiveness and ostentation of the merchant class.[3] But after the Restora-

---

[1] *The Vicar of Wakefield*, ch. IV.

[2] D. Ogg, *England in the Reigns of James II and William III*, p. 43.

[3] See e.g. Bernard Bailyn, *The New England Merchants in the 17th Century*, 1925, ch. II; Gustav Renier, *The Dutch Nation*, 1944, pp. 142–3; Sigmund Diamond, *The Creation of Society in the New World*, 1963, chs. II and III.

tion came a marked change in the social composition in Dissent. Some gentry were still to be found, down to 1700, in the ranks of Presbyterianism, Independence and even Quakerism. By 1740, social prestige had largely been eliminated from Dissent. Gentry were rarely found amongst its numbers. And as the fire left the belly of old Dissent and passed into that of the new — the Methodist 'enthusiasts' — the older sects became more and more the religion of those sober, energetic, single-minded and mostly self-made men of business of the industrial areas. At the turn of the century, Lancashire probably had some 20,000 Dissenters. Norwich, with its stuffs, its brewing and its market, still kept a sizable Dissenting element, descended in part from the sixteenth-century Calvinist immigrants from the Low Countries. Prominent amongst the Norwich Quakers were the Gurneys, cloth traders of old, bankers-to-be. But the strongest concentrations were the Quakers and Unitarians of the Midlands and West Country. From the Bristol merchant Quakers came some of the families of the Midland Association of Ironmasters of 1762 — the Darbys, Lloyds, Reynolds, Crowleys, as well as the Hanburys of Pontypool, the Harfords of Ebbw Vale. Everywhere in the Gloucester and Wiltshire cloth trade, as at Bradford, Quakers were strong in the woollen industries. The new unincorporate towns, like Manchester and Birmingham, had obvious and special attractions for them and the Unitarians. Hence the Gaskells, Phillips, Porters, the Chamberlains, Martineaus and Nettlefolds.[1] All these formed a social element *sui generis*. While the aristocracy and gentry spent the money they could spare, and some they could not, on the high living of the day — lavish building, *objets d'art*, gambling at Newmarket, high life at Bath, routs at Ranelagh, or hunting parties nearer home — the Dissenting entrepreneur did not seek, in the first generation anyway, much in the way of extravagant social pleasures. He did not yearn for a peerage for his son or want his daughter to marry into the aristocracy. Educated most often at one of those Dissenting academies that deserted Latin and Greek for Natural Philosophy, 'Mechanics, Hydrostatics, Pneumatic, Electricity and Airs, Optics and Astronomy', he emerged thrifty, cautious, prudent, more prepared to plough any money he made into his business than to spend it on luxury. From academies like Warrington — 'the Athens of the North' — came men of a severely practical education who were to play a

---

[1] See Wagner, *English Genealogy*, pp. 174–7; Robert Halley, *Lancashire — Its Puritanism and Nonconformity*, 1869, vol. II, pp. 228–96; Isobel Grubb, *Quakerism and Industry*, 1930, pp. 105–66.

great part in the preparation and execution of the Industrial Revolution.[1]

The concentration of Dissenters on the economic arts was all the stronger because they failed, after the Revolution of 1688, to achieve any political cohesion. 'The Dissenters', wrote Defoe (himself a Dissenter) to Harley in 1704, 'are divided and impolitic; they are not formed into a body; they hold no correspondence among themselves. ... They are consequently passive in matters of government; the most they ever do is to address their Ministers.'[2] Political persecution created Dissent. Political pressure and its own temper, contentious and fissiparous, kept it politically impotent. Frugal as the first generation might be, the second and succeeding generations were inevitably prey to social ambition. Thus the numbers of Dissent tended to dwindle as the sons and grandsons drifted away to join Anglicanism and scale the upper rungs of the social ladder. Those who remained were often professional or semi-professional men: part of the growing army of attorneys, lawyers, clerks, agents and stewards who also hovered on the fringe of the changing economy, attending at one remove as it were to the economic business. Along with them, small shopkeepers, tradesmen and manufacturers of all kinds. Their influence on the economic and social development of Britain was enormous. Even in mid-Victorian England, Dissent, the religion of trade and manufacture, the cradle of Philistinism, remained the principal and most impregnable fortress against Matthew Arnold's onslaught in *Culture and Anarchy*.

It is more difficult to prove any universal trend in the fortunes of the smaller landowners. Many contemporaries accepted the protests of the largely Tory squirearchy that it was oppressed and virtually bankrupt. Certainly there was widespread disgruntlement with Whig policies that seemed to load an ever-increasing burden of war taxes on the squire's shoulders. The Corn Bounty did not prevent him from arguing that the country danced to London's tune. It was such feelings that kept Jacobitism alive. But it was not only taxation that crippled many a squire and yeoman. Those very commercial conditions – the need to follow markets, invest capital and improve – which were making

---

[1] For the academies see H. Maclachlan, *English Education under the Test Acts*, 1931.

[2] G. H. Harley, *Letters of Daniel Defoe*, 1955, August–September 1704. See also the elaborate satire by Defoe, *The Consolidation or Memoirs of Sundry Transactions from the World in the Moon Translated from the Lunar Language etc.* The Crolians 'being generally the Trading Manufacturing Part of the World and *Very Rich*' represented the Dissenters. But unlike their earthly counterparts, they came to control the lunar economy because they were not rent by 'eternal *Discords*, *Feuds*, *Distrusts* and *Disgusts* among themselves ...'

merchants, manufacturers and the owners of coal, iron and timber resources rich, often worked against the squire. Not invariably. In the county where the Palgraves and Pastons were declining, the Walpoles and Townsends were rising on the profits of agricultural improvement. Everything depended on good management, but luck was welcome. A timely legacy or the appearance of an heiress opportunely saved many a squire from impending bankruptcy. Debt, 'the crushing, inexorable burden of debt',[1] extinguished not a few families. To others it was the whip that drove them on to exploit their resources with greater efficiency.

To generalize about the standards of living of the labouring class is the most difficult task of all. Conditions of employment and pay were subject to infinite variation. In many industries, the textile and mining industries especially, employment was rarely a full-time matter. Weavers and miners had their own small holdings of land. At harvest time they still worked in the fields. There was as yet no clear dividing line between industry and agriculture. In some industries, like coal mining, workers received part of their pay in kind. And throughout industry the shortage of coin made truck payment a common resort of employers, often of necessity rather than of malice or even choice. Wage rates in the same industry varied widely between one district and another. Allowing for all these variations, and for the insuperable problems of measuring incomes and costs, the historian is left with certain impressions. It was a common opinion that the lower orders generally were doing better in the first half of the eighteenth century than they had done in the previous century; and to this some historians would add, than they were to do later. Defoe — not a witness with any great care for statistical consistency — said in 1728 that the lower orders ate meat in plenty and drank profusion of beer. 'Even those we call poor people, journeymen, working and painstaking people do thus; they lye warm, live in plenty, work hard and know no want.' It was no doubt partly true. A skilled man in work benefited by the stable level of prices in these years, and the Hammonds, with their eye on later periods, were prepared to regard these years as a kind of Golden Age. The case for such a verdict is stronger in some areas than in others. Adam Smith later pointed out that it was 'less the volume of national wealth at any given time than its continued increase that accounted for a rise in wages. Accordingly it was not in the richest countries [i.e. counties], but in the most thriving, or in those which

[1] J. H. Plumb, *Sir Robert Walpole*, vol. I, pp. 14–15.

are growing rich the fastest, that the wages of labour are highest.'[1] This observation was to be most clearly borne out in the later decades of the century; but its force is visible even in the first half of the century. Some figures of annual wage rates show that the proportionate rise was already greatest in the northern counties where manufacturing was expanding most rapidly; lowest in the declining west. London experienced a gentler rise.

	London (£ p.a.)	West	North[2]
1700	25	17·5	11·5
1725	27	17·5	13·15
1750	30	17·5	15·0

These generalized figures can be made specific. An unskilled labourer in Lancashire in 1700 received 8d. a day, in Oxford 12d, in London 20d. By 1750 the Lancashire price was 12d, at Oxford it stayed at 12d, in London it had risen to 24d. It was in the areas of expanding trade and industry that the labourer was able to sell his labour most successfully.[3]

Such figures are not without their value. They should not be taken to portray a comfortable, well-ordered society in which the conditions of labour may be contrasted with the later conditions of exploitation, unemployment and misery. The permanent condition of the times was still that of underemployment. Those employments which arose out of the growth of trade and shipping in ports – the 'growth' industries of these years *par excellence* – were notorious then, as later, as precarious occupations. But in 'domestic' manufactures, too, the manufacturer liked to have more labour available than he normally employed, as an insurance against labour shortage in boom times. Moreover, the organization of manufacture by the merchant-capitalist, which was still the predominant form of textile industries, was inherently unstable. So long as the putting-out organizer's capital was still largely in the form of raw material, it was easy for him to increase his commitment if trade was good; but it was almost equally easy for him to cut back when times were bad. He lacked the incentive of the later factory owner, with capital invested in building and plant, to maintain a steady rate of production and a steady return on his fixed capital. Add to this seasonal variations in wage rates, and the effects of violent short-term

[1] Quoted T. S. Ashton, *The Eighteenth Century*, p. 231. See also J. D. Chambers, *The Vale of Trent 1670-1800*, p. 46, for a comment of 1768 on the rising living standards of farm labourers.

[2] E. Gilboy, op. cit., p. 220.

[3] Ibid., Appendix II.

fluctuations that arose from harvests and war, and the periodic outbreaks of violence are more easily understood. Spasmodic rises in food
prices provoked keelmen on the Tyne to riot in 1709, tin miners to
plunder granaries at Falmouth in 1727. There was a rebellion in Northumberland and Durham in 1740, manhandling of Quaker corn dealers
in 1756. More peaceably, skilled artisans in the cloth, building, shipbuilding, printing and cutlery trades organized friendly societies to
insure them against unemployment and sickness and sometimes, gild
fashion, against the intrusion of 'foreign' labour into their trades.[1]

The 'domestic system' had some compensations. It retained the
casual, leisurely flavour of country life and carried it over into this transitional phase of industrial life. Men worked when they chose and idled
or got drunk when they were tired or bored. It was this that brought
against them the common charge that it was impossible to pay them
higher wages than were necessary for their bare necessities because,
whenever the rates went higher, they immediately stopped work.
William Temple, a Gloucester clothier with a memory of labour
troubles, wrote in 1739 that the only way to make the workers tem-
perate and industrious was 'to lay them under the necessity of labouring
all the time they can spare from rest and sleep, in order to procure the
common necessaries of life'.[2] This gloomy theory ignored the appalling
conditions under which the majority had to work in their own cottages,
which were hearth and factory combined. A later horrific description
of the conditions in which the cottage wool-comber worked was
equally true in this period:

> The work people are obliged to keep their windows open in all weathers
> to prevent or mitigate the evil effects of the gas. They are roasted to perspira-
> tion on one side, and often have a current of cold air rushing upon them from
> the window. They look pale and cadaverous, few reaching the age of fifty.
> Their roasting employment and exposure to the gas gives them a desire for
> spirits and opiates.[3]

Plainly, many of the social evils of the day were rooted in the insecure
and revolting conditions of employment in the domestic phase of
industrial organization. By the mid-century, the opinion could be heard
more frequently that more incentives would improve the habits of the
workers. Was not 'the creation of wants', Bishop Berkeley asked in
1755, 'the likeliest way to produce industry in a people?' But it was

[1] T. S. Ashton, op. cit., p. 229.
[2] See J. Smith, *Memoirs of Wool*, 1747, vol. I, p. 30.
[3] *Health of Towns Commission*, 1845: Yorkshire, p. 19.

equally plain that the creation of 'wants' such as reformers had in mind must be preceded by changes in the system of education and training. Before 'incentives' could become effective there had to be radical changes in the conditions in which the working people had to live.

The merit of high wages was no new idea. It was in fact surprisingly old – surprising, that is, if we accept at their face value the contention that the harsh views on poverty described above went unchallenged. That it was held widely is unlikely. But there were always dissenting voices that softened the rough edges of the tougher brand of social opinion, and some of them were those of the merchant class itself. Josiah Child in his *Discourses* had paid increasing attention in successive editions to the social aspects of poverty. Child had his disciples in the new century. Even Defoe, though he deplored the shiftless drunken habits of the poor, did not favour the low-wage argument. To lower wages would reduce 'the value and goodness of the manufacture', and make them less competitive in world markets. For a nation that depended on the *quality* of its exports, such a result would be disastrous.[1]

The problem of wages and productivity merges at this point with the problem that most thinking men of the early eighteenth century regarded as the most serious of the day; the problem of that conglomerate mass of human misery they called 'the poor'. No controversy of the times is more illuminating than this great 'Debate of the Poor' which fills so much of the social literature of the day. This is the theme which unifies contemporary discussion of the balance of trade, wage levels, charities, above all the manifold and hotly debated proposals for and against workhouses and charity schools. The only conclusion that can be drawn is that a growing body of opinion was forced to believe that the economic growth described in earlier pages had brought no benefit to that large, perhaps still increasing, section of the population called 'the Poor'. The predominantly commercial character of that growth that benefited so handsomely the middle and upper classes had as yet failed, by its very nature, to provide adequately the opportunities for employment which were necessary if the poor were not to live largely off the charity of their own fortunate neighbours. If they could not be absorbed spontaneously, fruitfully, profitably into the economy, how should they be provided for? And if, as some influential writers suggested, the basis of wealth was labour, was it not scandalous folly that the means of wealth should lie idle, dissolute, untrained? But

[1] D. Defoe, *Plan of the English Commerce*, 1728 edn., p. 60.

how to devise incentives? The problem was real and intractable. It is familiar today to all students of backward societies. Did the answer lie in compulsion? Or in educating the poor to more useful employment? The two problems, social and economic, are mingled in almost every controversy of the age. They emphasize, jointly, the extent to which the economic achievement to date had fallen short of the task of utilizing that mass of unemployed or underemployed labour which observers like Gregory King had counted. The proportion of the total heads and hands of the nation – perhaps as much as a third or more – left stranded by progress in 1750 disposes of any lingering fallacy that unemployment is a creation of the Industrial Revolution.

Since the sixteenth century there had been marked indications of a changing attitude to the problems of poverty and charity. In the bad times of the early Stuarts especially, private benefactors had tried to combine their charitable benefactions with specific directions aimed at training the poor – especially the juvenile poor – in socially useful arts. Many charities continued on the old eleemosynary lines – beef or herrings for the poor, linen, woollens; coats, shirts and shifts for poor men, gowns for poor women; Bibles and books for both sexes, young and old. One village got an almshouse, another a fund for coal or bread. But the trend towards more socially constructive purposes was already emerging. Obviously a growing proportion of benefactors felt moved to endow some form of active apprenticeship or instruction for the juvenile poor, as distinct from the passive forms of relief common in earlier times. Such provision was commonly made in many of the numerous trusts endowed, especially by merchants, in London, Bristol, Norwich and other cities.[1] Much has been written of the social irresponsibility and harshness of the mercantile classes, especially after the Restoration. The allegations are not borne out by recently discovered facts. Of Bristol's surviving six hundred charities, about one-third date from the half-century after the Restoration. The thousand-odd trusts in the City of London contained about a third that were created between the Restoration and the Treaty of Utrecht: likewise at Norwich, where there were about a hundred and sixty trusts. It is easy to charge benefactors who founded such schemes as endowed apprenticeships with a desire to augment the supply of cheap labour, with a cunning and ignoble mixture of utilitarianism, self-interest and philanthropy. Such charges cannot be disproved. There was, probably, here as in most human actions, an element of self-interest. The modern habits of

[1] C. Wilson, 'The Other Face of Mercantilism', *Tr. R.H.S.*, 1959.

discriminating between deserving and socially useful beneficiaries may register a spiritual decline when compared with medieval almsgiving that aimed only at the moral betterment of the donor. Again, the historian can only form impressions of men's motives. But he has no right to deny the sincerity of the hundreds of benefactors who tried through private charity to alleviate the most urgent of social·problems by providing useful training. This was, indeed, as the historian of the charity school movement has reminded us, the Age of Benevolence, and its most ambitious philanthropic venture, the charity schools, was in its origin and administration animated by a genuine sense of pity and compassion.[1]

In this, perhaps the most striking social experiment of the century, private donors combined to set up thousands of schools in which hundreds of thousands of children, for whom no other possibility of education existed, received elementary but valuable instruction. Drawing their inspiration from Comenius and the reformers of Milton's circle, their methods came from Locke and on their modest level of reading, writing, arithmetic and handicrafts they gave the juvenile poor a practical education which helped boys to a variety of apprentice-ships, girls to work as domestic servants or sempstresses. From 1699 the movement was coordinated by the Society for the Propagation of the Gospel — a reflection perhaps of Josiah Child's idea of setting up boards of 'Fathers of the Poor' much earlier. Towards the end of the eighteenth century the schools lost both momentum and idealism, turning in some cases into mere juvenile workhouses. But by then they had contributed immeasurably to the social betterment of Britain, and their decline left a gap in the Victorian educational system that was not filled for a long time.

The charity schools themselves came under attack from the dogmatists who were already wedded firmly to the idea that social philanthropy was inherently wrong: a perverted form of self-interest. Mandeville's *Essay on Charity and Charity Schools* (1723), condemned them roundly as the product of the hopes of gain of their tradesmen sponsors who sold supplies to the schools, and of that 'satisfaction which delights mean people in governing others'. But any hostility aroused by the charity schools was negligible compared with the passions that raged round the proposal for workhouses. The Poor Law Act of 1601, codifying existing practice, had provided overseers

[1] M. G. Jones, *The Charity School Movement. A Study of 18th Century Puritanism in Action*, 1938, p. 3.

of the poor with power to set able-bodied paupers to work out of funds raised by the poor rate. The collapse of any central surveillance of social policy at the Restoration left parishes to their own devices, but the rise in the yield of the poor rate signified that parish activity was increasing and accounts in part no doubt for the alleged decline in voluntary private charity. The Law of Settlement (1662) which enabled parishes to eject immigrant paupers has often been taken as a sign of a harsher attitude towards the problem of poverty. This is doubtful. The preamble to the Act made it clear that it arose from the unequal provision made, as between one parish and another, for paupers, so that parishes which tried to do their duty were inundated with distressed paupers from other parishes which were less conscious of their responsibilities. In short, the Act did not arise so much from lack of concern as from the administrative difficulties facing parish governors, and though the enforcement of the Act led to some grievous hardships the system did not invariably work with the rigidity often assumed.[1]

The many schemes to combine poor relief with economic improvement of the Commonwealth period merged into the later proposals put forward from the 1670s by Josiah Child, Robert Harford,[2] John Cary, Francis Brewster, Charles Davenent, down to Jonas Hanway and Joseph Massie in the mid-eighteenth century. All the protagonists of a constructive policy of social relief shared in some measure Brewster's belief that 'the Neglect of the Poor seems the greatest mistake in our government' and applauded the rider that it was national disaster 'to have so many Thousand Poor, who might by their Labours Earn, and so eat our Provisions, and instead of sending them out, export Manufactures, and that would bring in double to the Nation, whatever our Provision doth'.[3]

The logic was plain. The idea that the employable labour of the poor was the nation's secret but unused weapon in the battle for a favourable balance of trade is common to most of the writers of the time. But how was it to be organized? Here opinion split sharply. Proposals for concentrating this labour potential in workhouses roused opposition from employers, ratepayers and philosophers. When Defoe attacked Sir Humphrey Mackworth's plan for parish factories in 1724, he did so on the grounds that this apparently cheap labour would lower the

---

1 E. M. Hampson, *The Treatment of Poverty in Cambridgeshire*, 1934, pp. 126, 267.

2 *Proposals for Building in Every County a Working Almshouse or Hospital, as the Best Expedient to perfect the Trade and Manufactory of Linen Cloth etc.*, 1677, Harl. Miscellany, vol. IV, p. 489.

3 *New Essays on Trade*, 1702, pp. 52, 122.

quality of English manufactures. 'If you expect the poor should work cheaper and not perform their work slighter and more overly (as we call it) and superficially, you expect what is not in the nature of the Thing – This therefore is beginning at the wrong end of Trade.'

Out of the battle between the workhouse enthusiasts and their opponents came a series of local experiments of which the Bristol scheme of 1696 managed by a 'Corporation for the Poor' was the most famous. Within a decade many other towns followed Bristol's lead. Where Mackworth's Bill of 1704 had failed, Sir Edward Knatchbull's Act of 1723 succeeded. This was followed by other Acts for joining parishes together to maintain workhouses. Altogether somewhere between 100 and 200 were established. Then in the mid-fifties the movement came to life again in East Anglia. This time it was Admiral Vernon, the victor of Portobello, who took the initiative in setting up a 'House of Industry' at Nacton, in Suffolk. Numerous 'hundreds' in Norfolk and Suffolk followed suit. In the first flush of enthusiasm the new effort promised well. The new factories (for that is what, amongst other things, they were) spun wool, knitted stockings, made socks, embroidery and lace. But their success was short-lived. As usual the troubles were administrative and human. It was not easy to find reliable officers to take charge of the difficult and disagreeable work of supervising paupers who ranged from able-bodied adults to children, criminals and lunatics. Funds and materials were embezzled. The hope of converting the drain of the poor rate into a profit dwindled and disappeared. Tiring of the failure of their good works, the guardians slipped back to the simpler palliative of outdoor relief. As an experiment in public industry, the 'Houses of Industry' failed because the overseers and officers lacked experience, enterprise and the organizing ability without which their small hand manufactures could not compete against more efficient private enterprise. While one aspect of their work was abandoned in favour of outdoor relief, another was taken over by the private employer. The private factory emerges imperceptibly from antecedents that include the workhouse – the first experiment in organizing labour in concentrated groups. These new factories often with their schools and dormitories for child workers closely resembled the earlier workhouses. Unlike them, they were equipped with machinery – spinning jennies, flying shuttles, power spinning. Unlike them they were made to pay. Their progress in the sixties owed a great deal to the hard times and high food prices which sent employers in search of mechanized means of reducing labour costs and at the same time forced the poor to face the hated prospects of disciplined work in an institution. Behind the mob that roared for Wilkes and Liberty loomed some simple material facts. 'We have', wrote Horace Walpole, 'independent mobs that have nothing to do with Wilkes and who only take advantage of so favourable a season. The dearness of provisions incites, the hope of increase of wages allures, and drink puts them in motion. The coal heavers began [it] and it is well it is not a hard frost, for they have stopped all coals coming to London.' Drunken coal heavers and dockers ('wild Irish boys mostly'), mutinous sailors and sawyers were an old story. Just off the London streets there was always this subterranean half-starved mob ready to riot. But in the sixties the riots were not limited to Spitalfields and Thames side. They spread throughout the Midlands and the north, and the unrest in Massachusetts and Virginia can be traced in part to the same source: the entire English economy and its colonial periphery was having to adjust itself to the conditions of peace, and the process was slow and painful. Yet from the travail was to be delivered a new and vigorous industrial society.[1]

Many who opposed the workhouse system did so on grounds of immediate expense, inconvenience and unfair competition with private industry. Others — and their numbers were increasing — objected on more philosophical grounds. They distrusted philanthropy out of logical principle, and hoped to see society's problems solved by Pope's social equation:

> That REASON, PASSION answer one great aim;
> That true SELF LOVE and SOCIAL are the same.

Here was one of the roots of later social *laissez faire* and the campaign against paternalism. Setting their face against the sumptuary puritanism of middle-class tradesmen for whom the social virtues were thrift and austerity, the new philosophers looked for salvation to that very luxury which was one established fact of contemporary living in the upper reaches of society. Dr Johnson often returned to the theme.

> Many things which are false are transmitted from book to book and gain credit in the world. One of these is the cry against the evil of luxury. Now the truth is, that luxury produces much good. Take the luxury of buildings

[1] For a full account of the Poor Law exponents see Sidney and Beatrice Webb, *English Local Government: English Poor Law History*. Part I. *The Old Poor Law*, London, 1927, ch. 3 *passim*; Wilson, 'The Other Face of Mercantilism', *T.R.H.S.* On the changes of the 1760s, A. H. John, 'Aspects of English Economic Growth in the first half of the Eighteenth Century', *Economica*, May 1961.

in London. Does it not produce real advantage in the conveniency and elegance of accommodation? . . . A man gives half a guinea for a dish of green peas. How much gardening does this occasion? How many labourers must the competition to have such things early in the market keep in employment? You will hear it said, very gravely, why was not the half guinea, thus spent in luxury, given to the poor? To how many might it have afforded a good meal. Alas! Has it not gone to the *industrious* poor, whom it is better to support than the *idle* poor?[1]

In an age of massive social inequalities, when the possibility of widespread mass consumption was still undetected by many, such attempts to rationalize the existing social framework into a solution of society's problems were natural. Yet, whatever was done, by organized charity or otherwise, the solution seemed as far off as ever. The social records of the age are full of the originals of Hogarth's horrific caricatures – Tom Nero, Mother Needham, Tom Idle and the rest. They are all there in the fearful annals of St Giles, Shoreditch, Drury Lane and Alsatia. When the Commons set up a Committee on the Care of the Poor in the Parish of St Martin-in-the-Fields in 1715, they found that 900 of the 1,200 babies born every year in the parish died. Many were exposed or overlaid by women euphemistically described as 'nurses'. Money was stolen, accounts falsified, paupers starved and murdered. When Jonas Hanway, a Russia merchant who helped to promote the Foundling Hospital and other charitable institutions, inquired into fourteen parishes in London, he estimated that the infant death rate in the workhouses set up since 1720 was 88 per cent. Some parishes admitted that 'no infant had lived to be apprenticed from their workhouses'.[2]

Such horrors were real. They have to be assessed against a background of contemporary facts and attitudes. The age was still in many respects barbarous throughout all ranges of society. Hygiene was hardly better amongst the gentry than amongst the poor. Violence was taken for granted. Boys at Eton were treated as brutally as the children in workhouses. Hanging, drawing and quartering was still a popular public spectacle. Men still lived cheek by jowl with death and disease in their most gruesome forms. Even a sensitive man (as Johnson was) had to grow a thick skin to protect himself against terrors that were otherwise unendurable. The other, practical, problem was the physical administration of poor relief. Until the Victorian Age, society understood little of the arts of administration. Large organizations, like the navy, were worked, as

[1] James Boswell, *Life of Johnson*, Oxford, 1927 edn., vol. II, pp. 37–8.
[2] J. H. Hutchins, *Jonas Hanway 1712–86*, 1940, pp. 47–75.

poor relief was, by indirect methods. The absence of a public service meant that almost all problems of large-scale administration were farmed out to contractors, and thereby the evils multiplied. Yet it was in this age that humaner voices were raised and the first fumbling steps towards a better order were taken.

This analysis of the social order helps to explain the persistence of the belief in balance of trade theories and policies. True, by 1752, David Hume had demonstrated, to his own local satisfaction, the absurdity of supposing that a favourable balance was anything more than a will-o'-the-wisp. For was not the economy perfectly self-regulating?

> Suppose four-fifths of all the money in Great Britain to be annihilated in one night — what would be the consequence? Must not the price of all labour and commodities sink in proportion and everything be sold as cheap as they were in former days? What nation could then dispute with us in any foreign market or pretend to navigate or to sell manufactures at the same price which to us would afford sufficient profit? In how little time therefore must this bring back the money which we had lost and raise us to the level of all the neighbouring nations? Where, after we have arrived, we immediately lose the advantage of the cheapness of labour and commodities and the further flowing in of money is stopped by our fullness and repletion.[1]

Intellectually, it is characteristic of the age and the growing partiality for mathematical and logical solutions of economic problems. Adam Smith himself could hardly have said more. Yet in a sense Hume was flogging a dead horse. The preoccupation with bullion flow, with international payments, with the currency, had been the motive force of mercantilist thought down to the Restoration. It was still a powerful element in such administrative moves as the establishment of the Board of Trade and the Office of Inspector General of Customs.[2] But there had been a marked shift of emphasis in contemporary thinking. Pamphleteers were now more interested in the relationship of the balance of trade and the volume of *employment* in Britain. A favourable balance was seen less as a source of bullion than as one yardstick by which men might judge whether manufacturing industry was developing satisfactorily. As the old concern with bullion, with strategic security and power faded concern with the balance of trade as an indicator of social health took its place. The notion was not in itself novel. The idea of increasing and diversifying employment was discernible in Mun and a number of his contemporaries. It assumes

1 David Hume, *Essays: Of the Balance of Trade*, 1752.
2 See G. N. Clark, *Guide*, pp. 2, 4.

much more importance in the writings of the eighteenth-century publicists. It was more characteristic of the times that most of them sought the solution of the leading social problem of the times through a regulated system of trade than that a few were losing faith in economic regulation of any kind. Few writers could pluck up their courage to abandon their belief in the importance of the balance of trade altogether. Although his logic pointed towards total economic freedom, Mandeville could enjoin statesmen that 'above all, they'll keep a watchful eye over the Balance of Trade in general and never suffer that all the Foreign Commodities together, that are imported in one year, shall exceed in value what of their own growth or manufacture is in the same exported to others'.[1] Defoe, who has sometimes been credited with precocious ideas on free trade, was in fact a thoroughgoing mercantilist who campaigned against an economic system that encouraged fine ladies to wear 'fine Massulapatam, Chints, Indian damasks, China atlasses, and an innumerable number of rich silks, the product of the coast of Malabar, Coromandel and the Bay of Bengal . . .' while the poor wore calico and 'our woollen industry languished, the poor want bread and butter and the nation is beggared'.[2] A score of other writers put the relationship between the balance of trade and the social welfare of the nation into more generalized form. The novel factor was an increased emphasis on the need for cheaper capital at lower rates of interest, and along with this the need to absorb the poor into the economic workings of society.[3] The transition from the older mercantilist thinking to the new is clearly visible in the title of the fifth of the *New Essays of Trade* (1702) by Sir Francis Brewster, Lord Mayor of Dublin: *That the full Imployment of All Hands in the Nation is the surest way and means to bring Bullion into the Kingdom.* Davenant pushed the argument a stage further in his *Essay upon the Probable Methods of Making a People Gainers in the Balance of Trade.* 'The bodies of men are without doubt the most valuable Treasure of a Country . . . *ordinary* people are serviceable to the country's wealth as the *rich* if they are employed in honest labour and useful arts . . . being more in number do more contribute to encrease the nation's wealth.' In the writings of John Cary, the Bristol merchant and philanthropist, republished twice in 1719 and 1745, translated into French in 1755

[1] Bernard Mandeville, *The Fable of the Bees, or Private Vices, Publick Benefits*, ed. F. B. Kaye, 1924, vol. I, p. 116.

[2] D. Defoe, *An Humble Proposal to the People of England*, vol. XVIII of *Novels and Miscellaneous Works*, 1841, p. 45.

[3] See *supra*, Chapter Eleven.

and into Italian in 1764, the argument was given a novel twist: that some trades were 'profitable to the nation' and should be encouraged, others were not and should be repressed. The criterion of judgement was no longer the effect of the trade balance on the flow of treasure or money but on the development of manufacture and employment and national prosperity inaugurated a new phase of what might be called 'social mercantilism'. It was to have a powerful influence outside as well as in England and its close correspondence with the ideas of the founding fathers of *Kameralwissenschaft* in Germany and Austria, and the very similar ideas of the later Neapolitan economists, is direct, not accidental. Joseph Becher and von Schroeder both lived in England after the Restoration. Sonnenfels's idea of the double trade balance — the 'monetary' and the 'employment' balances — comes directly from Cary. So does Genovesi's distinction between 'harmful' and 'useful' commerce, which sprang from his translation of Cary's *Essay*. These writers represented the 'underdeveloped areas' of the day. They were peculiarly conscious of the need to stimulate economic development by regulation and intervention.[1] But it was in England that the idea received its fullest expression in institutional form in the fiscal arrangements perfected by Walpole after the Bubble. There is little difference in principle between the basic ideas behind the protectionism and stimuli that became the leading characteristics of eighteenth-century economic statesmanship and those adopted by almost every European state from the 1930s onwards. The arguments for and against them remain much the same today as in the earlier centuries. They could claim to be dynamic, in the sense that they were a necessary means of effecting the transition from an agrarian society to a society based on a wider, more advanced and more profitable form of technology. Without them, new industries might not have taken root at all. But the errors were many. They sometimes encouraged hot-house growths that could not, in any circumstances, survive. Hare-brained projects received attention they did not deserve. Industries protected too long became lazy and inefficient. In societies where government was often insulated against opinion, criticism and public protest, abuses multiplied, lobbying and corruption became a normal method by which vested interests bought courts, politicians and bureaucrats for their own ends. Administrative offices were a tempting source of profit and political influence. There was force in the practical as well as in the theoretical objections urged by later eighteenth-century

[1] C. Wilson, op. cit., *Tr. R.H.S.*, 1959, pp. 97–9.

reformers. Yet it is impossible to read the later mercantilists, or to examine the system constructed from the interplay of interests with their ideas, without being impressed by the vitality and intelligence that they brought to bear on economic affairs as much as by the imperfections in their thinking.

Again, here and there, one glimpses doubts about the conventional theory that international trade was rooted in conflict and competitive force: that one state could only prosper at the expense of others. Hume's protest has often been quoted: 'I shall therefore venture to acknowledge that, not only as a man, but as a British subject, I pray for the flourishing commerce of Germany, Spain, Italy and even France itself.'[1] Such convictions were to be increasingly important, though even in their Victorian heyday, whatever economists might say or believe, statesmen never abandoned their concern for the balance of trade and the need of trade for physical defence.[2] Characteristically, the popular arguments for more commercial freedom and less monopoly were not based on logic or philosophy but on expediency. A pamphlet written by a 'Sincere Well-Wisher to the Trade and Prosperity of Great Britain' (in fact Josiah Tucker, Canon of Bristol and later Dean of Gloucester) in 1750 was entitled *Reflections on the Expediency of Opening the Trade to Turkey*. It was an attack on the monopoly of the Turkey Company on the grounds that by narrowing the outlet for trade the company was restricting exports and reducing manufactures, employment, shipping and national wealth. This empirical approach to economic problems was still more typical of popular thought than the philosophy of Hume or those physiocratic ideas discussed in 'the first political economy club in the world' by Adam Smith and others in the 1740s. For most people the virtues of a larger degree of economic freedom were still practical, not doctrinal. Equally, the eighteenth century did not witness anything like a complete divorce of liberalism and humanitarianism from the basic principles of power politics inherent in mercantilism. The majority of the social reformers and economic campaigners maintained their belief in the need for British power. Sea power especially was still the foundation of prosperity. Jonas Hanway, the most prolific and passionate of all the early humanitarians, could not bring himself to put his faith in the intelligent or moral interest of the nations in peace and

[1] D. Hume, *Of the Jealousy of Trade*.
[2] See Lord Keynes, *General Theory of Employment, Interest and Money*, 1936, Appendix on 'Mercantilism'; Gallagher and Robinson, 'The Imperialism of Free Trade', *Econ. Hist. Rev.*, VI, no. 1.

order: ' . . . more Kings are kept in awe by the combinations which are formed to restrain each other's passions and support an independency than by any sense of the moral duties arising from the common duties of mankind as founded in their original constitution . . . strength and power are the best rights of the sovereignties of countries.'[1] One of his works was dedicated to Anson, hero of the recent contest with Spain. Its theme remained the old inter-dependence of profit and power. 'The splendour of this Monarchy is supported by commerce and commerce by naval strength.'[2] There could be no divorce of nationalism and social welfare so long as an aggressive merchant body remained the largest generating force of wealth, private charity and economic ideas. Pragmatism remained the order of the day till after 1763.

[1] *Historical Account of the British Trade on the Caspian Sea*, 1744, vol. I, p. 421.
[2] Ibid., vol. II, p. 7.

Epilogue

IN RETROSPECT

EVEN at the end of the Seven Years War, the industrialized society was still largely in the future. The process by which it was to emerge – the contrapuntal interweaving of diverse but local economic themes into a national pattern of growth – was only just beginning. Yet the material for the later economic fugue was already present. Previous chapters have shown that the processes by which the economy was unified, diversified and expanded were not smooth. On the contrary they were jerky and discontinuous. The general movement of growth was punctuated by short, sharp crises like those of the 1620s and 1690s. But it was slowed down also by much longer pauses, like that which lasted from the 1720s to the 1740s, when all the forces of growth seemed weak. Always the forces of mobility and growth were balanced against the forces of inertia, the forces of enterprise against those of custom. This was still so in 1763.

Inventive ingenuity was abundant amongst a diversity of craftsmen – blacksmiths, clock makers, millwrights. Mathematical and elementary chemical knowledge of an empirical kind were already making their impact felt on the manufacture of instruments and textiles. Power for industry still meant, in the main, the water power that drove the small but spreading number of factories or mills like Lombe's silk mill at Derby; but the use of Newcomen's steam engine in the coal and tin mines pointed the way to an alternative. Mechanical inventions to increase output were widely used in the textile industries, but for the most part they were hand-operated. Neither Kay's flying shuttle to improve the weaving process nor Paul's invention intended to do the same for spinning had yet had much effect. The bulk of the textile industry still worked on the domestic system, dispersed and still essentially rural. Even the marked industrial expansion of the 1750s was achieved largely within the confines of the traditional economic organization: essentially, by multiplying the number of existing units of production and applying doses of fresh labour, and by borrowing processes (like dyeing) that were not in themselves new but added substantially to the profitability of the textile industries. This gain in momentum everywhere owed much to the abundant supply of enterprise, the growing numbers of capitalists with a keen eye to openings for profitable markets and the ability to organize production so as to follow market trends and satisfy the whims of fashion. Yet if some of the factors in large-scale production were still lacking — good internal transport for example — there were already signs that home markets as well as overseas markets were beginning to stimulate output.[1] Increased textile manufacture was already creating demand for the metal and fuel needed for machines and engines and this was reacting on the production of coal. The demand for skilled and unskilled labour was rising. Here and there production was already being concentrated in factories by men who were industrial rather than merchant capitalists — the Lombes at Derby from 1724, Wedgwood's first factory at Burslem in 1759, Boulton's at Soho in 1762. These were sizable establishments even by later standards, employing anything from 300 to 600 men. Typical as yet they were not: but the student of economic history must always balance against his measurements of averages the claims of innovation. If he must never cease to ask (in Sir John Clapham's words) 'How large? How long? How often? How representative?'[2] he must equally never forget the basic truth: *Ex glande quercus.*

To explain the remarkable if uneven economic growth of the period in the terms sometimes applied to earlier and later periods is not easy. There was no spectacular price rise such as has been invoked to explain the economic expansion of the sixteenth century. On the contrary, price levels were unusually stable, with only sporadic rises sufficient to cancel out sporadic falls.[3] But far from stifling economic enterprise, these problems of the market seem to have stimulated it, accelerating the quest for new markets for new products. In short, the price factor could work both ways. Another older explanation of the later industrial changes — the development of inventions in a new type of productive organization — can as yet have had insufficient effect to explain more than a part of the rise in production and trade. Was

[1] For details of the renewed upsurge of trade and industry between 1745 and 1763 see Deane and Cole, *British Economic Growth* . . ., chs. I and II *passim*.

[2] 'Economic History as a Discipline', *Encyc. of the Social Sciences*, vol. V, 1930, pp. 327–30.

[3] See Phelps, Brown and Hopkins, op. cit.,

there anything in the larger context of the nation's affairs that provided the opportunities or pressures that led to expansion?

First, it is easy to overlook the simple fact of geography. England,
on the edge of the western seaboard, was an integral part of the North
Sea economy, well placed to become the centre of the new Atlantic
economy that grew rapidly in the seventeenth century. The centre of
gravity of this rapidly changing area down to the middle of that century
was the Dutch Republic, far ahead of the rest of Europe in almost
every economic technique. One does not have to read much of the
abundant economic literature of the century, nor to examine many of
the advances in technology, commercial methods or public and
private finance to realize that much of England's progress had been
achieved by a simple process of borrowing from the Dutch. The essence
of much of the so-called 'mercantilist' literature was to commend a
programme of deliberate imitation of the Dutch, combined with
policies to protect the nascent economy from the effects of their powerful competition. From the time of Alva's persecutions until late in the
seventeenth century English industry was able to draw on the special
skills of entrepreneurs and craftsmen from the Netherlands. There is
hardly a branch of manufacture where we cannot identify technological
innovations, often individual innovators, from across the North Sea.
Agricultural innovators drew on the same source. And when this
stream of immigrants dwindled and fell away, the process was continued by another immigrant stream, this time the Huguenots from
Normandy, Guienne, and the Rhône Valley. The seas that divided
England from the Continent geographically were not a barrier but a
highway along which flowed not only a stream of goods but of people
and ideas. Slowly the centre of Europe's economic gravity shifted from
the Netherlands to England. Many factors contributed to the movement. They included the strategic control that England possessed in her
North Sea and Channel ports and bases, the naval power that made
this potential actual during the Dutch wars, and the increasingly
effective Navigation policy. But the process might have been longer
and more difficult without the access of economic skill that came from
foreign immigrants. Proximity to Europe offered England a rich harvest
of economic opportunity. Seventeenth-century Englishmen reaped and
gathered it abundantly.

Recent historians have assigned a less fundamental place to the
influence of taxation on the economic destiny of nations than was at
one time fashionable. Probably today we err in underestimating it.

Contemporaries grumbled against taxation of all kinds, and rioted against the excise which was especially reviled as a tax on popular consumption. The economic observers of the late seventeenth century could find little to cheer them when they surveyed the general superiority of their Dutch rivals except one thing: the burden that the excise placed upon producers, workers and consumers alike in that country. Gregory King thought that for every pound sterling paid in taxes by an average Englishman, a Dutchman paid three pounds.[1] The mid-eighteenth century saw the earlier neat balance of the tax burden in England between direct taxation on property and indirect taxation on trade and consumption to some extent upset. The steep rise in the public debt and the interest payable on it raised customs to the point where widespread smuggling became profitable, and general tax evasion a national habit. Even so, compared with every other fiscal system in Europe, the English remained relatively well devised and well administered. It did not strangle trade and industry with impossibly high costs, nor provoke deep social dissensions by its injustice. The two functions of revenue raising and the protection of home industry were as yet combined without apparent damage to the economy. Indeed, it could be argued that they were among the enabling conditions of its expansion.

Of the so-called 'pressures', the most debated is the pressure of population. Here, too, the period witnessed nothing like the rate of increase in numbers that was to occur after 1760. There had been, as we have seen, substantial additions to the population in the sixteenth and in the earlier and later seventeenth centuries. During the first half of the eighteenth century the movement seems to have been suspended until the 1740s at the earliest.[2] By a process of migration, mostly local, some of the surplus population of the countryside was being drawn into the new inland towns and growing seaports; just as men had, over a longer period and perhaps over larger distances, been steadily drawn to London. Almost everything about the early population problems, except the fact of general increase, remains doubtful and hypothetical. Some elementary principles can nevertheless be outlined. The size of a population in a given period is determined, if we exclude the factors of immigration and emigration, by the relation between the numbers of those who are born and of those who die. Immigration there

---

[1] See 'Taxation and the Decline of Empires: an Unfashionable Theme', a paper presented to the Royal Netherlands Historical Society at Utrecht, November 1962.

[2] P. Deane and W. A. Cole, op. cit., see pp. 6 and 103 for estimates.

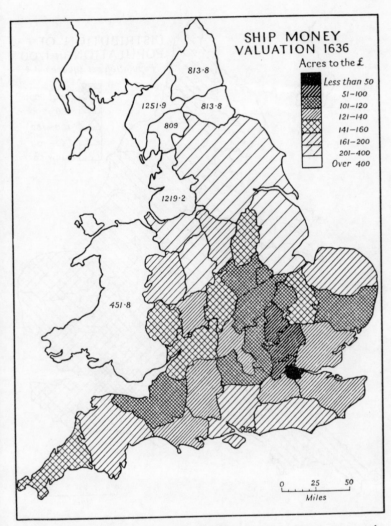

An approximate distribution of population in the first half of the 17th century may be inferred from this map which is based on the table in J. E. T. Rogers, *A History of Agriculture and Prices in England 1259-1793* (7 vols., 1866-1902), V, 104-5.

From Darby, *Historical Geography of England*, Cambridge University Press.

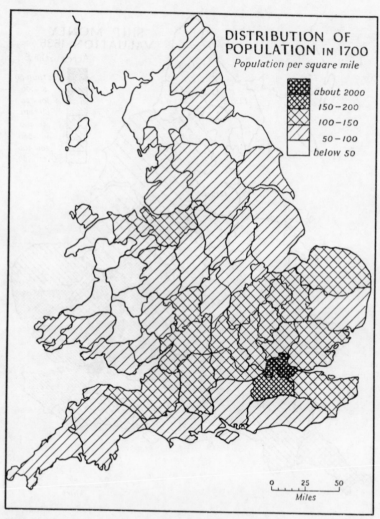

DISTRIBUTION OF
POPULATION IN 1700
Population per square mile

about 2000
150 – 200
100 – 150
50 – 100
below 50

0   25   50
Miles

This map is based on estimates contained in the 1811 Census Report, pp. xxviii–xxx. The distribution shown is only very approximate but the general impression is certainly correct: a broad well-settled belt astride a line joining Bristol and London: the north-west and Norfolk already showing rather higher densities than the other counties outside this belt.

From Darby, *Historical Geography of England*, Cambridge University Press.

certainly was, especially of Irish, who provided a supply of labour in the western ports and London, but this was counterbalanced by emigration to the colonies, and the final result must remain a matter of conjecture. The main attention of students of the subject has been focused on the birth and death rates as the principal determinants of population change. When, in the later eighteenth century, economists like Adam Smith, Malthus and Rickman came to examine the phenomenon, their main (though not sole) preoccupation was with births. John Rickman, a dutiful civil servant who worked on the first census figures of 1801, produced estimates of the population of England and Wales which suggested an increase from 5·5 million to 6·7 million between 1700 and 1760. A colleague, Finlaison, produced a table suggesting an increase of 5·1 to 6·5 for the same period. A twentieth-century scholar corrected these figures to 5·8 and 6·7 respectively. Population, along with many other things, was clearly beginning to grow again by the mid-century, but — as yet — slowly.[1] With population statistics, as with others of the time, we have to rely on calculations that were a by-product of other activities. Just as trade figures were a by-product of the taxation process, births, deaths and marriage records were a by-product of religious belief or public health policy. A proportion of all three must have escaped official notice. Some were too poor to inter their dead with religious ceremony. Babies born to pauper women in institutions were 'exposed' or overlaid by so-called nurses. *Pace* the optimism of some historians, it is difficult to believe that the 'statistics' can adequately reflect the social movements of such casual times.

Twentieth-century studies have nevertheless revealed one major factor to which eighteenth- and nineteenth-century students paid much less attention. From 1710 to 1720 the birth rate drew away slightly from the death rate. From the late 1730s, the divergence becomes even more marked; so that by the 1760s, while the death rate had fallen from over 33 deaths per 1,000 in 1730 to 26–27, the birth rate had risen from its lowest point of 28 per 1,000 in 1710 to over 33 per 1,000. Not all historians have felt able to accept the conclusion that the falling death rate must be regarded as 'the main cause' of the population increase.[2] For a century after 1720 the birth rate itself was remarkably high and buoyant. While the falling death rate must therefore remain an

[1] G. Talbot Griffith, *Population Problems of the Age of Malthus*, 1926, ch. I.

[2] Talbot Griffith, op. cit., p. 42; see also the diagram on p. 43. See also P. Deane and W. Cole, op. cit., for the most recent discussion and recapitulation of the whole population problem, pp. 122–35.

outstanding factor in the situation, the forces that kept the birth rate up seem as important as those which sent the death rate down.[1] Pushing the argument a stage further, one more recent authority has reverted to the older view, suggesting that 'the acceleration of population growth was primarily the result of specifically economic changes, and in particular of an increase in the demand for labour'.[2]

This argument for the primacy of the birth rate rests on the assumption that changes in the economic and social structure of England were making earlier marriage possible to a growing number of men and women. As the restrictive influences of formal apprenticeship weakened, as people moved into towns to earn higher wages at an earlier age, as more cottages were built in the countryside, the old inhibitions against early marriage (it is suggested) were removed, and the potential child-bearing period in a married woman's life was lengthened. Such assumptions have received support from more detailed regional inquiries which suggest that the number of marriages increased decisively after 1745 in, for example, Nottinghamshire, where slow-moving but powerful agricultural changes seem to have been amongst the generating forces of a demographic revolution. In Ireland, it has been argued that the steep rise of population was mainly due to a higher birth rate and this came from the greater ease with which a man could marry and raise a family on a very small acreage of potatoes.[3] If such experience were to be proved general, the old assumption that agricultural change led to depopulation would be shown to be wrong. Enclosure, so far from reducing rural numbers, could be shown to have released the countryside from the brake of the law that ruled 'no land, no marriage' and forced younger sons to stay celibate or emigrate.

Such theories have persuasive support. They are attractive to the historian with a natural wish to relate population increase to economic causes in a way not only plausible and logical but visibly rooted in the changing economic conditions of the time. What is more, they suggest in themselves a possible reason for the decreased death rate: for if the number of births rose, the age composition of the population

---

[1] See T. H. Marshall, 'The Population Problem during the Industrial Revolution', reprinted in *Essays in Economic History*, ed. Carus Wilson, 1954, p. 306.

[2] H. J. Habakkuk, 'Population in the 18th Century', *Econ. Hist. Rev.*, VI, no. 2, 1953. J. T. Krause, 'Changes in English Fertility and Mortality 1781–1850', *Econ. Hist. Rev.*, XI, no. 1, 1958, takes a similar view of the later period.

[3] K. H. Connell, *The Population of Ireland*, 1950, p. 240; J. D. Chambers, 'Enclosure and Labour Supply in the Industrial Revolution', *Econ. Hist Rev.*, V, no. 3, 1953.

would move in the direction of a younger population with (presumably) better chance of survival.

Yet where so much of the evidence is speculative, it would be rash to suppose that the debate is at an end. Admittedly, some of the reasoning put forward to justify the prime importance of the fall in the death rate has been hasty. Scholars have attributed an efficacy to human skill and medical progress that is almost certainly premature and exaggerated. It is improbable that improved medical skill did much directly to prolong life in the eighteenth century. That once much-favoured explanation of the decline in mortality – the reduced amount of gin drinking – is now less regarded.[1] But let us admit that the Act of 1751 that tightened up licensing laws and combined this with enforceable duties may have helped to reduce mortality. Better hygiene and more plentiful and varied supplies of food cannot be eliminated from the general if slow improvement of the social context which may have fortified men against diseases. Cheaper and more plentiful coal kept homes warmer and may have helped to prolong life young and old. But quite outside such ecological changes were those changes in the nature and impact of certain diseases which had been, in earlier times, killers on a mass scale. Those with personal or family recollections of the seventeenth century pointed to two major changes which they believed to have been decisive. Until the evidence is sifted more carefully than it has been, their opinion cannot be ignored. When Macaulay took Southey to task for an unwarrantably gloomy view of the new industrial age, he invited his readers to take account of the decline in disease and violence.

> Let them take into account the sweating sickness and the plague. Let them take into the account that fearful disease which first made its appearance in the generation to which Mr Southey assigns the palm of felicity and raged through Europe with a fury at which the physicians stood aghast and before which the people were swept away by myriads. Let them consider the state of the northern counties constantly the scene of robberies, rapes, massacres and conflagrations. Let them add to all this the fact that seventy two thousand persons suffered death by the hands of the executioner during the reign of Henry the Eighth. . . .[2]

Allowing for a measure of Whig rhetoric, the arguments were not contemptible. Plague, the greatest killer, had gone from Europe by 1700, not through better medicine but because the brown rat had

---

[1] See J. D. Chambers, op. cit., ch. III.
[2] *Essays*, 1854, vol. I, p. 260.

replaced the black rat through which the disease had spread. What the sweating sickness was we do not know, nor why it disappeared. Nor how the virulence of venereal disease lessened after its first onset. Nor the fortunes of the many other bacteria associated with epidemics – typhus, smallpox, dysentery, diphtheria and influenza. Nor the real nature of the 'relapsing fever' that struck London in the late twenties, nor the 'nervous, hysteric and putrid fevers' that ravaged the poor in Yorkshire and Devon at the same time.[1] Nor, with any precision at all, how the decline of casual or organized violence affected mortality as society became more orderly. Did the behaviour of some germs and viruses change by processes organic to themselves? Or did the causes of such outbreaks lie in starvation diets? We can only remember to ask such questions; they are not less important because they cannot be answered precisely.

Similarly with infant mortality. A verse on a tomb in a Monmouthshire church commemorates four eighteenth-century babies. Three died when they were six weeks old, the fourth in its seventh week:

> Ere sorrow, care or sin they knew,
> Their spotless souls from hence withdrew
> Just peep'd and uttered infant cries,
> Dislik'd the scene and shut their eyes,
> Shrank back from such a world as this
> To live in Realms of endless bliss.

Examples could be multiplied by the thousand. Perceval, the Manchester doctor, believed that half the children born in London before the 1770s died before they were two; in Manchester, the same proportion before they were five. When Johnson consoled Boswell on the loss of a child he reminded him that 'to keep 3 out of 4 is more than your share. Mrs Thrale has but 4 out of 11'. Before the 1730s, the deaths of children below the age of two were not recorded. Can we be sure that contemporaries were wrong in their belief that infant mortality was on the decline? It seems reasonable that even the slow beginnings of a more humane attitude to life, child life especially, in a slightly less insecure economic context, would reduce the 'overlaying', exposure and near-infanticide of more pinched and barbarous times. A child life saved was the equivalent of an extra birth, far more potent for the future than the prolongation of an old life.

Until the evidence becomes clear it seems wise to keep an open mind on the relative importance of the birth and death rates; allowing that

[1] See Chambers, op. cit., p. 29.

there may have been areas of rural England where conditions approximated to those of Ireland, and others where a fall in mortality was the dominant influence. The most recent writers on this subject have indeed cautioned us against seeking 'a single explanation of population change'.[1] An old city like London – dirty, disease-ridden, picaresque – naturally had a very high death rate as late as the mid-eighteenth century. Even a higher-than-average birth rate was not high enough to counteract the effects of disease and crime. The major force here after about 1750 was probably therefore the decline in mortality. But outside London – in the north-west of England, for example – very different conditions prevailed. Here, round 1700, both birth and death rates were relatively low. From 1710 to 1750 the main feature was a steep rise in births. Even the increase of deaths in the 1720s and 1730s did not wipe out the surplus of births over deaths, and by the mid-century this region enjoyed a sustained period of growth. Whether the increased numbers of children were due to earlier marriage, or to more fertile marriages, or even to illegitimacy, we do not know. We can guess that the rising tide of economic activity in the hinterland of ports like Liverpool or in the new manufacturing areas of the Midlands, created a demand for labour, raising wages on its way. This in turn may have encouraged earlier marriage. Larger population created the demand for food and goods. So the spiral rose.[2]

The issue – birth rate or death rate – is not merely a quibble of the demographic experts. It must influence powerfully our view of the economic changes that were already taking place and were to accelerate in subsequent decades. Population, it may be agreed, could be a cause, as well as an effect, of economic change. The view that the increase of numbers was merely 'the response to an increase in skill'[3] has its dangers. For it may lessen the dimensions of a social problem already acute *before* the Industrial Revolution. The population may well have increased by 50 per cent or more between 1600 and 1760, presenting a still pretty inflexible economy with a pauper problem insoluble within the terms of private or even organized philanthrophy. It is not altogether easy to reconcile this increase with the explanation of a rising birth rate conceived in terms of a later period of more rapid technological change and expansion. Many countries in Asia, and some in Europe, including Ireland, were to face the threat of 'Asiatic standards' imposed on those who suffer a great population increase without adjusting their economic

[1] Deane and Cole, op. cit., p. 126.   [2] Ibid., pp. 134, 135.
[3] A. M. Carr-Saunders, *The Population Problem*, 1922, p. 308.

system to the new demands for food, clothing and work. In short, the existence of the pauper problem *before* the Industrial Revolution underlines the truth that population is only a potential factor in economic growth. Given enterprise and the social framework within which it can operate, a growing population could provide the labour and the purchasing power necessary to maintain and improve its own condition. Without either, great numbers could remain simply useless mouths and hands, standards of living decline into standards of dying.

Aggregate increases or decreases are not the only important aspect of the population problem. Contemporaries could indeed live in total ignorance of such movements, fearing decline when in fact they were in the middle of growth. What they could see was local change. In 1700 only Bristol and Norwich had over 20,000 inhabitants. Birmingham and Glasgow probably contained 10–15,000. In general, towns of 5,000 or more comprised only 13 per cent of Britain's people. By 1760 the proportion had begun to rise. London's growth had slowed down, but Birmingham, Glasgow and Manchester had joined Bristol and Norwich in the 20,000 group. The transatlantic trade had trebled Liverpool's population by 1740, and the metal industries had quadrupled Birmingham's by 1760. The patterns of life of later industrial England were beginning, if but dimly, to appear.

One of the best established generalizations of the *laissez-faire* school of economic historians was the value of that economic freedom achieved during our period; the growing freedom of industry from gild restriction, from state paternalism, from internal tolls and barriers, from legal barriers between classes that characterized France, Germany, Italy and Spain. 'The economic historian', a great historian wrote, 'has to observe the gradual disentanglement of the economic motive from other motives with which it is at first blended, its early operation in the limited area of the civic economy, and its gradual permeation of the larger areas of the national and the world economy, by which the liberty of the individual has been enlarged and the wealth of nations increased.'[1] There is no need to challenge the assumption that England gained enormously by the much earlier achievement of this economic freedom and the appreciation of the nature and value of economic activity. A relatively high degree of social mobility, an unusually flexible system of national government capable of blending private mercantile interest with fiscal need, a rapid exploitation of sea transport, an effective and relatively equitable system of national taxation and a

[1] George Unwin, *Studies in Economic History*, ed. R. H. Tawney, 1927, p. 36.

well-managed public credit, all combined to weld Britain into a national economy at a time when most other states were still divided by internal barriers and by the relics of a medieval social and political system. Wealth in England brought its own rewards, including social prestige and political influence; it was burdened with few disadvantages. Yet economic progress was far from being the pursuit of easy profits by the capitalist. Each step forward represented the conquest of a problem – Dutch competition, food shortage, labour shortage, the burden of debt created by landowners and by governments. The weapons used in each contest were those of applied intelligence and enterprise. The entrepreneur was increasingly free to exercise his wit, ingenuity and resource to follow the market, organize new methods of production, change the type of goods he manufactured according to the needs of the day. Already before the Industrial Revolution and the general spread of the factory system and the new inventions, there were signs of the 'new man' in the north and Midlands: a family like the Crowleys, Quaker ironmasters, of London tradesmen stock, were manufacturers on a vast scale by the 1720s with a fortune of a quarter of a million that brought them on a level with the bigger city merchants and financiers who had hitherto dominated the business scene. Enterprise had increasingly been combined with an interest in scientific innovation, often rudimentary and naive but never contemptible. More than once in the period – in the 1620s, the 1690s, and the 1720s – it seemed as if the surge of inventive talent might carry industry through the barrier of customary methods to achieve revolutionary results. But the countervailing forces of custom or inertia were as yet too strong, the necessary social concomitants as yet too weak. Not till the 1750s did the average annual grant of patents exceed eight, and the steep continuous climb of invention finally begin. At last the inventor was in a social context congenial and stimulating to his talents. The Society for the Encouragement of Arts, Manufactures and Commerce (1754) symbolized the new and quickened spirit of inquiry and research. Although by later standards industry remained to a large extent empirical, some of the new men, like Matthew Boulton and Josiah Wedgwood, numbered contemporary mathematicians and scientists among their friends. Journals, encyclopaedias, dictionaries and yearbooks recorded technical advances and described economic and industrial processes. Some of the inventions were specifically directed to the saving of labour or the reduction of labour costs. The London Society of Arts offered a prize in 1760 for a spinning machine, observing that 'manufacturers of woollen, linen, and cotton find it extremely difficult in the summer season when the spinners are at harvest work to procure a sufficient number of hands'.[1]

How far the varying costs of borrowing money affected the rate of industrial progress can only be conjectured. The general tendency was for the long-term rate of interest (as indicated by the yield of interest on the Funds) to fall until the Seven Years War. The *price* of government stocks rose accordingly. A holder could therefore often realize his invested capital at a gain if he wanted to use it for industrial investment. The contrary effect was seen in 1757 when Jedediah Strutt found that a friend could not lend him money to finance a newly invested stocking frame because it meant selling his holding in the Funds at a loss.[2] The war had temporarily sent up the rate of interest, so that the price of existing stocks had fallen. But over the previous hundred years the trend of interest rates was downwards, as technical and financial improvements did much to dehoard capital and make it mobile. Much industry was financed from its own profits. The Walkers of Rotherham, iron masters, ploughed back their profits rigorously into their business in the forties and fifties.[3] So no doubt did many others. Upon larger, especially public, enterprises, the cost of borrowing probably had a substantial effect in deciding men for or against particular undertakings. It has sometimes been assumed that the Bubble Act, passed in the revulsion of 1720 against companies, transferable stocks and those who juggled with them, inhibited industrial progress. Certainly the prejudice against large companies persisted. Adam Smith could doubt their ability to carry on business efficiently. 'Negligence and profusion [he wrote] must always prevail more or less in the management of [their] affairs.' But most businesses could run their affairs on the resources of a partnership; where larger resources were needed, the lawyers managed to mould the partnership into the unincorporated association, with devices for transferring shares and sometimes limiting the legal liability of partners for debt. Thus any harmfully restrictive effects the Bubble Act might have had were circumvented. The foundations of the modern business company were laid.[4]

[1] See the graph of patents on p. 3 of A. and N. Clow, *The Chemical Revolution*, 1952.
[2] Dr Pressnell's chapter on 'The Rate of Interest in the 18th century', in *Studies in the Industrial Revolution*, ed. Pressnell, p. 184.
[3] A. H. John, ed., *The Walker Family Iron Founders and Lead Manufacturers, 1741–1893*, 1951, Introduction, p. v.
[4] A. B. Dubois, *The English Business Company after the Bubble Act 1720–1800*, 1938, pp. 1–38 and *passim*.

The period had seen England emerge from the stage when its financial arrangements were dictated by its condition as 'a parcellated jumble of little-related economic regions'.[1] If it did not yet possess a fully integrated money market, it is nevertheless difficult to exaggerate the effects of banking and of government investment. Jointly they redistributed purchasing power between the different sectors of the economy on a massive scale. They were important too as an educational factor. They had made men with money to spare familiar with the idea of investment, and the various loans that went to make up the National Debt gave investors a yardstick by which they could judge the relative profitability of alternative ways of employing their money. 'It seems safe to say that the rate of interest entered into a significant proportion of decisions to undertake economic activity.'[2] To go further than this is difficult. Lower rates of interest might help some entrepreneurs, some industries. But the point cannot be pressed too far. The falling rate of interest can no more be turned into a *deus ex machina* than population, invention or any other factor. It did not prevent the decline and virtual extinction of other old and well-established industries like the Old Draperies, or the Devonshire serge industry.

The expanding agriculture, trade and industry described in these pages was contained within a regulated economy. As the machinery of gild organization that had formerly controlled the organization of trade and industry withered away, it was replaced by new forms of regulation by the State. Characteristically, this was focused not on domestic production or trade (as it was in France) but on those commercial transactions that took place at the national frontiers. Industrial and social matters — standards of manufacture, conditions of labour, to some extent wages — were increasingly left to the play of market forces. The object, only gradually attained, was to control the movements of raw materials and manufactures in what was assumed to be the interest not only of specific individuals and companies but of the State as a whole. The *criteria* by which such controls were judged were modified as time went on. From the acquisition of bullion, interest shifted away gradually to industrial and commercial development, with a growing emphasis on social ends, especially the creation of employment.

The so-called mercantilist 'doctrines' were not in origin abstract or·

[1] Pressnell, op. cit., p. 203.
[2] Ibid., p. 210.

373

generalized. Their authors were for the most part practical men of business, not philosophers or economists. Their observations were provoked by the recurrent depressions in trade that occurred especially in the 1620s and 1630s, the late 1640s and 1690s. Mercantilist economics have for that reason been described as 'the economics of crisis'. Yet the articulate merchant like Mun or Child did more than merely apostrophize the image of his own immediate interests. In considering his own immediate problems he was drawn to consider the general context within which he and others like him had to operate. Imperfect as these economic arguments often were logically, they are not to be dismissed as merely ignorant, or illogical, or ineffective. No other European country can point to a contemporary economic literature so rich in ideas, so comprehensive or articulate within the limits imposed by the conditions in which it was produced. Alongside a system of government which allowed the merchant interest to petition, advise but not to dictate to government, it must be allowed to have played its part in shaping a system of economic policies which was appropriate to existing circumstances, successful in many of its objects and far ahead of most other such contemporary systems as an example of applied intelligence. The ministers and servants of the Crown, like Downing, who did most to put these ideas into legislative and administrative form, rarely accepted the petitioner's proposals *in toto*. Sometimes they rejected them. They cannot, that is to say, be regarded as mere puppets of a mercantile community which was itself fragmented into a score of warring factions. With the prestige they enjoyed, the Royal advisers could pick and choose between the petitioners' claims, and generally they chose and shaped their programme with a shrewd eye to the wider interests of the nation. Thus Downing, the architect of the Navigation Code, was the friend of the rising colonial companies and traders, the critic of the shipbuilder, no friend to the Merchant Adventurers and the sworn enemy of the bankers. The clash and ferment of economic ideas reflected the freedom of a society where trade was allowed to fight its case against the surviving remnants of feudalism: neither the freedom nor the ideas should be underestimated as a formative influence on economic growth.

Little more than a decade after our period ended, the whole of this 'system' came under the classic fire of the greatest economist of the age. In his celebrated chapter on what he entitled for all time 'The Mercantile System' Adam Smith attacked the 'principles' of the system as primitive ignorant trumpery, unworthy of serious attention; its practical effects as the sacrifice of consumption ('the sole end and purpose of all production') to the selfish interests of producers. The system therefore involved an unjust and improper discrimination by authority against certain classes of men in favour of other (and weaker) classes and was in consequence inadmissible. Such views have had a powerful influence on subsequent thought and policy down to our time. That they contained, by the 1770s, a considerable element of practical force and logic cannot be denied. But we live in a world of economics regulated according to ideas not altogether dissimilar from those attacked in *The Wealth of Nations*. The student can hardly be blamed if he feels less dogmatically certain that the traditional critical attitude of *laissez-faire* dogmatists can be accepted uncritically. That the 'system' was rigidly nationalistic in its primary aims goes without saying; that the means it adopted were exclusive, narrow, aggressive and sometimes brutal, that it led by logical extension of its principles to war and conquest also. But recent students have emphasized how naturally its ideas and devices grew out of contemporary economic and social conditions and in particular how its leading *motif*, the balance of trade, drew together aspirations and interests in an attempt to push Britain into a new phase of economic development. Given that the nation was in 1600 a still backward economy in leading strings to more advanced ones, notably the Dutch, the economic measures that were taken would not seem unreasonable to a student of modern policies in similar situations. Of a central part of the mechanism – the Navigation Acts, designed to protect and promote the English merchant navy against the superior knowledge and experience of the Dutch – the most recent and thorough investigator has said quite simply that they 'were successful'.[1] The other prohibitions and protections likewise aimed at nurturing infant industries. It is difficult to imagine that these could have prospered without artificial stimulus in the competitive conditions of the time. But the significance of the individual parts of the system is less than the significance of the whole. It rests in the last analysis not on the success of this Act or that proclamation, but on the belief, novel to this age, that material progress through state control and stimulus was not only possible but desirable. The idea, still strong in Tudor legislators, that the preservation of social order took precedence over economic progress, died hard. But even this gave place slowly to policies resting on the assumption that some men should be encouraged to better themselves, and by so doing, better society as a whole.

[1] Harper, op. cit., p. 377.

375

Traditional controls, whether by gild, municipality, or manor courts wilted and died. Inevitability, a hierarchical society based on custom and landholding faded imperceptibly into one based on enterprise, success, luck. Historians have often emphasized the misfortunes which the new commercial age brought to those who enjoyed none of these advantages. Such misfortunes were real. But they do not entitle us to regard the previous centuries as a Golden Age. The feudal order had its full share of poverty, brutality and victimization. Materially the new order promised a larger measure of wealth and welfare as well as insecurity. Its economic legislation, representing a flux of private and public interests, reflected and promoted change. Yet it cannot be torn out of the political and social context within which it was historically framed. If it contributed to the remarkable economic growth of the times, it was only able to do so because the system of government made it possible in a unique way for intelligence to be focused on economic problems. It restrained the damaging exploitation of the economy by absolutist dynasticism; and political order, social mobility and economic freedom made it possible for the innovators to enjoy the potential rewards offered to enterprise by expanding overseas markets and by an expanding home population. The eighteenth-century merchant, often charitable at home, did not yet believe that the meek inherited the earth abroad. Most, in this period, put their faith in protection and regulation backed by *machtpolitik*. The vision of Hume and Adam Smith remained for the most part a vision of intellectuals – logical, philosophical, but as yet prophetic. The groundwork of liberal Empire had been laid on foundations that defied their doctrines. In time, those foundations would be swept away as obstructive and inappropriate. By that time they had played their part and outlived their usefulness. Yet to understand their role in the indispensable expansion of the critical century before the Industrial Revolution, it is necessary to understand the entire complex of socio-political institutions which composed English life, and helped to convert England from semi-feudal into a semi-modern state.

In 1763 the social and economic changes which were to transform Britain – in transport, power, agricultural method, industrial organization, population – were only just beginning. Fortunately, earlier centuries had built up reserves of human skill and talent needed to develop Britain's rich natural resources and had created a political and social *ambience* in which such development could proceed. Few barriers of custom, class or law obstructed the industrialists, merchants and financiers, who mobilized the capital, labour, resources and markets to meet the challenges and opportunities of the new age. In the first instance they reaped the largest rewards of their enterprise. The mass of the people have often been represented as merely victims of the new system of industry. Yet, more distantly, more slowly, but in the end surely, it was this system which was to multiply the world's wealth and free a growing proportion of its peoples from the age-long threat of famine, starvation, disease and poverty.

Select Bibliography

The following list is not intended to be exhaustive. It contains a selection of those books and articles which have been most broadly useful to the author, which will enable the reader to deepen his knowledge of particular aspects of the period and guide him in turn to further detailed studies. Only those 'primary' sources which are accessible in print are included.

Some of the books listed appeared after the manuscript was complete. They have been included as valuable for subsequent reading, especially as in most cases some of their conclusions have been foreshadowed in earlier articles by their authors, which have been taken into account in the text.

PRINTED SOURCES OF STATISTICS AND CONTEMPORARY WORKS

CANTILLON, R. *Essay on Commerce*, ed. H. Higgs. London, Macmillan, 1931.

CLARK, G. N. *Guide to English Commercial Statistics 1696–1782*. Royal Historical Society, 1938.

DEANE, PHYLLIS and COLE, W. A. *British Economic Growth 1688–1959*. Cambridge U.P., 1962.

DEFOE, DANIEL. *A Plan of the English Commerce*. 1728.

FIENNES, CELIA. *The Journeys of Celia Fiennes*, ed. Christopher Morris. 2nd edn. London, Cresset Press, 1949.

HANSON, L. W. *Contemporary Printed Sources for British and Irish Economic History, 1701–1750*. Cambridge U.P., 1963.

HIGGS, H. *Bibliography of Economics 1751–1775*. Cambridge U.P., 1935.

KING, GREGORY. *Two Tracts*, ed. G. E. Barnett. Baltimore, 1936.

MCCULLOCH, J. R., ed. *Early English Tracts on Commerce*. Cambridge, 1954.

MITCHELL, B. R. and DEANE, PHYLLIS. *Abstract of British Historical Statistics*. Cambridge U.P., 1962.

MUN, THOMAS. *England's Treasure by fforraign Trade* (1664). Oxford, Blackwell, 1928.

SCHUMPETER, ELIZABETH B. *English Overseas Trade Statistics 1697–1808*. Introduction by T. S. Ashton. Oxford U.P., 1960.

SMITH, J. *Memoirs of Wool*. 1747. 2 vols.

Select Bibliography

WILSON, THOMAS. *The State of England Anno. Dom. 1600*, ed. F. J. Fisher. Camden Miscellany, 1936.

WING, D. *Short Title Catalogue 1641–1700*. New York, Columbia U.P., 1945.

AGRICULTURE

BARNES, D. G. *A History of the English Corn Laws 1660–1846*. London, Routledge, 1930.

CURTLER, W. H. R. *The Enclosure and Redistribution of our Land*. Oxford U.P., 1920.

DARBY, H. C. *The Draining of the Fens*. 2 vols. Cambridge, 1940.

ERNLE, LORD. *English Farming Past and Present*. 6th edn. with Introductions by G. E. Fussell and O. R. MacGregor. London, Heinemann, 1961.

HARRIS, L. E. *Vermuyden and the Fens*. London, Cleaver-Hume, 1953.

HOSKINS, W. G. *The Midland Peasant*. London, Macmillan, 1957.

HUGHES, E. *North Country Life in the Eighteenth Century*. Oxford U.P., 1952.

MINGAY, G. E. *English Landed Society in the Eighteenth Century*. London, Routledge, 1963.

ORWIN, C. S. *The Open Fields*. Oxford U.P., 1938.

RICHES, NAOMI. *The Agricultural Revolution in Norfolk*. Chapel Hill, 1937.

SLICHER VAN BATH, B. H. *The Agrarian History of Western Europe 500–1850*, trs. O. Ordish. London, E. Arnold, 1963.

THIRSK, JOAN. *English Peasant Farming*. London, Routledge, 1957.

TROW-SMITH, R. *English Husbandry*. London, Faber, 1951.

Articles

FUSSELL, G. E. 'Low Countries Influence on English Farming', *E.H.R.*, vol. LXXIV, 1959.

HABAKKUK, H. J. 'English Landownership 1680–1740', *Econ. Hist. Rev.*, vol. X, no. I, 1939–40.

HABAKKUK, H. J. 'The Rate of Interest and the Price of Land', *Econ. Hist. Rev.*, second series, vol. V, no. I, 1952.

HOSFORD, W. H. 'An Eye Witness's Account of a Seventeenth Century Enclosure' *Econ. Hist. Rev.*, second series, vol. IV, no. 2, 1951.

KERRIDGE, E. 'The Movement of Rent 1540–1640', *Econ. Hist. Rev.*, second series, vol. VI, no. I, 1953.

KERRIDGE, E. 'The Sheepfold in Wiltshire and the Floating of Watermeadows', *Econ. Hist. Rev.*, second series, vol. VI, no. 3, 1954.

KERRIDGE, E. 'Turnip Husbandry in High Suffolk', *Econ. Hist. Rev.*, second series, vol. VIII, no. 3, 1956.

MINGAY, G. E. 'The Agricultural Depression', *Econ. Hist. Rev.*, second series, vol. VIII, no. 3, 1956.

PARKER, R. A. C. 'Coke of Norfolk and the Agrarian Revolution', *Econ. Hist. Rev.*, second series, vol. VIII, no. 2, 1955.

PLUMB, J. H. 'Sir Robert Walpole and Norfolk Husbandry', *Econ. Hist. Rev.*, second series, vol. v, no. 1, 1952.

TRADE AND TRADE POLICY, TRANSPORT

ALBION, R. G. *Forests and Sea Power.* Harvard, 1926.

BAINES, THOMAS. *History of the Commerce and town of Liverpool and the Rise of Manufacturing Industry in the adjoining counties.* 1852.

BOURNE, H. R. FOX. *English Merchants.* 1886.

DAVIES, K. G. *The Royal African Company.* London, Longmans, 1957.

FRIIS, ASTRID. *Alderman Cockayne's Project and the Cloth Trade.* Copenhagen and Oxford, 1927.

GIBB, D. E. W. *Lloyds of London.* London, Macmillan, 1957.

GIBSON, JOHN. *History of Glasgow.* Glasgow, 1777.

GRAS, N. S. B. *Evolution of the English Corn Market.* Harvard U.P., 1915.

HARPER, L. A. *The English Navigation Laws.* New York, 1939.

HECKSCHER, E. *Mercantilism*, trs. M. Shapiro. 2nd edn. 2 vols. Allen & Unwin, 1955.

HINTON, R. W. K. *The Eastland Trade and the Commonweal in the Seventeenth Century.* Cambridge U.P., 1959.

HOSKINS, W. G. *The Industry, Trade and People of Exeter 1688–1800.* Manchester U.P., 1935.

MCGRATH, P. *Merchants and Merchandize in Seventeenth Century Bristol.* Bristol Record Soc., 1955.

PRICE, JACOB M. *The Tobacco Adventure to Russia.* Philadephia (Am. Phil. Soc.) 1961.

SCOTT, W. R. *The Constitution and Finance of English, Scottish and Irish Joint Stock Companies to 1720.* Cambridge U.P., 3 vols., 1910–12.

SUPPLE, B. E. *Commercial Crisis and Change in England 1600–1642.* Cambridge U.P., 1959.

WESTERFIELD, R. B. *Middlemen in English Business 1660–1760.* Yale U.P., 1915.

WILLAN, T. S. *River Navigation in England 1600–1750.* Oxford U.P., 1936.

WILLAN, T. S. *The English Coasting Trade 1600–1750.* Manchester U.P., 1938.

WILLAN, T. S. *Early History of the Russia Company.* Manchester U.P., 1956.

WILSON, CHARLES. *Anglo-Dutch Commerce and Finance in the Eighteenth Century.* Cambridge U.P., 1941.

Articles

COLE, W. A. 'Trends in Eighteenth Century Smuggling', *Econ. Hist. Rev.*, second series, vol. x, no. 3, 1958.

DAVIS, R. 'English Foreign Trade 1660–1700', *Econ. Hist. Rev.*, second series, vol. VII, no. 2, 1954.

DAVIS, R. 'Merchant Shipping in the Economy of the late Seventeenth Century', *Econ. Hist. Rev.*, second series, vol. IX, no. 1, 1956.

Select Bibliography

FISHER, F. J. 'London's Export Trade in the early Seventeenth Century', *Econ. Hist. Rev.*, second series, vol. III, no. 2, 1950.

WILLIAMS, J. E. 'Whitehaven in the Eighteenth Century', *Econ. Hist. Rev.*, second series, vol. VIII, no. 3, 1956.

WILSON, CHARLES. 'Treasure and Trade Balances', *Econ. Hist. Rev.*, second series, vol. II, no. 2, 1949.

WILSON, CHARLES. 'Cloth Production and International Competition in the Seventeenth Century', *Econ. Hist. Rev.*, second series, vol. XIII, no. 2, 1960.

POLITICO-ECONOMIC AND SOCIOLOGICAL

AYLMER, G. E. *The King's Servants. The Civil Service of Charles I 1625–1642.* London, Routledge, 1961.

BATHO, G. R., ed. *The Household Papers of Henry Percy, Ninth Earl of Northumberland (1564–1632).* Royal Hist. Soc., 1962.

BELL, H. E. *An Introduction to the History and Records of the Court of Wards and Liveries.* Cambridge U.P., 1953.

BRAILSFORD, H. N. *The Levellers and the English Revolution,* ed. C. Hill. London, Cresset Press, 1961.

BRUNTON, D. and PENNINGTON, D. H. *Members of the Long Parliament.* London, Allen & Unwin, 1954.

CAMPBELL, MILDRED. *The English Yeoman under Elizabeth and the Early Stuarts.* New Haven, 1942.

FINCH, M. E. *The Wealth of Five Northamptonshire Families 1540–1640.* Northampton Record Soc., 1956.

HEXTER, J. H. *The Reign of King Pym.* Harvard U.P., 1941.

HILL, CHRISTOPHER. *The Economic Problems of the Church from Archbishop Whitgift to the Long Parliament.* Oxford U.P., 1956.

HOSKINS, W. G. *The Midland Peasant.* London, Macmillan, 1957.

PEARL, VALERIE. *London and the Outbreak of the Puritan Revolution: City Government and National Politics. 1625–1643.* Oxford U.P., 1961.

SIMPSON, A. *The Wealth of the Gentry 1540–1660.* Cambridge U.P., 1961.

STONE, LAWRENCE, *The Crisis of the Aristocracy 1558–1641.* Oxford U. P., 1965.

TAWNEY, R. H. *Religion and the Rise of Capitalism.* John Murray, 1926.

TAWNEY, R. H. *Business and Politics under James I.* Cambridge U.P., 1958.

TREVOR-ROPER, H. R. 'The Gentry', *Econ. Hist. Rev.* Supplement, 1953.

UNWIN, GEORGE. *Industrial Organization in the Sixteenth and Seventeenth Centuries.* Reprint, with Introduction by T. S. Ashton. London, Cass, 1957.

WAGNER, ANTHONY. *English Genealogy.* Oxford U.P., 1960.

WILSON, CHARLES. *Profit and Power. A Study of England and the Dutch Wars.* London, Longmans, 1957.

Select Bibliography

Articles

COOPER, J. P. 'The Counting of Manors', *Econ. Hist. Rev.*, second series, vol. VIII, no. 3, 1956.

JOHN, A. H. 'War and the English Economy 1700–1763', *Econ. Hist. Rev.*, second series, vol. VII, no. 3, 1955.

KEARNEY, H. F. 'The Political Background to English Mercantilism 1695–1700', *Econ. Hist. Rev.*, second series, vol. XI, no. 3, 1959.

KERRIDGE, E. 'The Revolts in Wiltshire against Charles I', *Wilts. Arch. and History Mag.*, July 1958.

LASLETT, P. 'John Locke, the Great Recoinage and the Origin of the Board of Trade 1695–1698', *William and Mary Quarterly*, July 1957.

SUTHERLAND, L. S. 'The East India Company in Eighteenth Century Politics', *Econ. Hist. Rev.*, first series, vol. XVII, no. 1, 1947.

SUTHERLAND, L. 'The City of London in Eighteenth Century Politics', in *Essays Presented to Sir Lewis Namier*, ed. R. Pares and A. J. P. Taylor. London, Macmillan, 1956.

TATE, W. E. 'Inclosure Movements in Northamptonshire', *Northants. Past and Present*, vol. I, no. 2, 1949.

THIRSK, JOAN. 'Sales of Royalist Land during the Interregnum', *Econ. Hist. Rev.*, second series, vol. V, no. 2, 1952.

INDUSTRIAL STUDIES

CHAMBERS, J. D. 'The Vale of Trent 1670–1800', *Econ. Hist. Rev.* Supplement.

CLOW, N. *The Chemical Revolution*. London, Batchworth, 1952.

COLEMAN, D. C. *The British Paper Industry 1495–1860*. Oxford U.P., 1958.

COURT, W. H. B. *The Rise of the Midland Industries*. Oxford U.P. 1938.

DAVIS, RALPH. *The Rise of the English Shipping Industry in the Seventeenth and Eighteenth Centuries*. London, Macmillan, 1962.

ELLIS, COLIN. *History in Leicester*. Leicester Information Dept., 1948.

FLINN, M. W. *Men of Iron: the Crowleys in the Early Iron Industry*. Edinburgh U.P., 1962.

GILL, CONRAD. *The Rise of the Irish Linen Industry*. London, Humphrey Milford, 1925.

HEATON, H. *The Yorkshire Woollen and Worsted Industries*. London, Humphrey Milford, 1920.

HOSKINS, W. G. *Devon (Collins New Survey of England)*, 1954.

LOUNSBURY, R. G. *The British Fishery at Newfoundland 1634–1763*. Yale U.P., 1934.

MATHIAS, PETER. *The Brewing Industry in England 1700–1830*. Cambridge U.P., 1959.

MINCHINTON, W. E. *The British Tinplate Industry*. Oxford U.P., 1957.

NEF, J. U. *The Rise of the British Coal Industry*. London, Routledge, 2 vols., 1932.

RAISTRICK, A. *A Dynasty of Ironfounders: The Darbys and Coalbrookdale.* London, Longmans, 1953.

RAMSAY, G. D. *The Wiltshire Woollen Industry.* Oxford U.P., 1943.

REDDAWAY, T. F. *The Rebuilding of London after the Fire.* 2nd edn. London, E. Arnold, 1951.

WADSWORTH, A. P. and MANN, J. DE L. *The Cotton Trade and Industrial Lancashire 1600–1780.* Manchester U.P., 1931.

Articles

BOWDEN, P. J. 'Wool Supply and the Woollen Industry', *Econ. Hist. Rev.*, second series, vol. IX, no. 1, 1956.

CLARKSON, G. L. A.'The Organization of the English Leather Industry in the late Sixteenth and Seventeenth Centuries', *Econ. Hist. Rev.*, second series, vol. XIII, no. 2, 1960.

COLEMAN, D. C. 'Naval Dockyards under the Later Stuarts', *Econ. Hist. Rev.*, second series, vol. VI, no. 2, 1953.

JOHNSON, B. L. C. 'The Foley Partnerships', *Econ. Hist. Rev.*, second series, vol. IV, no. 3, 1952.

MATHIAS, P. 'Agriculture and the Brewing and Distilling Industries in the 18th Century', *Econ. Hist. Rev.*, second series, vol. V, no. 2, 1952.

PRICHARD, M. F. LLOYD. 'The Decline of Norwich', *Econ. Hist. Rev.*, second series, vol. III, no. 3, 1951.

SOCIAL AND DEMOGRAPHIC

BRETT-JAMES, N. *The Growth of Stuart London.* London, Allen & Unwin, 1935.

CLARK, G. N. *Science and Social Welfare in the Age of Newton.* 2nd edn. Oxford U.P., 1949.

DEFOE, DANIEL. *The Complete Tradesman.* 1728.

FURNISS, E. S. *The Position of the Labourer in A System of Nationalism.* New York, Houghton Mifflin, 1920.

GILBOY, E. W. *Wages in Eighteenth Century England.* Harvard U.P., 1934.

GRIFFITH, G. TALBOT. *Population Problems of the Age of Malthus.* Cambridge U.P., 1926.

GRUBB, ISOBEL. *Quakerism and Industry.* London, Williams & Norgate, 1930.

JONES, M. G. *The Charity School Movement: A Study of Eighteenth-Century Puritanism in Action.* Cambridge U.P., 1938.

JORDAN, W. K. *Philanthropy in England 1480–1660.* London, Allen & Unwin, 1959.

MACLACHLAN, H. *English Education under the Test Acts.* Manchester U.P., 1931.

SUMMERSON, J. *Georgian London.* London, Cresset Press, 1945.

Articles

CHAMBERS, J. D. 'Enclosure and Labour Supply in the Industrial Revolution', *Econ. Hist. Rev.*, second series, vol. V, no. 3, 1953.

Select Bibliography

COLEMAN, D. C. 'Labour in the English Economy of the Seventeenth Century', *Econ. Hist. Rev.*, second series, vol. VIII, no. 2, 1956.

GLASS, D. V. 'Gregory King's Estimate of the Population of England and Wales, 1695', *Population Studies*, 1949–50.

JONES, P. E. and JUDGES, A. V. 'London Population', *Econ. Hist. Rev.*, 1935. vol. VI, no. I.

HABAKKUK, H. J. 'English Population in the Eighteenth Century', *Econ. Hist. Rev.*, second series, vol. VI, no. 2, 1953.

WILSON, CHARLES. 'The Other Face of Mercantilism', *Trans. Royal Hist. Soc.*, fifth series, vol. 9, 1959.

FINANCE, CURRENCY, PRICES

ASHTON, ROBERT. *The Crown and the Money Market 1603–1640*. Oxford U.P., 1960.

BAXTER, S. B. *The Development of the Treasury 1660–1702*. London, Longmans, 1957.

CARSWELL, JOHN. *The South Sea Bubble*. London, Cresset Press, 1960.

CLAPHAM, J. H. *The Bank of England*. Cambridge U.P., 1944. 2 vols.

DICKSON, P. G. M. *The Sun Insurance Office 1710–1960*. Oxford U.P., 1960.

DUBOIS, A. B. *The English Business Company after the Bubble Act 1720–1800*. New York, 1938.

HARGREAVES, E. L. *The National Debt*. London, E. Arnold, 1930.

HORSEFIELD, J. KEITH. *British Monetary Experiments 1650–1710*. London, G. Bell, 1960.

HUGHES, E. *Studies in Administration and Finance, 1558–1825*. Manchester U.P., 1934.

KENNEDY, W. *English Taxation 1640–1799*. London, Bell, 1913.

SINCLAIR, J. *A History of the Public Revenue of the British Empire*. 1789.

WARD, W. R. *English Land Tax in the Eighteenth Century*. Oxford U.P., 1953.

Articles

BROWN, E. H. PHELPS and HOPKINS, S. V. 'Seven Centuries of the Prices of Consumables', *Economica*, vol. XXIII, 1956.

COLEMAN, D. C. 'London Scriveners and the Estate Market in the later Seventeenth Century', *Econ. Hist. Rev.*, second series, vol. IV, no. 2, 1951.

DAVIES, K. G.' Joint Stock Investment in the late Seventeenth Century', *Econ. Hist. Rev.*, second series, vol. IV, no. 3, 1952.

JOSLIN, D. M. 'London Private Bankers 1720–1785', *Econ. Hist. Rev.*, second series, vol. VII, no. 2, 1954.

PRESSNELL, L. S. 'Public Monies and the Development of English Banking', *Econ. Hist. Rev.*, second series, vol. III, 1953.

Select Bibliography

SCHUMPETER, ELIZABETH B. 'English Prices and Public Finance 1660–1682', *Review of Econ. Statistics*, vol. XX.

SUTHERLAND, L. S. 'Samson Gideon and the Reduction of Interest 1749–1750', *Econ. Hist. Rev.*, first series, vol. XVI, no. 1, 1946.

REFERENCE AND GENERAL

The following books contain a wide range of studies into many aspects of economic history. These can be usefully supplemented by the standard reference works e.g. the *Victoria County Histories* for local industries; the *Dictionary of National Biography* for individual merchants and entrepreneurs (though the older volumes deal with these but sparely); the *Encyclopaedia of the Social Sciences* (1930) and R. H. I. Palgrave's *Dictionary of Political Economy* (1901–1908) are still useful for the history of economic ideas and institutions. The *Journal of Transport* contains many useful articles on navigation and road transport.

ASHTON, T. S. *Economic Fluctuations in England 1700–1800* (Ford lectures 1953). Oxford U.P., 1959.

ASHTON, T. S. *An Economic History of England. The 18th Century.* London, Methuen, 1955.

FISHER, F. J. *Essays in the Economic and Social History of Tudor and Stuart England, in honour of R. H. Tawney.* Cambridge U.P., 1961.

LANE, F. C. and RIEMERSMA, J. C. eds. *Enterprise and Secular Change.* Illinois, 1953.

OGG, DAVID. *England in the Reigns of James II and William III.* Oxford U.P., 1955.

PLUMB, J. H. ed. *Studies in Social History. A Tribute to G. M. Trevelyan.* Longman, 1955.

PRESSNELL, L. S. ed. *Studies in the Industrial Revolution. Essays Presented to T. S. Ashton.* London, Athlone Press, 1960.

WILSON, E. CARUS, ed. *Essays in Economic History.* London, E. Arnold, vol. I, 1954; vols. II and III, 1962.

Contributions and Communications to the First International Economic History Conference at Stockholm. 1960. The Hague 1960.

Articles

JOHN, A. H. 'Aspects of English Economic Growth in the first half of the Eighteenth Century', *Economica*. May 1961.

Index

accountancy, 11
Adam, Robert, 257
Advice to the Stewards of Estates,
  251
Advocate, The, 61
Africa, 64, 67, 163, 165, 170; trade,
  172–3, 275
agriculture, ch. 2 *passim,* 69, ch. 7
  passim, 205, 237, 267, ch. 12 *passim;*
  arable, 23, 141, 145, 245; Board of,
  260; bounties, 147–8, 246; capital
  investment in, 120; changes, 20,
  245–6, 366; Corn Laws, 147, 148;
  crop rotation, 142, 143, 146; depression, 243–5; efficiency of, 246, 261;
  employment in, 21; 'engrossing',
  251; fodder crops, 143, 149; improvements in, 20, 27, 28–35, 87,
  120, 123, 141–6, 149–50, 151–5,
  245, 246–50, 260–1, 342; income
  from, 21; open fields, 33, 141, 146;
  output, 23; pasture, 141–3; prices,
  147–8, 149, 243; progress, 260–2;
  specialization, 27, 147; stockrearing,
  149; subsistence, 27; yields from,
  23, 33, 249. *See also* enclosures,
  farming, harvests, individual crops
  and livestock
agricultural reformers, 27–8, 125, 142,
  150–5, 246–51
Albemarle, Duke of, 165, 281
alchemy, 19
Alva, Duke of, 361
Amboyna Massacre, 64
Amelia, 254

America, 40, 56, 64, 161, 271; French
  threat to British interests in, 282–3;
  North, 165, 283; rebellion in, 291;
  trade with, 275, 276
Amicable Assurance Society, 335
Amsterdam, 41, 42, 50, 61, 123, 334;
  Bank of, 41, 209; Bourse, 221, 222;
  financial centre, 333
Ancaster, Lord, 244
Anglo-Spanish Treaty (1604), 52
antiquaries, 6, 14; Society of, 6
Antwerp, 41, 42
apprentices, 116, 136
Archangel, 272
aristocracy, 10, 14, 105, 150–1; and
  agricultural improvement, 151–2;
  and Civil War, 109–11, 114;
  economic fortunes of, 123–4; extravagance, 111–12, 154–5, 341,
  finance of, 155–6; wealth of, 338–9
Armada, 90
army, 128
Arnold, Matthew, *Culture and Anarchy,* 342
artisans, 22, 51, 340, 345; Huguenot,
  195–8; immigration of, 61, 75, 168.
  See also craftsmen
Arundel, Earl of, 87
Ashburnham family, 127
Ashton, 298
Asia, 41, 163, 369
'assarting', 33, 149
Assessment, 212
astrology, 6, 19
astronomy, 6, 19

387

coke, demand for, 82
Coke family, 115, 147, 151, 153, 320
Coke, Edward, 6, 7, 10, 153
Coke, Thomas, 247, 255, 258; marling, 248; improvements in husbandry, 248–9
Colbertism, 57
Colbert, Jean Baptiste, 282, 291
Colchester, 75; cloth industry, 75–6, 192, 293; Dutch immigration in, 75–6
coleseed, 31
Collection of Letters for the Improvement of Husbandry and Trade, 143, 222–3
colonies, 351; imports from, 272, 285; Plantation, 271; trade with, 179, 275
Colston, Edward, 51
commerce, policy, 135–6, ch. 8 *passim. See also* trade
commodities, tax on, 129
Commons, House of, 9, 54, 92, 109, 114, 129, 167, 293, 352
Commonwealth of Oceana, 109
communications, 42. *See also* transport
companies, 116, 132, 196–7, 221, 270, 272; bonds of, 223–4; capital investment in, 173–5, 315–17; control of commercial policy, 166–7; as credit institutions, 315; joint-stock, 56, 62, 135, 172–6; livery, 49–51; organization of, 135–6; promotion of, 113, 183; regulated, 62, 172–3; stocks and shares, 222–3, 315–17. *See also* individual companies
competition, for land, 159; in cloth industry, 290, 293. *See also* Dutch, economic rivalry with
Constantinople, 270
consumption, as basis of economic policy, 236, 237–8; 'conspicuous', 49; increase in, 264, 288–9; industries, 79, 83, 85, 195; tax on, 319–20
Cook, James, 39
Cookworthy, William, 310
copper industry, 202, 280

copyhold, 8, 134; conversion of, 251; decline of, 251–2
copyholder, 3, 7, 15, 16, 150; expropriation of, 251, fortunes of, 261–2. *See also* yeoman
corn, 44, 253; Bounty, 224, 246, 249, 339, 342; exports, 147–8, 170; laws, 147, 148–9, 236–7; output, 148–9, 261; trade, 36
Cornwall, 24, 133, 260, 304, 331; china clay, 310; tin mining, 68, 85, 87, 202–3, 205, 288, 304, 305
corporations, 102–3, 315; decline of, 269–71; finance, 315–17, 320; power of, 317–18
Corpus Christi College, 144
Corunna, 268
Cotesworth family, 260
Cotesworth, William, 249
Cotswolds, 32, 108
cotton, 56, 68, 160, 170, 200, 293; imports, 275, 285, 296
cotton industry, 296, 297; fustians, 193, 297, 298; legislation (1701), 297, (1721), 293, 297; protection of, 297
Cotton, Sir John, 156
Cotton, Sir Robert, 6
Court, the Royal, 14, 49, 113, 123; of Charles I, 95–6; and City, 15, 47, 48, 57; office holding, 115, 125–6
Courteen family, 125
Courteen, Sir William, 12, 115, 122, 158
Coutts family, 329
Covenanters, 128
Covent Garden, 47, 48, 177, 178, 330
Coventry, 69, 82, 296, 300
Coventry, Henry, 167
Coventry, William, 165, 167
craftsmen, 361; types of, 67–8, 116. *See also* artisans
Cranfield, Lionel, 10, 12, 51, 60, 96, 122, 212; and reorganization of finance, 93–5, 106, 160
credit, ch. 10 *passim*, 313; bills of exchange, 155, 207, 332–3; bonds, 207; crisis, 220; from corporations,

credit (*contd*)
315–17; land banks, 218; million
lottery, 218; National Debt, 218,
313–23; public, 313–15
crime, in London, 117, 369
crisis, 64, 87, 120, 182–3, 229, 359; in
banking, 219, 220–1; financial, 92;
in foreign trade, 53, causes of, 53–5;
liquidity, 259
Crisp family, 115
Crisp, Sir Nicolas, 212
Crommelin, Louis, and linen industry, 197–8
Crompton family, 331
Cromwell, Oliver, 30, 53, 61, 64, 114,
136; commercial policy, 58, 135,
165; financial difficulties, 130–3
Cromwell, Richard, 58, 131
Cross, John, 201
Crowland, Manor of, 31
Crowley family, 15, 341, 371
Crowley, Ambrose, 303, 312
Crown, 125, 127–8, 134, 167; poverty
of, 115–16. *See also* individual
kings
Crown Lands, 90, 134; loss of, 108,
111–12; manipulation of, 103–6;
survey of (1607), 30, 103
Crying Sin of England, The, 34
Culliford, William, 230, 234, 266
Culpeper, Thomas, 103, 233
Culture and Anarchy, 342
Cumberland, 251
Cumberland, Earl of, 87
currency, 78, 183; debasement of, 71,
74, 119; gold, 206, 220, 328; man-
ipulation of, 54, 59, 71, 74, 125;
paper, 206, 328; reform of, 220–1,
224; scarcity of metal, 328; silver,
206, 220, 328
customary tenants, 21, 35, 249
Customs, 53, 90, 96–8, 130, 216;
'Book of Rates' (1608), 91; farmers
of, 97–8, 115, 116, 212; House, 230;
Inspector General of, 353; London,
129; yield from, 146, 211

dairy produce, 44, 148

Dallam, Thomas, 68
Danby, Thomas, Lord Treasurer, 214
Danzig, 42
Darby family, 341
Darby, Abraham, 199, 301
Dartmoor, 189
Daubuz, Stephen, 327
Davenant, Charles, 155, 156, 167;
Discourses, 228; *An Essay on the
Probable Methods of Making a
People Gainers on the Ballance of
Trade,* 229–30, 354; and poor, 234,
349
death rate, bills of mortality, 46;
effect on population, 366–9; factors
influencing, 367–8; fluctuations in,
365–6; infant mortality, 352, 368
debt, ch. 10 *passim,* ch. 15 *passim,* on
landed property, 155–7; National,
132, 265, 313–23, 373. *See also* credit
Decker, Sir Matthew, 330; *Essay on
the Decline of Foreign Trade,* 266
deflation, 119, 124, 221
Defoe, Daniel, *Essay of Projects,* 7;
mentioned, 15, 29, 155, 178, 245,
275, 293, 295, 296, 317, 339, 342,
343, 346, 349, 354
de la Pole family, 9
Delaval family, 88, 340
'denshiring', 36, 142
depression, 47, 117, 124, 160, 182–3;
in agriculture, 243–5; causes of,
54–5, 277; in cloth industry, 40, 58,
67, 74–5; in trade, 52–4, 62, 70
Derby, 319, 331; industries of, 235,
299, 309, 310; silk, 359, 360
Derbyshire, 9, 82, 84, 201, 244, 260;
lead mining, 68, 85–6, 87, 205,
303
Descartes, René, 226
Devonshire, 66, 99, 260, 295, 296, 331,
368; agriculture, 30, 32, 124, 252;
cloth industry, 69, 77, 79, 86, 125,
146, 188–91, 197, 373; serges, 176,
235, 290–2
de Witt, Johan, 335
Dialogue of the Commonweal, 60
Diggers, 128

mercantilism, 42, 235, 236–8; aid to economic growth, 269; French, 65; German, 267; legislation, 135; social, 122, 353–7; theory of, 57–61, 233, 266–7, 373–6, change in, 353–7

Merchant Adventurers, 40, 52, 56, 59, 60, 63, 77, 116, 132, 172, 192; and Cokayne Project, 70–4; and monopoly of cloth exports, 54, 69–70, 270–1

merchants, 18, 22, 38, 45, 53, 92, 270, 272, 338; and agricultural improvement, 157–9; capitalists, 193–4, 298, 360; charity of, 121–2, 234–5, 347–9; and Civil War, 115–17, 127; of cloth, 190–1, 292–9 *passim;* Devonshire, 290–1; and Dissent, 340–2; Dutch, 189, 272, 322; economic interests of, 122–3; economic theories of, 59–61; families, 179, 275, 331; and Government, 12–13 58, 114, 126; Hanseatic, 69; houses, 146; in industry, 87–8; influence on economic policy, 11, 57–9, 63, 131, 135, 166–8, 285; of London, 9, 49, 116; and Navigation Acts, 165–6; protection of, 62–3; rise of, 5, 9, 14–15, 88, 116; and royal finance, 96–8; and social change, 20; wealth, 21, from land, 10, 123, 134, 340, mercantile, 51, 113

Merchant Taylors, 50

metals, imports, 85; industries, 68, 84–6, 136, 263, 280, 300–1, 303, 370; smelting, 198, 202–3, 312

Methodism, 137, 341

Meynell, Francis, 213

middle class, and Civil War, 109–11; in Parliament, 114

middlemen, 38, 50, 88, 119; Dutch, 61

Middlesex, 9

Middlesex, Earl of, *see* Cranfield, Lionel

Middleton, Thomas, *A Faire Quarrel*, 16

Midland Association of Iron Masters, 341

Midlands, 82, 86, 122, 303, 341, 351, 369, 371; agriculture, 24, 25, 26, 244; coal deposits, 84–5, 198, 204; enclosure of, 32, 141, 146, 250; improvement of, 260; iron deposits, 68, 152; metal industries, 68, 152; population, 295; silk manufacture of, 299–300; stocking frame, 194

Million Bank, 223

mills, 304, 359; construction of, 32, 43; fulling, 136, 190; paper, 66, 196, 197; slitting, 300, 301

Milton, John, 13, 348; *Paradise Lost*, 6

Mineral and Battery Works, Company of, 85

minerals, 36, 152, 267

Miners Friend, The, 203

mining industry, 69, 79, 136, 186, 267, 343; and landowning, 17; occupational hazards of, 87, 203; technical development in, 202–3, 303–5

Minorca, 284

Mint, 208, 220, 227

Misselden, Edward, 58–9

Mompesson, Sir Giles, 49, 102

monarchy, cost of, ch. 5 *passim. See also* kingship

Monasteries, dissolution of, 111

money, 224; bills, 129, 207–8, 214; cost of, 372–3; lender, *see* scrivener, lending, 206–7; market, 206, 373; paper, 219; supply, 209. *See also* coinage *and* currency

monopolies, 95, 100–03, 106, 129; monopolists, 116; reasons for, 102; statute of (1624), 102; trading, 172, 173, breakdown of, 270–1

Monson, Sir John, 104

Monson, Lord, 17, 244

Montagu, Ralph, 216, 219, 315

Montesquieu, 286

Moore, Edward, 200

Moore family, 340

Moore, John, *The Crying Sin of England*, 34

moralists, 17

Morse family, 16, 330

mortality, *see* death rate

Index

Quiberon Bay, 285

radicals, in Civil War, 128, 133
Radnor, Earl of, *see* Robartes, John
Raleigh, Sir Walter, 90
Ranelagh, 341
raw materials, 61, 66, 68, 69, 78, export regulation on, 267
Reade, Sir Compton, 156
Reading, 82
reclamation, land, 30, 32
re-exports, 160; growth of, 161, 169–70
Reflections on the Expediency of Opening the Trade to Turkey, 356
Reformation, 121
religion, as cause of Civil War, 108, 110; division in, 137. *See also* Catholicism and Puritanism
rents, 243–4, 258; from land, 21, 157, 158; rack rents, 254; rise in, 114, 248, 261
republicanism, 133
Restoration, as economic turning point, ch. 8 *passim*
retailers, increase in, 50
revenue, Assessment, 212; Customs, 96–8, 130, 131, 211, 216, 319; excise duty, 129–30, 131, 318, 319; 'extraordinary', 90–3; feudal dues, 95; Hearth Tax, 211; Knighthood, 105, 211; from lands, 103–5, from tax on, 130–1, 212, 216, 217, 318–19, 331; monopolies, 95, 100–3; 'ordinary', 90–3; prerogative, 96, 98–101; purveyance, 92; reorganization of, 93–4; royal, ch. 5 *passim*, 129–32, 225; Ship Money, 4, 7, 95, 99, 100; subsidies, 92–3; from trade, 92; wardship, 91–2, 211
revolution, 'Commercial', 161; Industrial, 202, 235, 264, 286, 288–9, 299, 341, 369, 370
Reynold family, 341
ribbon industry, 297
Richard II, 115
Rickman, John, on population, 365
riots, 34, 128, 291, 345

rivers, and development of ports, 44; economic importance of, 43; financial organization of, 278; improvement, 43–4, 278; navigation of, 36, map, 279; traffic, 277–8. *See also* transport
roads, condition of, 43, 44; turnpikes, 278
Robartes, John, 87
Roberts, Lewis, *Treasure of Traffike*, 61
Robinson, Henry, *England's Safety in Trade's Increase*, 61
Robinson, Thomas, 87
Rochester, Bishop of, *History of the Royal Society*, 7
Rochester, Lord Treasurer, 214
Rochester, Viscount, *see* Carr, Robert
Rockingham, Lord, 4, 256
Rodgers (Lord Monson's Steward), 17
Rodney, George, 1st Baron, Admiral, 338
Romney Marsh, 142
root crops, 23, 33
Rotherham, 372
Roundheads, 109, 110, 114
Royal Africa Company, 215, 270, 271, 329; growth of, 172, 173, 175–6; stocks of, 222–3
Royal Commission of Array, 110
Royal Exchange, 177, 222, 326, 334
Royal Fishery Company, 176, 188
Royalists, 108, 114, 115, 127, 128, 129, 212; lands of, 134, 157
Royal Navy, 283
Royal Society, 19, 73, 82, 138, 144; patron of agriculture, 144–5; scientific experiments of, 226–7; and technical innovation, 73, 186–8
Royal Society of Arts, 297
Rubens, Peter-Paul, 96
Rupert, Prince, 138, 173
Russell family, 14
Russia, 56, 70, 76, 272, 283, 284; Company, 270
Rutland, 15, 244, 257
Rutland, Earl of, 87
Ryswick, Treaty of (1679), 282